HOBOS, HUSTLERS, AND BACKSLIDERS

Hobos, Hustlers, and Backsliders

Homeless in San Francisco

Teresa Gowan

 University of Minnesota Press
Minneapolis
London

Parts of chapter 5 were previously published as "New Hobos or Neoromantic Fantasy? Urban Ethnography beyond the Neoliberal Disconnect," *Qualitative Sociology* 32, no. 3 (2009); reprinted with permission from Springer Science and Business Media.

Photographs in the book were taken by the author in San Francisco.

The maps were created by Jennifer Kotting. The map images are reproduced courtesy of Earth Sciences and Map Library, University of California, Berkeley.

Published by the University of Minnesota Press
111 Third Avenue South, Suite 290
Minneapolis, MN 55401-2520
http://www.upress.umn.edu

Library of Congress Cataloging-in-Publication Data

Gowan, Teresa.
    Hobos, hustlers, and backsliders : homeless in San Francisco / Teresa Gowan.
        p.   cm.
    Includes bibliographical references and index.
    ISBN 978-0-8166-6967-7 (pb: alk. paper)
    ISBN 978-0-8166-4869-6 (hc: alk. paper)
    1. Homeless persons — California — San Francisco.   2. Homeless men — California — San Francisco.   3. Homelessness — California — San Francisco.   I. Title.
    HV4506.S355G69   2010
    362.509794'61 — dc22   2010007699

Printed in the United States of America on acid-free paper

The University of Minnesota is an equal-opportunity educator and employer.

20   19   18   17   16   15
10   9   8   7   6   5   4

In memory of James Dezebee Moss
April 27, 1952 – March 28, 2005

Contents

Acknowledgments

THIS WORK WAS INSPIRED, PROPELLED, AND FREQUENTLY turned upside down by those living homeless in San Francisco. Some were patient interpreters and genial companions with whom I spent many hours talking and working. Others had little interest in my project but were nevertheless willing to let me witness scenes that could easily turn excruciatingly intimate or painful. Thank you, brothers, from the bottom of my heart.

I must give special mention to James Dezebee Moss, my wise and witty bodyguard. Before emphysema confined him to his wheelchair, James gave me years of his company in potentially dangerous situations. His loving friendship and generous trust of my motivations gave me crucial sustenance through periods of self-doubt.

Another great debt is to those activists and institutional players who helped me reach a better understanding of the field, either by giving me access to various programs for the homeless or drug addicted or by helping me to understand the complexities of social welfare policy. Again, in the interests of their privacy and that of their clients, professional ethics forbid me from identifying by name those who appear in the text, but you know who you are. "Sandrine" and Emma Bonacich, in particular, gave me vital help in making contact with shelter caseworkers.

This manuscript represents the combination of several years of difficult, often forbidding fieldwork and a tortuous writing process. I would have drifted to shipwreck long ago without the support of many friends and intellectual companions. First and foremost was Michael

Burawoy—incomparable teacher and friend—who gave me immense encouragement from the beginning. On my first day in the field, stuck agonizing about consent and the awkwardness of "coming out" as an ethnographer, I called him at least three times. As he would on countless occasions in the future, he pulled me clear and pushed me back out into the current.

Peter Evans, Raka Ray, and Michael Johns were of great help in designing the research and assisting me in thinking my way through the stumbling blocks that scatter the sociology of poverty. Loïc Wacquant, Mike Savage, Darren Nixon, Jeffrey Paige, and the generous and hardworking reviewers from two university presses all gave invaluable feedback at different stages.

The graduate students of the Berkeley sociology department offered intellectual companionship of the highest order. Our sustained collaboration over several years led to deep engagement with each other's work and, indeed, with those aspects of personal life that cannot in good faith be separated from messy qualitative work. Millie Thayer, Leslie Salzinger, Rachel Sherman, and Amy Schalet all have made an indelible impression on this manuscript. Christian Parenti, Sebastien Chauvin, John Gulick, Jackie Orr, Mary Kelsey, Sean O'Ríain, Lynne Haney, Steve Lopez, Joe Blum, Maren Klawiter, Sheba George, Zsuzsa Gille, Gretchen Purser, Ann Marie Wood, and Michelle Williams have been influential in important ways: some dived into drafts of my work while others shared conversations that fired my excitement.

More recently, my manuscript benefited extraordinarily from the expert commentary of my colleagues and students at the University of Minnesota. I thank Jennifer Pierce, Mary Jo Maynes, Rachel Schurman, Ron Aminzade, Michael Goldman, Doug Hartmann, Lisa Park, Josh Page, Jim Saliba, Helga Leitner, Sarah Whetstone, Kristin Haltinner, and (arriving in the nick of time) Guillaume Boccara.

I was nourished and encouraged through my fieldwork by a wonderful collection of friends outside academia. Elsie Büpp, Kevin Thompson, Xiu Min Li, Toni McCarty, Tricia Fallon, Christopher D. Cook, Amy Kipfer, Mark Kipfer, Ladan Sobhani, and the members of the bands Swarm and the Gated Community all contributed to the completion of this project in their own ways, if only by pulling me forcibly away from it when necessary, making music with me, and keeping my spirits afloat. As for my generous-hearted lover, caterer, and copy editor David Kaiser, his thoughtful support has rarely flickered, even though this project has constrained our lives and warped my temper.

Finally, I thank my mother, Tessa Gowan. Despite our turbulent life together, her yearning for intellectual development left its print on me. Without her passionate frustration with the "half-led life," my own odyssey into the world of scholarship would have been unlikely indeed.

Sin, Sickness, and the System

Charlie

"GOOD THING ABOUT SAN FRANCISCO, FOR THE HOMEless, it's that we've got enough people here that they can't run us out of town just for being poor, you know. Some of these small towns, you stick out straightaway and they come for you. Someone makes a call and the cops get on your tail. You could be just walking down the road like anyone else, no cart, nothing, and they pick you up. Now here, it's not like we don't have our problems with the cops, you know that—but all the same you are in it with other homeless folks, people that aren't scared of sticking up for themselves. And it's not a racial thing, generally speaking. We're all in it together."

Charlie Mack, a mustachioed African American in his late forties, had spent the last four years of his life buying clothes and appliances from dumpster divers and selling them on busy street corners. Charlie usually did not have a large stall, though. Things had been looking up. His favorite sister had given him her car. The transmission was gone, but he had it parked down south on Alemany Boulevard, a welcome haven in the evening.

Leaning against the wall of the Civic Center station entrance in downtown San Francisco, Charlie rolled an emaciated cigarette with his last scraps of tobacco. Most of the people walking by scanned his offerings out of the corner of their eyes and continued on their varied ways. Charlie didn't have much on his piece of carpet today: some ugly ties, a pile of aging computer textbooks, a blender, a couple of electric razors (one without a cord), and a neatly displayed selection of clean but faded sports clothing. Twenty minutes ago he had made five dollars on a Giants jacket, leaving him satisfied with the day so far.

Two men approached, parking shopping carts loaded with cardboard tubes to the side of Charlie's carpet.

"How ya doing?" asked a friendly looking Latino in a wrinkled Hawaiian shirt.

"Not so bad. Finally got that damn air conditioner off my hands. I'm not taking any more of those. What about you boys? How's the dumpster divin'?"

"It's OK. Haven't done much today. Yesterday we found a couple of phones you might like." He started rummaging in his cart. "I've only got one, Pipe. Where's the other one?"

His younger companion, a sharp-faced white man with a pistol tattooed on his hand, bent to retrieve a package from the rack underneath his cart.

"This one is the nicest," he said, pulling it out. "It needs a cord though."

Charlie looked the phones over. "You checked them out?"

The Latino, Manny, shook his head. "You want to try them now? I can mind your gear."

Charlie agreed and took off with the phones for a nearby clothes shop, returning a couple of minutes later.

"They're OK. But I'll never get this one clean. How about $3.50 for the two?"

They settled on $3.75, and Manny and Pipe turned back toward Sixth Street.

"Nice guys," Charlie commented, then returned to watching the world roll by. Streetwalkers, schoolkids, winos, punks, and lawyers; suits and cell phones, scooters and shopping carts; shouts, jokes, and traffic accidents: Charlie had seen it all and resumed his previous soliloquy without distraction.

"What was I saying? OK, yeah, Frisco. Now *here*, you can make a few bucks with sidewalk sales or selling the *Street Sheet* or canning, and if you don't go against the cops, they might leave you alone. And then there's other people too that know what's going down, people who have sympathies for our side of the situation—you know, the Coalition,

Food Not Bombs. A man don't feel so alone in the world. You don't have to hide. It's bad enough being homeless; you don't want to have to hide like an animal."

Charlie articulated an analysis of homelessness as "just poverty," a case of innocent people down on their luck being pushed around by merchants and cops. He saw some of the other people on the street as "bad characters," to be sure, including several who sold him items to trade. Yet he put faith in Manny, living out his claim that homeless people in general were a diverse group drawn together by economic hardship, neither inherently "sick" nor "sinful."

Lee

"I always liked your shady places—yo' pool hall, yo' juke joint. That's how I *always* was. That's what my grandma say. I couldn' be moochin' 'round the house, hanging 'round school. Seven, eight years old, I'd be already sniffing round Bullshead, down the pool hall. . . . Couldn't stick the teachers, the lame-ass bull crap. . . . So yeah, pool hall was the thing, watching the big boys. They got to know me. Told me bring them a drink, some food. Keep the change. Here's a smoke. Then I was running them reefer. This one O.G. [original gangster], Solo, decided to get me high. Gave him a kick, see this li'l carrottop white kid staggerin' around."

"Lame."

"Nah, was cool. Like I'm saying, it's in my nature. I didn't want that straight life. I was after the candy—getting high, easy money, freedom, ladies, getting high some more. All the good stuff. 'Da *life*,' you know."

I was huddled under the generous awning of the Essex Hotel with Li'l Lee, a twitchy, battered thirty-two-year-old originally from Prichard, Alabama. I welcomed the miserable rain, for it was hard to grab time with Lee, perpetually on the move.

"Shiii-it," he gestured at the silent, glistening sidewalks. "No action today."

Lee—Li'l Lee to many—had spent most of his life immersed in the drug economy. He had started dealing reefer at eleven and by fifteen had developed a heroin habit that eventually bought him time in three states. Like many other white cons, he had adopted elements of

African American style, his languid "Whassup, cuz" lying oddly with his frenetic, forward-leaning stomp up and down the drug markets of Eddy and Ellis streets. At the moment he was touting for a couple of dealers operating around Boedeker Park, copping heroin and sometimes crack for whites wary of the street scene, steaming off to shoot up as soon as he made a few dollars. Other times, when business was too slow, he spare-changed near City Hall, eyes down, sign flying: "Homeless, broke. Anything will help. God bless."

Back on his home turf, though, Lee fiercely rejected the victim role. He never referred to himself as homeless, for example, and in fact used "homeless" as a term of abuse for those unable to "keep theyselves together." He seemed to relish the perils of the Tenderloin streets, claiming that anyone and everyone was a potential predator. "Stay sharp and you jus' *might* survive out here," he warned me after seeing me talking to a friend.

"Linc's cool," I retorted.

"You wanna run with the wolves, you better watch your back," he snapped back.

Sure, the Tenderloin was dangerous, especially at night. But it was Lee himself, far more than I, who insisted on running with the wolves, foolhardily testing his street credentials over and over.

One night I found Lee kneeling in a doorway, trying in vain to save his jeans and shoes from the blood pouring from his nose and lip. One of the Turk Street dealers had caught him trying to steal a lump of black tar heroin and had beaten him to the ground, kicking him hard in the face and ribs. I persuaded Lee to get some stitches in his badly torn lip and found us a ride to San Francisco General Hospital. By then the bleeding had slowed, and he was consigned to wait his turn with a couple of aspirin. Two hours in, he was silent, sweating, and restless. He abruptly surged to his feet and sped around the corner. I followed him, but he was just looking for the bathroom. I could hear him ranting without consonants behind the closed door. He came out, slamming the door.

"You dope sick?"

Lee grunted. "I am so sick of this 'ullshit," he mumbled, trying not to use his aching lip. "Sometimes I wanna leave here so bad, I can't stand it."

"Could you go to Mobile?" Lee still called his mother in Alabama a couple of times a month. "There's ways to get Greyhound tickets, you know."

"Sure I know. And I *ain't* going to my mama. She's got Jesus, and Jesus an' me don't agree." Lee threw himself back in his chair and started to bang his head against the wall. He was a gruesome sight, with his bloodstained clothes and swollen, bloody face.

"Maybe you don't have to be a Christian to get clean?"

"There's no way," he muttered fiercely. "I screwed up every last chance way back. Ain't no way but down. Never done nothing but fuck up." Lee's voice, already quiet, dropped to a mumbling whisper. "Ain't got it *in* me. Ain't got the *will*. The dope . . ." He closed his eyes.

An hour later, his lip stitched and painkillers in his system, Lee had started to recompose his habitual pugnacious persona. He tried to wrest his bruised face into a fierce scowl. "I'll be making plans. That nigger gotta watch his *back*. He think I'm some kinda weak 'uhfucka. Unh *uh*. I don't *think* so."

Lee and Charlie Mack both were living hand-to-mouth in downtown San Francisco. They passed much of their lives within two blocks of each other, some nights sleeping on the same sidewalks and other times standing on the same lines for the massive downtown soup kitchens and emergency shelters. They had a nodding relationship, yet there was little sympathy there, and they had profound disagreements about the causes and significance of homelessness. Charlie presented himself as a fundamentally honest person whose homelessness was a product of a combination of personal bad luck and various social forces stacked against him, notably the racism of potential employers and a "beyond crazy" local housing market. The life he had created for himself went some way toward supporting these beliefs. He had a network of acquaintances, homeless and housed, who treated him as a legitimate trader, and a broad though watchful solidarity toward others on the street. Lee, on the other hand, alternately celebrated and occasionally castigated his wayward nature. In either register he attributed both addiction and homelessness to the willful hedonism of "the life," faltering to silence in the moments when his claims of self-sufficiency and control were disrupted by disrespect, violence, or dope-sick misery.

Timothy

To put it simply, Lee mostly saw homelessness as an outcome of his unchangeable orientation toward "shady places" and life's "candy," whereas Charlie's tendency was to blame a hostile, fiercely unequal society that left him few alternatives. These profoundly dissonant perspectives, which I call *sin-talk* and *system-talk*, dominated the sidewalks and encampments of homeless San Francisco. Many people were more ambivalent than Lee and Charlie. *Sin* or *system* could take hold in different moods, around different activities, and sometimes in different spaces. Off the street, though, in the shelters and in rehab, different stories were told. Homelessness was neither the result of criminality nor social injustice, reiterated the drug counselors and case managers, but a symptom—of addiction, mental frailties, post-traumatic stress syndrome, and other sicknesses.

This kind of therapeutic orientation, or *sick-talk*, offered little opening for self-respect to people still out there on the street, who tended to reference it primarily in mockery and insult; it was most solid among those who had come in from the cold. In a small studio apartment overlooking San Francisco's Polk Street, Timothy, a neatly dressed black man in his forties with a handsome, bony face, shook his braided head with disbelief. "I don't know who's up there, but someone is looking out for me. Should be dead three times over, the life I was leading, but somebody wanted me to survive."

Timothy smiled. "I think that the higher power, or God, or whatever you want to call it, it wanted me to help other guys in the same situation, that's what I think. That's why I became a counselor. Once I started to heal myself, I knew I had to work with this so-called homelessness problem, to get some of those people suffering out there into treatment and help them turn their heads around."

"So-called?" I said.

"Ain't no homelessness problem, in my opinion. The problem is addiction, period. Even those people that have schizophrenia or something else like that, generally you find they have a big problem with addiction as well."

"Is that how you saw it when you were out there?"

"Not really." Timothy caught my eye and broke into a chuckle. "My thinking wasn't worth shit. You know, when you are fully in the grip of the disease like that, you have it all backwards. I was hopping mad at pretty well everyone and mad at myself too, when I was big enough to admit it. But mostly I'd be thinking about my boss that fired me, my girlfriend that turned me out, how they destroyed my life. Plus plenty of blame for the white man, the system, how it wouldn't let me get ahead. You've seen it—you know that tired old BS.

"You let that shit go when you work the twelve steps, if you do it right. It's no good looking outside of you, and it's no use blaming. For me, I had to accept that my *mother* was an addict, and *I* have always been an addict, since I was a little kid. We have that addictive personality in our family, in our DNA, you know. It probably goes back all the way to Africa. Maybe they knew how to deal with it better in those societies."

Like many of his Narcotics Anonymous fellows, Timothy seemed to find comfort in a strongly sociobiological interpretation of addiction. If his problems were predetermined by his addictive personality, there was indeed no use blaming himself as Lee did. And once Timothy accepted that his homelessness was purely an advanced symptom of that addiction, it made little sense to fault social structures "outside of you," as Charlie did.

The highly contradictory discursive strands articulated by Lee, Timothy, and Charlie run deep through American street life, both highly local and specific in their particular character and at the same time deeply constrained by developments at the national, even global, level. The discourses are deeply rooted in specific spaces. For example, I saw a tight affinity between sin-talk and the ex-con milieus of San Francisco's Tenderloin; between sick-talk and the meeting rooms of its transitional shelters and rehab programs; and between system-talk and the outlier encampments of its homeless bottle and can recyclers. Yet the character of these different spaces was unmistakably formed in interaction with broad shifts in notions of governmentality, social entitlement, and social control. Without the imprisonment binge of the late twentieth century, there would be far fewer ex-cons bringing fear and defiance learned behind bars back out onto the streets. Without the vast expansion of therapeutic services since the 1987 McKinney Act, far fewer of the street population would be exposed to medicalized notions of homelessness. And without the massive rejection of broad-based social entitlement since the Reagan revolution, the system-talk of the San Francisco recyclers might be more widely diffused. But then again, without these transformations, perhaps the hundreds of thousands living on the streets of San Francisco and other American cities would not be homeless at all.

This book is organized in three parts: "Backstories," "The Street," and "Rabble Management." The first part lays the groundwork for the ethnographic discourse analysis employed throughout the rest. Accompanying the text are photographs taken in the early 2000s, toward the end of my research, when Gilles Peress helped me overcome a long ambivalence about bringing my camera into the field. Pictures should be understood not so much as direct illustrations of the nearby text but as a visual complement. By then many of my earlier informants had moved on, and there was only a minor overlap with those who later agreed to collaborate on the photographic work. Only James Moss, the friend to whom this book is dedicated, is identified by name and photograph. Many more of my informants pressed me to identify them by name and sometimes by image, but sadly, university human subjects research requirements forbid this. I have disguised their identities in the text with pseudonyms and occasional changes to intimate identifying details.

The first chapter, "Urban Ethnography beyond the Culture Wars," shows how the project developed from a study of homeless recyclers as workers into an ethnographic discourse analysis of several different homeless subcultures. Discourse analysis, I argue, opens a path around social science's interminable tussle between the concept of a self-reproducing culture of poverty and the nearly as old counterargument that deviant practices among the poor represent commonsense adaptations to difficult circumstances. Instead of asking whether the culture of the stigmatized poor might be immoral or pathological, discourse analysis suggests the more holistic project of tracing the intimate, if sometimes reactive, relationship between dominant and more marginal cultural formations. Rather than building (or refuting) an anatomy of deviance, this text investigates how competing discourses on poverty and homelessness affect poor people themselves, organizing and defining their existence and leading them to present themselves in archetypal terms upon the stage of the street.

Chapter 2, "Managing Homelessness in the United States," makes the case that three primary constructions of homelessness have historically dominated American understandings of homelessness: homelessness as moral offense, homelessness as pathology, and homelessness as the product of systemic injustice or instability.[1] Each of these discursive logics — sin-talk, sick-talk, and system-talk — represents a structure of meaning and intention, a magnetic force that lends coherence, authority, and legitimacy to everyday speech and practices within the field of homelessness. Each sets up antithetical causal stories about homelessness, and each demands of us fundamentally different strategies to deal with problem. Sin-talk summons up the twin strategies of exclusion and punishment, sick-talk calls for treatment, and system-talk recommends broader regulation, reform, or even transformation of the broader society. The chapter establishes the salience of this central conceptual schema and provides essential historical context for the ethnography to come.

The three chapters comprising the second part of the book move into the most autonomous spaces of homeless life: the sidewalks, alleys, and encampments frequented by homeless San Francisco men. Despite the constraining hands of the police and the shelter system, men living outside managed to make surprisingly different ways of life. Many pushed back against the degradation and anomie of life on the street, searching to bring together more bearable ways to be homeless. Chapter 3, "Moorings," shows how congregations of street dwellers separated into different subcultures and spaces, highlighting a dramatized semiotic divide between the Tenderloin, the geographic and symbolic center of the city's street scene, and Dogpatch, a more remote and peaceful edge zone. Chapter 4, "Word on the Street," roams more widely through the San Francisco street scene, uncovering a spectrum of street discourses on the causes and character of homelessness. Taking up popular discourses of sin, sickness, and the system, men on the street reworked, blended, and subverted their material. Sometimes they acted strategically, but just as often with passionate sincerity, fighting for some coherent understanding of their past and present experience that might reduce their confusion or despair.

The focus of chapter 5, "The New Hobos," is the lively homeless subculture built around recycling, through which hundreds of homeless pros laid claim to old-fashioned blue-collar masculinity. Spending their days energetically collecting bottles and cans, they developed a grammar of action geographically, economically, and culturally independent of the core skid row zones. Their faulty, addicted bodies were reborn into heroic manual labor, and this labor in turn opened the door to some positive, egalitarian reconnection with each other and the non-homeless. Within the niche economy of recycling, systemic critique took on a tone quite different from the sporadic hyperbole found among those panhandling or stealing, settling into a more coherent and a more feasible "design for life."

The men who gave life to this study led varied lives before becoming homeless. Though most of them had always been poor, they were by no means culturally homogenous. Indeed, the extraordinarily high cost of living in the San Francisco Bay Area squeezed an unusually diverse group of people out onto the streets. There were sociable enthusiasts and misanthropic loners, old cons and young hopefuls, sci-fi freaks and history buffs, football fanatics and rappers, new age philosophers and hobo historians, black nationalists and queer activists. Many had long careers as thieves, drug dealers, or rent boys, but just as many had spent years as soldiers, cooks, truckers, assembly line workers, and nurse's aides. One had been an aviation mechanic, another a municipal dogcatcher, and a third an archaeologist. But without place or possessions, their life histories, enthusiasms, and non-street expertise were gradually stripped away. As they circulated between the street, the homeless archipelago, and the jails, those who failed to get back off the street tended to become more alike, shrinking into stock characters: the manipulative system worker, the resentful panhandler, the menacing street robber, the obsessive recycler, the pathetic bum. The third part of this book turns to the institutions most immediately constraining homeless lives in San Francisco, showing more of how such stock characters get made.

The last chapters center on two pillars of what John Irwin memorably called "rabble management"—the arcane patchwork of institutional strategies we have developed to guide, heal, and punish the urban poor.[2] Chapter 6, "The Homeless Archipelago," follows the men encountered in Part II into the San Francisco shelter system, at that time in the process of shifting from basic or emergency warehousing to more service-rich environments. Here, social workers and counselors tried to help men and women by providing a safe island for therapeutic intervention, but their successes were fragile and often transitory, their sick-talk overwhelmed not only by the endemic sin-talk within street subcultures, but by the insult-laden and authoritarian behavior of many of the frontline staff. Sick-talk struggled to hold its own, sliding back toward the magnetic binaries of sin, further compromised by the paucity of long-term funding for the more healthy men exiting transitional programs. Only the seriously disabled or the few who successfully remade themselves into dedicated twelve-steppers could get enough financial help to actually quit the street. Even then, they were most likely to remain dependent on the treatment industry for their livelihoods.

Meanwhile, the city intensified the redlining of the homeless outside the shelters into a few skid row zones, ghetto neighborhoods, and a few scraps of low-value public space. The homeless clearances described in chapter 7, "The Old Runaround," fueled the alienation and mistrust of those living rough and further attenuated the possibility of community and mutual support by destroying edge zones that had developed relative stability and solidarity. Even those living inconspicuously in vans and cars found themselves further displaced and dispossessed, losing their cars to aggressive ticketing-and-towing campaigns or forced to move outside of the city.

At the level of official discourse, though, the punitive rhetoric of homeless clearance largely disappeared. Politicians' long-standing difficulty justifying high-profile police sweeps to their strong left-liberal constituency spurred them to recast the criminalization of homelessness as tough love in the face of self-destructive denial, a crusade to save the homeless from themselves. Gone was the polarizing struggle between the supporters and critics of Mayor Jordan's Matrix policing offensive of the mid-1990s. Instead, this historically radical city had become one of the central sites for the hybridization of sin-talk and sick-talk into authoritarian medicalization. Taking up the federal approach of narrowing attention toward the most expensive of the homeless population, pioneering mayor Gavin Newsom persuaded voters to pass both the 2002 decimation of relief payments and intensified police campaigns against panhandling and outdoor "lodging."

What was revolutionary was not the crackdown itself, but the way Newsom's team managed to frame it in terms of care and compassion for a chronic population seen fundamentally incapable of understanding their own interests.

A Plea for Patience

Social science pressures us to privilege history over biography, collective patterns over individual maneuvers. Yet ethnography, by immersing researchers for long periods in social spaces outside our control, forces us to recognize the specificity of each person's experience, the striking differences between people in similar social locations. Different people and different traditions have developed highly divergent approaches to writing up the fieldwork. Some adopt looser, more expansive forms of narrative, using the text to follow people, to create richer descriptions of certain individuals, milieus, and particularly evocative episodes. Other ethnographers, especially those of us within sociology departments, are expected to produce and substantiate tightly argued claims and thus tend to chop our data into bite-sized evidentiary segments.

I have always been frustrated by the latter, snippety method of presenting ethnographic work. By showing only decontextualized moments that appear to be emblematic of some collective tendency, this style runs the inherent risk of creating iconic subjects rather than individuals. People appear like stock characters on the news or reality TV, standing for particular experiences, particular positions taken. We smooth over contradictions, losing the uneven texture of the specific in the service of the generalization and oversimplifying complex relationships.

After spending years getting to know individuals, it feels like violence to subject them to this reductive process. The structure of this book, with its alternation between analytical chapters and field vignettes, reflects my own compromise with this particular ethnographic dilemma. Even within the chapters proper, I tend to move backward and forward, theory and evidence interspersed with less tidy, more organic detail. I hope my readers will have patience at the times when I hold off the inherent coercion of analysis to allow some room for the disorder, ambiguities, and ironies of real life.

Part I

BACKSTORIES

ONE

Urban Ethnography
beyond the Culture Wars

T HEIR NUMBERS STEADILY GROWING SINCE THE LATE 1970s, hundreds of thousands stir awake each dawn to the realization that this will be just another day where nothing can be taken for granted. Set fresh every day, the game of the street demands that they play their cards right for money, food, and some kind of shelter over the next twenty-four hours. Horizons shorten; it is hard to strategize beyond the moves of the day. Many hide away their misery, but thousands congregate in the public spaces of large cities, now well-established stock characters of the urban environment. Emaciated panhandlers display their sores and amputations, genial hustlers simultaneously entertain and disturb, and haggard men and bundled-up women stare off into space, jarring the sensibilities of more comfortable passersby.

Homelessness, though, is not a new problem. Mass migration for work was a commonplace of American life during the late nineteenth and early twentieth centuries, the hordes of the destitute on the roads and railways becoming a primary object of fear and political anxiety during periods of particular economic hardship.[1] But during the four decades between the Second World War and the Reagan Revolution, the large-scale homelessness of the previous years was pushed into abeyance. The Okies, tramps, and wild boys of the Great Depression were raised off the street by new social protections, the mass mobilization of the war, and the postwar boom. A few lived out their days in the single-room-occupancy hotels of the Bowery and other shrinking skid row zones, but millions more left destitution for jobs, homes, and

3

families. Many, especially African Americans, found themselves left out of the new prosperity, but utter destitution became rare. Poverty in the United States came to be seen in terms of relative deprivation, stigmatization, and cycles of abuse, not as a fundamental lack of the basic necessities of life: food, shelter, a place in the world.

Then, during the last quarter of the twentieth century, street homelessness rapidly resurfaced, first in the United States, then all over the industrialized world. The American middle classes of the 1980s were taken by surprise, shocked by the dissonance between the abjection of those eating out of garbage cans and their own air-conditioned affluence. Progressive activists and academics responded quickly, setting up thousands of small-scale volunteer operations and developing a systemic analysis centered on deindustrialization and the aggressive rollback of the welfare state by the Reagan administration. They campaigned tirelessly for an integrated federal homelessness policy and succeeded in pushing through the 1987 McKinney Act, which laid the foundation for a new, albeit small, branch of the welfare state. Heightening associations between contemporary street dwellers and the hollow-eyed shanty dwellers of the Great Depression, the activists made homelessness a touchstone for popular fears that layoffs, union busting, and welfare rollback were creating vast polarities of wealth and stretching the social fabric to breaking point.

Sociologists Martha Burt, Peter Rossi, and Joel Blau started work on a trio of landmark sociological studies that investigated both the vulnerabilities of homeless individuals and pursued the structural lines of inquiry raised by the advocacy movement.[2] They associated the growth of homelessness with the decline of industrial employment and the reduction of the social wage, defined as basic provision for those unable to survive from wage labor. Rossi argued in 1989 that there had been a 224 percent increase in extreme poverty since 1973, which he attributed primarily to the loss of manufacturing jobs, starting around 1975.[3] Large reductions in working class wages due to the shift from blue collar to service jobs had been accompanied by sharp reductions in welfare benefits during the same period, especially for recipients of (local) General Assistance (GA) or General Relief (GR). Blau argued that the housing market contributed to the problem and demonstrated a correlation between the return of mass homelessness and a nationwide shortage of affordable housing. Real estate speculation had driven up the price of housing since the late 1960s, while urban redevelopment sharply reduced the availability of affordable niches within central cities, especially the availability of cheap hotels.[4] According to Blau, the most significant losses in the affordable housing market occurred between 1970 and 1985, coinciding with the turn from manufacturing to service work and financial services and the progressive gentrification of the inner cities. A 2-million-unit surplus of cheap housing in 1970 turned into a 3.7 million unit deficit in 1985.[5] Yet, rather than intervening to protect poorer Americans from high housing costs, government bodies from the federal to the city level had steadily moved away from providing or subsidizing housing.[6]

Early investigations into structural causes of homelessness were soon outnumbered by a social welfare literature focused almost exclusively on individual pathology: mental illness, family dysfunction, and drug addiction. The vast network of agencies proliferating after the 1987 McKinney Act opened a massive new terrain for practitioner and policy research; some indicators even suggest that there was more research done on homelessness during the late 1980s and 1990s than on the poverty of the housed.[7] The bulk of this applied homelessness research zoned in on the multi-problem individual in a way that explicitly and sometimes aggressively denied any role for the broader social structure.[8] Baum and Burnes's widely cited *A Nation in Denial,* which came out in 1993, pronounced the whole category of the homeless as fundamentally wrongheaded and overpoliticized. Instead, the authors recommended dropping the term "homeless" in favor of clear medical descriptions such as "patient," "person with AIDS," "alcoholic," "substance addict," and "sexually abused child." The condition of homelessness, rather than taking center stage, said Baum and Burnes, would be better understood as a side effect of more individual-level pathologies.[9]

Sociology, cultural geography, and anthropology pushed back, the next generation of researchers developing a valuable field of what we might call critical homelessness studies. Many of these works take a closer look at the immediate institutions that mediate the experience of homelessness—"the homelessness industry," as the advocates of the 1980s named it. Snow and Anderson were pioneers in this regard, with their typology of different kinds of institutional responses to homelessness.[10]

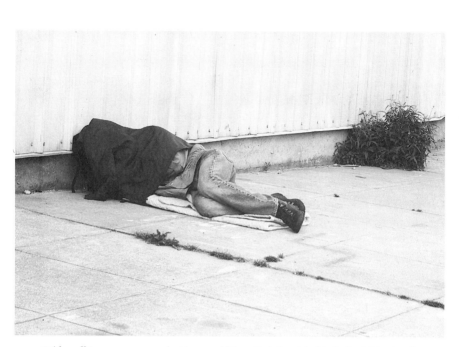

"Sidewalk's warmer come daytime, and if you find the right kind of neighborhood, people won't give you much trouble. It's nighttime you run into the real bullshit."

Golden, Liebow, and Passaro each produced rich studies of the gendering of homelessness and homeless shelters.[11] Later studies, notably those of Philippe Bourgois, Robert Desjarlais, Gwendolyn Dordick, Vincent Lyon-Callo, and Darin Weinberg further explored how shelters and other poverty agencies alter the lives, consciousness, and bodies of their residents.[12] Kim Hopper, who like Gary Blasi combined a prominent advocacy role with research, contributed invaluable work on the institutional circuits traveled by the mentally ill, his more recent work making a strong case for paying more attention to the racialization of homelessness, both past and present.[13]

As the homelessness industry has grown into a massive archipelago of warehousing institutions, several have raised the thorny question of how homelessness might be reproduced or even encouraged by the very institutions set in place to alleviate the problem.[14] Ida Susser suggested that shelters might be further breaking families.[15] Others took up Blau's early lead by extending to the structuration of homelessness by the broader political economy. Snow and Anderson, Waterston, and Duneier pioneered studies of the role of homeless people within street-level informal and illicit economies,[16] complementing analysis of the politics of homelessness within gentrifying and redeveloping cities by Gagnier, Mitchell, Vitale, and others.[17] In a similar way, work focusing on the forceful effects of the criminal justice system[18] and welfare policy[19] found its complement in examinations of bottom-up homeless activism and advocacy, including Talmadge Wright's groundbreaking study of tent-city activism.[20]

"Out There"

In the beginning, the phenomenon that captured my interest was the steady stream of shopping carts loaded high with glass, cans, cardboard, and scrap metal rolling past my door. My apartment overlooked the busy pedestrian corridor of San Francisco's Twenty-fourth Street, one of the main thoroughfares for homeless recyclers on their way to the recycling companies on the eastern edge of the city. Every few minutes I would hear the rising and falling rattle of a shopping cart along the sidewalk below. Often the person, usually a man, stopped to search the trash can under my window, rummaging swiftly into the lower depths with his battered hands.

I found that all sorts of homeless people collected bottles and cans for money, but most visible were a large core group who had created an intense web of meaning around their work as a kind of blue-collar trade. It was with these men that I started my research, interested in how their work seemed to be moving back in the direction of the rag-pickers of the pre–welfare state era.

I learned to do the job, exploring the specific knowledge and practical skills it harnessed and listening closely to how the men talked about it. My notebooks accumulated detailed scrawls about routes and routines, the mechanics of managing large loads, tactics and turf, the connections between the men, and their relationships with their suppliers. My rationale for this starting point was my belief that the recyclers deserved to be taken seriously as workers as much as did nurses, currency traders, bricklayers, or any other occupational group. In the first few months I learned only fragments about the men's more private lives, either by reading between the lines or by seeing things they did not have the resources to hide from me. My unwillingness to pry found willing partners in my new companions, most of whom were just as happy not to bring me into the darker side of their lives. It is not clear now how much of our see-no-evil double act was due to my fear of asking as opposed to their reluctance to show or tell me. Perhaps we shared a tacit assumption that work dignifies while homelessness degrades. Of whatever material this silence was made, we coasted along quite amiably, crushing cans and sharing stories from pre-homeless lives.

As I will soon explain, my focus gradually shifted from the work toward an exploration of how these men engaged with contending discourses about what it means to be homeless. This transition was propelled by the fieldwork itself. We could not maintain the double act forever. It became abundantly clear that digging recycling out of trash cans was fundamentally and inextricably connected to these men's homeless condition, something they would never do were they not living on the street. There was an intimate connection between the "dirty job" and the master status of homelessness, both in their eyes and in the eyes of those that saw them.

At first, the cultural and emotional workings of poverty and exclusion were undercurrents in my work, powerful reasons for my research but superficially examined. Eventually, immersion in these men's lives forced me to acknowledge the torture of being set apart, perceived as profoundly inadequate or irredeemable human beings. The recyclers' awareness of their outcast status slipped into view constantly, by virtue of the passionate exhibitionism with which they invested their dirty, low-paid labor.

One of my first work companions, Sam, clung to his work like a drowning man. He was a champion recycler, muscular and persistent, who often put in nine, ten hours on the trot. Marveling at his speed and stamina, others dubbed him "Robocan." Sam came across as a skillful, intelligent, confident person, whether talking about his past career as a mechanic or loading 200 pounds of cardboard, bottles, and cans onto a slender shopping cart. But when not recycling, his street life was spent skulking in a miserable encampment under a freeway, eaten up by irritation and self-loathing.

Sam had no doubt that his workaholic habits were, more than anything, his way of dealing with the horrors of homelessness.[21] About three weeks after we had started working together, I commented on his insistence that we keep working in heavy rain. "You prefer it when you're working, it seems?"

He looked at his cart full of bottles and replied with an angry laugh. "You could say that. Without this, I'd kill myself. Couple a days, I'd do myself in. . . . You get some guys, seems like they can deal with homelessness. I'm not one of them."

I had little to say. Moments like this swelled my uncomfortable feeling that my primary focus on "work" was leading me to avert my eyes from intense human suffering underlying the vigor of the recycling scene. I began to give more space in my field notes to signs of conflict, anger, shame, and misery.

Turning to the fast-growing literature on homelessness, I learned much of interest, but like other sociologists before me, found it hard to relate the inventiveness, humor, intelligence, and self-sufficiency of the men with whom I had been working to the fundamentally inadequate, socially incompetent multiproblem individuals emerging from the voluminous social welfare literature.[22]

Perhaps the recyclers were an exceptional group, I wondered. Maybe they represented some of the most "high functioning" homeless men. In terms of physical health, this may have been true. However, as my street companions gradually took me inside the city's poverty management apparatus — the hospitals, shelters, welfare officers, and law courts — I saw social workers treat them as chaotic addicts, doctors diagnose them as depressives, and police officers treat them as impediments to the quality of life of other San Franciscans. Perhaps they were not so unusual.

Nevertheless, my evolving line of inquiry required that I increase the scope of the project to get a broader picture of men living rough, and I gradually balanced the twenty "pro" recyclers with eighteen more men who made day-to-day cash from panhandling, stealing, drug dealing, or sidewalk sales. These thirty-eight became my principal research "companions." (They would hate the snitching tone of the term "informant.") Lee was the youngest at thirty-two, Navajo Joe was twice his age. Fourteen of the men were African American, another fourteen white, and seven Latino. Joe was indeed Navajo, Tony Silver a gypsy, and Emory a second-generation Chinese San Franciscan.

As the research grew from the recycling case study into a more ambitious analysis of male street homelessness, questions of representativity returned again and again. How did the idiosyncrasies of my research companions lie in relation to San Francisco's homeless men as a whole? By contacting people on the street I missed out on those currently going through rehab, working programs, and generally spending more time indoors. (This did not create a lasting distinction; over the years of my research most of my companions at some point tried such programs.) More significantly, I had pointed myself in the direction of people physically and mentally strong enough to sustain cash-generating activities. This precluded work with men who were constantly drunk or otherwise deeply incapacitated. Over time, two became severely physically disabled and three more were prevented from any steady working by continuous use of drugs and alcohol. Yet, on the whole, the group was somewhat skewed toward the more robust of the city's homeless men.

Even more significantly, none of my research companions suffered from the psychotic or delusional mental illness that torments a significant minority of homeless men. Six of the men had known several periods of depression or extreme anxiety in their lives, and the isolation, shame, sleep deprivation, and eternal worry produced by homelessness threw several more into periods of acute mental stress. None of the men, though, had been diagnosed with schizophrenia or any other psychotic or delusional disorder. My schizophrenic acquaintances among the city's recyclers sometimes commented on their lives in quite fascinating ways, but to work closely with people with such problems would have raised thorny questions about informed consent. For good or ill, I restricted myself to those who I judged to be sound of mind.

Between the mid-1990s to the early 2000s, I spent roughly 1,700 hours in the field with these men and their friends. I worked and fixed camp with them, and watched and listened as they hawked papers, panhandled, sold junk on the sidewalk, and dealt drugs. Downtime was equally important, whether watching freighters on the bay from the ruined dock at Mission Rock or sitting by as they shot up under a tarpaulin. I followed my street companions into emergency rooms, shelters, and soup kitchens. When I could, I went with them to their interviews with doctors, parole officers, and welfare caseworkers, observing how they were treated and encouraged to think of themselves. The focus of the fieldwork, though, remained their lives *outside* (as well as their *outside* commentary on *inside* affairs).

Relationships with many of the men were episodic and irregular, subject to the endless disruptions of street life and the obstacles of building trust and routine contact across the great housed/homeless divide. My longest sustained friendships developed with those who either lived nearby or came through my neighborhood regularly, as it was easier for them to drop in on me than for me to find them after a lapse in contact. Beyond regular field expeditions to certain encampments and zones of activity, I shaped the rest of my life around my fieldwork, trying to walk, bike, or take the bus through likely places, my eyes scanning carts and camps for familiar faces or objects. I used the street telegraph to good advantage, casual acquaintances often helping me to find people. My own way of life made it easy for my street companions to get in touch with me. They could wave me over on the street, call me, or find me working in my apartment on much frequented Twenty-fourth Street.

The peculiarities of the San Francisco street scene reflect those of the city itself. Unlike most of America's stagnant inner cities, the built environment is dense with both residential units and myriad small businesses, its sidewalks teeming with activity. The city has long been a refuge for artists, activists, gay people, and other nonconformists. Home to the Beats, epicenter of the Californian counterculture of the late 1960s, and crucible for a multitude of new social movements from gay liberation to La Raza, postwar San Francisco developed into one of the world's most culturally vital cities. The industrial crisis of the 1970s and 1980s hastened the collapse of the city's massive port, which had employed much of the working class, both African American and white. Large numbers of working class and poor residents, especially African Americans and Latinos, left the city for more affordable towns across the bay.[23] Yet as the labor market and, ultimately, the class structure shifted, the city held on to its commercial importance and skilled working population. Young, well-educated people in large numbers continued to arrive every year. By the 1990s, the Silicon Valley boom was propelling a second gold rush, making San Francisco into a networking capital and playground for the creative highfliers of the information revolution. If not quite a "global city," in Sassen's terms,[24] San

Francisco was established as a "technopole," a major node for increasingly mobile flows of information and international capital.

All of these conditions have played into the particular local shape of the homelessness problem. Since the 1980s, the extraordinary cost of housing in the city, and in the metropolitan area as a whole, has steadily exerted more and more pressure on those of limited means. Evictions from rent-controlled apartments gathered steam during the 1990s, swelling to a full-on panic during the dot-com boom of the late 1990s. (Condo conversions took nearly 900 units out of the rental market in 1998 alone.)[25] Beyond the immediate pressures of eviction, the high price of the housing market squeezed down on the large renting population (the overwhelming majority of the city's residents). Finding and maintaining housing created enormous financial pressures at people's most vulnerable moments: during family or relationship crises, psychotic breaks or crippling depressions, on release from jail or after losing their jobs.[26] Some managed to hold on; many left the city for Oakland and beyond. Others hit the street.

The political and cultural idiosyncrasies of the city also had their effect on the makeup of the street population. The city commands an intense loyalty from its denizens. For a fraction of its impoverished aging hippies and activists, gender outlaws and black nationalists, this loyalty trapped them between a rock and a hard place. Like the majority of the population, they were incomers, but many had not kept much in the way of ties to homes they had left many years ago. They had nowhere to stay and nowhere to go.[27]

Even in the 1980s, the city was already overcrowded and exorbitantly expensive, and had started to be nationally known for its extraordinarily large homeless population. By 1994, when I started my research, panhandlers worked every major intersection, while the shopping carts and encampments of the street homeless regularly punctuated residential and industrial streets alike. Although skid rows of some other American cities are highly dangerous,[28] the relative density and diversity of San Francisco's street scenes made them safe enough, and I roamed freely.[29] My existing mental map of the city became overlaid by a new one, in some ways a negative of the other, a map that highlighted places I had previously passed with indifference. My new San Francisco was the city's remaining blocks of traditional skid row character, vacant lots, back alleys, wasteland alongside freeways and railway tracks, (rare) abandoned buildings, a few parks, and those poor residential neighborhoods too overwhelmed with existing problems to react strongly to the presence of homeless people. If not exactly safe spaces, these liminal areas represented some measure of escape from harassment, places where visible homelessness was less likely to be perceived as a criminal offense.

Many of the street homeless did not abandon the central city, though. My new homeless map of San Francisco also gave prominence to the primary commercial strips, which functioned both as prime sites for panhandling during the day and as dormitories at night, when abandoned by the rest of the population. Along the busiest shopping streets downtown, every block, doorway, and heating vent was claimed by sleepers, with only a sleeping bag, a foam mattress, cardboard, or tarpaulins for shelter. Late each night the loading alleys behind San Francisco Shopping Center sprouted a tent city of several hundred, which melted away by seven o'clock the next morning. The shopping streets of more down-at-heel neighborhoods were equally popular sleeping places. Between the hours of midnight and six, those who were tired or sedated enough slept among the noises of the other people of the night, the patter of roaming thieves and clatter of garbage pickers, the boom boxes of the gang bangers and the bitter fighting of the neighborhood junkies.

I got to know many homeless San Franciscans in the course of my fieldwork. Besides my core research companions, there were some thirty other men and women whom I visited regularly in their encampments and hundreds more with whom I had the occasional conversation. Many of these fleeting relationships grew out of my volunteer work with Open Hand, a meal program for those with HIV and AIDS. I worked for Open Hand in the Tenderloin neighborhood for several years, delivering meals in the airless corridors of the cubicle hotels or staffing a pickup site set up in the lobby of a nonprofit hotel. In flush times of the month, before clients' General Assistance and disability checks were depleted, fewer showed to pick up their meals. On those days, I would bring my rusty yellow Heavy Duty delivery bicycle. Thirty or forty meals piled high in the front basket, I took the sidewalks out of the Tenderloin into the alleys and empty lots of South of Market, the North-East Mission, and China Basin, barking "Hot meals!" or "Want some food?" Most were eager for the food and many happy to talk. These encounters with hundreds of lonely men, tired prostitutes, shifty-acting plotters, and jumpy addicts provided a wealth of observation to draw on as context for more focused fieldwork. Gradually I built a broad picture of the spatial concentrations of the area's homeless subcultures.

Many of my street companions lived in and around the Mission and the Tenderloin. In the Mission, where I had started my fieldwork with the recyclers, were the enthusiastic pros Walter, Juan Carlos, Sam, Anton, Victor, Anthony, Javier, and Hilario, daily steaming across the neighborhood and nearby Noe Valley, Bernal Heights, and the Castro in search of their two loads a day. In the central Tenderloin were Del, JJ, Sammy, Junior, Li'l Lee, Valentino, Spike, Tony Silver, and Linc, all involved to some extent in more illicit ways of getting by. And out on its western edge, panhandling and shooting grotesque quantities of heroin, was Freddie. Then there were those I initially encountered in heavily touristed North Beach (Desmond), the farther reaches of South of Market (Derick and Julius, Dennis and Willie), the counter-cultural center of Haight-Ashbury (Ray and George), and the industrial streets of Bayshore (Wash). Another recycler, Dobie, lived and worked around the residential avenues of the Sunset district.

Perhaps the richest of my sites, though, was the area known as Dog-patch, an isolated industrial neighborhood between the great trench of the 280 freeway and the old industrial shoreline east of Potrero Hill. In this backwater hundreds of homeless people had collected, some hidden away, others in larger encampments or vans. Individuals changed, camps were destroyed, vans towed, but the area proved a consistently compelling place to study San Francisco homelessness. At different points during a six-year period, Dogpatch became home to several men who play important roles in future chapters—cons Pipe and Manny, unemployed painter Carlos, and the stalwart pro recyclers Clarence and Morris. There also was the more desultory Mexican can-ner Valentino, who also sold weed; his genial friend and lover, Spike; big Rich from Kansas; and Navajo Joe. Here were determined loners— Guatemalan marijuana dealer Pablo, depressed loner Tom, and cranky old Peter, desperately defending his right to moor his tiny houseboat. Here also migrated van livers Emory, Foxy, and Smiler, all of them exhausted with fighting the police in the Haight. Now parked on Illinois Street, they joined the neighborhood's earlier migrants from the Haight,

Neighborhoods of San Francisco.

including the countercultural quartet of dumpster divers known to their neighbors as Quentin's crew: Billy, Quentin, Ray (again), and Jaz.

I decided early to maintain my research focus on single men, who greatly outnumbered women on the street.[30] The conditions of life for homeless single women, and even more for homeless women with children, were strikingly different from the situation of single men.[31] Homeless services made a priority of female shelter beds, as women were often victimized on the street. In comparison, men received less financial support and were overwhelmingly caught up in the criminal justice system.[32]

Indeed, the specific form of poverty and isolation suffered by these men was intensely gendered. Since the colonial era, poor women, children, and the elderly have been the primary objects of both charity and

welfare assistance, while impoverished able-bodied men have been left to circulate between the street and the rougher mercies of the criminal justice system. In keeping with this broad historical pattern, the men in the study were both literally and metaphorically caught up in an endless drama of cops and robbers, screws and cons, their attitudes toward other forms of state intervention always overshadowed by the system. Their situation was further determined by their own and their families' notion of manhood. For example, several of the men had hit the street immediately after breakups, breakups often fueled by their failure to live up to the "provider" model of masculinity. Once they were homeless, similar notions both prevented them for asking for help and circumscribed their choice of means of survival.

If the experience of homelessness was heavily gendered, so was the ethnographic encounter. Even beyond the choice of the research questions themselves, any ethnography is bound to be highly colored by the personality and preconceptions of the researcher. When I started doing this research I was thirty years old, a small English white woman of muddled class origin. I had come late to university after playing music on the street, working as a trainee nurse and care worker, and using time on the dole (unemployment benefit) to volunteer as a welfare rights activist. What influence my life history had on my ethnographic role I do not know. It is always hard to *really* know what other people make of you. One thing I knew for sure was that several of the men appreciated my willingness to jump into dumpsters. I think it also helped that I had some acquaintance with drugs and squatting. I was not squeamish and adapted to the dirty and uncomfortable conditions of street life fairly easily.

Gender, on the other hand, set me fundamentally apart in these all-male spaces. I may have been butch enough to be out there with them, but I wasn't really that tough. My companions knew it, protecting me from individuals they knew to be dangerous, hiding my presence at times, and often telling me to go home to bed when it was getting late. I rarely stayed out all night. A few were flirtatious, clearly enjoying an all-too-rare chance to play the ladies' man.[33]

I have no doubt that my gender also played into my decisions about where, when, and how to do fieldwork. In return, being a woman seemed to have an equally important effect on the kinds of experiences, moods, and stories my companions were willing to share with me. Where the work of male street ethnographers has often highlighted rambunctious group life, my own field notes were thick with meditative, sometimes painfully confessional conversations with men on their own or in pairs.

A conversation with Dennis, a middle-aged white recycler, suggested something of the way that introspection and intimacy played into my own particular ethnographic quid pro quo. Dennis and I had been working together, talking, and hanging out occasionally over two months, mostly around the rapidly changing South of Market area. Today we made a good start, meeting at 6:00 a.m. by the Ferry Building. After good pickings in the alleys around Fourth Street, we pushed south toward the recycling center on Rhode Island.

"Do you mind if I get that down?" I asked after he had shared a story about his life working on the state highways.

"Go ahead," he said, looking a little uncomfortable. I grabbed my notebook from my back pocket and scrawled for a minute while Dennis walked across the street to check out a couple of trash cans.

As we set off again, I asked him, "So how are you feeling about this, about being part of my ethnography?"

"It's OK, I guess. Can't say it really makes any difference to me. Long as you change my name," he said and glanced at me questioningly.

I promised again that I would and he shrugged. After selling our first load and taking a cigarette break, Dennis was eager to get moving again. Last week he had decided to buy himself a tent, and I was saving the cash for him.[34] We set off for a residential trash run on the wealthier north end of Potrero Hill, slogging up in silence, the effort taking all of our breath. The morning mist had rolled away to hang above Twin Peaks and the sun was shining hot on our backs. At the top of the hill we paused for breath, sitting on the edge of the sidewalk. Dennis lit up the remains of a cigarette.

"Seriously, it's cool with me, this research deal," he said. "To be honest, it is a big relief to drop the bullshit. Just be *real,* you know. I can get kinda down out here."

Dennis started to complain about "BS" from his peers on the street. "Damn, there is a whole load of bullshit: 'Nah nah, the government this or that,' 'Yah yah, big plans, buying vans, setting up business,' 'Nah nah I useta be such a big fella.' Sometimes you just wanna say, 'Come on man, you fucked up, we all fucked up. And we are screwed, majorly screwed.' Sometimes I just got to *say* it. There's no chance, no fucking chance in hell, I'm gonna get my old life back. I. Am. So. SCREWED." Dennis's sudden shout startled a woman farther up the sidewalk, who turned an anxious face.

"Feel better?" We laughed.

"Dunno. Yeah. I gotta look it in the face, move from here, you know."

Confessional moments like this usually occurred one-on-one, often inside my apartment, in fact. Whatever influence my presence had on the tone of their lives was clearly limited. Within yards of the door, earnest introspection could turn to sarcasm or phlegmatic business as usual. Yet I think the particular kind of intimacy our relationship offered was significant for several of the men — another reason I have chosen to use the term "companion" rather than "informant."

I found this more small-scale fieldwork very rewarding. Ideas about "where the action is" are, of course, highly subjective. If I had been a man — or even a different kind of a woman — perhaps I would have been more excited about proving myself in the most rowdy situations. Or if I had been trained in sociology's symbolic interactionist tradition, for example, I might have approached the microfunctioning of street groups with a more driving interest and a richer set of research questions. But as it was, I was drawn to quieter forms of interaction.[35]

One advantage of spending time with individuals and pairs of buddies was the chance to discuss both my own evolving analysis and arguments developed by other researchers: Snow and Anderson's various typologies of homeless life; Passaro's explanations of the extreme gender separation among the very poor; James Q. Wilson's "broken windows" argument; Ida Susser's analysis of how shelter systems might distort family forms; or William Julius Wilson's claims about the "declining significance of race" or concentration effects in the ghetto.[36]

The project to take so-called folk theory seriously should be apparent in the text, particularly in Part III, where I treat the men's analysis as counterpoint to my own narrative. This kind of fieldwork is far from fly-on-the-wall ethnography; there is an inevitable trade-off between reflexivity and naturalism. Most of the time I tried my mouthy best to let my companions roll with their own subject matter, dedicating my energies to recording their lives and voices.

Wrestling the Post-Moynihan Syndrome

Like Lee at the beginning of the book, a good number of my research companions were convinced at heart that their own sinful ways had led them to their current poverty and degradation. This often defiant claim of agency, of making their own choices, echoed talk of intentional homelessness within the public sphere and forced me to think long and hard about how to represent their voices. My reflections were inevitably overshadowed by the persistent, sometimes paralyzing impasse within American research on poverty that I think of as the "post-Moynihan syndrome."

In any context, the awkward intimacies of ethnographic method have a tendency to bring up excruciating dilemmas, pressing us to wrestle particularly intensely with questions of representation, reciprocity, accountability, and other "power effects."[37] What makes the American social science of poverty distinct, though, is the way that culture itself has become so firmly attached to blaming the victim that generations of scholars have tied themselves in knots trying to undertake qualitative studies of poverty without giving cultural patterns any independent causal weight.

This is not a place for a thorough excavation of the history of culture versus structure in American poverty studies, a thread that stretches back through the nineteenth-century charity reform movement and beyond.[38] But for those either new to this field or rusty on the history, the defining moment remains the raging debate over the 1969 report on "The Negro Family: The Case for National Action" by Daniel Patrick Moynihan, which accounted for the poverty, unemployment, and violence that were plaguing African American communities across the country by pointing at problems on the family level. Dysfunctional values and behaviors at the family level, particularly a tendency toward matriarchal households and corresponding male irresponsibility, said Moynihan, were now more potent causes of black poverty than the vestiges of white racism. "Three centuries of injustice have brought about deep-seated structural distortions in the life of the Negro American," he wrote. "At this point, the present tangle of pathology is capable of perpetuating itself without assistance from the white world. The cycle can be broken only when these distortions are set right."[39] Oppressive social structures may have started the problem, but now the issue was one of pathology.

The central concept that Moynihan drew on, the self-reproducing culture of poverty, was first developed by Oscar Lewis in 1961 and taken up by several other sociologists and anthropologists during the following years. Like contemporary biological interpretations of addiction, Moynihan's "tangle of pathology" manifested in dysfunctions set in place early in life. According to Lewis, the "slum child" was already programmed for failure by the age of six or seven, unlikely to be able to take advantage of any opportunities that might arise later in life.[40]

Moynihan's report was released to a divided nation. The war in Vietnam was still raging, and at home the optimism of the earlier civil rights movement had become overshadowed by anger, despair, and violence. The previous five years had seen the assassinations of JFK, Malcolm X, and Martin Luther King Jr.; riot and rebellion in several major cities; and the rise of black separatism. In this volatile atmosphere, the widely publicized report provoked fury among civil rights activists and the left. The protesters included many of the younger generation of social scientists who were developing quite different analyses of race and poverty, ones that traced the social problems of the northern ghettos out to the broader social and economic structure (or political economy).

There was no sense, said Moynihan's critics, in attributing a "culture of poverty" to a population that had consistently been excluded from participation in the basic democratic institutions of American society by both terrorism and force of law. The Voting Rights Act, after all, was barely four years old. To focus on the reproduction of African American poverty when it was so obviously produced by forces beyond the control of poor communities was tantamount to collaboration with the racist establishment, they argued.

"Poor people tend to live in slums, to be oppressed and exploited and mistreated, and to experience enormous amounts of social, economic, mental and physical suffering as a result," argued popular sociologist William Ryan. "It is much more reasonable to conclude, not that 'family instability' leads to a 'tangle of pathology,' but that poor Negro families — that is, close to half of all Negro families — are bitterly discriminated against and exploited, with the result that the individual, the family, and the community are all deeply injured."[41]

Rarely has a government report raised such a passionate and sustained reaction from either academia or the general public. Not only did the reaction to Moynihan provoke intense soul searching within sociology and anthropology departments at the time, it has overshadowed the study of poverty and underdevelopment ever since. This post-Moynihan syndrome has particularly affected studies using ethnography and other qualitative methods, inhibiting up-close cultural description.

As Philippe Bourgois has said, it is not surprising that the culture of poverty concept was developed within anthropology, the original home of ethnography's method.[42] With an intimate focus on the texture of on-the-ground social life, ethnography necessarily pulls people's behavior to the foreground. Given that readers are highly predisposed to scorn and fear those at the bottom of class and racial hierarchies, ethnographies of the lifeways of the poor are highly vulnerable to being taken out of context and used against their subjects as evidence of cultural dysfunction, regardless of the nuances of the writer's own analysis. At the same time, the immediate character of the research means that it requires considerable skill, not to mention chutzpah, to mobilize ethnographic data into a convincing structural analysis.[43] In other words, ethnographers are most likely to be considered expert authorities to the extent that they are describing behavior, while our efforts to integrate structural analysis are dismissed as unconvincing due to lack of statistically significant sound-bites.[44]

Scholars pursuing qualitative studies of poverty and marginality in the intensely politicized post-Moynihan years in fact ran a double jeopardy. Not only did they need to preempt misappropriation of their work, but they also needed to win over colleagues eager to root out the "victim-blaming" scholarship that had given their disciplines a bad name. Among left-leaning social scientists, culture had become something of a dirty word and was allowed into the picture only when treated strictly as superstructure. Ethnographers willing to brave the field of poverty became more rare,[45] and in general, the sociology and anthropology of poverty suffered a crisis of confidence, which only hastened the loss of policy ground to economics, a discipline much less concerned about maintaining progressive credentials.[46]

Those persisting with ethnographies of poverty moved very cautiously, negotiating a tricky midground between structure and culture. Most followed the path laid by Hyman Rodman, Elliot Liebow, and Carol Stack, among others.[47] Like Lewis himself, these authors treated the beliefs and practices of poor African Americans and other poor people as cultural adaptations to hostile and unmovable external structures. But where Lewis had seen such adaptation hardening into pathologies with their own effects on the future, the post-Moynihan adaptation scholars saw reasonable behavior within unreasonable constraints.

The overt tension within the field may have appeared to abate over the years, but the culture wars continued to smolder beneath the surface. One particularly notable flare-up occurred in the late 1980s, in response to the work of William Julius Wilson. Wilson had made his name with *The Declining Significance of Race* (1978), an analysis of changing determinants of African American poverty, which he positioned firmly on the safer ground of structural analysis. Nine years later, with *The Truly Disadvantaged*, Wilson shifted cautiously in the direction of culture, turning to qualitative research on the reproduction of disadvantage within ghetto communities isolated from mainstream social norms.[48] Again, a lengthy debate and some hard words ensued. Wilson's analysis of local neighborhood effects on poverty and low labor market attachment was widely adopted as a framework for policy research, but Wilson was taken to task by several eminent sociologists for contributing to the pernicious notion of a self-reproducing underclass and, in the process, failing to sufficiently emphasize structural causes of inequality.[49]

The most recent exchange of blows in poverty research's culture wars was launched by Loïc Wacquant in his blistering 2002 critique of what he called "neoromantic ethnography." Contemporary ethnographers of urban poverty, he charged, are "locked within the prefabricated problematic of public stereotypes," so fearful of producing negative images of the poor that many of us are producing anodyne, moralistic pabulum. Focusing on a trio of recent works by well-respected ethnographers, he argued that the authors failed either to describe accurately the degradation and demoralization of the poor or to analyze how such degradation might be produced and maintained by the symbolic and economic violence of the neoliberal state.[50]

What few would deny is that qualitative researchers have had good reason to move cautiously. As the political movement to roll back the welfare state and institute harsh sentencing gained momentum during the 1980s and 1990s, there was more danger than ever that unflattering descriptions of the lives of poor Americans would lead to blaming the victim and only reinforce the popular concept of a depraved, self-reproducing underclass.[51]

The acrimony of the neoromantic debate aside, it follows that the hostile political climate has pushed ethnographers themselves to adopt a handful of their own strategies — often more than one at the same time.

Drawing broadly from ethnographies of inequality, I see at least six of these strategies, each providing some kind of solution, yet, inevitably, more problems of its own. Still most common in sociology is the adaptations strategy itself, pursuing the early lead of Ryan and Rodman by playing down cultural specificity and constructing difference in terms of rational behavior within unreasonable conditions.[52] A second approach has been to design research more likely to produce relatively positive images by studying less deviant segments of the poor population,[53] whether defined as the (black) "working poor" of Stoller or Newman or the struggling parents of Edin and Lein, Berrick, and Kaplan.[54] The so-called neoromantic strategy excoriated by Wacquant takes this approach one step further, fighting the moralists on their own terrain with an explicit emphasis on decency in the face of overwhelming odds. At the opposite pole is a fourth strategy, a refusal to engage at all with the inflated moralism of public debate on the subject, often expressed within a macho "ethnonoir" register that makes a virtue of deliberately gritty, sometimes overblown realism.[55]

In a quite different vein is the body of work analyzing deviant behavior as a collective rejection of hegemonic norms. Some scholars continue the resistance narrative developed in studies of the global south in the 1970s and 1980s.[56] Reading subaltern cultural forms and hostility toward hegemonic narratives as critique, the resistance model's pitfall is the temptation to optimistically slide from resentment to rebellion and from rebellion to social change.[57] Everyday forms of opposition may be creative, and even of great cultural significance, but if unconnected to a coherent strategy or the resources for social change, they are just as likely to reproduce inequality as to change it.[58] This idea that rebellion often feeds social stasis forms the kernel of a sixth strategy, one that owes much to Willis's *Learning to Labor*.[59] In the more recent formulation of Philippe Bourgois, for example, the agency of the young drug dealers in *In Search of Respect* comes down to the freedom to fashion their own destruction.[60] Again, though, with its emphasis on "bad" behavior, this focus pulls work toward the lowlife glamour of ethnonoir.

All these responses to the post–Moynihan syndrome are both tempting and problematic in their own way, and I struggled for some time to find a path that felt right. Indeed, the dangers of conceptualizing my work badly seemed far more forbidding than the dangers of fieldwork itself. A year in, I recognized that my initial study of the role of homeless people in the recycling industry had taken me much too far into the realm of positive images. Without a broader sense of the discursive logics of the street, my descriptions of the powerful work ethic I found among the pro recyclers seemed to slip into a normative tone, implying a certain moral approval by implication withheld from those securing their daily bread in more passive or more illicit ways.

My second response to the analytical and political dilemmas of studying poverty was to turn to an ethnographic form of discourse analysis. Discourse is neither culture nor structure but *cultural structure*. As such it challenges the old opposition between large scale (external) structural forces and cultures defined as small scale or local.

Instead, it encourages us to pay attention to the lines of continuity knitting elements of domination, reproduction, and even "resistance" together to form dense tangles of thought, speech, and practice.

What I try to demonstrate, therefore, are the commonalities linking each of the three primary American discourses on homelessness: the moral castigations of *sin-talk,* the therapeutic narratives of *sick-talk,* and the structural critiques of *system-talk.* These competing discourses were not only mobilized by experts and officials embedded in large-scale institutions, I argue, but they were also taken up, reworked, and performed by people on the street, sometimes in quite a direct fashion, more often in oblique, reactive, or strategic ways.

Yet the rich potential of ethnographic method seemed cramped by focusing on speech and text only. Discourse analysts in the social sciences usually address projects or practices that have been *flattened* into text, as representations, narratives, plans, or rhetoric. Another strategy is to flatten those processes ourselves by interviewing and analyzing the transcripts. Then we have to turn in the opposite direction, to *unflatten,* and show that our analysis has something to do with real-life practice. This roundabout process distances us from individual experience and action and nudges us toward functionalism, leaving our subjects themselves flattened in turn, lifeless puppets jerked around by forceful ideas.

My approach is to avoid the problems of flattening with an unusually *ethnographic* discourse analysis. Rather than treating discourse and practice as essentially different, I find it more useful not only to treat speech as action (like the symbolic interactionists), but also to understand action as a kind of "speech," a vehicle of meaning in its own right. A lot of behavior, like much talk, remains uncontentious, unladen with heavy symbolism or argument. Yet practices can become just as discursively charged as any verbal statement. For example, I described earlier how the hard manual slog of the "pro" recyclers became a defiant public reply to widely held assumptions about the incapacity or idleness of the homeless.

Discursively charged practices, just like speech, tend to congeal, different "grammars of action" pulling together specific physical styles, repertoires of skill, or ways of moving through physical and social spaces. Particular elements come to stand for broad orientations, just as a phrase like "multiproblem individual" or "playa" conjures an entire lexicon. For example, the street hustler's "cool pose" makes up a particular "grammar of action" — a physical style and repertoire of action that, whether intentional, unconscious, or something in between, not only sets strong limits around what the hustler can comfortably do, but directly constrains the semantic potential of his or her actions. Within the caseworker-client interaction, a knowing smirk or wary front, with its implicit retention of agency and rejection of the supplicant role, violates the therapeutic discourse on homelessness as much as any overt disagreement.

Though the men in this book disagreed passionately about the causes and character of homelessness, all agreed on one thing. For them, just as for the rest of us, homelessness constituted a rupture in the social order, an exceptional state that required explanation. The ragged external markers of living outside — the big bags and blankets, the shopping cart, the tattered or smelly clothes — all worked together to scrawl a large question mark over each person's head, compelling some kind of story of "the fall."[61] Within this context, the micropolitics of self-representation transmitted via different grammars of action took on weighty explanatory significance.

First, though, we need to move back a couple of steps. Homelessness in America is a long-lived phenomenon, a many-headed monster. Few of us can be unaware of the largest social policy turns of our era — the great imprisonment binge, the dismantling of the Keynesian welfare state. Yet the specific policies most immediate to this story — the medicalization of homelessness since the late 1980s and the simultaneous wave of quality-of-life legislation criminalizing panhandling and other status crimes — have probably become naturalized to many readers by this point. The next chapter aims to reverse this naturalization, clarifying the parallels between shifting ideas about homelessness and broader American constructions of inequality and citizenship, past and present. Our contemporary iterations of "broken windows" policing, transitional shelters, and social justice advocacy take on a richer meaning against the crucial backdrop of the great tramp scare, the "Wobbly" mobilization, and the powerful cultural and economic interventions of the New Deal. The history matters.

TWO

Managing Homelessness in the United States

FTER A THIRTY-YEAR PERIOD WHEN THE ONLY STREET people were a few chronic alcoholics, homelessness re-emerged during the economic slump of the late 1970s. Initially concealed by more flamboyant intentional dropouts of the counterculture, the new homelessness did not attract immediate public attention. By the early 1980s, large numbers of ragged people had moved into the downtown areas of large cities, sleeping in doorways and asking for change. An old social problem was reborn, and in time, also reborn, albeit in new forms, were powerful discourses on vagrancy developed over previous centuries.

This chapter lays the conceptual groundwork for the ethnography to come. Moving through some of the most important developments in American homelessness policy since the colonial period, it shows how broad, long-standing epistemic currents have fed into three primary discourses on homelessness: an ancient sin discourse gradually challenged, but by no means defeated, by notions of sickness and system.

The history of American homelessness management has in several respects run parallel to the country's broader stream of ideas and practices around poverty management. But at certain times in history, homelessness has become a more autonomous field of play. In an effort to keep this rather complex story clear, I differentiate between specific discourses on homelessness — *sin-talk, sick-talk,* and *system-talk,* in my terms — and the more far-reaching *constructions of poverty* to which each is related: *moral, therapeutic,* and *systemic.*[1] Each discourse on homelessness shares with its related construction of poverty the same fundamental strategies for managing the disruly poor. The moral construction and sin-talk are primarily tied into strategies of *exclusion* and *punishment* (although there is also the possibility of *redemption* for the more deserving); the therapeutic construction and sick-talk look to *treatment;* and the systemic construction and system-talk urge *social regulation* or even *transformation.*

Sin, Sickness, and the System

According to the *moral* construction of poverty, the miseries of the poor are the result of moral laxity. At best they give into laziness and hedonism; at worst they sell their souls to the devil. But whether demonic or merely disorderly, they willfully deviate from society's rules.

The essential elements of this discourse have remained markedly consistent between European and North American Protestants over the last five hundred years. The fundamental causes of poverty are found in the same character defects, and the primary strategies of control remain punishment and exclusion, although the earlier differentiation between the two has been progressively blurred with the rise of incarceration, a practice combining both strategies. Ideas about the instrument of punishment, though, have evolved more significantly. As the Protestant ethic became entwined with liberalism and social Darwinism, the drama of future hellfire gradually took second place to more mundane misery here on earth. God's judgment passed into the inexorable hand of the market, rewarding effort and dooming the feckless.

In comparison with most of Europe and Latin America, the moral construction of poverty in the United States has been extraordinarily potent and persistent. Many authors have argued that the persistent power of this premodern, crudely binary form of social control is rooted in the nation's history of settler colonialism. A capitalist powerhouse built on the frontiers of the preindustrial world, the United States was born of an uneasy marriage between two very different kinds of society. We tend to accentuate the modernity of America, the dynamism of its industrialization and the civilized political forms that

Constructions of poverty	Moral	Disease	Systemic
Discourses on homelessness	Sin-talk	Sick-talk	System-talk
Central cause of poverty/homelessness	Sin	Sickness	Characteristics of the social structure
Fundamental strategies for managing poverty/ homelessness	Punishment and exclusion	Treatment	Social change/ social regulation
Focus of causal narrative	Individual	Individual	Structural
Notion of agency	Strong	Weak	Weak

Euro-American constructions of poverty and homelessness.

nourished it. Yet equally important was the primary accumulation pioneered by the American colonists and their descendants: the native genocide, the forceful expropriation of vast amounts of land, and a prolonged reliance on slave labor and other violent forms of racial domination.[2]

It is to this second trajectory that the United States owes its continued reliance on punishment, incarceration, and even execution to control the behavior of the poor. Indeed, many make the case that these punitive practices depend for their legitimacy on demonic representations of African Americans developed during slavery.[3] Equally important, the widely held (erroneous) conception that feckless African Americans make up the majority of welfare claimants has weakened public support for antipoverty programs throughout the twentieth century, an abandonment that only reinforces desperation and criminality.[4]

Lying within the outstretched arms of this moral construction of poverty is the more specific moral discourse on homelessness — what I am calling sin-talk. Sin-talk has its own particular bogeymen: the lawless tramp, the inevitably criminal drifter, the fraudulent panhandler. Over the last four centuries these images of the undomesticated outsider have been mobilized in twin strategies: *clearance* of vagrants, or street people, by the police or private security forces, corralling them into marginal areas away from the rest of the population; and punishment of vagrancy by *confinement,* often including forced labor.

From the "Beggar's Book" to the Poorhouse

American sin-talk dates back at least as far as the great theological and ethical changes wrought by the Protestant Reformation. The significance of these Protestant innovations is hard to grasp in our own time. Before the Reformation, medieval European understandings of abject poverty were underpinned by a discourse now almost obsolete within Protestant countries: the Catholic transcendental discourse on poverty. The medieval Catholic believed that to refuse charity to the homeless beggar was to risk eternal damnation. Almsgiving was the principal practice associated with this discourse. Not every rich man was willing to give up his worldly goods, and almsgiving was a much less demanding alternative. The transcendental discourse did not construct poverty as a social problem. One could sympathize with wretched individuals, but the persistence of wretchedness was taken for granted. "The poor are always with us," says the Bible, and the possibility of achieving a blessed afterlife through almsgiving actually made the poor quite useful.

Although gift giving had the important effect of dampening potential conflict between rich and poor, ad hoc donations on the individual level were never enough to deal with large-scale crises. From the eleventh century onward, population growth and mobility created a series of epidemics across Europe, devastating newly urbanized peasants who lacked immunity to the common diseases.[5] Influential abbots exhorted their fellows in other monasteries and convents to provide help and shelter to the sick and poor, calling on the biblical story of Dives and Lazarus.[6] Eventually, rural and urban monasteries provided rudimentary shelters, known as hospices, which offered a degree of food and refuge for the indigent and sick. These rather chaotic Catholic hospitals all differed from subsequent European institutions for the poor in that they made little distinction between deserving and undeserving or, indeed, between poverty and physical incapacity.[7]

The Protestant Reformation initiated a sea change in how poor people were seen and treated. Work, not almsgiving, was now the road to salvation, and poor people who failed to work represented a disconcerting blot on the spiritual landscape. Protestant crusaders strove to discredit the transcendental discourse by associating it with the most corrupt aspects of the Catholic establishment.

The case against spontaneous almsgiving was made most forcefully by Martin Luther in his *Liber Vagatorum,* or "beggar's book." This apocryphal rant is written in the form of an encyclopedia of deceptions perpetuated by beggars. Presenting the beggar as the ally and lay counterpart of the fraudulent, licentious priests and monks he excoriated in other works, Luther aimed to cast suspicion on impoverished strangers of all kinds, whether peddler, blind beggar, epileptic, cripple, or wandering scholar.[8] The solution to the contemporary problem of beggars was strict monitoring of paupers by each parish and limiting aid to the deserving:

> Every town and village should know their own paupers, as written down in the Register, and assist them. But as to outlandish and strange beggars they are not to be borne with, unless they have proper letters and certificates; for all the great rogueries mentioned in this book are done by these. If each town would only keep an eye upon their paupers, such knaveries would soon be at an end.[9]

With Luther's help, the new sin-talk transformed attitudes toward beggars. For the first time, begging and impoverished wandering were primarily understood as indications of moral weakness or criminality and as major social problems. The new Protestant municipalities of Switzerland and Germany, for example, quickly outlawed begging and removed responsibility for welfare from the Catholic Church into rationalized secular organizations. Sixteenth-century welfare reforms were most far-reaching in Protestant-controlled areas. By the mid-1500s, for example, English vagabonds were liable to be branded and enslaved, the punishment for a second escape being death. Catholic elites followed suit, adopting the new antibegging laws to control the famine-starved peasants on their own lands.

In Reformation Britain, the new Protestant animosity toward beggars and wanderers came together with the needs of the aristocrats, launching a ruthless war on vagrancy. The centuries-long exodus of serfs from rural estates to the growing towns was accelerating, squeezing the resources of the aristocracy and providing the cheap labor to fuel the rise of the rival merchant class. In response, the lords instituted even stricter vagrancy laws. The justification for these extraordinary punishments was the same belief expressed by Luther in the

Liber Vagatorum: the notion that impoverished wanderers lay at the root of social disorder and criminality.

The moral construction of poverty thoroughly dominated American poverty management throughout the colonial period and beyond. The colonists of the seventeenth century reiterated the approaches to poor relief unfolding in Britain, combining limited relief for certified residents with stringent settlement laws denying entitlement to strangers.[10] Indeed, the sectarian insularity of the New England Puritans only intensified suspicion of newcomers without money, who were liable to be warned out of town or auctioned to local farmers as indentured workers.[11]

Over the next two centuries, poverty relief remained an intensely local affair. Colonial small towns spent a good deal of effort on shipping out both disabled and able-bodied vagrants to other municipalities.[12] For the poor who did qualify for relief, there were three possible outcomes. Those judged to be sufficiently deserving—mostly women—were given "outdoor relief," that is, aid that did not require them to be institutionalized indoors. The second option was the dreaded poorhouse, where vagrants and other indigent paupers were involuntarily confined and set to work. The third practice, and probably most abusive of all, was to auction off the poor to the lowest bidder, who would keep his or her charges as cheaply as possible, with little oversight from the parish. Treatment of the nonslave poor was worse in the South, where organized outdoor relief was very rare.

During the eighteenth and early nineteenth centuries, urbanization increased the numbers of people living in abject poverty, concentrating them in larger towns and cities. To deal with this new industrial poor, both more visible and rebellious, urban elites developed a sprawling patchwork of institutions: prisons, houses of industry, orphanages, asylums, poor farms, and jails. The central institution of this complex was the poorhouse, designed to warehouse all kinds of municipal paupers.

The expansion of the poorhouse system was broadly supported by the upper classes of the early nineteenth century. Many educated people were influenced by the work of Jeremy Bentham, Thomas Malthus, and David Ricardo, who saw the roots of poverty in insufficient discipline, illegitimacy, and the pernicious effects of relief on the labor market.[13] With the poorhouse, as with the new penitentiary, elites pursued social control over both vagrancy and demands for welfare. They hoped that a centralized institution of confinement and hard labor would deter tramping and applications for municipal relief.[14]

However gruesome the reality, the poorhouse was by no means a purely punitive development. The early nineteenth century was a period of great optimism, with hope that rational social engineering might solve all sorts of problems. The more sympathetic reformers were particularly concerned to finish with two of the infamous abuses common under the existing, more piecemeal system: the auctioning off of care of the poor to the lowest bidder and the endless transportations of paupers from one town to the next by municipalities unwilling to pay for their survival. On humanistic grounds alone, the imprisonment of the improvident in poorhouses was seen to open the greater possibility of treatment and rehabilitation. The future therapeutic discourse on homelessness — sick-talk — was already in the air.

In practice, however, the new institutions continued to be dominated by notions of sin rather than sickness, with the goal of deterrence triumphing over the ideal of rehabilitation. The poorhouses were underfunded, disease-ridden barns with terrible food and little heating. Any pauper capable of work was set to hard labor in farming or manufacturing by superintendents keen to maximize their profits.[15] Vagrants or drunkards shared quarters with destitute families, the mentally ill, abandoned children, the old and the sick, and the mentally and physically disabled.

The mid-nineteenth-century poorhouse may not have given much space to the developing therapeutic construction of poverty, but ultimately its failings made it a unifying focus for critics of punitive approaches. By midcentury, many reformers were arguing that the age-old division between the deserving and undeserving poor should be reconceptualized on medical grounds and the poorhouse population separated into multiple regimes. Children should be removed to orphanages and given a useful education, while the genuinely disabled, sick, insane, and elderly should be given decent medical care in almshouses and asylums. The physically fit, in contrast, would be more convincingly deterred from dependency if separated off to perform hard labor in houses of industry and poor farms.

As has often been the way with American poverty policy, poor funding trumped theoretical ideals. Asylums, funded at state levels, did indeed take over many of the mentally ill and elderly, but county houses could ill afford separate institutions for the other inmates. Instead, the poorhouses gave up on the project of disciplining vagrants. Between 1850 and 1870 they turned into infirmaries, ejecting all transients of working age.[16] Men and women on the streets now had nowhere to sleep but the station houses and jails.[17]

Even inside the highly controlled tutelage of the late nineteenth century's confining institutions, the medicalization of poverty remained patchy. Certainly, the classification and management of the poor began to take on a more medicalized character, but the therapeutic construction of poverty remained incoherent, with the concept of rehabilitation constantly undermined by the persistence of moral condemnation and punishment.

Outside of the confining institutions, sin-talk proved even more dominant. The migrant poor continued to be plagued by settlement laws that refused relief to outsiders without established residency and punished them for their indigence.[18] These laws had by now served as the benchmark of the Anglo-American distinction between deserving and undeserving poor for nearly three centuries. Each locality was free to set its own classification system and rules, creating a chaotic system that only encouraged the lengthening of settlement requirements as more generous locales tried to prevent immigration from those with stricter laws.[19] Even arguments from frustrated employers failed to shift the intensely local structure of welfare provision, and settlement laws remained the primary mechanism for adjudicating relief well into the twentieth century.[20]

Tramp Scares

Settlement laws utterly failed as a deterrent strategy, and the numbers of migrant poor swelled throughout the second half of the nineteenth century. By the 1850s, most manual workers had been reduced to wage labor, vulnerable to the unsteady business cycle. Independent journeymen artisans were slowly but inexorably losing their jobs to lower paid apprentices and unskilled laborers, and unskilled and seasonal laborers like threshers or ice cutters losing theirs to machines.[21]

The Civil War further disrupted employment and production, as well as leaving hordes of hardened ex-soldiers who refused to return to domesticated settled life under the old conditions. New immigrants from Europe and many thousands of freed slaves moved into the north and west of the country, increasing competition for both agricultural and industrial jobs. Both single people and families migrated frequently, struggling for a niche in crowded labor markets.[22]

Decades of immiseration and dispossession culminated in the great crash of 1873, the worst unemployment crisis in American history. Many parents pulled their children from school and sent them to work in mines, textile mills, and glassworks, where vacancies for children under the age of fourteen were more plentiful than those for adults. Other families made sweatshops of their homes, with all but the smallest children participating in making artificial flowers, clothes, or other piecework.[23] Yet even these tactics were often not enough to keep families afloat. Thousands wandered the countryside looking for work, and others gathered in the dense slums of the major cities, insistently demanding relief, the more submissive manner of the traditional small town charity recipient now replaced by assertiveness and hostility.

Their authority and legitimacy challenged, the ruling classes turned their attention to managing the disruly poor. Following the energetic leadership of Josephine Lowell, prominent ministers, professors, doctors, and industrialists developed Charity Organization Societies across the North. Their primary target was the indiscriminate giving of alms and outdoor relief; they believed that overgenerous handouts to alcoholics and immigrants who lacked the Protestant work ethic weakened the spirit of the American worker, creating dense neighborhoods of dependency and vice in the great cities.[24]

The new charity activists, like Martin Luther 350 years earlier, were nostalgic for a radiant past when rich and poor had interacted more intimately, with less overt conflict. They aimed to abolish dole giving and replace it with a carefully engineered gift relationship between upper and lower classes, where "good men and gracious women [would] inspire goodness and graciousness in other men and women."[25] This articulation of the benefits of charity demonstrates the distance between the Charity Organization Societies and the old Catholic transcendental discourse. Though intimate contact with the poor was still connected to spiritual salvation, the idea that the poor were closer to God was long gone. To the contrary, it was the "gracious" of the better classes who were to bring spiritual light to the benighted rabble.

The Charity Organization Societies combined nostalgia for noblesse oblige with modern record keeping and communications. They gave no direct relief themselves but made sure it was impossible for poor people to move between one benevolent society and another. Relief, according to the Charity Organization Societies' principles of "scientific charity," should be given only after a charity visitor had visited the household in question to probe into their attitudes and practices.[26] Charity visitors examined women as housekeepers and mothers, while their husbands had to undergo a stringent labor test. (This nineteenth-century "workfare" usually consisted of breaking stones or chopping wood.) Families of men who drank should not be helped unless they separated themselves completely from the man in question.[27]

The Charity Organization Societies' distrust of the male poor drew strength from the current popularity of social Darwinism, a philosophy that equated the labor market with the law of the jungle. The fit—that is, the hardworking and sober—prospered because of their moral and physical superiority, whereas poverty represented failure before both God and nature. With this hyperindividualist doctrine riding high, the semiotic division of American life into feminine and masculine spheres became more caricatured, with sympathy and pity only for the most passive and pure representations of women and children.

Charity reformers used pulpits and newspapers to paint single men asking for money as criminals and to warn would-be benefactors against thoughtlessly indiscriminate almsgiving. Yale's Francis Wayland, president of the American Social Science Association, was inspired enough to put his ideas in verse form:

He tells you of his starving wife,
His children to be fed,
Poor little, lovely innocents,
All clamorous for bread—
And you so kindly help to put
A bachelor to bed.[28]

Wayland's doggerel shows just how synonymous were bachelor-hood and unworthiness in those years, for his punch line would be meaningless without a shared assumption that helping to "put a bachelor to bed" was an outrageous waste of money. Men who should be rightfully striving for survival in the economic jungle had no legitimate claim to the comforts of domesticity in their own right.

The idealistic reformers of the Charity Organization Societies on their own could not have brought about the sweeping charity reforms of the late 1870s. Fortunately, their interests coincided with those of Republican politicians eager to destroy the working-class Democratic machines and their ward-level patronage base. Together, these two groups were able to act swiftly and decisively. By the late 1870s, provision of municipal outdoor relief had dwindled sharply, and numerous municipalities had divested all responsibility for relief into the hands of private religious organizations.

Michael Katz suggests that the reforms of the 1870s and 1880s highlight a perennial contradiction within U.S. poverty management. Concerned with fraud and cultural degeneracy, Charity Organization Societies replaced the relatively neutral financial support offered by ward-level outdoor relief with intimate investigations that invaded the homes and lives of the poor, demanding demonstrations of gratitude and convincing dramas of failure and tragedy. But by making people compete to present the most deserving, helpless case, these practices were likely to create habits of feigned deference, manipulation, and passive dependency, not the honest self-sufficiency that the societies theoretically desired. By adopting a set of discourses and practices that treated poor people as manipulative and dependent, they were likely to create their own reality.[29]

The stigma and powerlessness weighing on unemployed men after the abolition of outdoor relief led many to leave home and join the outlaw army of tramps.[30] Mobility was easier than ever before. The railroads that now crisscrossed the country made it possible for penniless migrants to cross vast distances, riding illegally in empty boxcars or hanging underneath the wagons. The unrestrained vagrant, always a cause of distrust and fear, could now cross the continent, stopping at any small town with a railroad station. Not surprisingly, the appearance of these ragged strangers eating and sleeping in the streets and roadsides ruffled the social order, and local elites fought back with an intensified crackdown on transients.

Vagrancy laws were both revived and newly invented across the country. Any form of begging could be considered evidence that a man was a tramp, and many state legislatures prohibited migration without "visible means of support" under penalty of imprisonment and forced labor.[31]

These legal developments were mirrored on the municipal level, where men suspected of vagrancy were arrested without warrants, tried without juries, and sentenced to up to three years' hard labor.[32] New York City and Chicago, as hubs of the migrant worker circuit, were particularly energetic in their attacks on the tramp population, with police in each city arresting several thousand on vagrancy charges every year in the late 1870s and 1880s. In New York City, police officers routinely roughed up unemployed men standing or sitting around in the street. Any loitering man without decent clothes was liable to be assaulted as a tramp, even, in some cases, sitting on his own stoop.[33] Reformers in several cities even succeeded in closing down the sleeping place of last resort, the police station itself, arguing that there was insufficient regulation and supervision.[34]

In their struggle to subdue the tramp population, the northern elites followed a road laid by landowners of the postwar South. Following emancipation, large groups of freed slaves fled their places of captivity. Some took the long roads north and west out of former slave states, while more took to moving frequently within the South to avoid the miserable debt peonage now imposed on them by the planter class.[35] Desperate to hold on to their cheap labor force, the cotton aristocracy cooked up a mixture of trickery, violence, and a plethora of legal bindings to control the penniless, and mostly illiterate, freedmen and women. Along with emigrant agent restrictions and enticement laws came harsh vagrancy statutes and tightly controlled relief administration.[36]

These southern strategies of racial control were swiftly adopted by northern charity reformers in their project of restraining the increasingly unruly northern working classes. Several of the most prominent charity reformers, including Josephine Shaw Lowell, Samuel Gridley Howe, and Edward Pierce, traveled south in the late 1860s and 1870s to observe or participate in the early efforts of the Freedmen's Bureau and Freedmen's Association before applying similar terminology and tactics to the native-born white and immigrant working classes in New York, Boston, and Chicago.[37] This translation of social control from South to North provides a compelling example of how both sin-talk and the American moral construction of poverty in general have been periodically reinforced and hardened by the harsh binaries and forceful techniques of racial domination.

The great tramp scare also spurred the development of therapeutic and systemic discourses on homelessness. Various theories emerged that defined even homelessness itself as a pathology. Following the prewar diagnosis of "dromomania" among runaway slaves, psychopathologists now discovered wanderlust and "fugue" among the tramps. Ideas attributing homelessness to psychological weakness or immaturity remained intellectually respectable for the next fifty years. (The founder of the American eugenics movement, Charles Davenport, went a couple of steps further, developing a theory of nomadism as an inherited pathological condition linked to racial inferiority.)[38]

Among poorer Americans, though, the 1870s spurred militant critiques of laissez-faire capitalism. For workers with experience moving backward and forward between wage work and dependence on alms, neither psychopathology nor sin-talk's fixed opposition of the honest worker and the devious beggar was likely to ring true. Workers and their advocates instead conceptualized a large class of men constantly vulnerable to unemployment, obliged to "either sell day work, or live on charity, or starve to death," as labor reformer Ira Steward put it.[39] Even as anti-tramp feeling erupted into violence and hysteria, the common plea of the down-and-out man for work surged into increasingly militant demands for relief, such as the celebrated march of Coxey's Army of unemployed veterans.

Organized labor mounted a spirited resistance to vagrancy laws and coerced pauper labor, using the labor press and federal committees to press their case. By imprisoning workers and making them labor for no pay, argued labor representatives, vagrancy laws threatened the livelihoods of wage workers. They pointed out similarities to the fugitive slave laws that had outraged northern liberals before the Civil War. Free men should be allowed to search for work without being thrown in jail. Unregulated boom-bust capitalism, they argued, was the primary source of vagrancy and many other social problems affecting the poor. With a crowded labor market forcing men to settle for wages barely reaching subsistence level, the declaration of a war on vagrancy was an insult to hard-hit workers, a mockery of the concept of free labor.[40] What was needed was not punishment but rationalized social protection.

For the first time in American history, system-talk was embraced within elite discourse. A minority of elite social reformers became convinced that unemployment itself was indeed a systemic problem beyond the control of poor people themselves.[41] Their ideas would have little immediate effect, but percolated within the progressive movement, preparing fertile soil for the New Dealers of the next generation.

But among working-class people themselves, system-talk continued to gain strength. Despite the high levels of repression, the union movement increased in confidence and scope. The far left of the movement gradually coalesced and rejected the compromises of the American Federation of Labor, founding the Industrial Workers of the World (IWW) in 1905. For the first time, the transient moved to center stage: the IWW developed a radical analysis of homelessness, eloquently blaming the greed of the employing class for the destitution of the hobo army. Hobos themselves, not the state, were not only the object, but also the revolutionary subject of "Wobbly" discourse and strategy. Unlike other unions, the IWW organized heavily among the hobos, recruiting thousands of them into their "One Big Union" every year between 1905 and the First World War.

The IWW produced weekly journals in many cities. In Chicago, the vital center of the railroad network and therefore the hobo world, the union put out separate papers in nine languages. Nels Anderson related (in a rather irritated tone) that newcomers to even remote "jungles" (hobo encampments) were liable to be asked to show the organization's red membership card.[42] Though the anticommunist purges of the late teens and early 1920s destroyed the IWW as a mass movement, its spirit continued to flourish among the hobos and other marginal Americans.

The Rise and Demise of the New Deal Era

The mass unemployment following the Wall Street crash precipitated a major battle between the moral and systemic constructions of poverty. As in the great tramp scare, homelessness became a crucial field of discursive dispute. Again, huge numbers of people traveling and living rough prompted an expansion of authoritarian practices of punishment and exclusion. As mass unemployment multiplied their numbers, the already unpopular "wild boys of the road" became seen as a major social threat. In only one month of 1932, the Southern Pacific estimated that it had driven 80,000 transients off its trains.[43]

Many of the destitute migrants made for the West, drawn by rumors of jobs in California agribusiness. They were met with extreme hostility. Mobs regularly beat up single men for trying to cross the state line, while the Okies traveling in families were similarly shunned, portrayed in the press as disease ridden, incestuous, ignorant, and inbred. Initial charitable attempts were overwhelmed, and many cities provided little support to homeless migrants of any description. The Los Angeles police department, for example, would regularly sweep skid row neighborhoods and book every vagrant for thirty days inside.[44]

As millions of workers lost their jobs, the traditional Protestant view of unemployment and vagrancy as the products of character flaws could not sustain its hegemonic position, and Roosevelt and his allies swept into power, promising large-scale government intervention to protect the population from the irrationalities of the economic system. The homeless people who named their tent cities for the laissez-faire policies of President Herbert Hoover now found elite allies in the corporatist socialists on the left of the Roosevelt administration. There remained considerable resistance, especially in hard-hit California, where the big growers and Hollywood came together to crush the populist Upton Sinclair in the 1934 race for governor. It took outsiders to the state's political structure, university professors and New Dealers with federal jobs, to set up the famous federal transient camps that ultimately improved conditions for some of the migrant families.[45]

The new order emanating from Washington required new ways of talking about poverty. The Roosevelt Democrats spoke of the "new unemployment" and the migrant worker as if they should be distinguished from the disreputable hobo or tramp problem of the previous decades. Some sought merely to establish yet another benchmark differentiating between the deserving and undeserving poor. Yet the more radical New Dealers were determined to establish categories uncontaminated by moral constructions of homelessness, treating both the "unemployed" and the "migrant worker" as inclusive categories. The job-creation programs of the Works Progress Administration and the Civilian Conservation Corps drew in not only the new destitute of the 1930s but many of the former disreputable poor.

Tim Cresswell has made the case that the Farm Security Administration photography program, in particular, played a vital role in this process. The haunting, dignified images produced by Dorothea Lange and the other FSA photographers reconstructed the rebellious tramp into the yearning, dispossessed migrant worker, a victim of social disorder who needed to be given the means for a settled, more regulated existence.[46]

The programs instituted by the Roosevelt administration and the massive World War II mobilization put an end to large-scale homelessness for the next forty years. The radicalism of the 1930s may have been dissipated, first by the war effort and then by McCarthyism, but the New Deal order of social inclusion via Keynesian economic policy remained in place, bolstered by the economic growth created by the Pax Americana during the postwar years, as well as the activism of African Americans and their allies. The tent cities and migrant labor camps seemed to be gone for good, and many who previously had been desperately poor finally obtained a stake in the society. A cluster of systemic interventions — labor rights, job creation programs, Federal Housing Administration (FHA) mortgages, the GI Bill, federally mandated cash transfers to poor families, and, above all, Social Security — created a substantial break with the past. Legions of white working-class families finally became the steady, prosperous consumers of Henry Ford's dream.

While not everybody became rich or even prosperous, the New Deal order greatly reduced the risk of extreme poverty. Even African Americans, cut out of many of the most important New Deal programs by racism within the Democratic Party, saw a modest but steady rise in living conditions over the first two postwar decades. The elderly, until then always the biggest demographic group of paupers, were rescued by Social Security from homelessness and destitution on skid row.

Yet the complex, unpredictable dialectic of history was at work, and the very successes of the New Deal laid the foundations for its death. Without the big government of mass mortgage subsidies, highway creation, legalized trade unionism, and Social Security, many of the white working-class bootstrappers of the 1950s would have remained in the cities, more dependent on urban public goods — public schools, hospitals, libraries, parks — and thus more willing to spend their tax dollars on them. Instead, in one of the great ironies of the twentieth century, the New Dealers created the conditions for a suburban exodus of white working-class city dwellers, whose subsequent embrace of privatized domestic nirvana and the Nixonian politics of resentment came to constitute a great bulwark against further investments in public goods.

The 1950s, 1960s, and 1970s saw the progressive abandonment of great swathes of white New York, Detroit, Philadelphia, and Chicago, as well as scores of smaller American cities. Left behind were African Americans, cut out of the suburban boom by the inequities of the FHA and other New Deal programs and by continued labor and housing discrimination. Even within the cities, the poorest African Americans were concentrated into the corrals of the great housing projects, the names of which became bywords for crime and misery.

As the civil rights movement gathered steam in the early 1960s, Democratic politicians finally attempted to address the exclusion of African Americans from the New Deal order. The Kennedy and Johnson years saw not only the extraordinarily late enfranchisement of African Americans, but also the Economic Opportunity Act of 1964, the Community Action Program, and companion elements of the Johnson administration's War on Poverty.

Through the new Office of Equal Opportunity (OEO), the federal government funded numerous community-based programs focused on education, juvenile delinquency, job training, and civil rights, improving the living conditions of many people living in poverty. The welfare rights activism sponsored by many community organizations sharply increased the number of recipients of Aid to Families with Dependent Children (AFDC). Widely available food stamps mitigated outright hunger, and Supplemental Security Income (SSI), Medicaid, and Medicare all were expanded to create better health coverage for welfare recipients, the disabled, and the elderly.

With the escalation of the Vietnam War, the poverty warriors lost much of their political momentum. Their already limited funding, never significant enough, slowed, and the only significant form of job creation became the draft. The desperation with which younger African Americans viewed their persistently blocked aspirations found expression in the urban uprisings of the late 1960s, and the destruction only further accelerated the exodus of those with the means to leave.

As urban manufacturing shuddered to a standstill over the next decade, the collapse of the urban tax base drove the older central cities of the nation into a fiscal vortex. Presidents Nixon and Ford refused to help, sticking to their developing political narrative of an injured white majority beset by a conspiracy between elite liberals and over-demanding people of color.[47] In 1980 Ronald Reagan took power, thoroughly rejecting the Keynesian principle of tax-and-spend and promising to revitalize American business by declaring war on antipoverty programs and a century of labor rights. During the following years, the systemic construction of poverty staggered from defeat to defeat, its political rhetoric discredited and its institutional power inexorably whittled away by decades of budget cuts and program abolitions. The New Deal order was over.

The Return of Street Homelessness

During the early 1970s, the social work agencies serving street people in cities across the United States noticed rising numbers of transient and penniless clients, substantially different from the more middle-class hippie dropouts many of these agencies were created to serve. Along with the counterculture's detritus of LSD casualties and heroin addicts, the agency workers saw increasing numbers of chronic transients. The Travelers' Aid Society noted large numbers taking to the road in search of work, once again heading for California and other places thought to be richer in jobs. But labor markets were tight across the nation, and after a short while in "crash housing," they would move on again. Many were small-town transients who had little identification with the counterculture.[48]

The numbers of transients and long-term street homeless continued to rise throughout the 1970s, but the phenomenon was slow to gain much media attention until the depression of 1982, when unemployment reached 11 percent. The number of people visibly homeless increased sharply, shocking the many Americans who had thought that sleeping in the street was as obsolete as the horse and carriage. The ancient social problem of homelessness had reemerged and with it the debates that had raged during earlier periods. Over the next decade, journalists and social workers, ministers and doctors, intellectuals and homeless activists, religious advocates and politicians struggled to control the definition of the problem.

The first discourse to be revived was system-talk. In fact, systemic constructions of poverty were already in crisis when large-scale street homelessness reemerged in the late 1970s. Yet in spite of, or perhaps because of, this crisis, system partisans fought vigorously to claim the new social problem for their own terrain, to present it as striking evidence of the dysfunction of contemporary social and economic policy and, in particular, the neoliberal policies of the Reagan administration.

In this project, system-talk had one great advantage. Although the meanings of homelessness had in fact been highly contested during the 1930s, the New Deal order saw old-fashioned sin-talk and sick-talk fall into abeyance. The problem had become defined in retrospect by the resonant legacy of Steinbeck's *Grapes of Wrath* and Lange's *Migrant Mother,* giving the homeless poor a good chance of being seen as "deserving." Outraged by the Reagan administration attacks on the welfare state and the unions, a group of longtime activists launched themselves into energetic anti-homelessness campaigns. Perhaps they could revive the nation's failing antipoverty impulses by showing them a group whose desperation and sheer deprivation seemed to be indisputable. They were joined by thousands of left and liberal religious advocates, ranging from the radical Catholic Worker organization, whose members had already been living with, feeding, and housing the impoverished for decades, to well-heeled congregations of various faiths and denominations, horrified by the human misery confronting them in the streets. This broad coalition took action at all levels of government, demanding that the homeless should be given the necessities of life: food, housing, and medical care.

On the local level, most advocates and activists focused on mobilizing sympathy toward immediate service provision and quickly made significant gains in terms of both municipal funding and volunteer mobilization. Early movement discourse converged around causal links between homelessness and large-scale layoffs, successfully drawing media attention in particular to white workers and their families swelling the lines at soup kitchens and food banks across the country. With these kinds of images, they hoped to get away from both the negative image of the ghetto poor and the idea of homelessness as a form of countercultural rebellion.

The anti-homelessness movement chose the term "homelessness" (as opposed to "transient," "indigent," etc.) for its implication that the biggest difference between the homeless and the housed was their lack of shelter.[49] The more politicized of the activists hoped that not only could they win lifesaving services for the very poor, but that increased sympathy for the homeless would add to a broad public perception of the inhumanity of the Reagan revolution. Perhaps they could turn the public against corporate downsizing, union busting, and welfare rollback, just as the homeless Hoovervilles had served the reform discourse of the depression era.

Despite early resistance from elected officials, especially in New York City,[50] the anti-homelessness movement was surprisingly successful. Washington, D.C.'s Community for Creative Non-Violence (CCNV)[51] led the way, with their 1981 "Reaganville" of tents, crosses, and plywood tombstones in front of the White House. Three years later, the first federal shelter opened in D.C. The activists had succeeded in making the homeless into the new "deserving poor," now perceived as more white, passive, and suffering than the unruly ghetto poor, who were once again being scapegoated by politicians and the popular press as an antagonistic, pathological underclass.[52] Their insistence on the basic human right to shelter resulted in the opening of thousands of emergency shelters across the country during this period, ranging from small volunteer-run operations in church basements to vast dormitories in hundreds of National Guard armories commandeered for the purpose.

The liberal mass media, always on the lookout for pathos, rushed to present sympathetic images of homeless people in films and television.[53] They followed the lead of advocates in presenting homeless people as regular Americans traumatized by disability or unemployment, especially emphasizing white people[54] and homeless two-parent families (which were, in fact, relatively rare).[55] Similarly, advocates and activists followed the lead of homeless panhandlers in drawing attention to the prior military service of many homeless men. Hollywood started pumping out tragedies featuring homeless Vietnam veterans.[56] In 1986, at what later proved to be the highest point of media sympathy, six million people joined hands coast to coast and raised $24 million for the "Hungry and Homeless."[57]

The Homeless Archipelago

Over the next decade, the radical anti-homelessness activists became victims of their own success. In the absence of strong government intervention, the emergency was mainly addressed by religious congregations with an existing tradition of charity work. Soup kitchens sprang up in countless church basements in one of the great volunteer mobilizations of the century. Every day thousands of high school students, seniors, and other volunteers prepared and served food to this new "deserving poor." While much immediate hardship was mitigated, the soup kitchen or emergency shelter tended, as ever, to institutionalize the problem of homelessness rather than prevent it. The vague good intentions of this large volunteer body drew more heavily on habitual discourses and practices of religious charity than on the traditions of protest and self-organization of the radical activists, whose network was far smaller and more sparsely distributed. Somewhere along the way, the systemic discourse of human rights violated had become lost in a sea of practices that implied very different ways of understanding the problem.[58]

Many of the multiplying shelters and soup kitchens developed the same moralistic character as the prewar rescue missions, combining elements of charitable donation and admonition. All over small-town America, homeless clients were required to pray before eating or sleeping. In small evangelical Protestant operations, fiery deacons jumped up and down in front of lines of food recipients, exhorting them to leave the ways of the devil. In Catholic soup kitchens the clients sat at empty tables, drearily intoning the Lord's Prayer with the nuns before receiving their mashed potato and mystery meat. Even in the more professionalized secular shelters of the larger cities, the frontline workers tended to treat homeless clients with a high degree of disrespect, reinforcing the stigma of homelessness with a presumption of guilt.

If the operations of many of the new homelessness institutions took on the sin-talk of the long-standing mission tradition, the more liberal institutions set up intimate connections between charitable volunteer and grateful recipient, creating ties of deference and obligation across social classes.[59] The liberal food programs and houses of hospitality run by the most fiery homelessness advocates settled into day-to-day practices that were fundamentally quietist, emphasizing volunteers' closeness to and acceptance of the homeless rather than the prevention of homelessness. Drawing on the pre-Reformation transcendental practice of cleansing one's spirit by "being with" the poor, middle-class volunteers found their own liberation from social guilt in friendly, superficially egalitarian exchanges with the less fortunate. Their ideas about homelessness may have emphasized "the system," but the practice of volunteering tended merely to "accommodate" the problem, to use Snow and Anderson's terminology.[60] Far from serving as living critique of a negligent social system, homelessness became the primary arena for the restoration of the old gift relationship between the indigent and the privileged that had served to stabilize the dangerous classes before the age of entitlement.[61]

The rise of small-scale charitable programs, whether of the hellfire or the quietist variety, did much to undercut the systemic focus of the advocates, but they lost even more ground to sick-talk and professionalization of homelessness services. Their great struggle to secure significant federal funding resulted in the 1987 McKinney Act, which in turn stimulated the growth of a massive bureaucratic structure for the management of homelessness, systematically favoring those with qualifications for social welfare or public administration over the religious or radical activists who led the earlier, more independent agencies.

Some system-talking activists resisted becoming too involved in the new archipelago of agencies managing the homeless and retained an emphasis on rights interventions, from squatting campaigns to tussles over anti-panhandling codes. But more could not resist the opportunity to draw on funding sources to create programs with a democratic, system-talking ethos. Once they got into the business of service provision, however, the leaders who had developed the radical systemic critique were in danger of turning into homelessness managers.

"You can't end homelessness, you know," said Paul Boden of the San Francisco Coalition on Homelessness. "You can impact the poverty programs and the education programs and the housing programs to the point that there's less homeless people. . . . I mean, we — we exist because the other shit wasn't working. . . . But you can't end homelessness until you've knocked down all those barriers. And by setting ourselves up the way we have, in the way Home Base and the National Coalition and the National Law Center have — and *us* — we've allowed ourselves to be become another tier and another player in the fuckin' arena."

Boden felt in retrospect that social justice goals were all too easily displaced by the business of daily social work. Surrounded by an ever-increasing army of salaried social workers and (mostly apolitical) volunteers, he saw the programs for which they had fought so hard become fixed into a sprawling holding mechanism that many on the street and off came to call the "homelessness industry." In the meantime, the defunding of broader-based housing and welfare programs continued apace, ensuring that the industry was here to stay.

The McKinney Act rapidly transformed the field of U.S. homelessness provision from a small network of voluntarist organizations focused on social change and emergency aid into a social service behemoth. Informed by the deliberations of welfare policy experts, the federal funding stream came to determine where and how to spend billions of dollars dedicated to shelters and transitional housing. The number of agencies multiplied from 1,500 in the early eighties to more than 15,000 ten years later, creating thousands of new positions for case managers and program administrators. An army of social work professionals trained in the language of disease and dysfunction designed and moved into the more comprehensive transitional shelters mandated by the Clinton administration's "Continuum of Care" plan, examining and categorizing their clients' capacities in terms of mental health, substance use, life skills, parenting, budgeting, and overall "housing-readiness."[62] Volunteers moved to the sidelines, now concentrated in the more discursively shallow field of food provision.

The growing homelessness archipelago powered the ascendance of sick-talk within both the academy and the media. A new lingua franca linked the hundreds of thousands of health-care professionals and nonprofit workers employed by the developing homeless archipelago, and researchers working within such programs turned out hundreds of studies of the pathologies of the homeless, establishing their high levels of addiction, depression, and family dysfunction. As sick-talk expanded into a large subfield across social welfare, psychology, public health, and other disciplines, researchers developed complex, multifaceted models of the causes of homelessness, and leading voices such as Alice Baum and Donald Burnes fiercely challenged the claims of the National Coalition for the Homeless (NCH) and other advocates.[63] From the point of view of many health professionals building expertise within the homelessness archipelago, homelessness was a symptom of the severe mental illness and substance abuse of the few and had little to do with working and housing conditions for the many. Some used the news media to criticize the ideological hyperbole of the activists' system-talk, arguing that their conception of a large working class pool at risk from homelessness relied on erroneous claims of similarity between the homeless and the general public.

The struggle between sick-talk and system-talk reached boiling point over the 1990 U.S. Census. After only a cursory attempt in 1980, the Census Bureau made a more serious attempt to count homeless people, both inside and outside the shelters. Two of the most prominent advocates — Mitch Snyder of CCNV and Maria Foscarinis of the National Law Center on Homelessness and Poverty (NLCHP) — went on the record before the count with their own estimate of two to three million and sharply criticized the Census Bureau's strategy. The count in fact came to only 228,621, and while some airplay was given to criticisms of the Census Bureau's operation, the credibility of the advocacy organizations with the mass media was significantly tarnished. Images portraying the dignity and resilience of homeless people continued to circulate in street newspapers, alternative newsweeklies, and art houses, but these kinds of representations became increasingly rare in television news and daily newspapers. The suicide that year of Snyder, the most well known of the radical anti-homelessness activists, was interpreted by many as some kind of verdict on the movement itself.

Editors gave more space to stories that conformed to the therapeutic and moral narratives, namely social welfare reports and policing issues. Sentimental stories about homeless people became confined to the annual Christmas and Thanksgiving holidays, the time when Americans traditionally set aside individualism and self-interest for expressions of community and compassion.[64]

In policy circles, the advocates' position continued to lose much of its early power, and discussions of homelessness increasingly focused on the grubby, addicted, and depressed poor themselves. The National Coalition for the Homeless, the NLCHP, and various city-level advocacy groups and organizations of the homeless continued to frame the problem in largely systemic terms, but strategically they found themselves on the defensive, reduced to rearguard actions against welfare cuts and the further criminalization of homelessness.

Far from inspiring a reassessment of American constructions of poverty in general, as the system partisans had hoped, the homeless gradually lost their mid-1980s image as the "deserving poor"[65] and followed welfare mothers, the ghetto poor, and the rest of the so-called underclass toward the land of the disreputable poor, their condition constructed first and foremost as a problem of immoral or pathological behavior.

"Quality of Life"

While sick-talk and system-talk on homelessness have very different narratives of the causes and cures of homelessness, they both imply a basically sympathetic orientation to people who are homeless, an assumption that they should be reintegrated into the broader society. From the late 1980s onward, the consensus on reintegration was challenged by advocates of clearance who focused their rhetoric on the noxious street-person, the revised version of the predatory tramp of the 1870s. Sterner voices demanded reinstitutionalization of the mentally ill and removal of the disreputable poor from public sight. Across the country, both the tourist industry and middle-class civic associations proclaimed compassion fatigue, lobbying for the police and other city workers to clean up neighborhood shopping strips and downtown streets and squares.

The primary object of sympathy was no longer the homeless themselves, but the decent citizen threatened by crime and unsightly disorder. Just as the New Dealers had repackaged the hobo as the migrant worker, those calling for police crackdowns distanced themselves from the homeless and adopted the term "street people," an ill-defined category suggesting a squabbling, hustling nuisance most likely to be African American. This rhetorical twist shifted images of the homeless much closer to the already discredited ghetto poor, directly counteracting the "whitening" strategy of the advocates.[66]

Central to revived sin-talk was what Gagnier and others have referred to as the aestheticization of homelessness, a shift in focus from the problems *of* the homeless to the problems *caused by* homeless people — chiefly, the aesthetic or economic problems created by homeless people panhandling or otherwise occupying public space, rendering it ugly or disorderly.[67]

Local governments introduced new techniques of exclusion, from alterations to the built environment to the proliferation of what came to be known as quality-of-life legislation.[68] Conflicts over public space reached the greatest intensity in places where commerce was heavily dependent on the fickle tourist trade. Orlando, home to Disney World, was an early leader and took the strategy further than any other municipality. Having tried unsuccessfully to completely ban panhandling in 1980, the city introduced complex, heavily enforced codes. Panhandlers had to obtain laminated permits; they were forbidden to work in stations, parks, stadiums, or near ATM machines; they were not to approach people in vehicles, follow people, or work in pairs; they were forbidden to make false representations such as claiming that a donation was required for a fictional need or wearing a military uniform; and they could not ask for money for one purpose and spend it on another.

The extensive detail of Orlando's quality-of-life legislation was unusual, but eventually most other cities followed its lead. By the mid-1990s, more than 75 percent of U.S. municipalities passed laws prohibiting or restricting panhandling, and nearly 70 percent forbade sleeping or loitering in public places.[69]

Contemporary sin-talk may have been relatively slow to cohere, especially in the more liberal regions of the United States, but ten years into the crisis it had made a forceful return. If we extend back out to the broader reconfiguration of poverty discourse during the same period, it is easy to see how the decline of system-talk was overdetermined by the weakness of the systemic construction of poverty as a whole. Like the roundups of the tramp scare, the contemporary manifestations of sin-talk were predicated on broader shifts in public orientation toward poor people in general. Particularly significant was the reconfiguration of three key institutional fields: welfare, policing, and community action.

The great welfare reforms of the 1990s demonstrated the completion of a broad, twenty-year shift away from service provision and cash transfers and back toward the punitive work programs and criminal sanctions that had proliferated in the United States between 1865 and the New Deal. By signing the momentous (Republican-sponsored) 1996 Family and Personal Responsibility Act, Democratic president Bill Clinton demonstrated the Democratic Party's relinquishment of the policy of using cash transfers to mitigate the effects of social inequality.

Clinton skillfully wove his acquiescence into a rhetoric of care and inclusion, claiming that he was honoring a moral obligation to help poor people help themselves. The new term limits, he said, represented not punishment but liberation for welfare recipients depressed and demoralized by their dependency. "The door has now been opened to a new era of freedom and independence," he intoned in a radio address shortly after the bill was passed. "We can make the permanent underclass a thing of the past."[70] Once liberated from their alleged passivity, the poor were to be energized by their tussles with the free market and thereby released from poverty, now defined chiefly as a state of mind.

The Clintonian articulation of poverty as depression might suggest that what was needed was not just work but therapeutic intervention. Yet the short-term pseudo-therapeutic efforts of the cheerleaders administering welfare reform were terminally hamstrung by inflexible rules, punitive sanctions, and extremely limited resources for long-term support. In the big picture of American poverty management, their efforts were vastly overshadowed by the far greater expenditure of energy and resources on the criminal justice system. Poverty as depression was trumped by the "moral poverty" delineated by William Bennett and other leaders of the war on drugs.

While media attention concentrated on federal-level legislation to reform welfare for women and children, an equally important removal of cash transfers was rolling forward on the local level. Between the early 1980s and late 1990s every major American city either abolished or reduced General Assistance payments to indigent single adults, often deploying the argument that recipients used the money to buy drugs.[71] In many places, recipients could now claim benefits for only one month out of any year.[72] Where the time limits were less restrictive, job search and work requirements served a similar function. In Los Angeles, for example, a third of the employable caseload were not receiving their benefits in any given month due to penalties related to job searches and work requirements.[73]

General Assistance benefits had always been locally funded and administered, a piecemeal and perennially inadequate last resort for those failing to qualify for federally mandated cash assistance. Nevertheless, something is always better than nothing. As Rossi has emphasized, even unequal relationships require some degree of reciprocity to survive, and armies of failing family members and other couch surfers who had given their hosts some money toward rent were no longer able to do so.[74] Altogether, the progressive loss of even these meager payments pushed more and more of those living on the edge into the homeless shelters.[75]

While welfare benefits and social service provision to poor people were steadily scaled back, punitive measures against the deviant poor moved to the center of new policing philosophy. This second broad discursive transition was initiated by James Q. Wilson and George Kelling in their article "Broken Windows: Police and Neighborhood Safety," published in the *Atlantic Monthly* in 1982. Considered by many police chiefs as the most influential text in modern American policing history, "Broken Windows" privileged a Main Street conception of the orderly community over the rights of individuals to behave as they choose, claiming that the relatively permissive responses to panhandling and loitering in the 1960s and 1970s had led to declining levels of civility and safety in public space.

The debate continues over whether there is much validity to the "broken windows" thesis.[76] But whether or not Wilson and Kelling were right that the prevention of panhandling could preempt more serious crimes, their theories were put into practice all over the country, in the form of both legislation and the policing to back it up. Police officers on the quality-of-life frontlines became full-time rousters of the homeless in a constant war of maneuver, a full-time job.

The third, and related, discursive transition that made it possible to crack down on homeless people was the transformation of the concept of community within the big cities. In the 1960s and 1970s unions and urban grassroots organizations developed a diverse, cross-class conception of community and neighborhood, which asserted the rights of the poor, disabled, and otherwise marginalized to be included in local decision-making.

With the turning of the political tide in the late 1970s, the progressive urban community organization began to lose its power. Slowly these organizations were superceded by thousands of associations of "homeowners" or "stakeholders" bent on bringing a "broken windows" policy to bear on local teenage "loiterers" or homeless "druggies." In general, the poor were increasingly treated as external threats to the social body rather than community members in need of help or integration.

Understandings of homelessness within the public sphere shifted with these broader currents. As the sense of emergency of the mid-1980s gave way first to the managed homelessness of the late 1990s and then to the chronic homelessness push of the 2000s, activists found fewer and fewer media outlets for system-talk. For their part, poor Americans had by no means given up on systemic interpretations, but these social justice interpretations now rarely found voice beyond smaller African American and left-wing media.

Reinventing the Poorhouse

The last quarter of the twentieth century saw the resurrection or expansion of many forms of poverty management characteristic of the sin-dominated mid-nineteenth century. The chaotic, diseased nineteenth-century poorhouse became the late twentieth-century homeless shelter, and the work test of stone breaking or wood chopping became the humiliation of street cleaning for General Assistance or food stamps. The children of the indigent were farmed out to inadequately supported foster homes, some not much better than the notorious "baby farms" of the nineteenth century. Evangelical skid row missions were even closer to their forebears, "pray to eat" remaining the time-honored rule of the day.

At the same time, mass street homelessness became the catalyst for one of the largest charity mobilizations of the century, reviving the Victorian gift relationship between rich and poor that had largely disappeared in the postwar period. Just as Lowell's Scientific Charity transformed more ad hoc charitable efforts into coordinated action under bureaucratic surveillance, the volunteer-run shelters of the mid-1980s were gradually professionalized and incorporated into a network of microsurveillance, where clients are fingerprinted on entry and compelled to construct their problems as bad behavior. Not surprisingly, Paul Boden is not the only anti-homelessness activist to have openly admitted to some grave misgivings about the unintended consequences of the big-hearted homeless advocacy of the 1980s.[77]

Where the psychopathologists of the previous century had prescribed moral cures for mental disorders such as wanderlust, the new homelessness experts locate the roots of dispossession in mental illness and inadequacy, demanding submission to medications, twelve-step doctrine, and housing-readiness programs. If the suspicious, intrusive practices of the Charity Organization Societies gave life to the dependent, mendacious paupers they feared, the authoritarian medicalization of the modern homelessness industry exerts a similar pressure. Those who fail to follow this straight and narrow road are subjected to tactics not so different from those of the great tramp scare. Contemporary forms of outdoor relief for single adults (General Relief or General Assistance) have been either abolished or decimated in every major American city, and police mobilized in large numbers to clear commercial strips and downtown areas.

Like the tramps a century before, legions of men, and not a few women, vote with their feet, trying to hold onto a degree of autonomy by roughing it outside, accepting only the most superficial relationship with service agencies. It is to their world, more specifically, to the skid row streets and the hidden camps of San Francisco, that I now turn.

Part II

THE STREET

Watch Out, San Francisco!
Ain't Gonna Get No Peace

THE HOMELESS MEN AND WOMEN WHO spent their lives drifting around the streets and parks of San Francisco's Tenderloin were streetwise. Most other homeless people came into the service-rich neighborhood to get what they needed, then bid a hasty retreat. Those who stayed tended to be the ex-cons, the former drug dealers and pimps, prostitutes and thieves. Each surviving local street entrepreneur was outnumbered by five losers, lining up for food or shelter, panhandling from the tourists nearby, and thieving "small shit." The condition of these down-and-out playas, riven with strokes and hepatitis, tuberculosis and AIDS, marked all too clearly the brevity and brutality of the hustler's life cycle.

One such was Del, homeless crack addict and sometime dealer. Del spent much of his days leaning against a wall on Eddy Street, his eyes scanning for drivers with that intense, uncertain look that might mean business. His spare frame was frequently shaken by violent coughing, which he did his best to ignore. I suspected tuberculosis, but he would not get tested.

Del loved the Tenderloin. The same place many homeless men strenuously avoided—a "pen for fuck-ups," Carlos called it—Del saw as the hot heart of the city, the place where the action was, the drama, "the life," and "the game." "Mm-*mm*. Place is jumping," he crooned appreciatively, scanning the crowded drug market on the Eddy Street sidewalk. He paused to bum a cigarette from one of the dealers, flashing me a knowing grin. "Sheee-it! Bunch of baad mofos 'round here."

"Watch out, San Francisco! Ain't gonna get *no* peace."

Del took pride in "slinging rocks," but he was the most small-time of dealers. Over a couple of afternoons when I watched him work from a cafe window, he made only three sales, all to whites in cars, hiding his own drug hunger with a flirtatious smile and a twinkle in his still-enticing green eyes. "They look on me a couple of seconds, I'll make a sale. I do the soft sell, smooth and swift, smooth and swift," he boasted to me, taking a break to drink a soda on my funds. "This my *game*, baby." But Del had no regular buyers. He was too shabby to inspire much confidence, and word on the street said he was his own best customer. In fact, nobody seemed to trust him much at all. No one, family or friend, would let him stay on the couch anymore, and by now he was inured to the discomforts of both shelter and sidewalk.

Del would never admit it, but he was only able to maintain his dubious claim to "sling rocks" due to the generosity of his supplier and nephew, Sonny, a sleepy sixteen-year-old giant. "See, my daddy always say, keep an eye on Uncle Del, watch his back," said Sonny. (His father, Del's older brother, was doing serious time in Corcoran prison.)

"So I let him have a few rocks. If I don't keep with him, I know he'll go get himself killed. Shit's got him bad." But Del himself would have none of it, insisting he was still in the game.

During those frequent periods when Sonny lost patience with him, Del turned to recycling, mostly in the form of collecting aluminum cans from public trash cans or the dumpsters at the back of the skid row hotels. He stayed within the bounds of the Tenderloin, venturing out only to sell his cans at a supermarket up the hill in the Castro. While he had got used to handling garbage, he didn't like the work and showed none of the vigor of the self-styled "pro" recyclers swinging their heavily loaded carts around the same corners.

Morris, a lanky, serious "pro," crossed the Tenderloin at least twice a day on a long journey between South of Market and Pacific Heights. Del might greet Morris with "Whassup?" and a wave, but Morris only nodded politely and moved on.

After watching me arrive with Del at the Safeway redemption center, Morris commented quietly, "I'd say you should stay away from that yellow dude."

"You know him?"

"Not really. I've seen him, of course. You get to know all the street faces after a while. TL's not such a b-big place."

"So why don't you like him? The company he keeps?"

60

"I don't know about his company. He just seems like he's g-got that BS smile, like he's trying to take you for a fool. A street guy, you know."

Del seemed offended by the unwillingness of the pro recyclers to give him the time of day. "They acting like they better than the rest. Always trying to look busy, like they got something real important to do," Del sneered. "You see them down St. Anthony's (soup kitchen). They sit on their own or with each other, ignore other folks, like they'd rather read the paper than look at you."

"And in the shelter, *that* guy," Del pointed to Julius, who was collecting cans in the distance, "he's been in Polk Street (shelter) a couple times, but he always gets into respite." (Respite was a part of the shelter set aside for those who were sick, giving them special privileges.) "He won't go in with the rest. Even on the street, you got those white-acting niggers."

"What's with this 'white-acting' shit?" I asked.

"I don't have a problem with white people if they don't have a problem with me. But when a brother gets him that white attitude, that hurts."

"Can't there be different kinds of black folk?"

"Sure, 'course there is," flashed Del. "But they still raggedy-ass black motherfuckers. Po-liceman ain't gonna see no difference," he said scathingly.

"See, like all sorts of guys do the recycling thing," Del continued. "Those old oriental people, they are doing the same thing. We all just making a few pennies. But those dudes"—he gestured at the corner where we had seen Julius—"they just making a big old fuss about it. Like they working for the *city* or something. And that other brother with the bushy head and his supersize rattling old smelly train he acts so proud of. No time to talk, and you should get out their way. Who the fuck they think they is? They're bums, dope fiends and bums."

"How do you know?" I said.

"They out here. They homeless." Del snorted dismissively. The connection was self-evident.

My long identification with the recyclers showed itself. "*You* don't know if they are fiends," I said. "They are people, that's all. If you stick in the Tenderloin, you haven't seen the half of it. You know, out in the neighborhoods, there's hundreds of those guys, working all the time, bringing in real big loads. They don't go down the supermarket because they can get more money over at the real recycling companies down Bayshore. You wouldn't even see most of them around here."

I had caught Del's interest. "How much more do they get?" he asked.

"Depends on the market. Sometimes twice as much, but not usually. They make maybe twenty, twenty-five bucks on a big load."

I had lost him. "And that's for heaving around a big old rattling buggy all day," he said pityingly. "I can make fifteen bucks insid'a two minutes."

"But what about all the time you're just waiting around?"

"That's the deal. If you wanna sell, you got to be there twenty-four seven."

"So you're putting in the same hours they do."

"I ain't heaving around a big old buggy. I be on the street, watching the action, you know. Which *you* wanna do?" Del sniggered.

"Too much hollering," I said.

"It just talk, most of the time, just talk." He flashed a gappy grin and sauntered over to the curb to pick up a just-discarded cigarette butt.

THREE

Moorings

The Tenderloin

"**W**HEN I WAS FIRST HOMELESS, I STAYED AROUND THE TL, you know, because that's where the food was, the shelters was. I was kinda knocked out, you know, stunned. I would just go where the homeless people were supposed to go. I mean, now I know other places, but it seemed like everything was there. I just lined up for St. Anthony's, the shelters, MSC, Hospitality House, like there wasn't nothing better to do." Ray, a bearded African American in a black leather jacket, stopped to examine one of the garbage bags tied on his shopping cart, which seemed to be leaking valuable aluminum cans onto the road.

"They say you go here for this, you go there for that," Ray continued, yanking a new garbage bag from a clump inside the cart. "Seems kind of convenient, like it's a supermarket, a supermarket for being homeless. Except you be waiting all day here, all day there. Wasting your life away. Getting pushed around. Getting ripped off, hustled, beat up, beat *down*. I hate the damn Tenderloin."

The hard-drinking sailors and wintering miners are long gone, but San Francisco's Tenderloin still holds the ghostly memory of old Barbary Coast San Francisco, the busiest port in the United States and the West Coast capital of prostitution, dope, gambling, and crimping. Over the last thirty years the city's other remaining strands of institutions catering to poor single people — the hotels and diners on Kearny, Broadway, Divisadero, Folsom, even the city's primary heroin market around Sixteenth and Mission — have steadily shrunk into smaller

Sixth Street, San Francisco.

pockets and strips. To the northwest, the seamy blocks of Polk Gulch are still gentrifying, while on the other side of Market Street only the tenacious finger of Sixth Street remains of the old South-of-Market "foreign quarter," which once held 40,000 units of cheap housing for single men.

The Tenderloin, though, still digs its heels into downtown San Francisco, a teeming ghetto of the dispossessed, home to thousands of poor whites, African Americans, Latinos, Southeast Asians, refugees and bohemians, swindlers and prophets. By concentrating many of the city's most disreputable poor, it stands as a bulwark against the engine of gentrification north and south, its rambling slum hotels, liquor stores, sex shops, low-income housing developments, and poverty agencies covering a good fifteen city blocks between Union Square and City Hall.

The persistence of this old-fashioned skid row in the center of what is now one of the nation's wealthiest cities is unusual. Other major American cities have impoverished, even depopulated neighborhoods near their centers, but the Tenderloin is not so much near as right in the middle of San Francisco's downtown. Dividing the corridors of government power in City Hall and the federal building from the financial district, it intimately rubs against the hotels and upscale stores of Union Square, forcing tourists and downtown workers to recognize the city's chasm between rich and poor. A big part of the answer, say San Francisco historians, lies in the extraordinary persistence of its warrenlike residential hotels.[1] In most cities, the single-room-occupancy hotel (or SRO) became largely extinct during the late twentieth century. San Francisco had a disproportionate number of these institutions in the first place, partly because the city was demographically dominated by single men during its first few decades, and also because the years when most of the housing stock was built, in the late nineteenth and early twentieth century, were also the high points of hotel living nationwide.

These hotels originally housed single people across the class scale. The city had whole neighborhoods of hotels and lodging houses, each area with a different character and constituency.[2] But the family-oriented cultural and demographic shifts of the 1950s and 1960s depreciated demand for hotel rooms, and the buildings became the refuge of the marginal: retired sailors, single immigrants, artists, addicts, transvestites and other sexual outlaws, ex-cons and bohemians. Over the decades, the hotels were steadily turned into apartments and office buildings, the process accelerating as the price of San Francisco real estate started to rise again in the 1970s. More than 5,000 of the remaining rooms disappeared during that decade, but the number of permanent hotel residents in 1980 still numbered 27,000, three times the population of the city's public housing projects.[3] Eighty percent of the remaining rooms have been lost to fires and tourism makeovers since the 1980s,[4] but tenants and their political allies (notably the Tenderloin Housing Clinic) have continued to fight back, holding landlords to the law and persuading the city to fund nonprofit takeovers of several hotels and apartment buildings.[5] San Francisco still retains a couple thousand of SRO units, far more than most cities.

On the face of it, the Tenderloin still has much of the look of the traditional "main stem," catering to the single person in straitened circumstances. But the remnants of old-fashioned skid row enterprise — the handful of cheap diners, check cashing joints, temp agencies, liquor stores, and locker services — can obscure the fact that the neighborhood has become the primary institutional ghetto of the city, with a host of nonprofits providing food, classes, medical care, housing referrals, and other services to the city's poorest residents. At this point, it is the agencies more than anything else that cement the Tenderloin's place as the epicenter of the city's street scene, bringing in thousands of migrants every day.

In most urban areas, people identifiable as homeless comprise a people apart, clearly and inexorably differentiated from the rest of the population. The Tenderloin and its outposts, however, represent a world of poverty, a layering of multiple and diverging forms ranging from the utter abjection of the most far-gone street alcoholics to the much more ambiguous situation of the long-term apartment and hotel residents.

Some advocates have defined everybody living in the hotels to be homeless — and indeed, the 1987 McKinney Act includes those living in "welfare hotels" in its definition of homelessness. In practice, though, few would include everybody in the Tenderloin hotels in this category. The hotels provide a setting for very different kinds of lives. Many Cambodians live in the neighborhood, together with other immigrants from Asia and Latin America, sometimes a family of five or six sharing a room. There are large numbers of ex-cons, some recently released and struggling to somehow reestablish themselves, many stalled in limbo, aged out of the illicit economy but unable to hook into anything legal. Impoverished drag queens, retired strippers, and call girls share the corridors with the many people who are mentally ill or physically disabled, some of them excruciatingly isolated, others gratefully treasuring their independence from institutional life. Most of the residents live on very low wages, Social Security payments, or disability (SSI), the last group including a large number of people living with HIV and AIDS. There is much misery in the hotels, yes, and often a sense of being caged or warehoused, but many American dwellings are wretched. The residents do have their own small space, of which many manage to make home.

Then there are the hotel residents, given a short-term voucher or enjoying a temporary spike in funds.[6] Unlike those staying in the shelters or sleeping rough, hotel residents have a refuge from the "BS" and violence of street life, a place to stay warm and to get clean. Many use the soup kitchens for their meals but can otherwise minimize time spent walking round the neighborhood, adopting that swift, business-like stride that sends the message, "Just passing through."

If we move further toward the street, toward homelessness in a more literal sense, the Tenderloin again plays a central and multilayered role. Historically a port-of-entry neighborhood for refugees and other impoverished immigrants, the TL has now taken on the same function for the Bay Area homeless. In search of food and shelter, the newly homeless are drawn into the neighborhood. Even though many of them later move, they often continue to migrate backward and forward, most of all to eat the large and high-quality meals provided by St. Anthony's and Glide Memorial.

The majority of the thousands of homeless people moving through the Tenderloin streets in any given week are there to eat, to obtain other services provided in the neighborhood, or to buy crack, speed, or other drugs. Some of them are sleeping in one of the large shelters that border the neighborhood, others coming in from other parts of the city. Everywhere there are tired or ragged-looking people, lining around the block for the soup kitchens or making their way fast along the sidewalks. They are given away by their backpacks and blankets, their shaggy 'fros, beards, and torn, dirty clothes.

As Ray said, the Tenderloin is where homeless people are sup-posed to go. The aggressive policing of its border streets and spaces, of Powell Street, Civic Center Plaza, and the adjacent stretch of Mar-ket Street, gives a clear enough message that ragged loiterers should stay within the Tenderloin's "rabble zone."[7] While many homeless people resist this corral, fearing and disliking the streets of the TL, not everybody feels that way. There are often hundreds of homeless men and women on the teeming sidewalks of Eddy or Ellis, Hyde or Leavenworth, many of them addicted to crack, most of them African American, who wander up and down, engage in desultory conversa-tions, and generally pass time around the neighborhood. It is these individuals, the archetypical and often self-identified street people, who have come to define the character of the neighborhood in the eyes of other homeless people, and, indeed, in the eyes of many San Franciscans.

This chapter takes a journey across San Francisco from the dense drama of the Tenderloin to what was then the sleepy refuge of Dogpatch, way over on the city's eastern shore. Knitting the chapter together is an attention to the intimate relationship between discourse and space in both neighbohoods, each of which took on a specific and resonant discursive charge in the imaginary of their denizens, symbolizing very different ways of both living through and understanding homelessness.

It took me a long time to get access to the Tenderloin street scene. I was several months into my fieldwork with can and bottle recyclers when I decided to try a contrasting case study of homeless hustlers, a prominent group universally maligned by the recyclers for their sneaky, predatory behavior. It was tricky, however, to move beyond casual encounters. I already knew something of the neighborhood. I had visited soup kitchens and other agencies with my recycling companions, and I was staffing a meal distribution point inside one of the hotels, often delivering meals to rooms in surrounding buildings. I knew a few of the program's clients living with AIDS and often visited with them. During this time I also developed close friendships with two men who lived on Eddy Street, Victor Asencio Cortez and James Moss, which brought me intimately into the life of the hotels. I had been bullied by sneering desk clerks, stepped over the bloody needles in the bathrooms, and sometimes tried to sleep in the dank, overheated rooms. My instinct told me to stay inside once the street turned dark, its late-night desolation peopled only by fidgety crack addicts and shifty-looking wanderers. Yet it was these much despised street people I felt I should be getting to know.

In the end, my opening came through the meal program. When demand was slow I would sometimes take surplus dinners out to the street. Ten or eleven scruffy, bleary-eyed men would suddenly appear in front of me, eagerly grabbing boxes, trying to get two. On one of these occasions, I heard a dry chuckle of "Bum rush!" to my left. I turned to see a slender man leaning against the wall, holding a half-covered bottle of malt liquor. I struggled to hold on to one of the meals.

"Want it?" I said to him.

"Don't mind if I do." The others quickly disappeared with their food, but the man on my left stayed where he was.

"You got a fork?" he asked.

I went to find one for him.

"So who are *you?*" he asked me as he started eating his meal. He still looked amused.

Lots of things amused Linc, it turned out. Luckily for me, he was also tickled by the idea that I wanted to do ethnographic research with homeless people around the central Tenderloin.

"I'll tell you what you need to know," he told me. "You leave those guys alone. They ain't gonna tell you nothing but bullshit."

"That's not really how it works. But, yeah, maybe we can chill a bit when I have closed up here?"

Twenty minutes later, we walked up toward Leavenworth and then sat down in a doorway. Linc had clearly decided to be generous with his time and commentary. He was mostly concerned that I might give him away by looking at somebody he was talking about. I gazed dutifully at the architecture opposite and he started to loosen up. Linc was curious-minded, funny, and bored out of his mind by the shrinking horizon of his life on the street. Over the next few weeks, he kept company with me for several days, telling me stories, introducing me to Del, Sammy, and several other street hustlers, and showing extraordinary tolerance for my fumbling attempts to understand what was going on. (You will see in the next chapter that he had an interesting and slightly idiosyncratic perspective on both homelessness and addiction.)

Sammy

A few days later, we were sitting in Boedeker Park when Linc gestured toward a rawboned, sullen man coming our way. "Now *he* is one mean-spirited mofo. Sammy Dinks. Back in the day, whoa baby, what a fighter. . . . If he coulda only follow the rules, might have won himself a title. He's all broke down now, but you don't want to give him a reason . . ."

Sammy saw Linc and moved toward us, limping badly.

"Whassup, Sammy?"

"Whassup," he grunted, giving me a hostile once-over. "Got a smoke?"

I gave him one. He was turning away when Linc said, "You hear Jackson's back?"

"Trey?" Sammy's face lit with curiosity. "Thought he got three strikes."

Linc shrugged. "Heard he's in the Delta."

Sammy abruptly turned back in the direction of Sixth Street and the Delta Hotel, leaving Linc smiling sardonically. "Now he knows you got smokes. You'll be seeing him." Linc was clearly enjoying his new job.

Although Sammy grabbed purses and picked pockets all across downtown and Chinatown, the Tenderloin was the center of his world. He steamed through at least twice a day to trade tales about the latest news from San Bruno (county jail), Corcoran, Pelican Bay, or San Quentin.

At night, his presence took a more sinister turn. Sammy didn't seem to sleep much. He used not only crack but also meth, sending what seemed to be his natural nervous energy into overdrive. He was often "86'ed" from the shelters for fighting or stealing and had become something of what they used to call a "jack roller," regularly robbing homeless people who were trying to sleep around Market Street, kicking them and threatening them with a knife. When I summoned the courage to question him about this, he shrugged silently. Then, with an amused sidelong glance, as if daring me to do something about it, Sammy told me about robbing an SSI check from someone I knew, a man with AIDS living in the Franciscan Hotel. "Sorry son of a bitch," he sneered. "I known him back in the day. He never done *me* no favors."

Sammy was indubitably an example of the "wolves" feared and loathed by more vulnerable homeless men. "*I* look out for my*self*," he told me, sucking his teeth. "If people gonna be weak motherfuckers, if they gonna be suckers, that ain't my fault. A black man's gotta look out for himself. No one else going to give a damn."

Like Del, Sammy sidestepped notions of deprivation in favor of claims to knowledge, competence, even possession of the Tenderloin streets. "A lot of folks can't handle the TL, you know," Sammy liked to boast. "But it's cool—these my streets."

Watch Your Back

Most of the local street addicts seemed to have lost the capacity to maintain relationships of trust with each other. They shared a common sense that the central Tenderloin was a jungle, a place where the strong abused the weak and the weak in turn exploited each other. Yet there were certainly moments of community. Men might suspend their wariness, sharing their cigarettes and their amusement at the regular spatters of yelling or other drama enlivening the sidewalk. Some would go further and commit random acts of surprising generosity. But lasting solidarity seemed almost impossible. Postmortems on encounters that looked friendly enough to me would morph into alienation ("Wouldn't trust him with a dime") or that constant obituary—"Crack," with a dry shrug.

Del, Sammy, and their peers tended to alternate between isolation and running together in short-lived pairings. Like those who feared them, they often referred to each other as "dog(g)s" or "wolves," but in this milieu, these metaphors carried a minimal burden of pack loyalty. Unlike the roaming "road dogs" of the smaller town tramp circuit, who might develop considerable reciprocity and affection, these crack-addicted hustlers paid little lip service to brotherhood and often stole from each other when they were asleep.[8]

Sin-Talk

The last chapter showed how three primary discourses have dominated Euro-American constructions of homelessness: what I call *sin-talk, sick-talk,* and *system-talk.* In the terms set by sin-talk, the oldest and most powerful of the three, homelessness is a product of past and present transgressions, willful choices to pursue self-indulgent, destructive desires. The bravado of the homeless hustlers expressed the street's own version of sin-talk, their view of the world organized across the same set of interlocking binaries. On one side was their turf, the street, with its main character, the wily, hedonistic, heartless hustler. On the other lay the straight world of domesticity, religion, and hard work, at its center a role of patriarchal provider formidably hard to achieve. Both their words and their deeds resonated in harmony with the voices calling for a crackdown on street people.

Laclau and Mouffe see the discursive content of action as something fundamentally fluid and unstable. Every articulation is unique, and every different combination of people, space, and time yields a set of actions with somewhat different discursive implications. There were indeed important instabilities in the hustlers' discourse, as the next chapter brings out. Yet most notable was its stability. The longer I spent with them, the more vividly predictable became the dichotomy between "street" and "straight." Each worked it in his own way, but these binaries remained imprinted on their narratives and behavior. It became easy to foresee, for example, that Del would construct every interaction with healthcare or service agencies as an opportunity to display his hustling craft. He adamantly refused to play the victim; to do so would violate the core of his way of seeing.

Furthermore, the limits of things Del might say or do were deeply inscribed in his very way of being. He was deeply rooted in a particular genre of expression; a lexicon, syntax, and style of talking anchored what he said to the hustler role. Similarly, he was unlikely to take on a strong identity as homeless. He would never use the expression "on the street," for example. Not only was this idea alien to Del's project of maintaining agency at all costs, but the phrase was also fundamentally dissonant with his own lexicon, within which the street represented an entire world of meaning, action, and self-expression. Much would have to change before he would reduce "the street" to a metaphor for his current miseries.

Just as important, Del's ground-in physical behavior and way of responding to the world was rooted in a specific and limiting grammar of action.[9] Even though he made money from recycling cans on occasion, he was unlikely to adopt the workerist body language characteristic of the city's pro recycling contingent, a group he found mystifying and self-deluded. Just as their ideas were not his, their muscular endurance was quite different from his own mastery of emotion work, and their strenuous body language jarred with his own languid physical repertoire.

Despite their defiance, the hustlers had long been drifting into decline. By the time they were homeless, they were making a poor show of fast living, easy money, or playing the ladies. Living was hard, money was rare. Once a wealthy pimp, Fox now depended for cigarettes on handouts from a high-school girlfriend working in the housing office. The closest he got to "playing the ladies" now was by wheedling spare meals, or cheating women riding the subway station escalators out of petty change with a flirtatious bait and switch.

"Homelessness is a time machine," Linc once said. Men and women on the street were liable to fall swiftly into deeper abjection, heavier drug use, declining self-respect, and, most of all, deteriorating mental and physical health. Binge drinkers turned into constant drinkers, the mentally fragile into the permanently delusional, the combative hustler into the broken-spirited panhandler. Yet many of the hustlers continued to adamantly reject the idea that they were despised, abandoned, and powerless, clinging to the strong agency of the willful sinner. Indeed, the worse things got, the more masculine defiance seemed to become their only comfort. They patently lacked money, personal space, clean clothes, shelter, reliable friendship, and functioning family ties. Their sins were all they had.

People of the Night

Some of the street's most scurrilous reprobates had only drifted into an outlaw identification as adults, but many more were like Sammy and Del, just continuing on a path set much earlier in life. The high proportion of African Americans among the latter group will surprise no one familiar with the history and current conditions of black America. Flirting with the dark side may run deep within American popular culture, but the decision to move beyond fantasy and actually live outside the law is always going to be stronger among those who have the least to gain from playing the "straight" game — namely, among those trapped in economic and social marginality. The humiliating job restrictions for black men historically pushed generation after generation of ambitious young men to try their hand in the illicit economy,[10] and this black male valence of the street hustler's game has only become stronger over the last century. While other groups previously connected with illicit economies — Jewish Americans, Italian Americans, Chinese Americans, for example — gained increasing respectability and some degree of success in the legitimate economy in the post-WWII period, large numbers of African Americans were left behind. In the great immigrant cities, new groups of hard-up incomers — Dominicans, Colombians, Russians — stepped on those underwater treads of ethnic succession, but across the nation as a whole, vice became more tightly racialized, with new generations of impoverished African Americans moving to fill the niches left behind by their upwardly mobile compatriots.[11]

The gap between the black poor and the rest of America has worsened since the great deindustrialization of the 1970s and 1980s, which devastated the black working class even more than their white peers.[12] Faced with a growing surplus labor force, the politicians of the new right turned to crudely punitive forms of social control: workfare, school exclusions, proliferating techniques of surveillance, and, above all, incarceration, nearly quadrupling the population behind bars between 1975 and 2000 and continuing to grow rapidly through the 2000s.[13] Often directly pushing the media to focus on crack dealing and other street crimes already coded black, they were able to mobilize the weight of American's racialized symbology in support of fierce new sentencing policies.[14] As John Edgar Wideman, Loïc Wacquant, and more have compellingly elaborated, the criminal has become "coded" African American and imprisonment one of the most important ways of "marking race," a bizarrely normalized rite of passage for ordinary black men.[15]

This *carceral* bent to social policy has not only warped the lives of several million individuals and their families, but further degraded the spaces where poor people are concentrated, especially the ghetto neighborhoods and skid row zones of the deprived central city that endlessly trade their population with the mushrooming satellite ghettos of the prison-industrial complex. Men and women often come out penniless and practically friendless. When I met Fox, for example, he was riding a night bus in nothing but hospital pajamas and sneakers way too small for his feet. After fourteen months in jail for crack possession he had been released at 11 o'clock at night with six dollars and twenty cents. The grandmother who had raised him was long dead, his brother was in prison himself, and the rest of his family had given up on him years earlier. He had absolutely nowhere to go and had defaulted to riding the bus all night.

On the Tenderloin streets, the workings of the carceral society were easy enough to excavate. The streets may have beckoned, but just as important, the men had known little but castigation and violence in other spaces. With fierce punishments at home, suspensions and expulsions from school, endless frisks and frequent arrests, low-paid work punctuated by firings, their behavior had consistently been found wanting and they had failed to prosper.[16] Time inside had only reinforced tenfold their sense of a world split into two hostile camps: cops and robbers, screws and cons, those who went to church and those who ran the streets.

After the high point of sympathy in the mid-1980s, representations of the homeless veered back in the direction of the racialized moral judgment dominant in most public conversations about crime and urban poverty. Though there was certainly still room for "deserving" categories such as veterans and the mentally ill, the urban African American homeless—the majority in most large cities—became increasingly defined as street people (fueled, in the case of New York City, by middle-class hostility toward "squeegee men"). This definition brought together two symbolic binaries: the foundational American division between black and white, converging on to the equally ancient polarity between the dangerous vagrants outside and the decent within.

In this respect too the Tenderloin hustlers mobilized the same symbolic oppositions as the authoritarian pundits and politicians who wanted to clear them out of public space. Blackness and the street converged. Never mind the cold; staying outside all night was a badge of black pride. "We the people of the *night*," Sammy told me with a half-smile. "Takes a *black* man to run the streets, night and day."

Fear and Loathing

As later chapters show, the service agencies could produce plenty of problems on their own. Yet the atmosphere created by Sammy and others like him was equally difficult to deal with. The suspicious, aggressive disposition of street hustlers and wolves was germinated in deprivation and alienation, articulated in a language that constructed each and every stranger as a hostile force. The hustlers' ways, learned in youthful gang-banging, then fixed and amplified by their experiences of incarceration, returned prison culture to the streets, reproducing a climate of fear and distrust across not only the skid row but also the shelters and soup kitchens.[17] Their competitive, dog-eat-dog worldview cemented its own reality, not just for the true believers, but for thousands more who were forced into the corral.

"You have to get wise, living on the street," said Mikey, a prematurely aged white man with mental health problems. We were standing in line on the Tenderloin's Turk Street, waiting to get into St. Anthony's soup kitchen. "I used to be a lot of a nicer person. But you learn you can't trust no one in this place. Not in the shelter, not here. There's too many people looking to rip you off. Mean, cheating, low-down kinds of people. And I'm not being racial. It's just a fact: this neighborhood is not safe, and I keep my head down, and keep my own company, and that is how I stay alive. For real."

Many talked of "keeping their heads down," and indeed eye contact was an area of constant tension. If a homeless man always avoided the eyes of other men, he came across as weak or scared and set himself up for later attacks. If he met their eyes in a nonhostile way he might be taken for a fool and fall victim to some hustle. But then again, if he held another man's eyes too assertively, this might well be taken for a challenge. People developed their own ways of negotiating this treacherous path. James Moss,[18] a six-foot-two, street-smart African American and a former Turk Street crack dealer, felt far more vulnerable on the streets after his crippling stroke. As he walked toward another black man on the sidewalk he would fix him with a flat, imposing stare for about two seconds, then acknowledge him with a reserved, formalistic, "How're you doing?" Finally he would end the interaction by firmly dropping his eyes.

The actions of the "wolves" directly countered the city's attempt to corral the homeless and very poor into the Tenderloin and the smaller skid row pockets of the city, instead fueling a steady centrifugal movement out to other spaces on the street. The exodus was just as much about the shelters and hotels themselves, which not only concentrated contact with other people on the street, but frequently added their own contribution of petty domination and symbolic violence. For many residents, the shelters are an unpleasant reminder of time behind bars. "I don't know what they're thinking, some of these shelters," said recycler Morris, who had done two spells in jail for drug possession. "You can't expect to put a load of people together and have them all respect each other, respect each other's personal shit. The few assholes will mess it up for everyone. And they do. Every night there is some bullshit. It's impossible to really sleep. You know, I have my earplugs, but all the same it always wakes me up, someone going off, something missing. And it stinks. Man, does its stink. Close your eyes, you're in jail again. Worse even.

"But I could stand the stink if they would put in some kinds of cages, you know like the old cage hotels. For security. Even some of the jails, they understand this. Like over in Contra Costa County, they give you the key to your cell. It's the only way to make it safe. So you don't have to fight, you don't have to get all your personal items lifted. But the last thing they seem to care about is keeping people safe. Instead it's rules and constant—I mean *everlasting*—disrespect. It knocks you down."

As Ray commented at the beginning of the chapter, his own migration away from the Tenderloin was driven by a similar mixture of alienation with the services and dislike of the wolves. "I soon got real sick of it all. It drives you crazy, man." Ray shook his head. At the time of this conversation he had been on the street for more than a year and joined the city's army of homeless recyclers. In the interim he had grown a jutting beard and large Afro. With his long, ropy arms tightly gripping a train of two large carts, he made an imposing figure. After collecting bottles since two in the morning, Ray and his companion, Clarence, decided to share a late-morning joint. Clarence, always a little foggy, was smoking a lot at that time, hoping that marijuana would help him cut down on his crack use. While Clarence tipped the last scraps into his pipe, Ray continued his complaints about the downtown homeless scene. (He had to go to the Tenderloin the next day to reapply for General Assistance, which he had not received in eight months.)

"Like with the shelter. I like to keep on the move. I've always been that way. But they have you standing, standing, *standing*—then having to deal with some nasty little crackheads hustling you every second you don't pay attention. One guy gets you talking, the other is in your bag, in your pocket, taking your shit. You stand in line forever, and when you do get in, those people do *not* treat you with respect. They let you know you are dirt. *Dirt!* Especially the monitors. You get some of the worst people in there and what do they do? They give them special jobs, special privileges, you know. 'cause they *work* it, they talk the talk. It makes you sick to your stomach. And outside it's worse. I'm not a straight kind of guy. I've been around. But I can't stomach the endless, endless BS. Nobody talks to you without they are trying to play you for a fool; somebody is always trying to fuck with you.

"So I go up Van Ness a few blocks, set me up in the bushes on one of those streets up there—what do I get, second night I'm there, a damn ticket."

"Uh-huh. Lodging, right?" asked Clarence.

"That's right. See," said Ray, turning to me, "That's how it is, you know. Once you been out here for a while you see that you ain't gonna get no peace round the TL, anywhere downtown. You got your thieves on your left and your cops on your right and whoa! You better watch your back in every direction you can. That's why you see the smarter people, or I guess people who have their shit together, they'll find something more private, more out of the thick of things, you know."

Ray himself, strong and relatively fearless, had launched himself toward the more obscure edges of the San Francisco street scene. Wandering over by China Basin he had met Clarence, who converted him for the moment into a pro recycler.

Where else did the shelter exodus trickle? Many stayed nearby, hanging in limbo in the downtown area. Despite the great police clearances of the 1990s, people continued to feel that this was the part of the city in which they had most right to be, where there were few residents to offend. Some found strength in numbers. Every night a scattered shanty village would assemble behind the San Francisco shopping center downtown, to be quickly disassembled in the early morning. Hundreds of frightened and lonely souls adopted a night shift, sleeping fitfully on benches and walls during the day and wandering at night. Sammy, whose ghoulish "jack rolling" made him an expert on the sleeping homeless man, called such people "ghosts," and it is true that they could look eerie to those around them. They had to sit, rather than lie, to avoid trouble with the police, but would rest motionless, their head and upper bodies covered entirely with a blanket.

Thousands more dispersed themselves throughout the city. Certain areas, such as tourist destination Fisherman's Wharf or the elegant sidewalks of Pacific Heights, were hard places to sleep unmolested by police or security guards. But everywhere else homeless people slept on the sidewalk, in alleys, doorways, cars, parks, beside and underneath freeways, on patches of waste ground, or in one of the city's rare abandoned buildings. Some put up tents on the sidewalk, many carried around sleeping bags and cardboard, others just crashed out on the ground, their clothes their only protection.

Then there were the more notorious concentrations centered on shared drugs of choice. West of the Tenderloin, on Van Ness Avenue and farther south around the busy heroin market of Sixteenth and Mission, congregated many of the city's self-described "dope fiends," in shooting networks or smaller groups with whom they could share costs

Looking out from homeless hideout near the Sutro Baths.

and watch out for each other in case of overdose or other dangers.[19] Out by the freeway South of Market became a similar concentration for homeless meth addicts. Quite a lot of these people kept bicycles, on which they would scoot into the Tenderloin to get both food and drugs. The young or counterculturally inclined gravitated to the long-standing critical mass on Haight Street, while many of those who got by from panhandling tried to "keep cool with the cops" in more lucrative middle-class neighborhoods like the Castro, Noe Valley, or North Beach.

Meanwhile, the so-called smarter people evoked by Ray made well-hidden encampments in the most remote thickets of the public parks, relishing the added privacy.[20] Clarence himself had spent several months sleeping in the damp ruins of the old Sutro Baths by Baker Beach.

Homelessness is all about being deprived of claim to place. Outside the designated rabble zones, many of these wanderers made nothing more than the most temporary mark on any particular city space. Someone might claim a piece of sidewalk for panhandling or sleeping, only to be moved away after an hour, a day, or even a week. Many people drifted, adapting or reacting. They might camp in a particular alley for a couple of nights, then leave it after a resident threatened to call the cops. They might, like Billy or Morris in the pages to come, move fast through the city, Billy's "art bike" and Morris' heavily laden cart speaking for them in spaces over which they otherwise made little claim.

Yet as streams of homeless life achieved a certain harmony of elements, they generally become written onto particularly important spaces within the street scene. The rest of the chapter follows Ray to Dogpatch, a temporary haven that took on a heavy symbolic load within the imaginary of its homeless residents. Leaving the intense street life of the Tenderloin's sidewalk drug market for the tentative reciprocity of the Dogpatch recyclers and "hunter-gatherers," we see how a pair of microcultures became rooted in a specific physical environment. Like the hustlers rooted on the seedy, seamy sidewalks of the Tenderloin, the Dogpatch residents created a discursive harmony between the place and their way of life, binding together their collective narratives, grammars of action, and means of survival.

On the Dock of the Bay

On the southern side of Dogpatch, a sleepy edge-zone on the city's postindustrial eastern shore, recyclers Ray and Clarence made their most long-lasting refuge. Along with a handful living in vans and cars, rough sleepers found this relatively underused part of the city rich in potential hideouts. Some put together camps by the Bay, finding refuge in the bushes by the tire-strewn Twenty-third Street "beach," in the concrete caves under the broken pier at Mission Rock, or on the vast waste ground across the road, from which point they could survey the wave of large-scale construction moving their way from downtown. A handful of more intrepid adventurers climbed onto the roofs of disused buildings or waded over the scummy inlet by the beach to sleep in the tram graveyard opposite.

Lefebvre makes a distinction between the trivialized spaces of everyday life and spaces that have heightened symbolic meaning, whether "desirable or undesirable, benevolent or malevolent, sanctioned or forbidden to particular groups."[21] It depends, of course, who is looking, but few would dispute the symbolic weightiness of the Tenderloin within the San Franciscan imaginary. Dogpatch, at least during the 1990s and early 2000s, had the opposite character. It has now been transformed by the construction of the UCSF Mission Bay campus and the new "T" line, but the area was in those years symbolically invisible to anyone but those who worked there and the small community of residents on the eastern slope of Potrero Hill. Other city residents seemed to see it as a space without place, a stagnant industrial zone lining the Third Street corridor to Bayview. I rarely got a glimmer of recognition when I told people I was doing fieldwork there. "Oh right, by the CalTrans station," they might say, or "by 280." For the homeless, this broader symbolic invisibility was vitally important, giving them long periods without the concerted police clearances that would have troubled them in many other parts of the city. This was a place that the homeless agreed was "out of the way," even a well-kept secret.

Within the little world made by homeless van livers and campers, though, the neighborhood became just as symbolically charged as the Tenderloin. In the early 1990s the area had been a quiet refuge for loners. The most notable resident was an imperious schizophrenic who had built a substantial shanty on a disused forecourt, complete with a large sign explaining why we should drink our urine. Most others were strictly keeping their heads down. During the mid- to late 1990s a younger, more sociable group of van livers moved in, for a while forming a straggling camper village around the garment factories and other small industrial enterprises along Illinois Street (see chapter 7). The area steadily swelled with other homeless migrants, and individual hideaways began to cohere into a collective refuge, a community.

Row of vehicular homes, Dogpatch.

Some started to talk about their camps as being "over in Dogpatch," rather than "'round Illinois" or "down past Mission Rock." As they used the neighborhood's name they began to conceive the place as their own, an embattled utopia sustained in explicit opposition to the life-world of the "hotter" parts of the homeless scene. "Out *here*, it's not like the TL. You can leave your shit for a while, you can wander around, you can watch the ships." Jaz, a middle-aged white camper, gestured out toward a couple of other camps and the expanse of the Bay. "Yeah, it's a whole different side of things, ya know, the Dogpatch scene," he said. "You're not watching your back every moment of the day and night. I am so goddamn tired of that shit."

Even though some of the residents were thieves — including Jaz himself — they agreed that it was not cool to steal from other people who were homeless. Exploiting the vulnerability of your neighbors was strictly against the rules, and a cautious courtesy prevailed that was very different from the hostile fronting and frequent fights on the Tenderloin sidewalks. Strangers were acknowledged, names exchanged, and small kindnesses offered.

Keeping It Cool

One of those most responsible for the communitarian ethic of the area was Morris, an angular, bespectacled African American in his forties who was a dedicated pro recycler, putting in seven to ten hours a day collecting bottles from dumpsters and trash cans across the city. Morris was a rare man on the street, a book reader and a true organic intellectual. As I describe in more detail in chapter 5, some of the homeless recyclers were very engaged by the idea that they were heirs to the honorable lineage of the American hobo. Morris spent hours trying to flesh out this idea, trawling the San Francisco public library system and the Internet for hobo arcana. In the evenings, he would read by torchlight from a box full of printouts and photocopies he kept stashed in his encampment.

In his own little corner of Dogpatch, Morris made strenuous attempts to create and maintain community. One evening a shouting fight broke out when black loner Tom tried to stop two newcomers from building a camp in his vicinity.

"Be cool, brother," Morris urged him, walking over to stand between Tom and the newcomers. "We have to respect each other. We are not d-dogs! We are men." He nodded earnestly at both parties in turn.

"That's right! And a man needs a bit of his own damn space," flashed Tom.

"We don't want nothing to do with your mangy crackhead ass," retorted one of the newcomers.

"D-D-D-Don't be talking like that!" thundered Morris, his anger inflaming his stutter. "We're not about that kind of b-b-bullshit, not round here. You want to beat each other down, there's plenty of places you can d-do that. We've been b-beat down enough."

Mustachioed Carlos, who had wandered over to see what was going on, nodded his agreement. "Yeah, come on now, keep it cool."

Morris brokered a compromise, whereby Carlos, who had only a small tent to move, would shift nearer to Tom, giving up his own space for

A bid for privacy: camping at Mission Rock.

the newcomers to pitch their shanty. (In return, one of the newcomers gave Carlos a small amount of marijuana, one of street San Francisco's primary currencies.)

The way that Morris and Carlos successfully mediated this conflict was, just as much as Sammy's brutal "jack rolling" of his fellow homeless, an example of discourse in action. Morris refused to believe that people on the street had to behave like "dogs" and, with the help of Carlos, accomplished a moment of community organization, which made his claim a reality.

Going Public

Morris sometimes took his strongly systemic interpretation of homelessness to an audience beyond his Dogpatch neighbors, stopping his work to elaborate his "new hobo" interpretation to suppliers and other homeless recyclers.

On one occasion, Morris saw an advertisement for a public meeting on the homelessness problem and showed up ready to talk about the hobo legacy, determined to put across another view of the homeless.

Standing shaggy and unwashed at the back of the room, he calmly waited his turn while some ranted about human refuse and others pleaded for patience and more outreach workers.

"I told them, 'I'm hearing all this about your so-called bad actors. But this is hard times, you know. We are not people that have had much of a chance, the people out here. You have your war veterans, your abused kids, your people with a mental illness. But a lot of this is about being poor, always being poor, and your family before you being poor, not having no rich aunt to pick you up. And there's us out there minding our own business. Like me, I work all day picking up cans and bottles. It's dirty, it's tiring, but there's nothing wrong with it. We are like your traditional hobos. We don't ask for much, but we would appreciate being left alone and not treated like trash.'

"I got a bit worked up," he said. "You know, in the newspapers and in that meeting, it's always about all the problems we make for the city. Well, yeah, I got a problem. Poor and homeless? It's not a great place to be. But like I say, things are hard for people that's poor, and it's always us that gets the blame, not people coming in, offering two g-grand for an apartment, not your contractor that only hires white only."

Morris may have been unusually articulate, but his invocation of the system was not uncommon in San Francisco, radical and counter-cultural capital of the West Coast. Morris's class and race-based analysis of homelessness resonated with the literature and statements put out by local advocacy organizations, such as the Coalition on Homelessness, and he found willing, even eager listeners among his suppliers, many of them bohemian types whose own tenure in the city was increasingly threatened by gentrification.

Nevertheless, I believe, Morris's cognitive map of homelessness would not have been sustainable, and he would not have been able to really make sense of the world of the street, if he was stuck in the Tenderloin, spending all day around the shelters and soup kitchens. The strength of his public persona was rooted in the recyclers' discourse of dignity and mutual respect—indeed, in their entire way of life.

Without their work, which allowed the recyclers to live homeless without being forced into more directly criminal or abject means of survival, there would have been little space for system-talk. Morris might dismiss men like Del as street guys—echoing the hustlers' own

"Oh no, you won't see me in a shelter. This is the best cart I've had in years. I'm holding on to it."

claim to be "of" rather than "on" the street—but without an alternative activity and source of income it would have been hard for him to avoid becoming "street" in *both* senses. I saw this happen too many times (see chapter 5). Those physically unable to continue recycling could drift away from their systemic analysis as quickly as they dropped their now obsolete worker identity, whether they subsided into drugged despair or shifted into a world of rehabilitation and recovery that redefined the slog of bottle-collecting as addictive compulsion.

Similarly, the survival of strong, coherent system-talk on the street was highly dependent on the existence of alternative street spaces such as Dogpatch. The ideas of Morris and other strong system-talkers had been developed and nourished over several years within the crucible of these outlier concentrations, places where they could congregate away from both the stigmatizing gaze of the housed and the Hobbesian war of the Tenderloin and other "hot" parts of town. When Morris saw this hard-won way of seeing violated in Dogpatch, he had allies ready to back up his attempts to "do" community—in this case, to enforce a degree of social regulation beyond the usual moral minimalism of the street, to get his neighbors to act like men rather than dogs or wolves.

Hunting and Gathering

Soon after Ray and Clarence moved to Dogpatch, Ray started to spend time with a fraternity of hippie heroin users quite different from the hardworking pro recyclers. His new friends, Quentin, Jaz, and Billy, had one of the most elaborate camps in the neighborhood, with a superb view onto the bay. They had made their shanties watertight and put together a well-equipped cooking station complete with pans, plates, and forks. Jaz, who had some skill with wiring, even managed to get electricity going some of the time, which they used to power a heater and lights. One August they put up a set of fairy lights and threw what became an infamous margarita party.

During the daytime, Ray and Jaz would put in several hours trawling around Potrero Hill or the Mission with a cart. Quentin, whose health was not good, mostly lay around and read books. He went into the city's central library a couple of times a week and maintained a lively Internet presence. Billy sometimes went with the others, but he mostly "biked around." On a vehicle strung with branches, silver foil, and the latest odd offerings from Jaz, Billy covered the city, charming his way to all sorts of free stuff: meals, magazines, groceries, clothes, clean drug paraphernalia. Billy was seriously bipolar and had found that exercise kept him "up."

Like Lars Eighner, the great homeless memoirist, Quentin's crew despised the wastefulness of consumer society and derived considerable self-respect from their ability to live outside the system.[22] They did collect cans, which were the most lucrative recyclables, but were more interested in finding food. They were less likely to talk about their activity as recycling than as dumpster diving—a term which for them summed up both a value system and an entire way of life.

If Morris was the organic intellectual of the recyclers, the Dogpatch dumpster divers had Quentin. A handsome man with intense dark eyes and mercurial moods, prodigal son of the old San Francisco oligarchy, Quentin advertised his calling with a necklace strung with teeth, foreign coins, and a china doll's leg.

"I was never really into work," he told me. "I've always been a treasure hunter. When I still had the house, I used to go on archaeological digs, you know? Spent two years in Cambodia, a year in Peru, six months uncovering cave paintings in France. In Cambodia we were so way out there we didn't have a shower in six months, just bathing in the river. I always liked to be free of all that, the daily grind. I drove my father wild. . . . Dumpster diving is like archaeology, really. You are looking for treasures other folks can't see. Like they would rather go out buying some ugly crap from Target or Bed, Bath, and Beyond when they could find something funky and actually have some fun making something of it. But that would involve actually opening their eyes and using their brains. . . . And they are just buying more and more junk every day, even though the planet is choking with all of this crap."

Quentin's upper-class background and good education set him apart from the rest of my research companions. He was a formidable street lawyer, civil and indefatigable in defense of his neighbors and friends when threatened by the police. He was well liked by his immediate camp partners, Billy, Jaz, and eventually Ray. They listened eagerly to his stories about indigenous people's ability not only to survive without modern technology and a wage economy, but also to enjoy themselves doing so. In particular, they seemed to appreciate Quentin's suggestion that homeless dumpster divers like them were the contemporary version of the hunter-gatherer. They seemed grateful for his suggestion about how to understand themselves beyond the overdramatized binaries of moralistic sin-talk.

Ponytailed Billy told me earnestly, "We are something like those bush people Quentin talks about, you know. We don't buy into some big old economic system, work for the man, buy a bunch of crap. We just go out foraging for stuff."

Billy and his older friend Jaz were archetypal "California boys," with their mellow friendliness, their tales of epic acid trips, and their common reverence for Mendocino weed and the Grateful Dead, Sly Stone, and vintage motorbikes. Though none of them identified as gay, they all admired Quentin, who was not only openly gay but suffering from symptomatic HIV. They were fascinated by his ability to dredge up interesting tidbits about anything from the kinship system of the Hmong to the sexual perversities of the California aristocracy.

Quentin's crew oriented their lives on the basis of two principles. The first was that it was not only necessary but desirable to get by without the tawdry comforts of the domesticated masses. The second was that the demands of dope should not be allowed to overwhelm the important business of play and creativity. Rather than demonstrating any serious dedication to the thieving arts, their escapades often had a childlike, anarchic spirit. Treasure hunting was always a high priority. One night Ray and Jaz broke into a storage cellar at a hospital, looking for aluminum to sell. They came back with various metal pans and trays, but their largest and by far most awkward burden was a full-size plastic reproduction of a skeleton, which they gleefully hung in a tree next to their camp and nicknamed "Mama." "Not in front of Mama," Billy joked as Jaz was shooting up.

There was a world of difference between this group of dumpster divers and some of their neighbors, particularly the fiercely "decent" Clarence, who sent in every receipt from his recycling to General Assistance. Yet Clarence shared with Willie and Quentin's crew the project of creating and maintaining an alternative homeless social space, distinctive from the "BS" of the Tenderloin and the humiliation of panhandling the neighborhood commercial strips. This was both a literal space, in terms of new territories where they could sleep without interference from either predatory jack rollers or the police, and a space of practices and relationships that separated them from both sin and sickness.

Now forty-seven, Jaz had been a heroin addict since he was twenty-two years old. A farm boy from the Bakersfield area, he had developed his habit while stationed with the military in Korea and never managed more than a couple of months clean. He had spent much of the last twenty-five years in San Francisco and Oakland, where he had gone through two marriages. Jaz was a skilled electrician, but the unreliability caused by his habit had cost him dozens of jobs, pushing him down the wage scale until he could get nothing but the occasional handyman gig under the table.

"Those first few weeks I was homeless, I was ready to cut my throat," Jaz told me during an extemporary interview in his camp. "It was a couple of years ago. I was all busted up anyway about losing my place, about screwing up my job. And I hated the fucking shelters. Couldn't stand being cooped up with all those people. Still can't. Worse than the army. I knew I had to figure something else out, but I just wasn't sure what to try. First of all, I started hanging out in this shooting camp over by the Central Freeway. Heroin Central. I was so miserable, I wanted to get wasted all the time.

"Then I totally ran out of cash. I was stealing stacks of CDs every day but could barely get my hands on any cash for them. The people in the used shops were onto me. So I was down Sixteenth and Valencia every night trying to put together ten, twenty bucks. Trying to smile and not look too desperate. OK, I thought. What's the point of being proud? Started panhandling down by the Bank of America ATM at Van Ness and Market. My hair was sticking out on end and I had this nasty bushy beard. So what, I thought. Least none of the boys from work are gonna know you. It was like I could barely feel anything. I was kinda numbed out, in a way.

"But it was a miserable time. Beyond miserable. And I couldn't stand those people in the camp. They were pretty broke down, and it was a nasty scene. They were doing everything—dope, crack, malt liquor, you name it. Sticking a needle anywhere you can stick it. And at some point I guess I just woke up and I thought, jeez, what the fuck am I doing? What a fucking lowlife! So I went back to the shelter, tried to cool down my habit.

"Then I hit a kind of turning point, I guess. Calmed down. And I always think like maybe I had a little bit of karma left, you know, 'cause that's when I ran into Billy. And I just knew right off he was gonna be cool. And things started coming together. Might sound idiotic to you, seeing how we live."

"Not really," I said.

"I don't want you to think I'm gay or something." Jaz looked at me quizzically.

"OK."

"Look, you wouldn't believe how important your buddies are when you're on the street. It's make or break. And until we hooked up there

Camping in the shadow of the Central Freeway.

was no question of buddies for me. I didn't trust anyone, and that was right. There's not so many people you can trust. This kind of shit does not bring out the good side of the human temperament, if you ask me. I'd rather be around a pack of dogs."

"So did you and Billy take off together?"

"Yeah, right, we figured some stuff out, and we got the hell out of there. And I never go back. Only time was after I went to jail this spring, and that was just a couple of days till I figured out where Billy was."

"When you first left MSC (the shelter), where did you go?"

"It's a long story. We've stayed in a bunch of places. Try to stay away from the cops, away from the jerks who wanna rip you off. It's not bad when there is a crowd of you, like here in Dogpatch, as long as people stay cool. You get a certain kind of safety in numbers. But the best thing is finding somewhere that's got a bit of space, trees, the ocean, the bay. That's what we look for. Our favorite place was out at the ocean, way down by Daly City. But it was too much effort coming into the city all the time. If we weren't dope fiends . . ." He grinned and raised his eyebrows at me.

Jaz's journey from the Heroin Central west of the Tenderloin to the Dogpatch dumpster divers exemplifies the men's desire for a coherent map of the world, for some sense of authenticity that could save their embattled self-respect and make sense of their difficult ways of life. His story is particularly enlightening about how different microcultures developed distinctive ways of using drugs. I imagine many readers to be skeptical that street addicts can exercise any control whatsoever over their drug use. As Darin Weinberg has described in rich detail, drug rehabilitation facilities and the twelve-step movement have combined with other cultural strands to produce a popular construction of the street addict that stands for utter chaos, loss of all regulation, and a constant threat of quite heinous criminality.[23] In Jaz's case, though, you can see how a new relationship of trust enabled him to move into what he considered a much less degrading form of drug-addicted homelessness.

Jaz was not trying to pretend he was not an addict. In fact, he was unusual in that he often wore a T-shirt that revealed his tracks and burns to all and sundry, only slipping on a long-sleeved shirt when leaving the neighborhood. What he wanted was not denial but other people with whom he could get by on the street in a way where he could still feel cool rather than a "fucking lowlife." Around people like Morris and Carlos, as well as his own crew, this had become possible. Most, though not all, of the Dogpatch street homeless were drug users, but underlying their ethic of cool and respect was an agreement that they were not dogs but men, and that they did not have to give themselves up completely to the dark side of sin-talk by subordinating every element of their existence to getting high. Surely this project of balance also gave extra intensity to the elements of play, the appreciation of nature, and the passionate friendships among Quentin's crew.

Ray

Jaz's camp companion, Ray was another restless drifter. He had moved within all of the street microcultures mentioned in this chapter—from the hustle of the Tenderloin to pro recycling with Clarence—ultimately joining the more laid-back scene of Quentin, Billy, and Jaz. Ray had never known much of a settled home. As a kid in the late 1960s he had drifted with his mother and sister through a couple of Oakland Black Power collectives, learning to question the extent to which a black man should tangle with the white man's world. The family also wandered through Los Angeles, the Bronx, Philadelphia, and Tucson, leaving Ray with vague memories of hundreds of housemates and no idea of the number of schools he had attended. What stayed clear in his mind was the high school in South Philly where he got into heroin. His mother dragged him back to a clean house in Oakland, but Ray could never quit for long.

In his twenties he spent a couple of years in Morocco, Senegal, and Liberia, where he sold hashish to white travelers. Ray's dream, though, was to trade African crafts. He brought a few boxes of carvings back to the United States and tried to set himself up with a market stall, but he never kept enough money to return to Africa. He reluctantly worked on and off in parking or security, staying with girlfriends here and there. In his thirties he did two stretches for heroin possession, which did not help him improve his position in the labor market. While serving a third stretch, this time for a minor marijuana offense, his mother died. His sister was somewhere in Philly, and his ex-girlfriends were sick to death of bailing him out. For the first time, he had absolutely nowhere to go.

Ray's broad life experience helped him to ease through the varied ecology of the San Francisco street, slowly gravitating toward a way of life that felt, if not exactly acceptable, at least less painful or difficult than other choices and toward companions of the street to whom he felt better suited.

Since joining Quentin's crew, Ray had become uncomfortable with the idea of being classed as a victim of homelessness. "I don't really think of myself as homeless," he said earnestly. "OK, I know I am officially, and it's not like I could afford to live inside in this city. All the same, homeless doesn't sound right for me. It was different when I was in the Tenderloin, you know. Even in the Haight. But now I'm camping out—that's more what it feels like. Like if they drove us off of here again, you wouldn't see us in the shelters. Billy and me, we're thinking we might go up to the Sierras, see the mountains. But the others don't wanna go."

"How would you do that?" I asked. "You need money; you need money for dope. How would you do that outside the city?"

Ray shrugged and looked out toward the Bay. "I dunno—cut down, clean up for a while, maybe get a few weeks in rehab, then skip. I am getting more of a handle on how to deal with shit, with my habit." He caught my eye. "Honestly."

"If you could clean up, you would stay outside?"

"Sure. Might go down to Mexico." Ray mused.

"You don't want to get straight?"

Ray shrugged again, and then smiled. "I didn't do so well when I was trying to go straight. Miserable mofo. Miserable, mean, and sneaky as hell! Started rehab eight, maybe nine times. Gone through it four."

Ray paused. I must have looked confused. "It's hard to explain. You know how in rehab there's all this about being realistic, not getting into denial. Well, I am trying to be realistic—realistic *my* way.

"Give me more money, some kinda job, and I'll just get me a monster habit. That ain't just opinion, I *know* that. Honest to God, that's just how it *is*. So I am better off out here, living simple. I used to shoot a lot more dope, you know. But Quentin, he has really come through for me. I don't mind saying it: I never thought I would be so tight with a white guy, with a bunch of white guys! If my sister could see me, it would blow her mind. But you know, you gotta keep an open mind. Quentin, he has been real cool. He talks me out of it, he says, 'Come on, Ray, keep it mellow.' I start jonesin', he finds me some weed. Keeps me eating, stuff like that. Call me crazy, but I feel like I got it all a li'l bit under control this way. It's been, I dunno, six weeks, since I really binged out. We just keep it cool, share one bag a day. Keep off the crack, off the speedballs. We don't go crazy, I guess that's what I'm saying.

"Once you get used to living out, you don't need so much." Ray gestured at the lean-to in which he and Quentin were keeping each other warm at night.

"I spent too much time *wanting* things in my life. Wanting good money, wanting nice clothes, then wanting dope, and more dope, and more dope. Wanting too hard, not appreciating what I had. Like my daughter—I never used to think how lucky I was to have a beautiful kid like that. I didn't spend that time, now she don't wanna know. You know what I'm saying?

"Now I'm trying to get more in touch with my gut, like Quentin says. It's like I'm Rahim again. That's what I was called when we was with Uhuru. Rahim. Before I got all tangled up in *society*. I feel like I'm goin back twenty, twenty-five years ago, but less stupid. Slowing down. Wasting time. In a good way, I mean. Trying to slow my head down. *Think* about stuff. Sitting on the dock of the bay." He whistled Redding's tune, something of a theme song in Dogpatch.

Already we have seen some very different responses to the stigma of being homeless. While the hustlers tended to deny that they were homeless at all, Morris and his companions deflected the shame of homelessness back onto the cruelties of the system. The Dogpatch dumpster divers developed a different response, hence the claim that they were to some extent intentionally homeless, or at least "not really homeless," as Ray put it. In Quentin's case there was probably something to this. With the others, though, intentional homelessness seemed better understood as a perspective developed on the street. Like the hustlers, they were trying to wrest back some sense of agency, of having a say in the shape of their own lives. Yet their notion of the street was a very different one, defined in terms of a quite different grammar of action—an intimate and trusting collectivism unusual in the "TL."

The dumpster-divers had worked out their own way of dealing with homelessness, a countercultural hybrid that took on elements from both sin-talk and system-talk without fully taking on either way of thinking. From sin-talk they took the strong agency, the sense of actively choosing the street over worse alternatives, while from system-talk they took both social critique and absolution from guilt, refusing to see themselves as immoral. At the cost of relinquishing claims on the broader society, Quentin's crew's hybrid philosophy escaped the personal dead-ends set up by both sin-talk and system-talk. Their freewheeling moral agnosticism bypassed the hustlers' confused, even schizophrenic relationships with good and evil. At the same time it avoided the fetishization of hard physical labor common among the pro recyclers, whose efforts to maintain self-respect through work could easily fall into the old moral template, leaving more conservative men like Clarence crushing his body with continual hard labor to hold on to his honorable exceptionalism.

Ray still spent time with Morris and Clarence, but he had never really adopted their strong work ethic, and he now seemed profoundly relieved to find others who were cool—distanced from the "crazy" death quests and Hobbesian war of the street—yet still fiercely critical of straight life. He appreciated the playful, less morally laden perspective of Quentin's crew, their refusal to pity themselves or to be ashamed of their heroin addictions. Neither the "wolves" of sin-talk, the enslaved addicts of sick-talk, nor the noble victims of systemic injury, his new friends gave him a space to revisit the radical critique of his youth in the 1960s, albeit in a very different key. His long ambivalence about the entanglements of marriage, work, and materialism had come together with his desire to keep steering his own destiny. "Homeless doesn't sound right for me," he said. Instead he was recreating himself in a form that let him "be Rahim again." Sure, he was older, drug-needy, and battered, but for the moment he seemed to have found a way to feel more at peace with himself.

Something Left to Lose

As we have moved from the hustlers of the Tenderloin to the Dogpatch recyclers and dumpster divers, we have seen how specific city spaces become discursively "charged" within the homeless scene, concentrating, nurturing, and symbolizing different forms of street existence. This intimate dialectic between spatialized practices and discourses on homelessness became particularly noticeable when men from the Tenderloin and Dogpatch moved into each other's orbit.

The vignette preceding this chapter, "Watch Out, San Francisco!," shows something of the hostility between hustler Del and the black recyclers who pushed their loads through the Tenderloin. From the perspective of Del, leaning nonchalantly against a wall for much of the day, the pro recyclers were suckers in that they worked harder than they needed to. Worse, they were suckers with attitude. They deluded themselves by thinking they were like real workers when in fact they were "dope fiends and bums." In Del's world, homelessness happened only to sinners, by definition. This meant that he himself was ultimately far more honest than Morris, for example, because he *knew* that he was fundamentally on the street side of the street-straight line rather than trying to pretend that he was "working for the city or something."

Del's ridicule of the earnest efforts of the black pros was incisive in its own way. He was certainly right that the honor of their dirty work lay mostly in their own eyes.[24] But at the same time, what Del did not seem to see was how his defiant orientation to the street represented a twisted form of consent to his own social exclusion. Del, Fox, and Linc's San Francisco was tiny compared with the city of the recyclers or Quentin's crew. Sammy roamed a slightly wider circle, but rarely ventured more than fifteen minutes' walk away from the central Tenderloin. All of them carried the ghetto walls with them, feeling little desire and no sense of entitlement to move outside of what for them was a safety zone. Just as their discourse of sin reproduced their socialization in carceral institutions of punitive neoliberalism, their attachment to the Tenderloin tidily reproduced the city's attempts to corral the indigent away from tourist zones and middle-class neighborhoods.

In the meantime, while Del was wandering back and forth around the drug market of Boedeker Park, Morris and Clarence were out on what Clarence called their "patrols," pushing through not only the Tenderloin but Pacific Heights, Russian Hill, Chinatown, or North Beach, passing the time of day with regular acquaintances among the broad variety of bar staff and city residents who saved them bottles. Their home turf, Dogpatch, was not an island so much as a relatively safe base for more expansive activities. What Del saw as slavish behavior brought them not only some spatial freedom but a degree of social integration, even a sense of citizenship.

The Dogpatch community did not last. First South Beach, then the entire eastern shore of the city exploded in a millennial development frenzy. Quiet dead-ends, stagnant basins, and ancient bars and restaurants disappeared under new townhouse and "live-work" villages, the 3Com Stadium, a college campus, and enterprises from golf drives to biotech start-ups. The area of Morris's first camp became an Esprit outlet store, and successive ticketing and towing campaigns drove out the van livers.

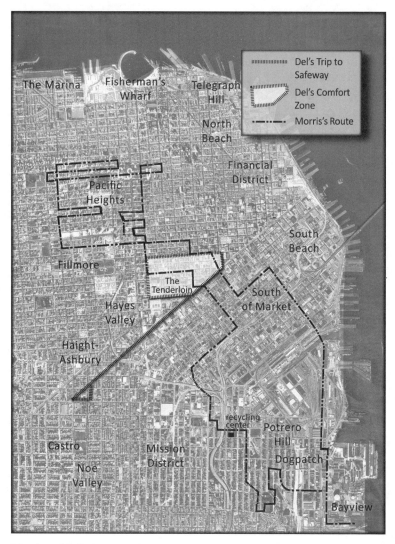

Morris and Del's San Francisco.

Yet even before all this, the area's homeless camps had been severely shaken by an event that showed the limits of the social control exercised by the more community-minded residents. One of the groups camping in the area made the dubious decision to engage in major mayhem on their own turf. Over a couple of nights they broke into a pier where several new city buses had recently arrived from Italy.

They swiftly stripped them of their shiny aluminum rims and trim, which they hauled away for scrap. The city was quick to retaliate, razing much of the undergrowth that had sheltered the nearby camps and changing the relatively hands-off policy toward the area.

Like the homeless shanty dwellers in Dordick's New York study, the Dogpatch campers had "something left to lose": safety, human connection, place.[25] Clarence, for one, returned to sleeping without a camp, crashed out on the sidewalks around Division Street. A few months later, he had taken to talking to himself.

"What would you say? Yeah, that's seven pounds, that's right, seven pounds," he was muttering as I pulled up on my bike.

"Yeah, I can't say I don't miss making a camp," he said when I asked him about Dogpatch. "Over there, you could have something to come back to. Most people would look out for you, you know."

"You haven't found anywhere else decent lately?" I asked.

"Not really. I get sick of trying to get myself together. I am out working and then, shit, my place is trashed! Like by the freeway, they come by every couple weeks and just break everything down, like it's not already trashed out enough. It's not worth it, making anything. . . . And it was cool to be around other guys, around other recyclers."

"You lonesome?"

"I'd say I'm just about as lonesome as a man can be before he goes crazy."

Some Other Kind of Life

IN THE SPRING OF 1976 Manny Vitello waded over the Rio Grande to join his sister's family in Los Angeles. He had already seen a lot of the world for a twenty-five-year-old. Son of Italian-Peruvian factory workers in Lima, Manny had started working in construction at thirteen. At nineteen he hit the road, peddling jewelry from Iquique to Santiago, Montevideo to Medellín. He had settled a while in La Paz, working for an operation processing cocaine for export, when the news of his sister's marriage inspired him to take his own chances in the United States.

Manny's fantasies of coming prosperity took an immediate knock when his middle-class Cuban brother-in-law met him with distrust and disdain, refusing to let him stay more than two nights and forbidding Manny's sister to lend him any money. But Manny decided to try his own way. He wandered north to Santa Barbara, found himself a cash-in-hand job as a gardener, and developed himself a sideline dealing marijuana to high school and college kids. Three years later he persuaded his Anglo girlfriend, Sandy, to marry him.

"I thought I had finally made it when that green card arrived." Manny chuckled, crinkling his well-worn crow's-feet. "But now I can see that's when my luck *really* turned to shit. Sandy got into speed.... She got fired for acting weird, freaked out her family. I was bagging groceries, all set to go straight, but I couldn't pay the rent. Landlord threw us out.... Sandy didn't wanna leave town, so I started making a run up here every five, six weeks. I had a connection with one of the growers in the hills.... Then we found another apartment, up the coast. Real nice, but we were there maybe two months and I got busted with a big, fat bag. And that was it. I spent the next eleven years in the pen."

In Corcoran prison Manny found himself cellmates with Pipe, a jumpy, disturbed white Californian. Pipe was a former foster kid who had spent much of his life locked up for theft or drug possession. His face and neck advertised his con status with the wavering lines of prison tattoos, and the only work he had ever known was prison labor and a couple of training schemes long ago. Manny met his nervy aggression with amused patience, slowly winning Pipe's trust and fierce attachment.

When he got out, Manny made his way to San Francisco and to Pipe, who was subletting a small room in the apartment of another prison buddy, TJ. Manny was determined they would find work, Pipe less optimistic. Six weeks turned up nothing but irregular day labor, and Pipe slipped back into stealing. Then TJ got evicted. The friends tried in vain to find something they could afford on the few hundred dollars a month they were putting together from Manny's General Assistance and Pipe's stolen car radios.

There was no way they were going to use the shelters, so they scoured the city for good places to camp out. They had "slept out," as they put it, although never before in San Francisco. Their first encampment was deep in the woods of the Presidio, the former army base near the bridgehead of the Golden Gate. Hoping to get back into small-scale dealing, they planted some marijuana nearby. Before the first harvest, though, workers from the parks department destroyed their camp and their plants. After finding their camp destroyed the fourth time, they gave up. They schlepped what remained of their possessions over to Golden Gate Park. Growing marijuana was not too promising there either. The city was making a concerted effort to rout druggies and their plants from the undergrowth, and between the city sweeps and depredations by their neighbors, Manny and Pipe found they couldn't keep a camp going for more than a few days.

Pipe didn't like the scene on Haight Street anyway. "Manny thought it was cool enough, but he's Mister Mellow, ya know. To me, it's kinda weird. The shops and houses are all fixed up, and then you got a bunch of kids—half of them run off from nice places in the suburbs, you can bet—hanging out, whining about Jerry Garcia and make-believing they got some great scene . . ."

"Hey, come on! Be nice, for a change," interrupted Manny.

"... like they got some kinda summer of love rerun. Which is such bullshit."

Manny shoved Pipe firmly enough to get his attention. "Thing is, we couldn't get our shit together there. We couldn't get no peace and quiet, set things up nice. If I'm gonna be homeless, at least I've got to have a decent camp. So I was bitching away to this dude, and he said a bunch of people he knew had gone over the other side of Potrero, mostly to get away from the cops. They hadn't moved back, so he thought maybe it was worth checking out."

Manny and Pipe took the 33 bus to Potrero Avenue, found a cart, and rattled their possessions through a tortuous zigzag up and across the hill, finally dropping down over a high freeway bridge. Manny seemed struck by the contrast between the cars roaring beneath him and the promise of haven ahead. "As soon as we were standing on that bridge, I got that feeling—this was the right place. Here you are, right on top of the freeway, but just over there you got the bay, you got quiet little streets. When most places in the city are people, people, people! I like quiet!"

That evening they set up camp between some bushes on a piece of wasteland by the bay. They walked over to St. Martin de Porres for food, and no one bothered them or their camp. One of their neighbors was Clarence, the gentle, vague master recycler of the neighborhood, who cautiously welcomed them and gave them a tip about a mattress he had seen on the sidewalk the day before. Couple of days later they saw Clarence come back from the city rolling a massive "train" of recyclables behind him. Clarence went into his camp for a couple of cookies to give him energy for the last haul. Intrigued by the scale of Clarence's operation, Manny asked if he could go along to the recycling company with him and check out the scene. Clarence (he later confided) was concerned that Manny might want to rip him off after he got paid, but he decided to play friendly. Manny came back from his trip interested in trying out the "dumpster-diving gig," as he called it.

Gradually Manny and Pipe became recyclers themselves, spending their days pounding the streets for bottles and cans. Sitting by their fire at night they made endless jokes about being honest working men or reformed characters. They got to know the other recyclers of the area and bonded over dumpster stories. Clarence, straightest of the straight, seemed to be convinced, moving his camp nearer to theirs so they could watch out for each other.

Living by the Bay turned Manny and Pipe's attention toward a bigger canvas: nature, adventure, travel. Manny recalled crossing the Andes, bouncing on the back of a vegetable truck, while Pipe listened hungrily. Pipe, for his part, seemed to be going through some kind of epiphany. He became desperate to escape the city. One day the three of us climbed Twin Peaks, the highest of San Francisco's hills, a windy hilltop with vast views over three counties.

As the ocean clouds slowly rolled in, covering the white city below, Pipe was musing over the possibility of getting work on a ship. Suddenly he changed the subject.

"It's cool to be around those dumpster-diving guys. . . . What is coming to me is how the system—you know, the system doesn't want us to trust each other, to treat each other with respect. You know in the system, in the prisons, in youth authority, they make it dog eat dog, like they encourage all this violence and petty bullshit between the inmates. That's what Manny was always sayin' in the joint. And he's right. . . . You don't really think about it beyond this or that guy you are avoiding or this deal you're making. You don't think about the system, the real system, the system that has, you know, two million of us locked up. And me, a lot of years, all I've been doing is staying in their stupid little system, like there was nothing else out there. You forget you could have some other kind of life."

Protected by his buddy and able to make some limited licit cash, Pipe felt more and more distanced from his small-scale maneuverings within the criminal economy. He was surprisingly quick to drop his old cat-and-mouse games with neighborhood cops. Equally significantly, he lowered his guard to embrace the communitarian vision of Clarence, Morris, and other Dogpatchers.

Manny appeared to have noticed this as well. "Pipe's chilling out over here," he told me. "He's always been cool, you know, he's got a good heart, but he is usually kinda jumpy. You know, I'm the easygoing one, and he doesn't trust people one second! I used to say, *hombre* did all that crystal when he was a kid and it got into his system. But is true, he's chilling, he's not, like, turning round or looking over my damn shoulder every three seconds. It's good. It's relaxing!"

A different geography, a different social milieu, and Pipe's petty criminal habitus did not seem so fixed after all.

FOUR

Word on the Street

THE 1980S RESURRECTION OF THE OLD SOCIAL PROBLEM of homelessness set off a fierce clash of interpretations. As I argued in part I, debate and policy gradually solidified around three discursive logics, what I call sin-talk, sick-talk, and system-talk. The powerful social justice advocates kept system-talk influential throughout the 1980s. The activists were quickly reminded, however, that social movements produce many unintended consequences. The most substantial end product of their tireless lobbying, media work, and hunger strikes was the great homeless archipelago, a network of depressing and often degrading emergency shelters and soup kitchens. While the activists succeeded in creating national concern about homelessness as a social problem, they gradually lost their purchase on both news media and policy development.

Many of the advocates, along with sociologists like Snow and Anderson, came to feel that the emergency shelter system they had initiated was ultimately accommodating the problem of homelessness more than solving it.[1] It is true that their activism did, by way of the McKinney Act, hasten the progression toward multiservice or transitional shelters with better physical conditions. But the new institutions were steadily permeated by the therapeutic interpretations—or sick-talk— proliferating in social work and public health circles. In the meantime, sin-talk reminiscent of the great tramp scare of the 1870s developed and spread across the entire country, materializing in mass legislation and police campaigns aimed at the clearance of homeless people from public space and their forcible corral into the shelter system.

Chapter 7 describes how San Francisco's prominent homelessness problem became a flashpoint for changing notions of citizenship, entitlement, and community. In 1991, liberal mayor Art Agnos was defeated by former police chief Frank Jordan, who had campaigned on a "revanchist" program to clear the homeless and lock them up in work camps out by the county jail.[2] San Francisco's long-standing progressivism was vigorously confronted with the neoliberal turn in national political culture. Newspaper columnists, drug counselors, city officials, academics, and mental health workers all struggled to stamp their own interpretation on the problem of homelessness. A strong position could make or break a political candidate, but also inject conflict into any casual gathering. Over the next decade the continual homelessness debates propelled a protracted struggle for the heart and soul of the city, resulting in a profound "crisis of urban liberalism," as Vitale has described it.[3]

In the midst of this turmoil, what went unnoticed was how San Francisco's passionate debate about causes and solutions to the homelessness problem made its way onto the street itself. As partisans of sin-talk, sick-talk, and system-talk battled for mastery within the public sphere, homeless people themselves pursued their own parallel projects to define, reject, or complicate "homelessness" in both words and deeds.

This is not a romance of resistance. Whatever discursive independence these men showed was reactive and fractured. Already in acute personal crisis, they were confronted continuously by forceful iterations of elite sin-talk and sick-talk in the form of rabble management by obligatory medicalization. In these contexts, their actions become highly strategic. People on the street learned fast how to position themselves when quizzed by shelter workers, police officers, welfare officials, nurses, lawyers, or activists.

Yet the men's iterations of dominant discourses on homelessness ran far deeper than the purely instrumental. Shame, stigma, and isolation kept these ideas twisting and turning in the minds of their objects. Out in the more autonomous spaces of street life — among sidewalk sleepers, corner "bottle gangs," panhandlers, recyclers, and thieves — multiple answers to the ever-implied question, "Why are you homeless?" hung in the air.

Homeless men's struggle to place themselves manifested itself in profoundly different strategies. Many were used to embracing criminality;

they had been chasing "bad boy" cool since they first sneaked into the street to play marbles and smoke cigarettes. At their most defiant and shameless, they claimed the streets for their own, reworking the sin-talk of the city's political leaders into a glorification of their deviant ways. In more vulnerable moments, though, they might relinquish the burden of agency and welcome the poverty agencies' offer to exchange culpability for narratives of helpless addiction, trauma, and mental illness. Others strove to separate themselves from the stigmatized status of "lazy bum" with hard physical labor, deploying a kind of "value stretch" to lower the bar of decency. At times any of them might pick up the trail of embattled system-talk, building passionate critiques of oppression and betrayal.

The last chapter showed homeless men writing their presence and way of life onto different city spaces. This one is driven by a different organizing principle. Traveling through a spectrum of street discourses on homelessness, I show how the men combined, blended, subverted, and reworked popular narratives and schemas to make sense of homelessness, both as everyday life and as extraordinary stigma.[4] Many of the most significant moments in street life, though, never reached the point of a sustained verbal articulation. Many of my street companions, especially the white men, seemed suspicious of too much talk, implying with their studied disinterest that talk was cheap and that actions spoke louder than words. In that, I suppose, they were like many white working class men. Yet commentary about homelessness was everywhere—in the downcast eyes of the panhandlers, in the assertive swing of the heavy-loaded recycling cart into traffic, in the angry stare that men bedding down on Market Street might return to curious tourists. To explore such discursively charged action requires moving beyond the text. Indeed, moving practice closer to discourse, getting at "lived discourse," helps us hold on to the concrete moorings—political, economic, cultural, institutional—that overshadow and channel the street's potential ways of seeing.

Sin

"I was always way outta control," said Fox, the African American crack addict raised in the Bayview neighborhood. "I always wanted to be outside, in the action, so's to speak. My grandma, she tried to keep me on track, but there was no way. Now I'm talking when I'm just a little kid, first, second grade. The street was, like, *magnetic* to me. I couldn't stand sticking indoors."

Their language, style, and behavior might violate countless rules of respectable society, but the disreputable poor of the Tenderloin and other "lowlife" concentrations closely echoed the rhetoric of the public figures pushing for the criminalization of homelessness. Like those who would clear them from the city's valuable public space, they disdained the term "homeless," instead identifying themselves as life-long street people.

"I be always poking my head out the door, out the window, running right on out when my grandma wasn't looking, when she was in the bathroom. I had this thing: I had to know all the playas, all the girls, all the pimps, the big boys. I would run out and sit on some stoop down by the corner of Third and watch and watch, all big-eyes." Fox laughed, his gummy smile decorated with a couple of sparse teeth. "I can't barely remember before I wanted to be a gangster. I'm telling you, it's like I was born that way. Running the streets—it's in my blood."

Within a flipped version of contemporary sin-talk, a homeless hustler like Fox understood his situation as not so much a radical break with the past as a fairly unsurprising consequence of his childhood choices. Indeed it was common to talk as he did about "running the streets" as a kind of life course, a deviant moral career driven by a powerful disposition toward all things street going back to early childhood.

From escaping onto the sidewalk to play with other "bad" kids, the hustlers had graduated to drug sales, pimping, or thieving. The adrenaline of teenage gang banging and the rite of passage in juvenile hall[5] were sweetened by the consuming pleasures of getting high, getting laid (frequently, if their stories had any truth), and "easy" money. Often they described an arc peaking in their early twenties and tailing steadily into failure over the ensuing years. In the context of such a career, homelessness signified rock bottom, a point when the shifting balance of power between man and street turned dramatically, even irreversibly, against the individual. Homelessness was a sure sign that he was losing or had lost the game of street life. Those men who had lived their lives wandering this particular semiotic grid were therefore likely to consider homelessness as retribution, divine or not. These grisly late chapters—few saw any escape—were only filling out the details of a script sketched out many years before.

Despite their losses, the homeless hustlers often remained loyal to the game. They wallowed in nostalgia for the wild lives they had led before hitting the skids—the time Del scored a three kilo heroin deal, Fox's former glory pimping young white women in the Theater district, Tony Silver's trade in stolen luxury cars. Even now, they would insist that they were still in the game in some minor way, that they were still of (instead of merely on) the street.

Clinging to a sense of agency, the hustlers presented their identification with the street as a fundamental moral orientation more than deprivation. Though they casually wandered through the food programs and often the shelters, they smirked at the professionals and volunteers who tried to help them, preferring to think that they were astutely working the system.

The great seduction of such homeless sin-talk was its extraordinary potential to turn sludge into gold, anomie into bravura. By dramatizing the street as a jungle, battered and broken men could stride in big boots across a stage set, congratulating themselves on their ability to survive. Yet at the same time, the hustlers were reinforcing the age-old demonic construction of deviance, drawing a dramatized line between two kinds of people, the saved and the damned, or, in their own language, the straight and the street. The primary difference was that this indigenous version of sin-talk "flipped" elite discourse, reversing the normative value of the binaries. Bad became "baad," and the street career that they called "the game" was sacralized into a quest for pleasure at any cost.

The diversity of the San Francisco street milieu made it possible for homeless African Americans to maintain some distance from the binaries of sin-talk and orient themselves by different principles. Veterans and ex–blue collar workers tended toward this direction. Refusing to participate in their own "blackening," many avoided the street scene of the Tenderloin and other hot strips and distanced themselves both narratively and practically from the game. Yet there is no denying that the strong agency of sin-talk had great appeal, and most homeless men, regardless of race, took some refuge in flipping the sin discourse and claiming the street as their own.

The Racialization of Sin-talk

Poverty, racism, and harsh sentencing policies had given the African American hustlers limited openings beyond the criminal economy, but the relationship between defiant individual and hostile system had taken the form of an intricate, mutually confirming dance. Adolescent dispositions that might in other boys in other times or places have been left to dissolve into adult conformity were instead intensified by incarceration and the increased difficulty of finding work after release.

The hustlers had seized from their turbulent experiences the attribution of the "outta control" other, the shadowy threat, and taken it for their own. They continued to live out the fundamental ambivalence about notions of good and evil that has sedimented itself into many African American cultural forms over centuries of violence, stigma, and disrespect. Explaining their lives, they drew on the great, ever-evolving countercultural lexicon of black English. More than anything else, they hovered around its one constant: the ambiguous and ambivalent reversal of the standard white usage of "bad," claiming to be "bad boys" grown into "bad-ass mofos."[6]

The street's flipped version of sin-talk, like its straight mirror image, is made of boldly drawn oppositions: the city street versus the domestic home, excitement versus responsibility, the wily "playa" versus the responsible patriarch, hustling versus straight work, and so on. Not only is this discourse constantly reinforced by authoritarian institutions, but its simplicity and coherence as a system of meaning creates a substantial obstacle for those trying to patch together a less bifurcated map of the world. Even when acknowledging that they lacked the youth and strength to push back in as successful "playas," the homeless hustlers could see little alternative to their current existence, given the patent impossibility of succeeding on the patriarchal straight path.

In the last chapter, Sammy, the pickpocket from the Western Addition, defined himself as someone who could handle the Tenderloin.

One of the "people of the night," he aggressively took what he needed for himself rather than wait for someone to give it to him. In his mind, a survivor like him was by no means homeless, though he had bounced between alleys, shelters, and other extremely marginal sleeping situations for several years now. He treated the term "homeless" as an identity more than a condition, one that he was determined to stay away from. He thoroughly despised anybody wandering around with a cart. "I don't get why those weak motherfuckers want to *advertise* like they homeless. Ain't got no self-respect," he said. Sammy kept himself neat and relatively clean and enjoyed melting into the crowd as much as he could, especially if he could get his hand on someone's wallet in the process.

"Takes a black man to be cool with the dark side," went Sammy's refrain. "You see how Lee and those other white dope fiends stay in their camps come midnight?" He certainly had a point about the disappearance of anyone but the most hardened (or crack-crazed) African Americans from the Tenderloin streets in the small hours.[7] But he was also claiming for his own America's ancient and persistent coupling of blackness and deviance. The black "people of the night," in his mind, were part and parcel of the dark side, the essence of sin itself.

Men like Sammy saw themselves as the most street of characters, and many of them boasted of committing quite heinous acts. But although they generally claimed a highly nihilistic, fundamentally suspicious relationship to others, the attitude of "dog eat dog" and "watch your back" could get old. While there was a certain awed admiration for the "cold" psychopaths of the street, Sammy and Fox's claim that the hustlers were unambiguously dedicated to the "dark side" proved unstable in various ways. Their outlaw street version of sin-talk remained tied to its straight twin, and any form of resistance that stays so close to its template is liable to suddenly capsize, to do a normative flip into straight turf and exchange bravado for guilt and regret. The weakest point of outlaw sin-talk was nostalgia for family. Even Fox, who seemed to have lost little sleep over exploiting teenage runaways and introducing them to heroin, could get maudlin at the thought of his grandmother. "I wish I hadn'ta given her such a hard time. She worked so hard to raise me, and what did she get? A pimp. I wish she had never known about all that shit. She was a *good* woman." Fox, usually so disparaging of domesticity, hard work, and indeed women, still held fast to this icon of decency, fourteen years after her death.

As Kim Hopper argues in *Reckoning with Homelessness,* the severe effects of deindustrialization, drugs, and incarceration on the black working class have strained to breaking point the formidable African American kinship systems that mediated poverty and unemployment in the past, resulting in a flood of utter destitution and homelessness.[8] These men knew that they had exacerbated the difficulties of their families with their wild ways, and I suspect felt a good deal of guilt about it. Certainly exhortations to atone to abused family members created some of the most powerful moments of collective effervescence in substance abuse meetings.

Public guilt and nostalgia about family members did not usually last long, whatever the men might have been feeling in private. But there were other strains on sin-talk. An unmitigated reversal of standard morality was a hard project to sustain, and only a few seemed to have the will to take it to the limit. The competitive, suspicious nature of their existence endangered needs most of us think of as universal—the desire for love, loyalty, and mutual care—providing only the frequently instrumental companionship of those chasing their own desires. When the men were feeling strong, they thought they could still handle it. But as they got sicker and older, locked up and knocked down, the hustlers were more likely to doubt their own bluster.

Upon reaching a personal and cosmological nadir, some die-hard hustlers finally turned to rehab with desperate sincerity. As old warrior Sling said in a Mission District twelve-step meeting. "I'm tired. I don't want any of it any more. All of that junk, playing this shit, shootin' somebody, *killin'* somebody. I'm tired, people. God knows I am *tired.* Just get me out of this place."

His eyes wide and his tone earnest, Sling went on to lament the lack of true companionship on the street. "I'm looking for help, people. From young, from old, wherever I can get it. We gotta stick together. We done too much of this takin' each other down, playin' each other for a fool. I always wanted to be cool with somebody or killin' somebody or, scarin' somebody—you know, 'Get outta my face.' Messing with the cluckers (crack whores). Pushing people around. Well, hey, maybe I finally growed up, 'cause you know what? It ain't cool. It just *stupid* shit."

James Moss, another Tenderloin crack dealer, had suffered a horrific stroke in a cheap cinema, a cocaine high boiling his blood pressure well beyond the level his hardened arteries could take. Years later he was still bitter that his companions Del and Mike had meticulously robbed him and left him sprawled comatose without calling for help. "Cold," he said with disgust. Now that he was disabled, he wanted nothing to do with such people, but continued to dwell in the stinking purgatory of the Cadillac hotel, warily limping to the soup kitchen and back.

Those living homeless were already financially broken, and if their health was not already in a precarious state, the street would take it to new lows. The oldest, sickest hustlers became riper for apostasy, for betrayal of the game, than they had ever been before. Maybe, like Sling, they would "flip" sin-talk back to its judgmental twin, repenting of their ways, or maybe like James they would wearily turn to the absolution of disability.

Even well before apostasy, though, the edifice of sin-talk was frequently shaken. Claiming the streets for their own gave the crucial sense of power to these scorned and destitute men. Where it could not help them was in those moments when they felt themselves ruined and helpless, with nowhere to turn, thrown about by powers far beyond their control. There was a fundamental discursive dissonance here. If Sammy really owned the nighttime, why was he facedown on the sidewalk at Leavenworth and Ellis, stammering lies to the police? If Del was so great at working the system, why was he regularly turned away from the shelters to sleep on the sidewalk? And if Fox and Sammy were such self-proclaimed dirty bad asses, how could they expect sympathy for their persecution by the police and other white institutions?

I found Fox meditating on these kinds of questions early one February morning. The previous evening the weather had been filthy and the shelters full. Fox had finally fallen asleep around two in the morning, finding some precious heat coming out of a sidewalk vent on Market Street, only to be awakened at five by a blast of freezing water courtesy of a Department of Public Works truck.

"What the hell? I mean, what the goddamn motha-fucking . . ." Still damp and shivering, Fox shook his head, his eyes speaking his misery and fury. "They treat us like animals, those assholes, like they wouldn't treat a *dog*. What have we done to get that kind of low-down shit? Why's it make you a criminal if you a poor black man?" Fox faltered, giving me a tired and confused look. "Why the hell are those white mofos sitting on their truck and soaking the hell out of us and laughing on back to their condos, and I'm going through the damn garbage looking for cigarette butts? I don't get it. Sometimes don't get *none* of it." In such moments, when the fantasy of bad-boy agency fell around their feet, the hustlers shifted toward systemic critique.

The System

Sin-talk, whether on the street or the television, put considerable barriers in the way of seeing homelessness in terms of inequalities of race and class. The same was true of therapeutic interpretations, which backed off from heavy moral judgment but still concentrated on the fallibilities of the homeless individual.

Nevertheless, this was San Francisco. Not only were there a handful of homeless men who were themselves longtime radicals, but a score

of organizations and numerous other sympathizers were elaborating arguments upon which like-minded homeless people could draw. The Tenderloin's Coalition on Homelessness, People Organized to Win Employment Rights, the Tenderloin Housing Clinic, and several other activist and advocacy organizations fought fiercely to keep alive a social justice perspective on homelessness. Despite many defeats, they succeeded in preserving thousands of SRO units, preventing various quality-of-life propositions, and retaining one of the highest remaining General Assistance rates in the nation.

Ironically, perhaps, the Coalition found a stronger audience among the radical middle class than on the street itself. But though their social democratic discourse struggled to gain resonance with a homeless population steeped in mutual suspicion and self-castigation, it had a notable effect.

Most immediately, the *Street Sheet* and other offshoots of the Coalition provided meaningful, nondegrading work in the form of newspaper selling or office workfare to many homeless people on General Assistance. These pseudo jobs represent an ecological niche similar to the can and bottle recycling described in the next chapter. Though homeless, people could still establish a dignifying identity around work, staving off the extreme alienation suffered by many on the street. Such workers were exposed to simple, strong, resonant articulations of system-talk. The *Street Sheet* printed many first-person articles by homeless people decrying policing practices, GA policies, and work-fare, for example. Sellers from the Tenderloin, predictably, showed less interest in the paper, but some of the vendors working in other parts of the city were much more engaged with its content.

Yet as we have seen, homeless men attracted to the social democratic discourse of the Coalition were unlikely to stay in the Tenderloin unless they banded together to pay for temporary rooms inside. Generally they voted with their feet, removing themselves as much as possible from both the BS of the Tenderloin and the areas most likely to be targeted by the police.

The Genocide Trope

More powerful on the street than the Coalition's primarily class-based analysis was a version of system-talk that placed race at ground zero. It was easy enough to make sense of the degradations of homelessness in the context of commonsense black understandings of racial oppression. If the disproportionate number of African Americans on the street has been undertheorized by scholars of homelessness, it certainly did not go unnoticed by homeless black men themselves.[9] Everywhere I heard them argue that black homelessness provided just another way for whites to exterminate troublesome black men no longer needed for menial jobs.

Even the most defiantly individualist hustlers veered into these waters occasionally. Remarking on the death of an old companion, Sammy muttered, "It's genocide, that's what it is. We all getting wiped out."

Sammy swung from sin to system and back again according to his mood. Though he was a particularly volatile person, he was not alone in this. Leaving undisturbed the identification with sin, the genocide trope was connected to a particular emotional register—someplace between impotent fury and despair. It was to this brand of system-talk that they would turn when interrogated by officious nobodies, defeated by the police, or humiliated by injury or sickness. At times like these, their desperate efforts to feel masters of their own destiny proved too difficult. The notion that their difficulties had been determined in the workings of some inaccessible totality could be a great consolation.

I was talking on Turk Street with Clarence, who was passing through the Tenderloin with a huge load of recyclables collected in the theater district, when I saw Market Street panhandler EJ storming up toward us. It was evident half a block away that something was very wrong. His fists were clenched and he was scanning the street furiously for someone to whom he could vent.

EJ had been given his second ticket for urinating out of doors. As he had also been cut off GA for failing to provide evidence he was looking for work, there was a very real danger that this minor violation would land him in jail. "Those motherfucking assholes!" EJ was breathing hard, his usual muted grumpiness replaced by patent fury. "They ain't got no *work* for us, ain't got no *welfare* for us, ain't got shit for us. Hell, they don't even got no damn *bath*room for us. But come to giving us hell, they's in the *mo*ney. All these po-lice to watch where you go take a piss. All these new prisons, this 'three strikes' bullshit. All our people locked away, that's where we're headed. Locked away or wound up dead."

Clarence nodded sympathetically. "You wanna share a cigarette, brother?" he offered.

"Yeah."

EJ lit up, his fingers trembling, and inhaled deeply. "You know, I'm trying to stay cool. But *damn,* they don't make it easy. What am I gonna do? Eighty bucks! I ain't seen eighty bucks together in a goddamn *year.*"

EJ sighed, and then shot Clarence an inquiring glance. He seemed to be concerned that he was coming over as too desperate.

Clarence, a muscular man with a large Afro and a benign, vague manner, was ready to commiserate.

"Times sure are hard."

"I gotta get me a lick," muttered EJ. "It ain't no use." He needed, that is, to do some thieving to get the money. He handed the cigarette back to Clarence. "Thanks for the smoke, bro," he mumbled without looking at him again. Shrugging himself back into his usual sullen affect, he sloped off toward Eddy Street.

At times the genocide trope could be built into a powerful analysis of the imbrication of race and class in America. But the latter incident shows something of the way that it was limited by the strength of sin-talk, particularly in the Tenderloin and other primary drug markets. Generally the hustlers made frequent but only glancing forays into system-talk. First, they were uncomfortable with the emotional register in which such talk was habitually voiced. Fulminations and despair worked against the hustler's obligatory "cool" masculinity. EJ's habitual grammar of action—his distrustful manner, his unwillingness to make eye contact—worked against more than a momentary solidarity with the "straighter" Clarence. Second, the hustlers seemed to recognize that the coherence of their discourse on homelessness was destabilized by system-talk. The more they evoked victimization to justify their actions, the more they endangered the core comfort of sin-talk, that precious idea that they exercised some kind of choice or control over their destiny. Without channeling their energies into collective action, system-talk sent them spinning into despair, violating their commitment to seeing life as a drama in which they played the lead role.

The third reason, I think, for the fragmented character of system-talk among the Tenderloin hustlers, was the dissonant note sounded by this kind of talk within a field of action that functioned on thievery, drug trading, and manipulation. To make sense of the world, most of my companions seemed to desire not only a rough coherence to their belief system, but also a cognitive map that wove feasible connections between discourse and action. The level of violence and mutual exploitation in the most intense "sin" zones of the city radically undercut the collective potential of system-talk. It was hard to feel brotherhood when immersed in manipulation, aggression, and physical violence from or against other African Americans.

Even in the Tenderloin's drug markets, though, a more coherent embodiment of system-talk occasionally surfaced. For some people an admixture of system-talk seemed to soften the bold binaries of sin-talk into a more livable form. The genocide trope opened a way to live on the "street" side of the line without losing all claims to be a good person; men could position themselves as victims of the broader system who had no choice but to adopt the deviant moral code of the street to some extent.

Best representing this position was Linc, who combined panhandling, stealing, and collecting cans to get by. Like Del in the previous chapter, Linc preferred to see himself as a hustler rather than a recycler. "I guess you might say I'm a professional alcoholic, not a professional recycler... I've sold the *Street Sheet* and clothes I've found on the sidewalk or taken from the wash-dry.... One time I had this charity jive going. That's some cold shit, and difficult. I shoulda been an actor.... I guess you could say this recycling, it's just playing safe, when a person's too tired to hustle. Hustlin' in my blood, you know, but there is times you get tired."

For Linc, ad-libbing came easily, though not necessarily painlessly. Seeing himself as a smart-talking, adaptable trickster, he prided himself on his wide repertoire of interpersonal skills, his ability to dress his persona for the requirements of the moment. Unlike Del, though, his hustler identity did not go "all the way down," and he did not decisively flip the moral discourse by choosing the *street* over the *straight* version of sin-talk. Rather than rejecting completely straight values, he saw them as a luxury he could ill afford as "another poor black man trapped by the system." He classified his "charity jive," which involved soliciting funds for a fictional organization, as "cold" with a flicker of distaste, but claimed the system gave him no choice: "You gotta do what you gotta do." Petty thievery from white tourists, on the other hand, Linc considered utterly harmless, and he took considerable pleasure in his sleight of hand. Unlike Sammy, he tried to get by without victimizing others on the skids.

The code of the street was, in his mind, precisely that—the law of gravity that governed behavior in a particular environment. But it did not encompass his entire sense of self. His winning charm, humor, and generosity remained distinct from his crafty emotion work when on the scam.

Linc's perception of the fundamentally limited possibilities for African Americans not only allowed him to make sense of the world, but also enabled him to hold onto the strong sense of his own basic humanity, which he had preserved from his moderately happy early childhood. "I don't lie down and take it, but I ain't *mean*," he said as he reprimanded Li'l Lee for ripping off Domenico, a rather pathetic alcoholic with AIDS.

Interestingly, Linc's ability to integrate sin and system, to play both sides of the line, cushioned his material experience of homelessness. He could turn his hand to various forms of petty crime, but still "be sweet" and maintain genuinely reciprocal relationships. Unlike shifty, bitter Sammy, for example, Linc was often able to find a temporary place to stay when he couldn't get a shelter bed. This was quite an achievement, for most of his friends lived in SRO hotels that either forbade overnight visitors or required advance notice of their arrival. At one time, apparently he had managed to use his money from General Assistance to sublet a couch or space on the floor for longer periods, but by the time I got to know him, he had been cut off GA and seemed to have given up trying to find a place. "I'm tired of trying to get my shit together," he said with a rueful smile as he sat on the ground in a dirty parking lot. "This city make it too hard. Ain't no damn use."

Linc's combination of sin-talk and system-talk was unusually stable and integrated. At this point in his life, any previous attachment to the glory and bravado of sin was far behind him. He was willing to acknowledge defeat by the system without experiencing any fresh wound to his masculinity. In a sense, his worldview was now much closer to system-talk than sin-talk, and he was only a hustler in a shallow sense.

Linc's disposition toward street life is a good example of how narratives, personal dispositions, and means of survival congeal more closely than poststructuralism may lead us to expect. While hard-core hustlers like Sammy painted the world as a jungle and did in fact get by in an almost entirely predatory manner, Linc created a workable blending of sin and system broadly consistent across speech and action.

Vietnam Nostalgia

If homeless African Americans struggled to articulate a strong systemic, collective analysis, whites and Latinos often had an even harder time. Disqualified by race from the genocide trope, the attrition of class-based analyses of poverty in American popular culture left them discursively floundering. Most were uneasy with the Coalition on Homelessness's demands for social provision, which they often connected to the demands of "system-working" African Americans. All the same, they felt abandoned and betrayed by the government, with its homeless clearances and demoralizing shelters.

"Sometimes I can't believe this shit," mused Kansan recycler Rich, complaining about the conditions in the MSC South shelter. "This is America? This is the best they can do? I dunno when this country got so heartless. You see people coming in there, they just hit the street, it's their first time, and they get all freaked out, and the guys on the desk, they just yell at them. Like there was a guy a couple days back, got his car stolen, with all his crap. Spent a couple of nights out, and he gets his face smashed in and his last twenty bucks ripped off by some jerk. Then he comes in the shelter and they turn him away, like it's just *fine* for him to sleep on the street again after that. I just don't get it. What do you have a government for anyway?"

The search for a way to understand working-class masculinity betrayed often led men toward the trope of the Vietnam War. They found much to identify with in the idea of vets who had suffered in the service of their country, yet had been abandoned to pick up the pieces on their own, often ending up homeless. The fact that vets were soldiers, archetypes of hegemonic masculinity, could mitigate the implicit feminization of seeing oneself as a victim. Of course, for hundreds of the men and women on the San Francisco streets, this was not a story, but an all too real experience, yet the symbolic resonance of the neglected soldier echoed far beyond the "legit" vets.

Sometimes the Vietnam identification could be instrumental. Many men on the street would introduce themselves as Vietnam veterans, especially if panhandling. Most were in fact too young to have fought in the war, and they often enough turned out to be veterans that had not seen active service.[10] But the "Vietnam veteran" claim was far more than a mere ruse. Unlike most panhandling lines, the resonance of Vietnam went deep, and "legit" vets were treated with genuine respect by all.

The topic of Vietnam would resurface at the most surprising times. One of these occurred when I was with Victor, the heroin-addicted carpenter from New Mexico. With his long hair and tolerant, laid-back attitude, Victor was not someone I expected to join forces with the über patriots. But while he was living with a couple of older white men near the Cesar Chavez Street underpass in the Mission, he started to echo their stories of the government's betrayal of the (putative) MIAs.

"I wish I'd a fought in Vietnam," he told me one day as we were sharing breakfast in his camp. It was six-thirty in the morning, and I was cranky and barely awake.

"You do?" I was surprised. "Wha' for? Fight the commies?" I asked in a sarcastic tone. "I don't get it, man. That experience really messed a lot of people up."

"Yeah, well, they were screwed, you know. Those guys in Vietnam were screwed by the government."

"So why do you wanna go then?"

"You know, do your bit, serve your country."

"And get screwed."

"You don't get it," he said irritably.

I realized I was being nasty. "I'm sorry. I'm just trying to understand," I back-pedaled. Pleading ignorance seemed like the right thing to do. "I'm not American, you know. Maybe I don't really get the whole Vietnam thing. You gotta educate me."

"It's difficult to explain." Victor was silent for a while, and I could tell that he was wondering whether he should just drop it.

But he continued. "See, like, when you're in the army, you do what you gotta do, you know. You ain't got no choice." He looked up at me.

"So, what, you like that idea of being on the edge? Surviving in the jungle?" I was thinking of the survivalist trope popular with some of the men. But I was on the wrong track, I think. Victor shook his head from side to side in a "maybe" gesture.

"I dunno. It's not so much about killing people. That don't light my fire personally. Those guys had to do that, and then they just got shafted, they got no respect. They got left behind, or they come back here and they got left behind here as well. Like the American society, the people back here, they moved on, and the guys ain't got no place. That's why you got so many of them on the street."

Victor clearly felt stabbed in the back by the government, and yet he had very limited ways to express his sense of betrayal of being left behind and having no place. His wish that he had fought in Vietnam, it seemed to me, was little about the glory of serving and more about finding a language with which he could legitimately criticize his abandonment by the government.

Vietnam nostalgia was the first articulation of system-talk that really had struck a chord with Victor. Now, for the first time since our first meeting several months before he was talking about homelessness as a collective injury rather than as the product of his own personal cocktail of woes.

Homeless people hungry for meaning did not invent this idea of an intimate connection between the Vietnam War and homelessness; in fact, it was a common theme in media representations of homeless people during the 1980s. In Hollywood, the pioneering work of this genre was Ronald Reagan's favorite movie, *First Blood* (1982), directed by Ted Kotcheff and starring Sylvester Stallone as the misunderstood hero, Rambo. *First Blood* re-created the Western's man-without-a-name, a penniless drifter set upon by corrupt local elites. Opening with the unfair arrest of a misunderstood Vietnam veteran for vagrancy, the film escalates into unrestrained warfare. The traumatized hero turns back into the killing machine his country has made of him, slaughtering the local forces of law and order with abandon.

Over the next few years, the damaged yet deserving homeless Vietnam veteran became a stock character, taking lead roles in the thriller *Suspect* (1987, dir. Peter Yates and starring Liam Neeson and Cher) and the action film *Hard Target* (1993, dir. John Woo and starring Jean-Claude Van Damme). Such representations of the Vietnam veteran as an enemy in his own country resonated deeply on the street. Eventually Hollywood moved on, yet several of my companions tenaciously clung to the figure of the homeless vet, making it into a primary metaphor for their own homelessness. As Abby Margolis argues in her ethnography of homeless Japanese neo-"Samurai," by creating homeless identities that draw on culturally valued archetypes, homeless people can push back against dominant representations of their cultural difference and marginality. Ideological stock characters such as samurai, or, in the American context, Vietnam veterans, are likely to take on particularly strong meaning among the homeless.[11]

Both on and off the street, then, the "betrayal" of those who fought in Vietnam became a key trope of homeless system-talk. Like the genocide theme, however, the Vietnam connection generally proved to be insubstantial as a way for homeless men to challenge the power of either sin-talk or sick-talk. The problem with each of these tropes was that they remained at the narrative level. Divorced from both the everyday lives of the men and from their more intimate conceptions of themselves as individuals, both tropes were reduced to fractured, shallow stories that were easily discounted as mere posturing, more street bullshit, in fact. This was the kind of talk that came up in group situations, often connected with alcohol, and was not necessarily taken completely seriously by the same people when sober.

Beneath the froth of system-rants, the taken-for-granted undercurrent of sin-talk pulled hard, consistently overwhelming alternative ways of seeing. Men often approached me individually after a system-talking session and expressed deep skepticism about what had been said. Willie, one of the white recyclers, introduced such a postmortem when we were sorting our recycling together.

"What do you think of that crowd on Bryant Street?" he asked.

"What do you mean?"

"What Ronnie and those other guys were saying when we went over there last week."

"About Vietnam and that?"

"Yeah—all that bullshit about the government causing all their problems."

Willie himself had been a far from passive participant in this discussion, making extravagant claims about the proportion of homeless vets on the San Francisco streets. This was the first time Willie had ever brought up politics, and I was eager to get his own perspective. I tried to reverse the interrogation, saying, "I dunno, really. What about you?"

Willie wasn't having it. "I say BS! But what do *you* think? You are the college student."

"I don't know about the Vietnam deal. Doesn't seem like there are so many real Vietnam vets out here. But what Ronnie was saying about housing . . ."

Willie interrupted, determined to talk about the "bullshit." "Yeah, that Vietnam talk. People's always trying to pull that one. Seems like you get a bunch of guys and some liquor and suddenly everything is someone else's fault. Don't get me wrong. Sure the government should have looked after the vets, but seems to me like people would be better off trying to sort out their own shit instead of blaming everything on the government. It ain't much use complaining, and most of it's BS anyway."

What should be made of Willie's discomfort that I had seen him on a Vietnam rant? Maybe this is one more case of my companions assuming that an ethnographer—perhaps especially a female ethnographer—would be bound to the perspective of sick-talk. If this was the case, I would have been likely to write off the belligerent complaints of Ronnie and company as system-blaming BS, as refusal to take responsibility. Yet Willie was hardly slavish to my way of looking at things the rest of the time. I feel sure that his insistence on distancing himself from the encampment system-rant demonstrated some genuine ambivalence on his part, some skeptical voices in his own head. His belief in the futility of critique, that "It ain't much use complaining," was shared by many of the men. If anyone was going to pull them out of the gutter, it would have to be themselves, they believed.

Those who by one means or another had created some distance from both the sin-dominated hustling economy and the sick-talk promoted by the shelter system voiced the most coherent and consistent articulations of system-talk. They might be working off their GA with one of the better agencies, or perhaps traveling out to a neighborhood commercial strip to sell the *Street Sheet,* but most likely they would be members of the city's several-hundred-strong league of homeless recyclers.

The economic niche of recycling provided a grounding of everyday behavior that proved fertile for systemic understandings of homelessness. It enabled a spatial expansiveness, regularity of routine, and a form of self-sufficient, noncriminal activity strikingly different from either the Hobbesian battle of the hustlers or the limbo of "shelterization." Recycling logistics were the topic of many casual conversations between acquaintances, whether working or not, shifting the terrain away from the standard themes of sin-talk: possible property crimes, personal vendettas, impotent furies. Within this calmer context, episodes of system-talk took on a deeper, more organic resonance.

The serious recyclers, or pros, congregated in the more peaceful edge zones of the city—Dogpatch and other less frequented parts of the shoreline: the more remote stretches of South of Market and China Basin. The recyclers understood the roads by which they had reached the street in a variety of ways. What many of them shared, though, was a claim that the depth of their current abjection was not their fault, but produced by racist or corrupt elites, which consistently foiled their attempts to get themselves "on their feet." Unlike the many panhandlers who saw their "lines" in purely instrumental terms, men like Clarence, Ray, and Victor drew from their work a

Packed up for the day.

strong sense of legitimacy, constructing it as a blue collar trade rather than a desperate hustle.

The recyclers' identity as struggling workers surfaced noticeably in their responses to nuisance policing, which were both calmer and more assertive than those of their peers. Where EJ or Sammy would have cursed and fulminated, Raymond and his companions were cooperative yet unyielding in the face of police questioning.

"Sure, you go through my cart," Raymond muttered quietly as two officers took his bundles apart in search of contraband. "I got nothin'. Period. So I got nothin' to hide." One of the officers asked for his ID. "Ain't got no ID. If the DPW[12] would stop trashing our gear, maybe we could keep hold of our papers."

Ray held himself straight and stared at the officers in silence, daring them to give him more trouble. His patience seemed to make them uncomfortable. Foul-mouthed resentment was easier to deal with. The female officer apologized to him for wasting his time, even helping him replace a bag she had taken from under his cart.

Sickness

Within the service agencies, however, social workers and advocates attempted to mitigate the sin-talk of the streets with an alternative institutional culture based on the disease discourse on homelessness. In this, San Francisco was in line with the Clinton administration's "Continuum of Care" strategy, mandating a shift away from basic emergency shelters toward multiservice or transitional shelters, which would offer clients various rehabilitative services in exchange for program compliance. With the rise of the transitional shelter and other agencies aimed at changing rather than merely serving the homeless population, the Tenderloin became a battlefield where the two major discourses on homelessness met head-on, drawing a line in the sand between the agencies and the street, *inside* and *outside*.

This stark spatial division was mirrored in the way the agency workers (like the LA drug counselors studied by Weinberg) characterized the street as "out there," an unhealthy chaotic zone where people were dominated by their addictions and lived in denial of their sickness.[13] What the caseworkers of the service agencies offered was a form of absolution from sin, an opportunity to exchange one's career of vice and self-indulgence for a case history, to give up the dirt and danger of the street and remake one's life "one day at a time" through a lengthy process of introspection and self-reform.

"You are not a *bad* person," as former homeless addict and drug counselor Timothy would tell his clients. "You have a serious, life-threatening disease."[14]

By far the most powerful strand of sick-talk within the homelessness industry is the language of the twelve-step movement, institutionally mandated as the approach of choice for homeless addicts and lent added legitimacy by the strong social movement base of Alcoholics Anonymous and related groups. Almost everybody I knew who was admitted into the transitional shelter program was required to attend numerous twelve-step meetings as part of the action plan laid down by their caseworker. Even admitting to very occasional use of narcotics led to "the whole nine yards," as they called it.

Various elements of the sick-talk promoted within the multiservice shelters and rehabilitation facilities did manage to permeate street discourse, at least among the (large) sector of the street population who regularly circulated through such institutions.

"Drug of choice," "That's the disease talking," and several other twelve-step catchphrases have become essential elements of drug users across the nation. However, as this conceptual vocabulary was transferred from the islands of rehabilitation onto the street, its character changed in a fundamental way. Instead of the serious, world-weary, confessional tone of the twelve-step meeting, the street version of sick-talk was more likely to take a form of parody or insult. As in the discourse of the drug rehabilitation facilities, every impoverished man or woman was branded as an addict, first and foremost, but the rest of the fellowship's construction of addiction was lost.

Rather than inciting sympathy for homeless addicts as victims of a disease over which they had no control, the hustlers enjoyed the idea that everyone "out there" was a willful sinner like them. Men like Del and Sammy would lean against the wall, classifying every derelict passerby by "drug of choice," whether they actually knew them or not. "Crack—crack—wines—herone—CRACK—Lord Al-mighty!" Del cracked up at the sight of an unkempt woman who looked like a particularly obvious case.

Sammy was especially judgmental. One time his friend Tony asked him to help carry a woman who had collapsed on the sidewalk. Sammy walked over to have a look. The woman was unconscious and bleeding from the nose. Sammy turned away.

"Ain't gonna have some dope fiend bleeding on me."

Tony was indignant. "No, man, I know her. She cool."

"Then she should stay away from that shit."

"She got fits, that's what is."

"Right." Sammy walked off, radiating disdain.

Rather than offering an alternative to sin-talk, then, street usage of twelve-step terminology merely confirmed the moral deviance of the very poor. Indigence was always a product of drug use, drug use was defined in terms of willful choices, and all and everyone wandering the Tenderloin sidewalks could blame nobody but themselves for their misfortunes. At the risk of repetition, note how the hustlers' version of personal responsibility again echoed the arguments of William Bennett, Charles Murray, and James Q. Wilson, intellectual architects of the punitive turn in American late twentieth-century social policy.

In chapter 6 we will see something of how different discourses on homelessness played out inside the shelter and rehab institutions. For now, the key point is how hard it was for therapeutic professionals to effect any lasting reorientation on those used to hustling for a living. The hustlers' determination to see themselves as competent, self-sufficient takers stood in the way of the institutions' project to get them to confront their problems and acknowledge that they were in need of help. Indeed, the "programs" provided a chance to show their skills at manipulation.

A "soft" hustler like Linc, who excelled at emotion work, could adapt to the discursive requirements of an interview in a heartbeat. I once went to a shelter intake interview with him. He worked his gentle smile on the intake worker, talked about being "ready for a big change," "wanting to look at his issues," and being generally "sick and tired."

He expressed enthusiastic interest in an employment training program run by Goodwill. "Yeah, that sounds interesting. That might be just the ticket for me," he said earnestly.

I was unsure how to take what I had seen. Did Linc indeed have some motivation to get clean and join the recovery community?

He stayed for a couple of weeks, attended the required drug and alcohol meetings patiently though silently, then walked out, taking a better set of "threads" furnished through one of the shelter programs.

"Why did you quit?" I asked him.

"Aagh!" He chuckled. "Can't stand that joint."

"What did you think you would get out of it?"

Linc looked confused. I tried again, "I mean, did you hope it was gonna be different?"

"Oh, please, baby!" he exclaimed. "Ain't *nothin'* new in those places. Nah, but I was looking into stuff, you know. SSI, mostly. But I don't see it right now. Peoples was sayin' some folks could pull down SSI on accounta being addicted — get yourself a room, you know. Thought maybe I could work that, but I guess it was just idle words, idle words from idle peoples." He fell silent, musing. "Now I guess you could go further, get into the whole mental thing, but that's a longer game. I don't see myself going that way."

For the right result, Linc might be willing to work the addiction apparatus, but becoming mentally ill seemed to be one step too far.

The fact that Linc was an accomplished trickster and liar made it second nature for him to work the system, which he saw as just another form of hustling. This is not to say that he was immune to change. He was indeed sick of his life and, in the right circumstances, might have been able to make changes. But, as I argue in chapter 6, the potential of sick-talk was substantially weakened by the paucity of resources offered to able-bodied men like Linc. The shelters may have used their considerable power over their clients to get them to "talk the talk," but they offered little in terms of material resources that could encourage men to give up the money they made from stealing, panhandling, or even recycling. SSI (disability) was Linc's best chance for getting off the street — unlike General Assistance it paid enough to support a basic room — but it remained out of reach.

Spare-changing and Boosting

The vulnerability of the disease discourse to distortion by sin-talk was compounded by its relationship with panhandling. Many panhandlers, especially white panhandlers, presented themselves as helpless victims of homelessness, trying to get themselves together. In effect, they had learned to use sick-talk in a purely instrumental way, evoking depression, HIV, and various physical injuries as their primary obstacles to a normal life.

Deathly thin, his left arm stinking from an infected abscess, heroin addict Freddie "flew" a sign from a windy median on Van Ness, one of San Francisco's busiest streets. On the large cardboard sign he had inherited from an acquaintance now in jail was written in red "Homeless and Hungry. Anything helps. God bless!" Freddie, long tangled hair streaming in the wind, would walk along the median next to the waiting drivers, fixing his intense blue eyes on them like a prophet of disaster. He made from two to four dollars an hour, more when traffic was heavy.

While I was working with Freddie's people, Freddie added "HIV+" to his panhandling sign, so that it now read: "HIV+, Homeless, and Hungry. Anything helps. God bless!"

"Are you HIV-positive, Freddie?" I whispered to him, horrified.

"I dunno," he shrugged with a half-smile. "Could be, I guess." Freddie, thirty-one years old, looked at me through the detached, ancient eyes of a man with little left to lose.

Freddie's three "H's" were couched in the language of homelessness as victimhood, but it was quite clear to him that this was only another hustle. He had no idea about his HIV status. He also did not consider food to be much of a problem. St. Anthony's dining room was not so far away, and he and his friends only rarely "wasted" money on food. The "H" that most concerned him was heroin, period. In the context of his so-called death quest, his homelessness itself felt more like bad behavior than a genuine misfortune. Others might fall for his sign, but he was never going to take it seriously himself.

Again, we see how the ways that men raised cash from day to day circumscribed the ways that they could coherently understand themselves. Freddie's need to portray himself as a victim to make his living, if anything, blocked any desire for serious self-investigation. Given that he lied for a living, the easiest way to maintain self-respect was to take pride in his ability to manipulate and "snow" his donors.

To some extent, though, everybody trying to work their way through the arcane agency runaround was subjected to the same effects. They had to learn to tell the right kind of story for each given situation—to emphasize job possibilities here, disability there, to talk of a waiting family to get a bus ticket to see an old girlfriend, but then disavow any potential family support for GA. It all took its toll, as beautifully told in Lisa Gray-Garcia's Kafkaesque saga of managing multiple identities to fix painful teeth.[15] Stories of deprivation and disability inevitably became a skill, and "getting over" one of the few satisfactions in enormously frustrating lives. Sin-talk's small consolations drew everybody in to some extent.

Wash, a self-styled "equal opportunity drug addict" and consummate shoplifter, took sick-talk more seriously. Although Wash was over fifty years old, he had the lively eyes and pure skin of a young man. His angular face was clean-cut, with small nose and pointed chin. Sometimes he looked strikingly beautiful, other times blank and eerie. A certain

Division Street village in the evening sun.

ageless quality was common to many longtime heroin addicts, but Wash had far more style than most of the homeless guys, with his black trilby and hair neatly braided by his sister every few weeks. Like Linc and Del, Wash was another occasional recycler, who rarely brought in more than five dollars' worth of cans. It took me a while to figure out why he did recycling at all, as he was clearly a prolific and expert thief. Once I got to know him slightly, he used to beckon me over and produce all sorts of goodies—cakes, beer, candies, beef jerky, vodka, toothpaste, shoelaces, prepackaged sushi, cookie dough, slices of ham.

Wash had a way of wandering off if I started asking questions, but I eventually caught him in an expansive mood and persuaded him to explain why he did recycling. We were sitting on the sidewalk, leaning against the chain link fence of a lumberyard in industrial southeast San Francisco.

"So what's the deal with the recycling? You just like doing it? I don't get it."

Wash laughed. "No, baby, this is for show money. I just come down here when I got no cash to get me some show. So I can walk in the store, flashing my money, then they won't be watching for me."

"You don't spend it?"

"Not in the stores, you know what I mean."

"Horse?"

"Nuh-unh. (Winks.) Reefer."

"You quit heroin?"

"Taking a break. I'm trying to be a good boy. Stay on top of my habit. Don't want that AIDS."

"Right on. You do crack?"

"Yeah, well, there's a strange drug. Couple years back I had me a run-in with the pipe . . . but don't like crack much. I like time for my money. Got too much of it anyway. I want to waste the whole day, and I mean waste." He swept his arm across the sky, wiping out some imaginary days.

Wash pulled two bottles of beer, two bags of trail mix, and a piece of prepackaged carrot cake out of the sleeve of his puff jacket. The trail mix was hot from lying against his arm. "Saved this rabbit food for you," he teased. We drank the beer slowly.

"I guess that would be a good stealing jacket?" I asked him.

I got a gleeful laugh in reply. "This is THE stealing jacket, baby." His lively eyes sparkled with pleasure as he pulled out yet another item, this time a jumbo pack of candy sours.

"You like this dark beer?"

Wash gave me a sad "you-just-don't-get-it" look.

"I've never refused an alcoholic beverage in my life. I'm a chronic alcoholic, I mean chro-nic." Wash took on a deep, doctorly, white voice and said, "This man is a chronic alcoholic with sclerosis of the liver and a history of blackouts, DTs, the works. There's no hope for him, I'm afraid. If only we could have reached him earlier. It is a sad case." (Wash reverted to character.) "Yeah, baby, I've climbed the whole ladder—the twelve steps to o-blivion. From beer to malt liquor, reefer, dope, crack, Hennessy, speedballs. For me that's the twelve steps."

"You ever want to quit?"

"Look," Wash sighed. "It's too late for me to change. I've been hooked on one or other since before you were born."

Halfway through the second beer, Wash put the bottle down on the sidewalk with affectionate distaste. "I don't even need this shit. I shoulda kept it. Now I'll have to go out again this afternoon."

Despite his playfulness, Wash did seem to believe that homelessness was purely the product of his drug-using career. Ever since he first succumbed to the pleasures of beer and reefer he had been a useless case. While he was definitely attached to his skills as a "booster" (shoplifter), his belief in his powerlessness in relation to drugs and alcohol went a long way to mitigate the intensity of sin-talk. He rarely talked himself up as any kind of "playa," and he observed the fronting of others with amusement. Wash never deified hard drugs in the feverish way of Freddie and his friends. For Wash, drugging was at best about losing time and place in pleasure. His metaphors for drug use were all about leaving his social location: "flying," "spacing," achieving the state of "gone." In comparison, the pleasure of getting away with illegal behavior was less passionately important.

Wash was similarly uninterested in invocations of "the system." One time, his acquaintance Big T was on a roll, crying genocide: "And you've got all these brothers out on the street. They give us this cocaine, this malt liquor, hope we will kill each other, kill ourselves. We got to get away from this shit."

Wash snorted. "Maybe we *like* that shit too much. I keep it real, brother....This all between me and...." Wash waved expansively at his bottles.

The Street Ain't No Place to Show Yo' Weakness

In general, sick-talk moved beyond humor only when the men were alone with me. I by no means thought of myself as a representative of the disease discourse, but some of the men would treat me as such, probably by virtue of my education, gender, and race.[16] White recycler Walter, for example, used me as a sounding board for exploring some ideas brought up in a rare meeting with a doctor.

"And she said I'm depressed, I've probably been depressed a real long time, from what she can tell. And, you know, that makes sense to me, because it feels like, oh man, years and years and years since I remember any real happiness in my life. So maybe this drugs thing is more about that, more about trying to force happiness....I don't know. How do you say what comes first?"

It is unlikely, I think, that rough-and-ready Walter would have indulged in such explorations in front of his street acquaintances. With his closest buddy Sam, for example, Walter seemed to have a tacit agreement to camp together with a minimum of talk. Even with me, Walter explored elements of sick-talk only when inside my apartment. Otherwise, when we were working together or even sitting in his camp, he stuck solidly to his regular street persona—the strong, self-sufficient worker. As another recycler, Luther, told me once, "Get beyond that fronting, and we all weak, believe me. But the street ain't no place to *show* yo' weakness." Self-doubt and introspection were dangerous luxuries.

Though someone like Walter was attracted to certain elements of sick-talk, and had a strong desire to leave the street, he felt that there was no way he could do this as an autonomous, mature person. The only route securing medium-term accommodation and food would have been one of the intensive drug rehabilitation institutions in the city, and he feared that this was not realistic for someone of his age and independent spirit.

"I may be depressed, I may be fucked up, but you know, I don't need to sit around with a lot of weak-minded dope fiends and be treated like a child. I don't see how that is going to help me. It never did before.... You know, I could go to meetings. Every day, if necessary, I could go to meetings, I think. But twenty-four seven, I don't think so." Walter thumped my kitchen table in frustration. "I need my fucking *privacy,* goddamn it. I need my own space to get my shit together. That ain't gonna be rehab and sure as hell ain't gonna be out here."

There was little chance of Walter getting his own place. The Clinton administration's "Continuum of Care" plan was designed to provide long-term housing or employment support for able-bodied men trying to leave the street, but this third phase of provision was given low priority within an already stretched homelessness budget and quickly disappeared into the archive of noble intentions. What were left were caseworkers who encouraged their clients to examine how their problems might be rooted in addiction or mental illness. What the caseworkers were unable to offer were the material resources to lift their clients permanently out of homelessness. The primary therapeutic exit from homelessness remained what it had been for decades: disability payments for the minority who could prove that their physical health had been permanently ruined by street life. Robust sloggers like Walter were unlikely to escape the street in this fashion.

I have been discussing how the uptake of sick-talk was disrupted by both the sin-talk endemic on the street and the lack of long-term resources offered by the shelters. Yet in some ways, the most vociferous explicit resistance to sick-talk came from the direction of system-talk. The system-talk circulating out on the street came into sharp, often explicit conflict with the insistence on individual and family-level causation inside. Indeed, for the many counselors specializing in substance abuse in particular, one of the first lines of action was to directly confront and neutralize elements of system-talk in clients' stories about themselves.

Shelter caseworker Valerie was trying to persuade white recycler Dennis to take computer classes.

"I don't see the point of these classes. They ain't gonna hire no one like me to work on computers," he grouched.

"Well, I'm sorry, Dennis, but if you are going to think like that, you will never get yourself a job. It's childish," she said firmly.

"I just think it's the truth," he returned. "I'm trying be realistic. I'm a forty-six-year-old man who didn't finish high school, who reads for *shit*. No one is gonna hire me for no office job, no computer job, no retail job, whatever. What I need is forklift, receiving, something like that. And I know how to look for work. It's getting work that's the biggest problem." Dennis was clearly trying to control himself, but his voice was rising.

"Don't be getting ahead of yourself. I think you need to take some time, work on your substance issues, and work on your anger. I would like you to try a couple of sessions of anger management."

"It's being in here makes me angry," he muttered.

"Uh-huh, that's what I'm saying," she said, looking out in the hall for the next client.

Dennis lasted twelve more days, then made his way back to his old encampment at China Basin. He seemed embarrassed that I had seen the interview with Valerie. "You didn't like what she was saying, I could tell," I said.

Dennis shook his head. "Talk about a fucking double-bind! They make you so mad, poking at you like — aagh! Then, hey, you're messed up because you're some kind of psycho. Oh, *please*. If I wasn't homeless, I wouldn't be getting that kind of bullshit. Anyone 'round here who knows what they're talking about, they would get it. I screwed up my last job, I've been out of work a long time, and it is hard as hell to get back in. That's reality. It's not all about me. At this point, my psychological state doesn't have a hell of a lot to do with it, I would say."

Dennis was in fact interested in "dealing with his issues," and squarely confronting the obstacles to getting off the street. What he would not accept was how Valerie dismissed his worries about prospects in the labor market as childish.

The same turned out to be true of Linc. Though he had a very different understanding of his homelessness than Dennis, a white man with a long work history, he was also alienated by the way the shelter staff left no room for systemic understandings of homelessness. A couple of months after the incident I described above, Linc revealed more about why he was unwilling to extend his shelter stay into a "longer game." Despite the superficial acquiescence we saw earlier, he was in fact adamantly resistant to the sick-talk of what he loosely called "those programs."

"You know I been in rehab a couple of times, one of those diversion programs. The second time I was thinking I would rather go to jail, but when it came down to it I thought, 'Be real, You wanna do thirty days or six months, you crazy?' So I went back again, only they kept me in sixty days."

"Warm and dry."

"So they say. But I hate that bullshit. I really can't stomach it. All these people in there playing this shit, this social worker talk, like black people start all their own problems. I don't think so. You wouldn't have all this crack, all this family problems, all that, if we could get ahead in this system.... Drugs and alcohol, that ain't the half of it. I know my own deal. I don't mind fooling around, but I ain't no fool," he shook his head distastefully.

It is not surprising that Linc was thoroughly uneasy within the disease model of rehab. Just as he thought that he had no choice about becoming a hustler, he attributed his fondness for "wines" to the adversity of his life rather than seeing substance abuse as the cause of his poverty. Having made system-talk the foundation of his self-respect within difficult conditions, Linc was extremely unwilling to shelve his invocation of institutional racism.

Irritation over the silencing of system-talk in the shelters gathered more weight when people on the street looked at local homelessness policies as a whole. The extensive shelter funding in place by the early 1990s was accompanied by concerted campaigns of quality-of-life tickets and homeless clearances. Those who stayed within the tacitly acknowledged limits of the Tenderloin were less affected, but as the last chapter shows, men living in other parts of the city became highly critical of the city's homelessness policy as a whole. In particular, the frequent assertion by politicians that there were enough shelter beds and that therefore nobody should be sleeping outside did much to undermine the idea of the homeless shelter as a refuge. "City wants us out of sight, shelter wants to get paid by the city, simple as that," was a common sentiment. Without the cold weather that drives rough sleepers inside the shelters in less temperate parts of the United States, many saw the shelters as meager inducement to offset the danger of getting drawn into a half-life of "shelterization," spending days waiting silently for something to happen, and nights tossing to the snores and coughs of the multitude.

Those who embraced this perspective most deeply might, even still, be open to working the programs in transitional shelters. Most wanted passionately to get off the street and knew the shelters offered important resources. Yet, like Linc, they entered suspiciously and held on to their system-thinking once inside, ever resentful of the individualistic emphasis of "social worker talk."

Recovery

Another response was to appropriate and subvert the idioms of sin-talk to their own ends. Some thoroughly rejected the twelve-step orthodoxy that held that staying "out there" represented complete abandonment to chaotic addiction. They described their street homelessness as a deliberate and relatively healthy choice. "I lose my mind in there, all bunched up with hundreds of other mofos, bowing down to the poverty pimps," said Derick. "It sets me off. I've gotta watch out for my mental health." This narrative of choice within intolerable constraints sometimes developed into a novel construction of street homelessness itself as a form of recovery, during which ex-cons could relax after the tension of prison and prepare themselves for the uphill struggle to get back into society.

Dobie, the powerful, brooding recycling giant of the Sunset, laid out this perspective one evening while out collecting.

"Prison is bullshit, you know. They talk about rehabilitation, and that is the biggest joke in the world if it wasn't so mother-fucking cold." Dobie swiftly sorted some bottles from a large dumpster into the three bags slung around his cart. "No one leaves with his head straight. . . . There's something about being locked up. . . . It breaks you down, your confidence, your get-up-and-go, your social, like, your social instincts, your health, all of it. It's such a strain, and you have to hold yourself high, like you don't give a damn."

Dobie's friend, Maddox, agreed from inside the dumpster. "Yeah, that crazy fronting. Makes you psycho."

Dobie continued, meditating on his time since prison. "For me, it held me in a time warp. I mean, I came out and I was still angry at Denise. Six years and I still wanted revenge. I dreamed of killing her. . . . I knew I had to chill, and, well, this homeless thing, that's one thing you can do, you can take some time for yourself. You stay out of the shelters, you sleep in the park, do some good honest work . . . and you can start to get yourself back to a better state. So you would be more ready to deal with people without losing it."

One afternoon I told Julius that I hoped Morris, a literate man with a two-year college degree, might someday be able to use his considerable talents to get himself a decent job. Julius shook his head. "He ain't ready to put himself on the line, you know. He's gotta get his strength back, take some time for recovery. The system's messed him up, you know. He needs to get his head straight, chill for a while."

Julius probably spoke for himself as much as for his friend, as he clearly took personal comfort in talking about street homelessness as sober self-care rather than the chaotic self-abandonment it represented within shelters. This surprisingly optimistic recovery narrative had become part of the project of hope, empathy, and mutual respect he shared with Morris, Dobie, and many of the other pros. The decision to stay outside was generally condemned as a self-evident bad choice, obvious "stinking thinking." When they turned this common sense upside down and constructed it as a rational response to trauma inflicted by the system, they directly pushed back against sin-talk and sick-talk, transforming deviance into self-help and critique.

Here, we come again to questions of "lived" discourse. As Morris and Dobie invoked recovery, they simultaneously cited their practice of recycling, the active, semi-legitimate "job" that took them outside the confines of the "rabble zones" and enabled them to make money without manipulating or victimizing either the public or each other. In conjunction with this work, which gave them a certain autonomy from the indignities of the homeless industry, the narrative of street "recovery" let the men combine critique of the system with some sense of agency. Men like Dobie and Julius felt driven down by the economy, the criminal justice system, and, more immediately, the police and the homelessness industry. In the absence of more significant forms of empowerment, the idea of street recovery was a crucial way they could still claim to be exercising free will.

This chapter has turned through the spectrum of street discourses on homelessness, from *sin* through *system* to *sickness*. Overall, though, I suppose I should reemphasize the vitality of the antagonistic sin-talk dominating the ghetto and skid row spaces of the city. It was hard for men on the street to find geographical spaces where their relations with other homeless people could move beyond a war of all against all, and equally hard to find discursive configurations where the bluster and cynicism of sin-talk did not either co-opt or undermine the other discourses on homelessness. Nevertheless, there were important ways in which the sin-talk of the street was itself modified by aspects of system-talk and sick-talk, and not just among the recyclers of Dogpatch. The men used evocations of both the inexorable workings of the "sickness" of addiction and the arbitrary power of a heartless "system" to create some distance from the most dramatized versions of sin-talk, opening a more complex repertoire of ways of seeing and behaving.

Literary theory's most influential writers on discourse—Kristeva and Bakhtin in particular—emphasize fragmentation and change.[17] And it seems true that statements about ourselves have an inherently unstable character, many-voiced, hybrid, and changing as we move into different social contexts. "Alongside verbal-ideological centralization and unification, the uninterrupted processes of decentralization and disunification go forward," in Bakhtin's words.[18] Yet even the battered souls on the San Francisco streets seemed to desire to make some coherent sense of their homeless condition, one which would reduce the assaults of stigma and somehow unify their narratives about themselves with their day-to-day means of getting by.

The different discourses on homelessness nestled in intimate relations with the material conditions of street life. The power of sin-talk was rooted in the practice of hustling (which included panhandling, in most people's eyes) as the primary way of making money from day to day. It was equally reinforced by the dangers of the street. Certainly in the more dense "rabble zones" of the city, the adoption of a cunning, potentially fierce street persona was the only way to hold on to one's meager resources. The sick-talk circulating in the agencies, on the other hand, required a vulnerability badly at odds with self-protection on the street. There was no street space within which to take it seriously, and mostly people reworked its terminology into the moral model of sin-talk, whether in jest or in anger. Even the transitional programs had limited resources for potential converts unless they were mentally or physically broken, or willing to enter the intensive self-reformation programs of the drug rehabilitation facilities. While one hustler, Junior, eventually "worked" a program to renewal and rebirth, most of my research companions slipped back through the revolving door onto the street.

System-talk, while it could be shallowly combined with forms of sin-talk, was ultimately contradicted by the daily hustle. The implied innocence, or normality, of the victim of larger social forces was hard to sustain when much of the day was spent lying or stealing. Equally, the combination of regular police clearances and attacks from other homeless men created large obstacles to building solidarity and pulling together anything but ephemeral collective action. The exception to this rule was the anomalous social world of the recyclers, which I explore further in the next chapter. Even though many of them voiced a relatively undeveloped narrative of system-talk, the recyclers were able to develop a set of daily practices supporting a collective sense of purpose, a common injury, and most important, a project of solidarity that provided a lived discourse in striking contrast to the Hobbesian tussle of the "wolves."

No One Loves a Loser

WILLIE, A LANKY, GRAVEL-VOICED WHITE MAN with a stoop, came from a hard-drinking "hillbilly" family in Stockton. His mother ran off when he was seven, leaving him with his older brothers, who beat him frequently and taught him to skip school. On New Year's Eve, 1973, fifteen-year-old Willie witnessed one of his brothers attacking a man in a drunken rage, smashing his head with a heavy chain. Overwhelmed by fear and disgust, Willie ran off early the next morning and caught the bus to Fresno, the nearest sizeable town. There he slept rough for a few weeks while looking for work. Lying about his age landed him a factory job, and he soon found an apartment to share with a couple of other young men. He never went back home.

Willie could move, but he couldn't change California's passionate affair with chemically enhanced experience. Early life had left him with a great fear of out-of-control drinking and drugging, a fear tinged nonetheless with desire and curiosity. Not only the bad times but the good had been charged by drug use. In Fresno, it proved hard to stay away from the constant drinking and drugging of his friends and coworkers. It was the 1970s, the height of American drug consumption, and it seemed like everyone Willie knew was involved with drugs one way or another, using marijuana and Quaaludes to chill, PCP and coke to fly, poppers for sex, and heroin—why, with heroin you didn't even need sex, so they said. Willie tried them all, thinking he would just experiment. Heroin proved too strong for him, holding him in a bitter and sordid embrace that steadily led him to unemployment and petty thievery, and then to jail. When he came out a year later, Willie decided to move to San Francisco, thinking that the variety and opportunities of a big city might help him steer a new course.

He worked a few temporary construction jobs and stayed out of jail for a couple of years, but his hold on himself was fragile, and he failed to land the kind of work that could anchor a new life. He started using heroin again in 1988, and his shoddy collection of part-time jobs was woefully inadequate to feed his habit. Again he turned to stealing, this time motorbikes, which he sold to a fence for between $50 and $200. Within months he was in jail again.

Willie told me this backstory one day when heavy rain prevented us from recycling. Giving up on making any money that day, we had gone to the St. Francis, a two-dollar cinema on Market Street, to see some second-rate action movie. It was warm and dry, and one of the only places in town where you could get away with smoking inside. I remember Willie's low voice and the glow of his cigarette in the dark as the gunfire rattled and the explosions roared around us.

I met up with Willie again a year later, a couple of months after he landed a dishwasher job at a small hotel. His clothes were cleaner and his beard was gone, leaving a handlebar mustache and sideburns that suited his angular face.

"Remind me how it was you got to be homeless in the first place," I asked him.

Willie leaned toward the tape recorder. "I got clean in the county jail in 1991, and I stayed that way for a while. I was a dishwasher and short order cook at the Shamrock, on Harrison. I was there seven years."[1]

"Where were you living?"

"I had a room in the Delta Hotel."

"Eww."

"OK, it was a dump, but I had one of the best rooms, up on the fifth floor, with a window looking out right over the corner of Sixth and Mission. I had a girl who didn't do junk, a nice colored girl.... She was only twenty-three when we hooked up, but she really liked me. She was a cocktail waitress in North Beach....We wanted to see the West, the mountains, Vegas, the desert, you know. The plan was to buy a van, something we could live out of. We had about $600. Then I lost the money and most of my things in the fire in 1997.[2] You heard about that fire?"

"Sure, it was a bad one," I said. "The place is still empty."

"The top floors were hit the worst, you know. All my shit was destroyed. I had to move into the All-Star, in the Mission. It was all I could find, a stinking little hole with no air, no windows, crackheads roaming the hallways, partying." Willie paused. "A few weeks later my girl dumped me."

"Do you think it had anything to do with the fire?"

"It felt like that. You know, no one loves a loser. She was mad with me over losing the cash, said I shoulda put it in the bank. Like I had enough money for a bank account. I was paid in cash, never had that much."

"You took out your disappointment on each other?"

Willie shrugged. "I guess. I wasn't great company. I was in a dirty mood. Then she caught me with a rock in my pocket, and that was it. Her parents were dope fiends, and she wasn't gonna tolerate me using."

"Were you using a lot of crack?"

"I wouldn't say a lot. Couple of times a week maybe. I was trying not to, that's for sure. But I could feel her drifting, flirting with other guys, dressing up more sexy when she was working. And when I talked about getting our shit together again, getting out of town, she wasn't interested. She would just watch TV when I was trying to talk to her. It made me feel like shit. I mean, this was the best thing I ever had, and I knew it was over. . . . And I was worried about my job. Some developer was trying to buy out the boss so he could tear down half the block for some of those new condos. The boss was giving us a good line, but we all knew he was going to take the money. It was obvious, the way he started spending more on his car, his clothes. He was just waiting on a better price.

"I needed something to look forward to. I was getting so angry, bitter angry. I thought I might hurt somebody. I wasn't going to go near heroin, I knew better than that. But I thought, well, cocaine, that's not my drug of choice, I can take it and leave it. I had done it before a few times, before I got with Theresa. And there was this guy at work, we would go up on the roof sometimes after our shift ended. I tried to keep it to a couple of rocks. I knew it was foolish, but I couldn't do any better. I didn't have the strength in me. It was a bad time.

"After the bar closed, I went on GA, started looking for another gig. But GA barely covered my rent. I had to get some money for my daily expenses. So I started panhandling on Market Street, by one of the entrances to Montgomery BART Station. I didn't know what else to do. My idea was to panhandle in the morning, then go out looking for work. I wasn't looking for a hustle. I'm too old for that. I just figured panhandling was the most honest way, you know—I need money, I ask people to spare a few pennies."

"Had you ever done it before?" I broke in.

"Panhandling? No. And it wasn't easy.... You get to hate the people marching past."

Willie cleared his throat and glanced up at me, a strained look in his eyes. "I was having dreams of being invisible, really invisible, like I couldn't see my hand. One dream I had, I was standing on a big staircase somewhere, and all these people, this whole line of people I used to know, they came down the stairs past me, and not one of them said a word. They didn't even seem to see me.

"And then I had to get up and try to find work. Except I had to go back to the hotel and change my clothes to look for work. It all took time, and I was so down, it was hard to come into a joint and ask for work. And they didn't seem like the right kinds of joints for me." Willie hesitated, struggling for the right words. "You know how the city, it's become so yuppie? Like, I'm too old, not educated enough.... Seems like it's not good enough to be just a regular guy.... In the end I gave up on looking for work, and I was just sitting out all day panhandling."

"Did you ask people for money?" I asked. "Or just fly a sign?"

"At first I had me a sign, and I would just sit and read a book, but you don't get much if you don't ask. Then I used to give people this intense look, just say, 'Please, anything helps.' I figured people should like that, showing you're not fussy, you'll take the pennies.... The thing is, after a while, you hate them, you hate everyone, and they feel it, they know."

"So how did you come to recycling?"

Willie was silent for a moment, casting his mind back. "See, I was watching Julius every day come past me with this big load. We would say hi. He lived on Sixth Street at one time, you know. I realized that he was having a better time than me. It was that simple. He seemed OK, less depressed than I was, for sure. Then it took a while for me to get used to the idea of pushing a shopping cart. Seemed to be like saying, 'Look at me, look at this poor homeless motherfucker.' And I wasn't even homeless. I still had my room, just. . . . But what's worse than sitting on Market Street begging? So I asked him could I go out with him, figure out if I could make it work for me."

"Did you like it?"

"It was OK, but the money was bad, worse than panhandling. I couldn't see it, working all day, and it's hard manual labor, pushing that bone-shaking cart. You know you should be getting twelve, fifteen bucks an hour and you're getting maybe one or two bucks an hour if you're really going at it. It wasn't till I lost my room that I went back to it. The thing is it's real different when you're homeless. For a start, you've got nowhere to go, so you don't care if you're working a lot of hours."

"The more the better?" I asked hesitantly.

"Yeah, just about." Willie turned to grin at me. "And it took me a while to realize that. I'm in this mentality of 'I'm not gonna work for nothing.' But with recycling, you're not working for someone else; you're working for yourself, so you don't have to feel like someone's getting rich off you. There's no boss. No one's making you do it. OK, the money's not going to do much for you, but it's something, and it gives you something to do that's not just sitting around. I got stronger than I had been for maybe ten years pushing that cart, slinging those bags of bottles. It kinda hurt my shoulder, but otherwise it was real good for me physically. I started cutting down on cigarettes because I needed my lungs for my work, and I wanted to save."

"Did you manage to?"

"Not much. But the recycling did get me off the streets. I really think it did. See, I met this buddy of mine back from my Fresno days, and I arranged to stay with him and his girlfriend and put something toward the rent. So I was recycling and every day I'd give them ten bucks. My mentality was so much better. I would go look for work in the mornings, then do a big load of recycling in the afternoon. And it paid off, at least for now. I moved with Wayne and Sherry, we got a place in East Oakland now, got my own room. Things are coming together again, I hope." Willie resolutely tapped the oak bar with his open hand.

Recycler powering down Harrison, with a homeless "ghost" across the street.

"Couldn't you have stayed with them anyway if you weren't recycling?"

"I dunno. No, I don't think so. They could see I was doing something for myself, like I wasn't going to be just hanging around with a long face, getting wasted. You know, I had this routine for myself, work times, work gear, it was like I was working."

"You just weren't making much money."

"Yeah. But money's not everything, you know."

FIVE

The New Hobos

THOUGH SAN FRANCISCO STREET LIFE OFTEN COULD BE nasty, it was far from being reducible to a war of all against all. This chapter turns to a relatively harmonious subculture within the city's homelessness scene—that of self-styled pro can and bottle recyclers. Turning their back on the dense, drug-infested Tenderloin, these men roamed the city for recyclables to exchange for much-needed cash. In doing so they exchanged the inaction of "hanging" for vigorous physical labor, making of their quest for bottles, cans, and cardboard a structured, even satisfying daily routine.

Getting By on the Street

As in San Francisco, most people living rough in the United States receive nothing in the way of institutional support[1] and are obliged to raise cash in a variety of ways, from regular wage labor to petty crime. Studies in the 1980s and 1990s estimate that a quarter to one-half of homeless Americans performed some kind of wage labor,[2] although there are clearly regional variations. A more recent study estimated that 13 percent of the homeless population was regularly working.[3] However, much of this wage labor is radically temporary. There are no reliable large-scale figures, but case studies in various cities have suggested that there is a large overlap between homeless wage earners and day laborers. Many, perhaps most, homeless wage earners seem to work by the day, and a majority of day laborers appear to be homeless or marginally housed.[4]

Outside of legal wage work, homeless survival strategies swarm within a gray area between illicit and licit, between indubitable criminality and street entrepreneurialism. According to Snow, Anderson, Quist, and Crest, homeless people are typically "bricoleurs," resourceful improvisers who respond to the different ecological niches in which they find themselves with different "adaptive repertoires" for acquiring money:

> The homeless trade or sell their possessions, peddle illegal goods and services, sell their plasma, solicit donations from passers-by, scavenge through refuse in search of usable and saleable items, and steal on occasion.... As need and opportunity arises, he or she combines a number of them into a distinctive repertoire of shadow work.[5]

My own interpretation is somewhat different. In my fieldwork across several different street milieus, not only in San Francisco but also in St. Louis, I saw a good deal of variety in what people did to get by and in the collective meanings they gave to those different activities. First, much depends on the local economic opportunities available on both sides of the licit-illicit line. Just as important is the way that police and other influential public officials position, interpret, and enforce that line. Third, what people do to get money when they are homeless is much influenced by the character of local street subcultures. Fourth, and not least, those on the street are deeply affected by local people's ideas about the moral standing of the homeless.

This chapter draws out the local specificity of orientations to shadow work with a case study of a relatively law-abiding group: homeless men who spend much of their time collecting recyclables for redemption. Within that aforementioned gray area between wage labor and criminality, recycling, or "canning," has become one of the most widespread activities. As I write, thousands of homeless people across the United States are pursuing their regular routine, collecting bottles and cans from dumpsters, curbside bins, and garbage cans, and then carrying, pulling, and pushing their loads toward redemption centers and scrap companies in exchange for a handful of dollars.

Many elements of Snow and Anderson's description of the unpredictability and constant crisis of homeless life rang as true in San Francisco as it did in Austin.[6] Yet, like Duneier's New York homeless street vendors, the San Francisco pro recyclers complicate the "bricoleur" model of homeless workers, suggesting that it may be shortsighted to characterize the very different moneymaking projects of homeless people as survival strategies driven by opportunity alone.[7] As will become apparent, moneymaking rarely appeared to be the sole purpose of the work. In fact, those most heavily involved used their scavenging work to combat stigma and create a space for self-respect and solidarity.

The Return of the Trash Pickers

An early morning visit to Bryant Salvage, a Vietnamese-owned recycling business, finds a multitude of San Francisco's scavengers converging to sell their findings. Vehicle after vehicle enters the yard to be weighed on the huge floor scale before dumping its load in the back: ancient pickup trucks with wooden walls, carefully loaded laundry carts, rusted old Cadillacs stuffed to overflowing with computer paper, the shopping carts of homeless men, a 1950s ambulance carrying newspaper, and even the occasional gleaming new truck. The homeless men unload their towers of bottles and cardboard while young Latino van recyclers shout jokes across them. Middle-aged Vietnamese women in jeans and padded jackets buzz around on forklifts or push around great tubs full of bottles and cans, stopping occasionally to help elderly people with their laundry carts. The van recyclers repeatedly honk their horns at the homeless people to get out of the way. The shopping-cart recyclers, silently methodical in all their work, rarely respond.

Equivalent scenes can be found in Jakarta, San Salvador, or Calcutta. The collection and sale of other people's trash has long been a

common means of survival for very poor people all over the world. In the global south, a huge variety of people collect, sort out, and clean rags, paper, cardboard, metals, and glass, often living on the dumps where they work. They either sell these materials for recycling or directly recycle them into new products themselves. The United States and Western Europe have had their own share of trash pickers. The wharf rats and the tinkers, the rag and bone men, the mudlarks and ragpickers, all lived off working the garbage of industrialization until the early twentieth century. However, in these countries welfare capitalism eventually absorbed most poor people into the waged working class, replaced by waged municipal garbage workers and an insignificant scrap economy supplied by eccentric junk lovers, school-children, and the occasional part-time cardboard or can recycler.

The trash pickers are back, all over the United States. As state laws over the last twenty years added redemption taxes to the costs of beverages, recycling became an important source of income for poor people. The U.S. recycling industry mushroomed on both the for-mal and informal levels, taking the form of a double-tiered system. While larger capital enterprises moved into reprocessing and import-export, various groups of informal scavengers took over the task of initial collection and sorting. Trash picking of all kinds spread out to cover many residential neighborhoods, especially on the more toler-ant streets of the major cities and their working-class suburbs.

Pickings are particularly good in California. After passage of the "Bottle Bill," the 1987 state law that instituted the redemption scheme, the informal economy in recycling took off fast, fed by an abundant supply of willing and impoverished labor, together with an easy cli-mate that makes outdoor work relatively painless all year long.[8] By the mid-1990s, more than 2,000 recycling centers were each buying between ten and twenty-five tons of recycling per week from a combi-nation of pedestrians and drivers.

The recycling boom coincided with the mushrooming of homeless-ness, and the homeless recycler with his shopping cart full of bottles became a stock character in many large cities. So much did recycling become associated with homelessness that in a few places nonprofits even set up their own recycling centers, aiming to provide a convenient service for poor and homeless redeemers. In California, homeless men moved into recycling in the thousands, most of them operating around the 700 or so recycling centers located in San Francisco, Los Angeles, San Diego, Oakland, and their working-class satellite communities.[9]

In San Francisco, the greatest volume of recycling is brought in by immigrant van recyclers, known to their competitors in the city's offi-cial recycling company as the "mosquito fleet."[10] But equally visible, and indeed quite audible, are the homeless recyclers. In the central and eastern neighborhoods of the city, the sound of rattling glass can be heard every five minutes or so from early morning to late evening and, less frequently, through the night. Working hard and fast, they collect bottles, plastic, cardboard, and aluminum cans from unsorted public and private trash. Making between five and twenty dollars a load, many of them put in more than twelve hours a day, taking in two or even three loads of 100 to 200 pounds each. The twenty-six recyclers of my core sample and my twenty or so other recycling acquaintances represented only a fraction of at least 500 other homeless San Franciscans at any one time making the majority of their income by collecting recyclables. There were several hundred more "casuals" like Wash or Del, "bricoleur" types who recycled as one moneymaking strategy among many, but here I will focus on the self-identified serious or pro recyclers.[11]

The typical homeless pro recycler was a man between thirty-five and fifty, most often African American or white, but also Latino. The racial breakdown of recyclers was therefore not dramatically different from that of the general homeless population, although there were perhaps slightly more white men and Latinos. Gender, on the other hand, was extremely skewed. Out of several hundred homeless recyclers on the San Francisco scene, I encountered only four women.

The lack of women in recycling was not surprising given the far greater numbers of men on the street.[12] But just as important, the work process itself—dirty, heavy manual labor—fell unambiguously into commonsense notions of "men's work." This assumption was vividly illustrated by those homeless women who accompanied their menfolk but generally ignored the work. They would rarely touch the cart, let alone jump into dumpsters and search through garbage. Recycling repulsed women with mainstream conceptions of femininity. Janice, a white woman who sold clothes on the street and turned tricks, described recycling as a "filthy job." "No woman should have to do that," she said.

Those few women who did take up recycling were classically "butch"—physically strong and good at watching out for themselves. Kay cursed her way through the Mission streets for a while, a tall, scowling white woman who carried her hunting knife prominently. According to Walter, she died in jail of symptoms related to heroin withdrawal. JT, who I met in Oakland, was a black lesbian car enthusiast, living out of an old Buick that she kept in great condition. She worked some of the time as a security guard and recycled when she had no money. I heard tell of two other African American women, no longer on the scene, both lesbians known for their physical strength. One of them was apparently a former traffic cop, and another had managed to return to wage labor and was now delivering refrigerators. The exception among recycling women was Denise, a slender, gentle black woman who worked with her boyfriend, Johnny. But Denise and Johnny were a little different. Their work was less heavy and their lives more comfortable than most of the homeless recyclers; they had a pickup truck.

The Peculiar Pleasures of Trash

Snow and Anderson's notion of the homeless as bricoleurs is a reasonably accurate description of how some homeless San Franciscans get by, yet it fails to capture the orientation of the pros toward the ecological niche of recycling. Far from being jack-of-all-trades, they saw recycling as their main gig and they threw themselves into their work with exhilaration, even love. Many welcomed the physical effort, pounding up the hills and along the sidewalks at great speed, stopping only a few seconds for speedy collection. Toward the end of the route, the loads could top 250 pounds, but those in better health found even the last slog pleasurable in its own way.

"I can kind of lose myself in the effort. You forget everything, and it's good for your health, you know, when you really pound the pavement. It's your body...you realize you are strong after all. Maybe it's going to be OK."[13] Hilario, a twenty-three-year-old Mexican immigrant, was sitting on the grass in a small neighborhood park, explaining the charge he got from recycling, his pleasure in the work. He was still covered in dirt and sweat from his morning's exertions, but he seemed truly at peace for a moment, gesturing at the city around him as he voiced his cautious optimism. His older friend, Anthony, teased him for taking the hills. "Little horse" — caballito — he called him. But Anthony too, cursing and gasping for air, had his own moment of jubilation earlier that morning with his first good find of the day: fifty beer bottles waiting outside an apartment building. "Now we're rolling," he had said. "Watch me now, gonna be my day." He whistled as he swung his cart back onto the street with renewed vigor.

The pleasures of this dirty, low-status, unprofitable work can be fully understood only in the context of repression, degradation, and anomie. "Seems like you gotta be down for a while before you appreciate this recycling gig," was the way Derick put it. "Sometimes, I see

Slogging up Potrero Hill.

someone I know from before—before the street, you know. That can be awkward, but then I say to myself, if you ain't here, you ain't got no idea. Recycling is all right. So I got my hands dirty. Right, but I didn't have to deal with any bullshit poverty pimps to get my money. I've got my own. No police, no questions asked, no supervisor, no motherfucking workfare jacket."[14] Derick, an African American loner in his early thirties, fiercely rejected the welfare bureaucracy with its humiliating "workfare" requirement and prying questions. He was equally adamant that he was never dealing drugs again. "Jail is *not* an option," he would say.

Caught between two arms of the state, Derick experienced recycling as a vital free space, a narrow line he could walk that freed him from having to deal with welfare and shelters and did not increase his risk of incarceration.

He was also avoiding a third fate: the humiliation and anomie of panhandling. Derick, young and strong, claimed that he had never countenanced panhandling, but for most homeless men panhandling was the most obvious alternative existence, the oft-mentioned "other" to the recycling life. The pros knew that panhandlers on Haight, Grant,

Market, or Castro street made the same kind of money as they did with far less effort. But they reassured one another that those resorting to panhandling were in a much worse state than themselves. "If you go on the bum, that's about as low as you can go," said Luther feelingly. Most talked only reluctantly of any panhandling experiences of their own. While a few regularly congratulated themselves on their superiority to bums, it was clear that the specter of the supplicant life haunted most of them, either as memory or nightmare of horrors yet to come.

But the pros rarely fell in love with recycling straight away. The stink of stale beer and the bone-rattling haulage of the recycling life was an acquired taste, one that started to look good after more insidious forms of purgatory. As Derick's comments suggested, most of the pros embraced recycling only after being "down for a while" and, in many cases, surviving on handouts.

In the vignette "No One Loves a Loser," Willie recounted his journey from the ghostly half-life of panhandling into the sweaty physicality of recycling. Though he still had his own place, Willie thought recycling beneath him, but once homeless, he came to understand it as a vital means of both economic and psychic survival. While Snow and Anderson separate verbal identity work from the opportunistic ways they see people on the street getting by, Willie's story brings such a separation into question. Recycling became more appealing once he needed it as an "identity resource" as well as a way of making a little money.[15] On the street, one's standards change rapidly, and it is only from within this desperate place that rooting through garbage and pushing a 200-pound load of bottles on a rickety shopping cart began to seem like a good way to spend the day. Willie and his peers on the street now gratefully appreciated the freedom to choose and structure their own activity, the comfort of street entrepreneurs the world over. Conditions might be rough, but they were at least doing what felt like their own thing.[16]

The Recyclers' Routine

The recyclers spent most of their work hours pushing their loads along, stopping briefly to check the contents of trash cans and dumpsters. In denser areas with substantial foot traffic there were more public trash cans, making those neighborhoods attractive to the less dedicated casuals. The pros, though, ranged out to cover the whole city, from the quiet residential streets of the outer Sunset and Richmond districts, fogged in by the Pacific, to the industrial areas bordering the western shore of the San Francisco Bay. In the residential neighborhoods they monitored street trash bins, the dumpsters behind apartment buildings, and recycling put out on garbage day. Many of the men knew the pickup days and times for certain blocks and would pull "early birds" before the garbage trucks came, taking their pick from the blue bins put out by the residents. Julius had a spiral notebook in which he had written the garbage pickup schedule of the entire eastern half of the city.

The pro recyclers tended to sort their findings as they went, separating plastic, cans, and different colors of glass into various plastic sacks tied around the edge of the carts. (The less Taylorist casuals, on the other hand, were more likely to fill up a shopping cart and maybe one or two extra bags of unsorted recyclables and then to sort at the recycling company.)

As only a minority of them had any place remotely secure to keep their possessions, many people carried a double load of recycling and their own things: bags, jackets, sleeping bags, boom boxes, books, and magazines. Pentacostalist Juan Carlos, for example, tied under his cart a great sack of dumpster-found clothes, which he was hoping to send to his sister in Honduras.

During a recycling run, the cart swelled into a wide, unstable monster, requiring considerable isometric strength to hold on course. Those with two carts had to pull with a strap, straining forward to shift the train behind them. Fully loaded, they would swing their carts onto the street, claiming the uncluttered space they needed to maneuver. At this point, it became important to plan the route to the recycling center, avoiding high curbs, uneven ground, hills, and streets with excessive camber.

The San Francisco pros thereby used this heavy, intensely public work to create a noncriminal, nonsupplicant public role without hiding their homelessness. Rather than skulking in alleys they were proudly claiming the roadway and forcing cars to make way for them—the bigger the burden, the more confidently they would hold up traffic. One man would regularly pull a three-cart train for two miles down

Third Street, the main north-south artery on the far east of the city. In the early morning a stream of overladen carts processed from the downtown area toward the recycling companies to the southeast, while in the late afternoon scores of men maneuvered trains of heavily laden carts eastward through the Castro and the Mission, sweaty and straining.

There were various choices of where to sell recycling in the city. Many of the supermarkets had small redemption centers, where residents went to sell their aluminum cans. (Among the homeless men, casuals who brought in only a small amount tended to go to the supermarkets, as it was not worth their while walking to one of the recycling companies.) The more hard-core pro recyclers, though, converged on the recycling companies on the east side of town along with the rickety pickups of the mosquito fleet.

Once at the yard, the cart recyclers sorted their loads into trash cans. (The men and women of the mosquito fleet, with their larger loads, used small dumpsters.) The process of sorting could be an occasion for greetings and talk, but often people were in a hurry. The end was in sight, and they were eager, sometimes desperate, to get their money. Once the recycling was sorted, there was nothing left but to wait in line to be weighed and paid. The trash cans were loaded onto the great scale, and the worker writing the difference between the overall weight and that of the trash cans on a slip of paper for the cashier. Occasionally conflicts would emerge at the weighing point when someone would claim that the scale had cheated them, but most of the time the operation ran smoothly, with a minimum of conversation.

Some of the pros brought in a broad range of materials, with an eye on changes in the purchase rates of glass, aluminum, cardboard, plastic, computer paper, and, in some cases, for copper and brass. When cardboard was doing well, for example, they would turn their energies to the back of shopping strips in hopes of finding cardboard. In such times the shopping carts shifted from a horizontal to a vertical axis. No longer wide barges slung with bulky bags, they became rickety towers of folded boxes slatted upward eight or nine feet, wound around with yarn or elasticized cables. The jarring rattle calmed, while the direction of the wind and the tilt of the road became major considerations.

Those most uncertain of their right to the streets especially loved the quiet of good cardboard times. Victor, a shy isolate, generally uninterested in making any public statement with his work, was the greatest cardboard enthusiast, always the first to switch over and the last to return to glass.

The first time I saw him with a load of boxes, I asked him, "You just doing cardboard at the moment?"

"Right."

"You found a good price somewhere?" He shook his head. "Not really. It's just one cent more than glass, six instead of five a pound. But it's just better. Glass is a mess."

"What's the big problem with glass?"

"The noise, going down the street." Victor looked uncomfortable. "Waking people up. Getting in the bins, all that. With the cardboard there's stores giving it to me."

Note that Victor, who had not been on the streets long enough to develop a strong homeless identity, saw only inconvenience in dumpster diving and embarrassment in rattling along the sidewalk with a huge load, both aspects of the work which longtime pros had come to appreciate. If he had remained homeless (which he didn't), perhaps he would have changed his attitude and turned to bottles.

The other mainstay, aluminum cans, paid up to twelve times as much per pound as glass, but here the homeless men were competing with many other would-be collectors and redeemers—not just the elderly Asians who specialized in browsing the public trash bins, but the many thousands of residents who saved their own cans to sell.[17] Outside of cardboard boom times, bottles remained the core product.[18]

Most of the pros had become habitual scavengers, so it was impossible for them to pass any dumpster or pile of rags without close examination. Much of what they scavenged was barely sellable, but they did not like to let it go to waste. As a housed friend, I often received presents: ancient blenders with no knobs, blown stereo speakers, faucet attachments, costume jewelry, garish sweaters, microphones, half-burned candles, telephones without receivers, office chairs missing wheels, mysterious computer parts, and obsolete software manuals. I was uncomfortable putting things back out in the garbage as I didn't want anyone who had gone out of his way to give me something to find it again in my trash. Beyond that immediate concern, I found myself ashamed of my unwillingness to spend time drawing life out of once valuable objects, embarrassed by my reliance on brand names, manuals, and warranties.

Some maintained a sideline in resalable junk—mirrors, working stereos, curios, smaller appliances, records, and Victorian house fittings. These treasures were mostly found in dumpsters, although sometimes residents gave them away. The pros usually resold them to dealers or sidewalk vendors rather than setting up their own sales. In some cases, the division of labor between scavengers and vendors evolved into a well-established relationship. Sally, a street vendor who circulated between various hipster playgrounds of the Haight and the Mission, regularly bought junk and clothes from several pros. When I first knew her in the early 1990s she kept in touch with her junk suppliers through voicemail. Later she got a mobile telephone, which greatly increased her business, bringing in money for a better van. She distributed hundreds of business cards to down-at-heel Tenderloin dwellers and homeless scavengers under the logo "Sally's Sales: Clothes, Appliances, Collectibles." Sally was a forty-something African American hippie with billowing skirts who made heavy use of eyeliner and the concept of karma. She claimed not to deal with thieves, although some of her merchandise was in such good condition it was a stretch to believe it had been found in the trash.

The recyclers didn't seem to mind Sally's huge markup. Luther, who had a knack for electronics, spent the best part of a day mending a boom box and then sold it to Sally for only two bucks. I asked him if he thought she had given him a fair price. "Selling shit gets in the way of your work," he replied. "I'd rather take a loss, you know, than stand around trying to hustle people. I just like fixing things. She's gotta live too."

Within the limitations of the street economy, Luther found scavenging and fixing things the best way to pass time and make pocket money. Unlike some of the recycling white men, he was not critical of "hustling," but he found the "emotion work" more tiring than pushing a heavy cart.

Making "Downtime"

Once they had their pay, the men scattered, heading for smokes, drugs, or beer. Some with encampments left behind their carts and moved fast, knowing they could find another one when they needed it. Even those without an illicit drug habit would not sit and smoke or drink in the open, but hastened to out-of-the-way places. This evasiveness was partly pragmatic. Certainly drinking alcohol in public was not a good idea, although it was easy enough to get away with it if one was discreet.

Julius, like a couple of other men, found it difficult to enjoy time off from recycling, even if he managed to hide away from the eyes of the street. For him the misery of homelessness required constant activity, and he worked all the time he was not sleeping, visiting Burger King once a day so he could avoid "wasting time" at the soup kitchens.

Sam, or "Robocan" to his colleagues, was equally unwilling to let downtime get in the way of his constant motion. For him, time not working meant time contemplating his situation, whereas when he was working he lost himself in the flowing physicality of the job, moving fast and smooth, always scanning ahead. I found it exhausting working with him. He sustained himself throughout a day with a couple of liters of malt liquor hidden in his cart, but would swig them only on the run, never while sitting down.

Sam and Julius were clearly concerned about city residents and workers thinking that they were lazy. Just by being homeless and inactive, they automatically entered the zone of aimless "bum," even if they had been working all day.

One time, a worker from the nearby bakery passed Julius and me sitting in an empty lot on some old railroad ties. "So this is where you hang out," he said.

Julius responded sharply: "I ain't hanging out, I'm resting." A minute later, he suggested we move to a more private spot.

Unlike Julius and Sam, many of the other recyclers very much enjoyed their leisure time. Yes, they stayed out of the public eye, but had their own ways of enjoying themselves, whether socializing in a well-hidden encampment or watching the sunset from the cliffs above Baker Beach. For some of my companions, the potential for genuine leisure seemed in fact one of the most compelling benefits of the "worker" identity. They could see a clear separation between work and leisure, and experience moments of inactivity as rest rather than limbo.

Outside of sleeping, getting high, or eating at a soup kitchen, the most common activity was reading. Reading cost nothing, as going through trash provided enough free books, magazines, and newspapers for anyone's needs, and many men said that they read more on the street than in the past, in the days they had owned TVs. Victor's interest in the Civil War was set off by finding a set of popular history magazines in a dumpster. Luther rediscovered science fiction after coming across a used bookstore that regularly put damaged copies into the alley behind the shop. When the price of paper took a dive, he stopped bothering to recycle them, but still went by regularly to hunt for new novels.

After several hours of manual labor, time off was experienced as genuine rest. Whether spent partying or as downtime, it provided relief from the unstructured anomie of hanging out "on the bum."

The most fragile point of the work project of the new hobos was that most were addicted to illegal drugs or alcohol. There was always the danger that, despite their efforts, the stigma attached to them as homeless addicts would contaminate or undermine their efforts to generate self-respect through work. In other words, spending their cash on heroin or crack cocaine could easily tarnish their hard work as a means to a shameful end.

Most of the recyclers were indeed heavy users of alcohol or drugs, and they quickly spent their earnings on their cravings — smoking crack, nodding on heroin, or, in a minority of cases, drinking themselves into a stupor. The partying varied according to the substances used, from the passionate singing of Latino drinkers Javier and Anthony to the wordless shooting ceremony of Walter and Sam. In each case, the construction of their partying as a complement to work lessened the centrality of drug use as a core identity and organizing principle, making it very different from out-of-control "missions" pursued by some of my non-pro companions.

For example, as Valentino and Rich lay in their sleeping bags behind the Twenty-second Street power plant, they discussed drug use in a far less apocalyptic register than the standard AA trope of the addict as moral imbecile. Rich, a lanky redhead from Kansas, told us how he had worked as a plasterer for one of the large construction teams throwing up flashy condos across the South of Market area. They would work nonstop from 8:00 until 1:00. Then, as they sat on the roof, letting lunch settle in their stomachs, the boss would say, "Candy time!" and they would snort enough company-funded cocaine to propel them for another seven hours of high-speed work. Two years later, Rich had a substantial coke habit and insufficient funds to finance it. Now he was doing similar hours for the fleeting charge of crack.

"That's modern life," he sighed. "We are all busy-busy, pumping ourselves through the day with drugs. If you take it too mellow, you get left behind."

Valentino was nodding in the half-dark. "Too true, my friend. All those yuppies downtown, you know they're doing big-time snow. And the speed freaks, they are the worst. The bike messengers, whoa!"

Here again we see how the pros reconstituted the zone of the street as part of a broader continuum of work, refusing to see themselves as set apart by criminality or deficiency. Many of the pros explicitly resisted sick-talk, denying that their homelessness was due to substance abuse. They would admit that they were too dependent on drugs, but, like Willie, they also took it as common sense that what their friend Morris helped them rationalize as "down-and-dirty comfort" was a symptom as much as a cause of extreme poverty. Their stories of decline were more complex, often involving a toxic cocktail of intersecting problems with work, relationship, housing, *and* drugging, as we saw in Willie's account. These more complex narratives of decline drew strength from evidence that not everyone was heavily addicted.

The new drug users gave extreme collegial respect to the work of known clean recyclers like Dobie, Julius, Morris, and Hilario. I didn't see much difference in loads or earnings between these four and men like Sam and Clarence, and it seemed to me that this approval was an expression of gratitude for what the clean recyclers represented on a symbolic level. Surely their companions on the street were aware that the existence of such colleagues disproved the sick-talking slurs of those drug counselors and outreach workers who wrote off the whole crowd as addicts involved in compulsive behavior.

Equally important in shoring up the pros' worker identity were the recent immigrants from Latin America, mostly always-poor men relatively unaffected by the stigma attached to both homelessness and garbage in the United States. Javier, for example, had grown up near a Mexico City dump, where many people from his neighborhood made a precarious living from scavenging. The Latinos' attachment to the worker model was often completely taken for granted, uncontaminated

by internalized sin-talk and sick-talk, and they unconsciously reinforced the more tentative claims of their colleagues.

"I got to get me some better work than this, I need good work," I
heard Javier tell Sam one day, oblivious to the usually weighty treatment of "getting off the street" or "getting yourself together." For him,
homelessness was simply a result of inadequate income, and it did not
occur to him that others might attribute it to his rather heavy alcohol
consumption.

The different language the recyclers used to talk about drugging
was partly reflected in their concrete drug practices. I came to see this
after getting to know nonrecycling street heroin addicts like Freddie.

Freddie and his friends Jim and Sass routinely binged away Jim's monthly SSI check within three days. The rest of the time they lived hand-to-mouth, ceasing to panhandle as soon as they made enough money for one bag. Similarly, casual bricoleur recyclers like Del or Wash would collect only enough for the next fix, even though this pattern was ultimately wasteful of the time spent walking to the redemption center and back. In contrast, the addicts among the pros had a longer consumption cycle. They worked until they had a full load, sometimes doing two shifts before "copping."[19] Some of the heroin users, including Walter, consumed as much heroin over a one-month period as any of Freddie's people, but they were steadier in their consumption, much less prone to bingeing. Even heavy crack users like Clarence and Desmond bought and smoked crack only once a day, gaining a certain sense of control through subordinating themselves to the work routine.

As I described in chapter 3, the concentration of several recycling companies in the east of the city encouraged many of the pros to make their encampments in the isolated industrial haven of Dogpatch. This special separation reinforced the worker project, as "other guys" camping out nearby were less likely to be a threat, representing instead a degree of security and fellow feeling.

"Being out here reminds me of when I first went to work," Mike once told me. "It's like that feeling when I would wake up work mornings and hear my dad and my brother in the kitchen. You know, you hear everything outside — so I hear the other guys getting themselves on the road and it's like, hey, time to go! Being homeless don't creep me out so much since I moved out here. You don't have to be so goddamn paranoid all the time."

The spatial separation of Dogpatch cemented the alternative character of its recycling pro denizens. Camping out in scattered tents and shanties around the Twenty-third Street "beach," in the bunker beneath an old railway line or in the quiet network of streets between Illinois and the Bay, they gained the sense of a common project through strength in numbers. Together with similar groups in the Presidio woods and Golden Gate Park, they formed a critical mass within which their worker claim and other elements of system-talk could feel more real.

Not only did the pros and their allies create small corners of homeless community, they also used their work to make spatial claims on the rest of the city. Instead of skulking in alleyways and vacant lots, they claimed the sidewalk, even the roadway itself. Indeed, the collective assertiveness of the pros was changing not only the microspatial order of the sidewalk but also the map of homeless San Francisco, otherwise densely concentrated into a few neighborhoods. Particularly important were the many who moved into wealthy residential areas to do their routes. African American Dobie was the foremost such pioneer among my sample. With his high, customized "buggy," his stylized hand gestures, his straight-shouldered, dignified attitude, he took the broad, quiet streets of the Sunset as his own. Through their display of competence and "decency," Dobie and his colleagues made a (mostly successful) spatial claim, resisting the corral of the street rabble into the Tenderloin and other poor neighborhoods.

The Hobo Thing

For the pros (unlike the casuals), recycling functioned as both primary activity and central identity. In the process of spending a large proportion of their days on the job, the men saw themselves as "doing" rather than "hanging," earners instead of supplicants, and increasingly referred to themselves by an occupational name, whether pro, dumpster diver, recycler, or canner. As they came to define their lives primarily in relationship to the work they were doing, they forced the shameful master status of homelessness into the background.

Many of the recycling men sought to give their alternative homeless existence a name with broader social resonance than recycler. Struggling to explain the difference they claimed in positive terms, they lit on the image of the hobo, the penniless migrant worker who rode the rails in the years between Appomattox and the Second World War. "We're more like hobos, really," they would say, or "We're doing more of a hobo thing out here." During my odyssey across San Francisco street subcultures, I found references to hobos surfacing again and again as recycling men all over the city claimed to be the true inheritors of the hobo dream.

The most passionate of the new hobos was Morris, an earnest, rather awkward African American with a stammer. As he searched to move beyond individual fallibilities to understand homelessness in relation to the workings of the system, Morris had discovered a great deal about the old California hobos, their considerable racial diversity, their routes and occupations, their jargon, and the rules of the hobo jungles.[20] Morris adopted the hobo vocabulary for many elements of his life, referring to his camp as his "jungle," the sheltered homeless as "mission stiffs," and the recyclers as "the hobo element."

"You hear folks talking about hobos. Most of it's BS," said Morris firmly. "People think that the hobos were these free spirits, you know, hopping trains, traveling the country, living rough, the open road—it's all got the Disney treatment now. Now that was the g-good times, and I ain't saying that there wasn't good times, but you gotta remember, the freedom had another side, and most of those guys worked very hard, just like we do. A man that would not work, they would call him a tramp, a yegg. He was no hobo. Hobos, they were working men, and people forget that. They weren't bums. In actual fact, they were the ones that took on the most difficult and dirty work. L-lots of them were black men too. . . . The lumberjacks, chopping down trees, that was very dangerous. Or m-mining, or working in the fields. What those Mexicans do now, that was the hobos, the hobos that would follow the harvests.

"Now you still got some g-guys ride the rails, and they think that they are like the hobos." Morris shook his head. "But they ain't looking for work—more like just tramping. I say it's really the recycling guys. We are the true hobo element. We do this hard, dirty work, we have nothing, but the good side is that we are free. We don't have to take too much bullshit." Morris trailed off, looking down at his hands. Only a couple of weeks before, city workers had slashed his tent to pieces. "Or maybe, well, it's not that c-completely," he stumbled, "but we know if they give us bullshit that it's their problem, you know, that they are full of shit." Morris found his voice again and looked at me directly. "You know what I mean? The shame is on *them*. Anyone can g-go down these days. It's like it was in my granddaddy's time."

The other "new hobos" among my street companions had neither Morris's historical knowledge nor his ambivalence about the romanticization of the hobo life. Indeed, their articulations of hobo identity were suffused with standard cowboy mythology. Sleeping on the hard ground became a sign of strength and resilience, of closeness to nature, while their very isolation from mainstream society was evidence, they claimed, of their iconoclastic pioneering spirits. Recycling, above all, was a vital proof of independence and resourcefulness in the face of difficulties.

In their own version of the common street claim to "take no bullshit," the new hobos saw the hardships and dangers of their street life as the inevitable cost of a deliberate and principled choice to reject the ignominy of the shelters. "Go to the shelter, you living around bums all the time, a man loses his self-respect, becomes a bum himself.... Stay out here, do the hobo thing, make your own money, you got a chance to stay strong," explained Dobie, another enthusiastic new hobo.

Like the worker project in general, the hobo claim was a collective project. Even though people more often worked alone than together, they seemed to recognize that their individual claims to strength and self-respect were fed by each other's endeavors, and they made strong efforts to be generally positive and respectful to other recyclers. While there were certain resentments over turf, competition was deliberately underplayed by most of the pros and rarely openly articulated. In fact, the tacit agreement not to create dramas over turf was one of the only rules holding together their loose, laissez-faire collectivity.

Probably the lack of vigorous competition was heavily conditioned by the fact that there was little sense of scarcity. The manageable size and high population density of San Francisco created a sense of abundance in recyclables. But abundance was not the whole story. I felt that those with whom I worked closely sometimes made a point of telling each other stories of good hauls or unusual finds. For example, one day at the yard I listened to Sam tell Dennis, another white ex-mechanic, a detailed story about how he had found enough bottles in one spot to load up the entire cart in fifteen minutes.

Afterward, I asked him, "Why did you tell Dennis about the FedEx building? What if he gets there before you tomorrow?"

"Well, a man like Dennis wouldn't just take that information and go and clean up ahead of me," Sam explained, "I mean, well, he would be embarrassed."

"How do you know what kind of man he is? Do you know him well?"

"I don't know. Sometimes we sit together at the nuns'. He's an OK fella. Used to be a welder at Del Buenos (a local bump shop). And he was on the highway crews. He's all right."

"So those other guys that were down at Bryant Salvage, you wouldn't have told them about the FedEx haul?"

"Nah, I guess not. But I've got nothing against them. There's enough out there for all of us."

Unlike some of the other new hobos, Sam never explicitly defined the collectivity as a cross-racial one. But although he did not offer his African American fellow recyclers the same easy trust that graced his interactions with Dennis, he did give them considerable credit for being "serious" recyclers, respect he certainly did not extend to non-recycling homeless "bums" of any race. The work of Clarence, the African American ex-soldier who brought in some of the biggest loads, inspired Sam to demonstrate uncharacteristic enthusiasm.

"You should check out Clarence's wagon," he told me. "That fella knows what he's doing. He's strong, but he's smart too. You won't see a better setup in this city."

As Willie explained in "No One Loves a Loser," the generosity and benefit of the doubt given to new recyclers could have a profound effect on people who felt they had hit rock bottom.

"It blew me away," said Dennis. "First time I went out, I was wandering around, picking up all the wrong kinds of shit, you know, like wine bottles,[21] and I ran into Anton. Didn't know nothing about me, but he showed me—well, everything, the whole deal. Ya know, when people are ripping you off, picking fights, and you're *so* sick and tired you're ready to blow, and then whoa—suddenly you get treated like a man again—Jesus Christ! It makes one hell of a difference."

Did the recyclers develop the worker language and grammar of action because this was who they already were? Many of the pros had at some point held blue collar jobs with a modicum of skill; they had been truck drivers, mechanics, lumberjacks, cooks, carpenters, and welders. According to Clarence, a handful of the more mechanically minded had been responsible for pioneering "serious" recycling during the mid-1980s and had later helped him and others to "make decent money." Even though these pioneers were now a tiny minority, they had given the recycling scene a particular character, most evident in the forthright physical style and determinedly comradely attitude adopted by the pro en masse.

The physical demands of the job suited people used to getting dirty and working with their hands, those with a blue collar habitus, in other words. And blue collar men like Dennis, Walter, Julius, George, Rich, Anton, and Sam had gratefully adopted this particular street survival strategy as one that they considered self-evidently better than their other limited possibilities. Like Luther, they found it a great relief that they did not need to hustle, for they found such emotion work unfamiliar and discomforting.[22]

Yet the resurrection of these blue collar ways in the recycling trade was no simple transposition. For a start, there were several among my recycling companions whose employment history was sketchy in the extreme: Derick, Anthony, Pipe, Manny, Spike, Valentino, Raymond, and Big Joe. And in between these extremes, several of the men had played both sides of the line; even when working, they had not exactly been model citizens. In this, of course, they were no different than many working-class men, but my point is that their worker identities may have been claimed more enthusiastically in retrospect than they had been at the time. Clarence, for example, was far more obsessively honorable and hardworking as a homeless crack addict than he had been as an army supplies clerk tangled up in the black market.[23]

Self-sorting according to cultural background and habitus, then, was important, but by no means all-determining. I think a better way of seeing it is that the recycling way of life in San Francisco tied together various forms of survival. On the most basic level, they could make money and keep physically safe by camping near each other, but they could also exercise a grammar of action and way of talking that drew on the more extensive cultural trope of "blue collar decency" to restore masculine worth. This project was certainly attractive to men already strongly invested in working class masculinity, but it also attracted men of much more ambiguous identity who were just flailing for psychic survival.

I saw plenty of proof that the subculture could draw in quite unlikely converts. In a couple of cases, recycling seemed to transform people's attitude to work altogether. Spike was a white hippie nomad I knew before he took up recycling and whose long career dealing marijuana and mushrooms had been derailed by the War on Drugs. He had always been scathing about work, which for him was tied to insult and boredom. One day he amazed me with an eloquent meditation on his new pleasure in hard labor.

"I know this sounds weird," Spike mused, "but I am happier doing this shit than I have been in years. You get such a sense of achievement out of it. Set off in the morning with nothing, then you find all this cool stuff, and people even appreciate what you're doing half the time. It's like I get high from it, a real buzz. But it is a buzz that lasts, not some quick high. It puts me in a good, mellow mood all day, especially when the weather is good. . . . I'm starting to see what I've been missing out on in my life. I always thought that I hated work because I hated the fucking supervisors. So now I'm seeing that it's not the work I hate. Not all work, anyway. In fact, I'm a damn good worker, in my own way."

Reading my field notes on this conversation in the light of Wacquant's critique of neoromanticism, I am struck by the grounded, practical character of Spike's comments. Like most of the talk about the benefits of recycling, Spike emphasizes the physical and psychological healthiness of the work more than its moral superiority. Similarly, several of the others talked about how working at recycling kept them from getting drawn into heavier drug use.

I saw evidence for this last claim in the sad decline of friendly, optimistic Javier, the recent immigrant from Mexico City. After a couple of years of recycling, Javier wrenched his knee jumping out of a dumpster. The occasional crack indulgence he had developed since hitting the streets now became far more problematic, and he seemed to feel in need of constant drink to put up with the humiliation of panhandling from fellow Mexicans. (Being undocumented, Javier was frightened to venture outside of the Latino neighborhoods, concerned he would be snatched by *la migra*.)[24] Javier was rarely sober now. His once bright eyes were bloodshot and unfocused, his rapid speech now slow and slurred. His former acquaintances among the recyclers were shocked at his quick degeneration into a "bum." Most deeply affected was Anthony, an older Mexican who had been on the streets for eight years. I asked Anthony if he thought what happened to Javier could happen to him. "I don't know. Could happen to a lot of people. You lose your hope, you know. . . . But you know, I think, I hope, I'm stronger than that. Or maybe I just have too much shame. It's too shaming to me, the begging, I can't deal with that." Anthony, not one for much street bluster, was hesitant. Having already slipped so far down the social ladder, he knew better than to be sure he would not fall farther.

Ultimately, Anthony explained Javier's transformation not by moral evaluation but by talking about the death of forward-moving time for those caught in structureless, stigmatized limbo. "See, that's what happens when you don't keep going at something," he said. "You lose heart, and you lose that sense of getting through the days, that's the worst thing. You have to be able to get through the days or time stops. Then you're fucked, really, because how can you think you will get off the street if your time is dragging so slow? That's when you become a real bum, I don't mean that to be cruel, you know, but to me that's the difference between someone who happens to be homeless and someone who is a bum. They have just given up trying; they're not really trying to live anymore. . . . With us recyclers, it's different—at least you're doing something and you can live with yourself. You can be OK with yourself."

Like survivors of other extreme forms of social suffering, Anthony and Javier's other former buddies among the pros learned to abandon companions in free fall, seeing all too clearly the hand of death. Within a year of this conversation, Javier had drunk himself to his final resting place.

Neighborhood Effects?

The previous section showed some of the ways that my companions used their recycling work to take on an identity as a "new hobo" or "honest working man." This project nevertheless required some help from others.

If they had found no confirmation from people outside their own ranks, I wonder if the recyclers would have been able to sustain their self-respecting self-image. As it was, they regularly connected with sympathetic residents and workers in neighborhood businesses in their search for empty bottles and cans. The friendly treatment they received made it feasible to interpret the transaction as an exchange or even a service. Certainly in the neighborhoods most heavily covered by recyclers, there was never any need to wait for the weekly municipal recycling run.

The pros talked up a storm about the importance of routinized relationships with suppliers. "That's what this business is all about," they would say, "finding and keeping your suppliers." Some even called the bars and restaurants they regularly stopped at their "accounts." Others framed their visits in terms of obligation, explaining that they needed to keep to their "schedules" or their "patrols."

If this was solely an interviewing project, I would not have had the means to question this common wisdom, but my experience working with the pros eventually convinced me that cultivating relationships with "suppliers" served almost no economic function. Even business suppliers were not usually particularly worth cultivating. The reality was that workers at many bars and restaurants were willing to give recycling to the first person to ask at a convenient time, but very few of the businesses we visited actually kept their bottles for any specific recycler, so most of our visits were fruitless.[25] We made far more money from those larger establishments where we could go around the back and get the recycling ourselves without contact with workers.

The resident suppliers were more reliable but no more economically important. Most of these were childless white or African American apartment dwellers with only a few bottles to offer.[26] They seemed to be somewhat more loyal to "their recycler" than were the businesses, although often not at home when their street buddies came around. When they were in, they would usually invite the recycler into their apartments, chatting about the weather, the news, local politics, or sport. After a few social niceties, the recycler would leave with maybe eight beer bottles and a few cans—less than a dollar's worth of recycling.

Once I realized that the suppliers actually supplied only a small fraction of recyclables, I wondered if visits to suppliers represented a subtle form of panhandling. Were they getting vital handouts from their suppliers, I wondered, even when bottles were in short supply? The answer seemed to be no. The issue of money rarely came up, and many of them would not even accept gifts of food.

To the contrary, the participants explicitly treated the transaction as an exchange, with each thanking the other for his or her role. It seemed to be a great relief for everyone concerned to feel genuinely useful. Recyclers often tried to increase their own contributions within these precious gift relationships. Clarence would help students clean up after parties in exchange for bottles and cans, while Morris sometimes took out the garbage for a supplier sick with AIDS. Sam and Walter gave competent advice on car problems and plumbing to clueless young bohemians.

These symbolic and social aspects of the relationships were ultimately far more important than either material gain or convenience.[27] The recyclers pushed themselves to make relationships with suppliers because they desired or indeed desperately needed social connection outside their own degraded social strata. They could enter residents' private space as neither supplicant nor marauder, and during these brief encounters they could talk about sport, city politics, or car maintenance, reentering the public sphere as "regular guys."

The conversations often turned around questions of public ethics and in particular around the politics of public space. To some extent, the recyclers talked to their suppliers in terms that reflected their ideas about what residents might want to hear. The claim that they were looking after the neighborhood by cleaning up potentially dangerous glass, for example, was something I heard of only in this context. Yet this was not any purely strategic vocabulary, but a genuine search for common ground and recognition. After all, these were men who fiercely resented having to "talk the talk" within poverty agencies and had made a particular kind of street life out of their refusal to do so.[28] Many of the suppliers were openly left wing or black nationalist in their sympathies, just as inclined to take a systemic line on the causes of homelessness as the recyclers themselves and eager to believe that their homeless acquaintances could be "decent" men.

The validation given by their interactions with suppliers gave the recyclers the sense of being public servants, or at least good citizens, rather than despised or feared outcasts. Without this recognition (tacit or spoken) from other residents of the value of their work, they would have found it much harder to shout back when people complained of the noise or to generally assert themselves in neighborhood space as workers rather than public nuisances.

New Hobos or Neoromantic Sociology?

In what must surely be one of the most widely discussed book reviews in the history of American sociology, Loïc Wacquant has made the case that increasing attention to work and mainstream cultural orientation

173

in U.S. ethnographies of poverty represents a "neoromantic" sociology.[29] Where the ("romantic") ethnographers of the 1960s and 1970s enjoyed *deviance,* he argues, those of today inflate and romanticize those aspects of the poor that illustrate how *similar* they are to other Americans—their mainstream aspirations, their law-abiding behavior, their conventional morality. The neoromantic sociologist, says Wacquant, has capitulated to the moralistic discourses of poverty promoted by the New Right. He "takes the statements of his informants at face value and conflates 'vocabularies of motives' with social mechanisms, reasons invoked to make sense of their actions with the causes that actually govern them."[30] What might Wacquant make of the "good worker" claims of Sam, Clarence, and Walter, I wonder? It's true that others within the San Francisco homelessness scene interpreted their activities in a very different way. Drug counselors saw it as drug-fueled compulsion overlaid by rationalization, and the Tenderloin hustlers similarly scorned it as self-deluded posturing. Why, as Del says in "Watch Out, San Francisco!," did "those dudes" act like they were working for the city when they were really just bums?

The recyclers' generally upbeat evaluation of their difficult and ill-paid work was by no means just a self-serving "line" designed for middle-class consumption. To see it in such terms strips all the discursive resonance from the practice itself—all the meaning from the action, to put it more simply. Why should we stuff whatever poor people do into the black box of survival strategies? A more plausible argument is that their worker project might reaffirm the grip of moralistic ideas about poverty and homelessness. Perhaps they were only shifting the line between "street" and "straight," between the sinful underclass and decent society. Were the hardworking, comparatively self-sufficient, no-BS recyclers claiming the high ground of the deserving poor, presenting themselves as a decent minority among the morally dubious hustlers, dealers, and panhandlers of San Francisco street life?

This analysis seems true enough of "Robocan" Sam in particular and to a lesser extent of Willie's friend Julius—although Julius was equally likely to evoke systemic explanations of black poverty. But for Morris, Dobie, and the other, more politically radical recyclers, their recycling became a grounding in praxis, an activity that spurred them toward a stronger, more convincing systemic critique.

Derick, for example, saw no contradiction between his dedication to recycling and his critique of the political system. Sloping along the empty sidewalks of South of Market with his huge load, he muttered angrily to the strain of the Run DMC buzzing through his Walkman. Derick's vigorous labor seemed to energize his rants against the local power structure. "And they say *we* a menace to society," he liked to say. "Fucking politicians. Motherfucking yuppie corporation assholes. They the problem." Similarly, pothead Spike and light-fingered Valentino would have been highly amused to be read as embodying Victorian values. Even as Spike embraced and articulated the "solid joys and lasting pleasures" of the work ethic, he was distributing (radical queer) *Act Up SF* manifestos from his cart. The recycling subculture tugged Spike *away* from the moral binaries of sin-talk, showing him for the first time that hard manual labor could be pleasurable.

It is true that the recyclers tended to construct their physical labor as a sign of moral capital. Like the rest of us, homeless people struggle to see themselves as ethical subjects. Indeed, the extreme stigma attached to homelessness means that homeless identity work is bound to be heavy laden with moral interrogation.[31] However, the right has no monopoly on morality tales, and the valorization of hard manual labor within Anglo-American culture goes far beyond the castigations of the idle poor by Victorian elites and their contemporary descendants. Its roots stretch just as deep in the Marxist tradition and the labor movement. Even the radical anarchists of the IWW (the union of the hobos, among others) celebrated the laboring feats of the muscular male worker and drew their sense of legitimacy as a universal class from their contribution to the American economy.[32]

The left-liberal discourse on homelessness established in the early 1980s—*system-talk* in the terms of this book—also contains its own moral scenario, one of "ordinary Americans" abandoned by employers, displaced by yuppie gentrifiers, and hounded in the streets. And indeed this story, strongly articulated in San Francisco by the radical Coalition on Homelessness, surfaced regularly in the encampment of the pros. To really believe in such a touchstone narrative, the pros needed to prove to themselves that they were, as Morris put it in chapter 3, "men, not dogs"—people with certain basic moral standards of honesty and consideration toward others, with a capacity for give-and-take and

"I kinda dig this recycling thing. You see all sorts of shit."

acts of generosity. This kind of project has no necessary connection with the moralism of sin-talk. To the contrary, it is only on the basis of self-respect and trust that sustained collective action is possible.

What seems most interesting here is not to try to evaluate the precise truth of these moral claims, but to understand the conditions under which these ragged outcasts could see themselves as more than mad or bad. Rather than the disconnect between "vocabularies of motive" and "real" causes of action suggested by Wacquant, the ethical claims the recyclers made around their work made sense because they were intimately tied in to day-to-day practice, which they found healthier for body and soul than the alternatives. Spike, for example, was converted to being "a damn good worker" because it enabled him to maintain a substantial distance from both the aggression of Tenderloin street life and the exhausting and demeaning process of dealing with poverty management agencies. Most of all, he liked recycling in particular because it was unsupervised, creative, and something he experienced as a choice. It was only in the context of these elements of autonomy that someone like him found the work aspect so liberating.

In a similar way, if we return to Anthony's discussion of time, he may have drawn on the work ethic to protect his sense of self from the stigma of "bum," but his argument was much subtler than a simple claim to be on the side of the deserving poor. Without sufficient action and structure, he said, you lose the forward momentum of time. It becomes impossible to see beyond the endlessly dragging tableaux of the street scene. In this situation, all sorts of people can become "bums." Anthony was not claiming that he recycled because he was better than a bum. To the contrary, his point was that the economic niche of recycling, and the life the men build around it, was one of the very few ways to avoid that resentful, dependent limbo out of which the "bum" was born.

Part III

RABBLE MANAGEMENT

Like I Need More Drugs in My Life?

SOMETIME AROUND 2:00 A.M., Carlos jerked awake as a hunting knife ripped through his homemade tent. He staggered to his feet, fighting awkwardly. It was the tarp that had sheltered him, but he did not move fast enough. A few hours later he regained consciousness, covered with urine and beaten so badly he needed eight stitches on his scalp. His attackers—he thought there were two of them—had found the $48 in his back pocket and, worse, made off with a backpack loaded with personal gear, including his last remaining photos and proofs of ID.

Afraid to return to the street, Carlos let a hospital social worker find him a place in a transitional shelter. Initially he was happy enough to be somewhere he could recuperate from his injuries in moderate safety. The program offered various classes that sounded promising, including basic instruction in Windows and various Microsoft programs. Carlos also seemed relieved to be forced to stay clean of cocaine. "Just as well," he said with a significant look, though he quickly claimed that staying clean was "no big deal." With clean clothes and a fresh shave, he looked ten years younger.

A couple of Sundays into the program Carlos took the subway to Oakland to see his cousin Lucy, his only Californian relative. Lucy was doing well, married to a wealthy Filipino restaurant owner called Ronaldo. Ronaldo, a large, loud man, slapped scrawny Carlos on the back and gave him a huge meal at the restaurant. Carlos got the impression that they were feeling guilty for not doing enough for him in the past. A few days later, Ronaldo called him and offered a week or two's work decorating two apartment buildings belonging to an acquaintance.

When Carlos requested permission to take the job, his case manager shook his head firmly. "Unh-uh. No way. It's not work you need right now. You are provided for here. *You* need to work on your *recovery*."

New lofts and street camping, North-East Mission.

But according to Carlos, work was exactly what he needed. He called me from the shelter, nearly crying from frustration. "I don't know what to do. They are going to kick me out the program if I take the job. It's so fucking stupid. Like this guy Wayne, the case manager, he wasn't so bad, but he is so sure that it's all about drugs, you know. Ain't so simple. Sure, I know I've got a cocaine problem. And I take that very seriously, you know I do. I've been honest about that with you. But I really need to work. It's work which will get my head straight. You know how I am, how recycling keeps me in line. I just have to work, be doing something with my hands. That's why I started doing crack in the first place, because I just couldn't find any damn work, didn't have the money for blow [powder cocaine].

"So I try to explain, look, there's people who use, and there is people who is used, like the people you see running around the streets begging, bugging out, jiggling around, lying, and stealing. I've never been there, I never will. You know it, right?

"I mean, I've been on the street two years, a goddamn dirty difficult life . . . kicked around by the police. Got robbed, got beat up. But I'm

182

still a man. I still got my limits, you know. . . . I'm out there working every day, not working a line, not playing the system. I just try to survive. . . . The whole thing makes me sick."

"Have you talked about it to your case manager?" I asked. "About how important it is for you to get work?"

"Sure I have. I've really tried to work with these people, straight up, but Wayne, he just laughs at me, says he's been there himself and he knows I'm full of shit. Denial, everything is denial with those people. 'You've got to work on your issues,' he says. All I know is, for me, work is a big fucking issue, the biggest. I came to this town for work, and this is the first decent work I find, and they won't let me stay in the shelter if I don't go to fucking AA every day. Wayne says it doesn't look like you are trying to *make changes.*"

I could tell that Carlos was about to blow. "Jesus Christ, it's like, it's like all the change has got to be you. You're the *asshole,* everything else is just fucking *dandy.* Well, maybe it's not that simple." Now Carlos was talking so loudly that his voice turned into a distorted buzz. "Maybe I just need a *fucking break!*"

He lowered his voice. "I'm sorry. It's getting me so frustrated. It's fucking crazy. Work is a big change. This guy could get me a lot more work if I do good. And he's providing the tools. This could be my break, and they won't let me go for it."

Carlos was very reluctant to leave the case management program, as they had promised to help him find affordable housing. Yet the insistence that he put recovery before employment eroded Carlos's trust that Wayne was either competent or "gave a damn." This particular case manager was steeped in the Alcoholics Anonymous perspective. For him, Carlos's drug use was by definition the root of his problems. Carlos had admitted to using crack, although he was, in my opinion, quite justified in claiming that his drug use was "moderate." I have encountered many people holding down jobs and apartments who smoke far more crack than he did. Wayne was sure that Carlos would go on a crack binge with the money he earned. In this case, at least, twelve-step dogma was proved wrong. Carlos walked out of the program and made enough on the painting job to stay in a hotel room for six weeks. When his money ran low, he spent the last of it on a tent and sleeping bag. Ronaldo had promised him more work in the future, but for the moment, he was back on the streets.

Carlos called me to meet up in the Burger King on Market, where we mused about the pros and cons of the transitional shelter model. "This whole new case-management program.... I don't know what to think," he said with a shrug. "The new shelters—they are definitely nicer inside than your old-school lottery deal. [Half the local male shelters still ran a daily lottery for the night's lodging.] You get some kind of bed, real deal, somewhere to put your clothes. You can keep yourself clean. That's all good. But it's like they want to control you, everything about your life.

"They don't know you, but they think they do. And it *gets* to you.... After a while you start thinking maybe they're right, maybe it's all about *me*, my *bad* attitude, my *drug* use. Maybe I'm depressed, like they say. This one woman was saying I needed antidepressants." Carlos gestured toward a hooded dealer on the street corner opposite. "What the fuck! Like I need more drugs in my life?"

SIX

The Homeless Archipelago

IN 1993 APPEARED A MANIFESTO, AN ENERGETIC ATTEMPT to corral the public's understanding of homelessness into a solely therapeutic register. With *A Nation in Denial: The Truth about Homelessness,* Alice Baum and Donald Burnes set out to discredit a decade of work by the National Coalition for the Homeless and other advocacy organizations—organizations that argued that the homeless were suffering primarily from poverty and the lack of affordable housing, and that they were therefore more similar than different to less hard-up Americans. To the contrary, wrote Baum and Burnes: "America is in deep denial about homelessness.... The primary issue is not the lack of homes for the homeless; the homeless need access to treatment and medical help for the conditions that prevent them from being able to maintain themselves independently in jobs and housing."[1] The homeless were *not* ordinary people down on their luck, but the victims of serious mental and physical illnesses—alcoholics, psychotics, and drug addicts. Instead of worrying about housing costs or unemployment, those who really cared about the homeless should be getting them treatment for their diseases.

The previous three chapters, set out on the sidewalks and encampments with San Francisco's rough sleepers, suggested the relative weakness of *sick-talk,* or the therapeutic discourse on homelessness. The claim that homelessness was the product of addiction and mental illness was "out there," all right, a nagging whisper or an unspoken accusation, but the men had their ways of neutralizing its impact, in public at least. When we move inside to the great homeless archipelago, the picture is very different.

Before moving to the men's experience "inside," though, it is worth returning to early 1990s to look at the process by which the proponents of sick-talk came to marginalize the system-talk of the advocates, bringing the "transitional" shelter into what seems now to be a permanent position as the centerpiece of American homeless programming.

Baum and Burnes made a passionate argument that Americans should acknowledge the deep pathologies of the homeless, specifically their high proportion of mental illness, alcoholism, and drug addiction. Most interesting, the authors blamed the low provision of therapeutic services on the excesses of the advocates. By portraying the homeless as ordinary people, they said, homelessness activists made it possible for politicians to ignore the incapacity and sickness of the homeless population and deny them the services they desperately need.[2]

They were not alone with this analysis. Many of this period's texts written within the register of what I have been calling sick-talk positioned themselves firmly in opposition to system-talk—arguments that the return of large-scale homelessness was a reflection of systemic factors such as deindustrialization, institutional racism, low pay, and high rents.[3]

The strong emphasis that writers such as Baum and Burnes placed on the error of systemic arguments seems puzzling in retrospect. Why did they find the advocates so pernicious? Was this small network of underfunded activists really more dangerous than the far more powerful neoliberal ideologues busy dismantling core elements of America's patchy social service provision? What was going on here?

The Rising Archipelago

Starting in the early 1980s, an ad hoc network of advocates, many of them members of activist churches and religious orders, had responded to the rising demand for emergency shelter by opening basic, no-questions-asked overnight accommodations in church halls and basements, armories, and warehouses. As the decade progressed, this bare-bones homeless provision gradually developed into a new branch of the American semi-welfare state. While Section 8 housing vouchers and the provision of public housing continued to shrink, the rough dormitory-style accommodations of the emergency shelters proliferated into an archipelago — islands of deprivation, mundane and ubiquitous yet socially apart.

The archipelago was filled by not only the many who had lost footholds in private accommodation during the rapid rent hikes of the 1980s but hundreds of thousands of people who had been previously in public housing or who would have been eligible for it. Most pertinent, more and more women with children showed up in search of shelter. Ten years into the crisis, the demand from emergency housing for both single adults and families was rising every year.

Following the milestone 1987 McKinney Act, the federal government moved to fund development of more permanent, professionalized facilities across the country. Thousands more shelters opened every year, and thousands of social workers shifted into a new field rich with jobs, if not with particularly high pay.

The arrival of President Clinton in the White House added new impetus to what some had already started calling the homelessness industry. Clinton had promised serious attention to homelessness, and during his first year in office the Department of Housing and Urban Development (HUD) rolled out a substantial funding initiative called the "Continuum of Care," which prioritized rehabilitation services and caseworkers for homeless shelters. Again, advocates played a key role in preserving elements of systemic analysis. The 1994 Interagency Council on the Homeless (ICH) report explicitly recognized the connection between loss of direct housing provision and subsidies, criticizing the cuts of the previous twelve years and demanding extra measures to repair the "damage caused by the misguided and harmful housing budget cuts of the 1980s."[4] The War on Poverty clearly off-limits, the authors called for the Democratic administration to pursue a War on Homelessness. HUD, though, had no intention of getting back into the business of housing provision, said director Henry Cisneros. That next year, HUD issued two major reports calling for the adoption of the new Continuum of Care approach across the United States. The agency did, however, reiterate criticism by advocates and academics that the huge amount of federal and local money being spent on emergency shelter did little to produce long-term solutions given

In limbo after a missed appointment: "Lady on the desk said maybe I can catch him later this afternoon."

the steady shrinkage of affordable housing. Hundreds of thousands of single people and families were circulating in and out of the emergency shelters and other marginal living situations, unable to make the transition into long-term regular housing. The emergency shelters were merely accommodating homelessness — and were by no means ameliorating it.[5]

The Continuum of Care

The Continuum of Care plan implicitly gave a role to both individual frailty and systemic dysfunction. The ICH conceived Continuum of Care as a holistic safety net encompassing three phases of support to homeless individuals. In theory, the new plan would move homeless shelters away from their simple corralling function, transforming them into gateways out of homelessness. Federal funding would guide municipalities and nonprofits away from emergency shelter provision toward transitional or multiservice shelters with a more comprehensive rehabilitative emphasis. The McKinney Act was expanded to provide supplementary services, including addiction treatment, counseling, and budgeting and parenting classes, as well as some funding for child care services, housing subsidies, and rental assistance to help people make the transition into employment and permanent housing. The idea was that individuals and families could graduate through the first two stages of support, being ultimately rewarded with subsidized permanent housing. The first phase would provide basic shelters; the second would help the individual become "housing-ready." A third phase would address the lack of affordable housing in the market by providing subsidized apartments to those who graduated successfully through the second phase.

All proposals for federal funding were now required to address homelessness in the terms set out by the Continuum of Care, ensuring that this framework entered policy debates in every county and municipality. But within three years it had become clear that the ICH's stated goal of providing "a decent home and a suitable living environment for every American" was not supported by the legislature. Federal funding not only dropped away from its initial high point in 1995, but it shifted in emphasis. The Healthcare for the Homeless program retained its funding, while the most significant cuts were made to HUD's Homeless Assistance Programs and Projects for Assistance in Transition from Homelessness, the programs designed to provide permanent independent housing. A 1999 report on transitional housing provision, commissioned and published by HUD, illustrated the frustration of social welfare professionals at higher levels of the homelessness industry. The authors, Susan Barrow and Rita Zimmer, made it clear that the lack of affordable accommodation was blocking the potential of transitional programs across the country. "Expanding the supply of affordable housing should be the highest HUD priority. The inadequate availability of affordable public housing limits the effectiveness of all efforts to support the transition from homelessness to housing," they stated.[6]

Those funds that were still available for funding permanent housing were now overwhelmingly directed toward families and single people

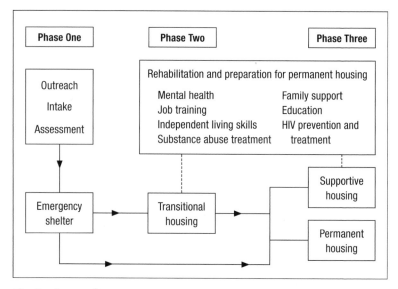

The Continuum of Care.

with mental or physical disabilities. A few of the new transitional shelters specialized in treating either male addicts or men with severe mental problems, but since the late 1980s the majority of shelter beds had been given over to the fast-rising population of homeless women with children. In many municipalities there was still nothing for able-bodied men without serious addictions or mental problems beyond extremely basic emergency shelter. Single men or women unwilling or unable to lay claim to such disabilities continued to be shut out of the third stage of the process, permanent housing.

In the context of the underfunded third phase, the notion of transitional housing became fraught with questions. To *what* exactly were clients to transition? Unable to work on systemic solutions to the problem, service providers were bound to turn to the programs within reach: the diagnosis and treatment of individual pathologies. The transition from homelessness became defined almost exclusively as a change within the individual, from being unhouseable to being housing-ready. Without the support of Congress, the system-talk evident in the original Continuum of Care report, with its assertion of the federal government's responsibility to promote housing rights, was gradually overtaken, drowned out by discussions of individual pathology.

Returning to Baum and Burnes's manifesto against system-talk, we can now see how some of those engaged in developing policy expertise on homelessness may have decided that continued federal support of their efforts (not to mention research) would require distancing themselves from the critical language and ideas of many homeless advocates. Perhaps they also acknowledged system-talk's continued resonance with much of the population and saw the need to shift public opinion about how to help the homeless. Taking advantage of the radical advocates' media missteps over the 1990 census,[7] ideologists of medicalization wielded the gathering weight of their research to claim the social problem as their own, positioning themselves as truer advocates than the policy outsiders who were "perverting science by stirring up prejudicial statements."[8]

In San Francisco many service providers were ambivalent about the causes and solutions to the problem of homelessness. Yet in practice they followed Baum and Burnes, downplaying the third phase of the Continuum of Care and using studies of the special needs of their clients to push for more transitional services. As I was told by Tom, a housing social worker since 1991, activist system-talk was not going to help service providers secure funding for what was becoming a hugely expensive social problem.

"Look, once we got into the early '90s, after Frank Jordan was elected [mayor], it was clear enough that there were limits to the kinds of arguments that we could usefully make if we were going to carry on pulling down public money for our programs. And that is *here*. The situation was worse for the folks working in other locations, believe me. But even in San Francisco, there really wasn't much point to us as an organization to be raising hell about rent subsidies, about the problems with the Section 8 vouchers, for example. These issues were not going anywhere, and we were not going to do our clients any favors by pushing too hard. And there was already criticism of the shelters for 'enabling' certain kinds of antisocial behavior, and we had to show that we were trying to deal with that issue. We had put a huge amount of energy into getting our services in place, and obviously our number one priority had to be keeping our shelter operational, keeping our caseworker positions. That was our first responsibility. If we lost our funding, we would be failing our clients on an enormous scale.

"Personally, I agreed and still agree with some of the arguments made by the advocates, or at least I agreed with the more moderate folks. But we had to be realistic about current thinking on the problem, about what kinds of demands we could legitimately make and what kinds of talk were just going to create problems, make us look too political, too pie-in-the-sky. We needed to establish a solid reputation as an organization.

"But, yes, I would say that there is a momentum that gets put in place. Ten years in, we have caseworkers specializing in substance abuse, which is very important, but on the other hand we still don't have housing vouchers for 80 percent of our clients. And I don't feel great about that, to be honest."

Little by little, the ascendancy of quality-of-life policing campaigns came together with the funding emphasis on transitional programs to marginalize the early social justice orientation. Advocates' suggestions that the homeless were injured citizens endangered the more politically diplomatic claim of sick-talk that the homeless deserved services because they were not competent to help themselves. Although the radical homeless advocates were few, they had shown themselves adept at reaching public opinion, and there was the risk they would contaminate objective science with unpopular leftist rhetoric. Perhaps the social workers' decision to downplay systemic analyses of homelessness made more sense than tilting at the neoliberal windmill.

With its large, visible homeless population, its fiery advocacy movement, and its progressive electorate, San Francisco presents a striking, even emblematic case of the medicalization of homelessness. As the interview extract above suggests, systemic arguments were not only given strong voice by the Coalition on Homelessness and radical politicians such as Tom Ammiano (and later Chris Daly), but were also taken very seriously by some of the leading service providers. The triumph of authoritarian medicalization in a place that was uniquely primed to resist it speaks to the power of sick-talk within American homeless policy as a whole.

Medicalizing the San Francisco Shelters

After the massive increases of the 1980s, the number of shelter beds in San Francisco remained stable at around 1,400 throughout the 1990s.

The handful of city shelters, including the multiservice centers, were far from adequate to house the homeless population, whether it was 5,000 (the lowest city hall estimate) or 12,000, as claimed by the Coalition on Homelessness at this time. Basic shelter continued to be allocated by lottery, and in 1997 the biggest shelter was still reporting 1,200 turn-aways every month.

But as San Francisco implemented the Continuum of Care model, the bulk of shelter places gradually shifted from basic cots or mats in generic shelters to "case management" beds in multiservice shelters with more comprehensive services.[9] Clients now had to go through a waiting list, but once admitted were guaranteed beds for at least three months, on condition that they participated in various rehabilitative programs.

It is this second manifestation, the transitional shelters and their rehabilitative programs, that is the focus of this chapter. I do not offer a detailed ethnographic account of the workings of medicalization within the homelessness industry, a subject well covered by Vincent Lyon-Callo and Darin Weinberg, among others. Instead, I draw on a mixture of my own street-based research and supplementary interviews with caseworkers and other shelter staff to bring out the ways that homeless men experienced and understood the ostensibly therapeutic approach within the transitional shelters and related institutions.[10]

The Persistence of Sin-Talk

The form of medicalization applied to able-bodied, nondelusional homeless men is usually only medical in the broadest sense, in its assumptions that individual pathology was the root of homelessness. Like motivational Welfare-to-Work programs and other manifestations of the contemporary medicalization of poverty, the inexpert, meeting-based therapeutic forms instituted by the shelters had very little to do with the expert-led, intimate, individuated process of classical doctor-centered medicalization. Similarly, the conceptual content, a one-size-fits-most mixture of pop psychology and moral tales, drew little on more complex models of mental illness or depth psychology.[11]

Even if it was only medicalization on the cheap — "pop medicalization" — the sick-talk articulated by caseworkers and drug counselors of the new transitional shelters could provide immense relief to men and women tortured by guilt and self-loathing. It could be quite wonderful to be convinced that one was sick rather than bad. But there was no free absolution. In exchange, "clients" had to be willing to relinquish their "street" agency and instead acknowledge pain and helplessness.

The self-examination required by sick-talk is a highly feminized and middle-class cultural form, a requirement to investigate and expose dirty laundry in public, to demonstrate honesty through self-revelation. It is not surprising that those most attracted by the disease discourse were far more likely to be female, white, gay, or from more middle-class backgrounds.

Authentic take-up of sick-talk was far less common among working-class men, whether unemployed manual workers like Willie, Carlos, and Derick or longtime hustlers and ex-cons like Del, Freddie, or Linc, who had spent many years honing a stripped-down survival masculinity centered on refusal to acknowledge pain or weakness. African Americans and Latinos in particular were often fiercely loyal to their families of origin and extremely resistant to the idea that their problems might stem from neglectful or abusive child rearing. As I described with Walter, even addressing the idea of being depressed seemed to be a risky activity he could approach only when in my apartment. Once in the shelters, these kinds of men might be amenable to opening up in the direction of sick-talk with the help of the right staff member. What they found very difficult, though, was that they did not have access to much time at all with their caseworkers and instead were asked to show their vulnerability in the much less protected environment of group meetings.

Lyon-Callo's work suggests that the medicalization of homelessness may work in a more powerful, unambiguous fashion in smaller city shelters. But in the big cities, the modest resources of pop medicalization—a handful of caseworkers serving hundreds of clients—are facing an ever-increasing tide of angry, rebellious souls who have lost to prison and jail much of their youth, their lovers, their families, their hopes, and often their mental health.

I found it to be taken for granted by both clients and staff that the violence, distrust, and alienation some men and women bring into shelters was the product of prison culture. Outside of meeting times and one-on-one casework sessions, there continued the low-level warefare that I described in chapters 3 and 4. There was perhaps less threat of serious violence, but more danger of being yelled at or robbed by a fellow client. Paul Boden, director of the San Francisco Coalition on Homelessness, described the intense mutual distrust among users of the old Hospitality House basic shelter: "I was at Hospitality House for seven years . . . my office was right off of the drop-in center shelter area, and it had a window looking to the drop-in center, and these guys would come in, person after person after person after person, and say, 'I ain't like them motherfuckers. Those motherfuckers out there are all crackheads, rip-off, cheating-ass motherfuckers.'" The shelter felt little safer than the street, and in some respects the level of conflict and fear was actually intensified because the down-and-out and desperate were concentrated in confined spaces.

"Holding the Line"

The therapeutic discourse the social workers were trying to promote was undermined not only by the mutual distrust of the clients, but by the authoritarian behavior of the badly paid frontline staff, who were more likely to shame or blame than to offer solidarity. Homeless shelters are difficult places to work as well as to stay, and adequate staffing is a constant problem. Frontline workers are badly paid, if at all, and often recruited directly out of the client base. The lowest level of authority staff, as in missions and poorhouses for hundreds of years, are clients themselves. Such monitors or coordinators may have their own little room or a separate dormitory, but these perks and a few dollars a week are all they get for their work. For some, there will be promotion to low-wage employment, but most remain in limbo, covetous of their tenuous privileges, yet still a long way from a home of their own. Shelter managers are canny about the obstacles to social control in these environments, and most seem to believe that those best equipped to exert immediate control over hundreds of ex-cons and other members of the disreputable poor are going to be insiders, tough "sin-talkers" who can, if necessary, use their own street capital to enforce law and order.

The consistent hostility projected by many of the monitors and frontline staff was a constant topic of conversation among the men who used the shelters. Here, for example, is a powerful anonymous letter titled "To Monitor in Training," published in the *Street Sheet* of June 5, 2001:

> You think, because I am in the same place where you would be if it were not for your cunning manipulative behavior, that you can falsely accuse me with your non-responsive stare....Your response to my refusal to join your illegal games, and attempts to attribute your motives to me, results in your insinuations and management by innuendo.
>
> I am in a shelter. You are the monitor.
>
> This week.
>
> Next week our roles may be reversed.
>
> GUEST IN RESIDENCE

Many of the men were critical of shelter managers for hiring workers out of the pool of residents. "The negative atmosphere in the shelters, in my opinion—I think the monitors are responsible for a lot of it," said Willie. "A lot of those guys are real major assholes. They give you this stare, like a cop, never smile at you. Then if you ask a question or something they act like you are the scum of the earth.... Just because you're in there you're *guilty* of something, it's all your fault.... I'm not saying everyone is like that, but there's enough negativity in most of those places to make you never want to go back. And half those guys, they hire them right out of the line, just because they know how to work the system. They are no better than the rest of us—worse, if anything. It's pathetic. All this money is spent on the shelters, you know, millions of millions of dollars, and they hire those jerks to push us around. Can't they get some better staff?"

Derick, an African American recycler in his thirties, said that the main reason he stayed out of the shelters was his fear he would "lose it" and attack one of the frontline staff. "The BS you get from the monitors, the guys on the desk, gotta be seen to be believed," Derick said, shaking his head. "It's in-fucking-*credible*. Those brothers take themselves entirely too seriously. I feel like hurting someone, I get so angry. It's hard out here, and then I go down the shelter and I get that kind of disrespect. You don't need that kind of infantile bullshit tearing you down even further, the way they treat you like a child, like you're

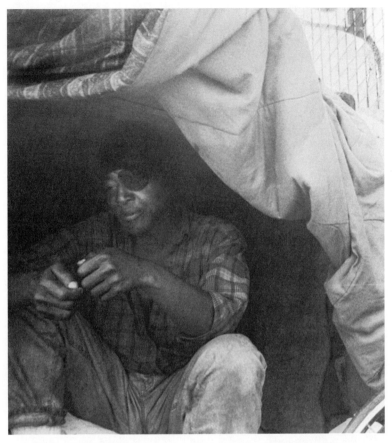

"Am I such a bad guy? I dunno . . . yes and no. One thing I do know — if I'm gonna get out of this hole I'm in, I need space, and I need a bit of respect."

nothing, worse than nothing. No, it's more than disrespect — it's plain hatefulness. I can't do it. Or some day I'm gonna hurt someone."

Hilario, the young Mexican recycler, suffered the humiliation of being treated like a child. "The Spanish [speaking] shelter's the best. It's much more friendly, but man, the rules. You wanna think you have your own life — forget it. Like my buddy buys me a nice burrito — *carne asada, aguacate,* the works. I save half of it for my dinner, but no, they say, put the burrito in the garbage or get out. I say, how about I just go out and eat it outside? They say no. The man is like, he is yelling at me: 'Put it in the garbage *now* or you are eighty-sixed.' It's embarrassing, being treated like a kid. . . . No one talks much to each other. They're all embarrassed. They are humiliated, man."

The slow up-and-down inspection of the incoming client, the skeptical eyebrows and expressionless response to any question or request, the gleeful maintenance of rules to the exclusion of humanity or even common sense — the intense culture of insult maintained by many monitors and front desk staff had to be seen to be believed. I myself certainly found it extremely hard to handle. Once, I visited Luther in a shelter when he was sick with pneumonia. He told me that another man had openly robbed him of thirty dollars and his state identification card from under his pillow when he was too weak to fight back. When I managed to get a monitor to come over and talk to us about it, the man just smirked at us. "I had thirty dollars there," said Luther. "You say," said the monitor, shrugging. Luther told the monitor that he had a witness. "Uh-huh. And?" The man walked off, seeming amused at Luther's illusion that the word of a derelict could account for anything.

The patchy quality of all levels of shelter staff is clearly related to low pay. The large population of young college graduates eager to "make a difference" mitigated San Francisco's caseworker shortages, yet notions of professional behavior reached few of those running the front desks, dormitories, or kitchens. As Evan, a caseworker in what was supposed to be a state-of-the-art multiservice shelter, told me, "We have no support, no kind of counseling for the workers on the desk, the monitors, the shift managers even. There is nothing to stop them venting on the clients, to educate them a little about what might be a better way to behave."[12]

Junior

I saw something of the making of a frontline worker when disreputable street criminal Junior progressed from street addict to gatekeeper. When I first met him in early 1996, Junior was a menace to other homeless people. A purse grabber in his youth, he now raised the cash for his crack addiction by robbing weaker men and women in the shelters and out on the streets. Eighteen months later he was trying to move out of the illicit economy, selling the *Street Sheet* by the Powell

Street escalators. He coughed all the time and a scuffle on some stairs had left him lasting lame. He had numerous family in the Bay Area, but they had little time for him and no one was going to take him in. While staying in one of the transitional shelters, Junior got on the waiting list for a residential drug rehabilitation program. He had been in rehab six or seven times before and had spent three years in and out of the transitional shelters. This time, however, he was able to stick with the program, finally proving receptive to the therapeutic community model. Over a two-year period he made the difficult transition from client to frontline worker. While living in a "clean" after-care house, he managed to land a job as a security guard in another institution run by the same nonprofit organization.

I ran into him by hazard and he told me where he worked. The next week I went to find him.

"So things are still going well?"

"Yeah, yeah. It's good. Can't complain."

He arranged to take a break and we stood out on the busy corner while he hungrily smoked a cigarette.

"This job OK?"

"Yeah, it's all right. I know what they need. Keep the crackheads out the building. I ain't scared of their bull crap. I know their game. I done played *their* game," he said contemptuously.

"You sure did," I said. As soon as I had said it, I thought I sounded mean and tried to smile it off. But I think we were both thinking of the evening James Moss and I had come upon him in the act of robbing Li'l Lee on Hyde Street. Catching my eye, he had let go of his half-strangled victim with a kick. In fact, right now I was wondering if his bullying ways from the street might have translated all too easily into his new role on the front line of the heroin zone.

"I was lost," he said somewhat truculently. "I was lost in the wilderness, as they say. I don't barely remember nothing from being on the street." He glanced at me. "I was not myself. I had not been myself for a long time. I do not have a tolerance for drugs and alcohol. I was out of my *mind*."

"I know, I know you were." I tried to placate him. He still had his notorious temper. "It's gotta be hard, dealing with folks who are still out here."

Junior fiddled with his cigarette packet, counting the remaining smokes. "Oh yeah, it's hard, all right. But I can take it. You gotta hold the line. There's brothers and sisters in there doing their best. They don't need any more of this shit."

"Yeah. It's a shame these places have to be right in drug central like this."

Junior shrugged. "That's right, but you can see how it is. Other people don't wanna be around this kind of low-down behavior. And you can't blame them." He drew himself up. "It's all right. I ain't tempted, not one little bit, not now. I left *that* man behind."

Junior turned to intercept a scruffy-looking white man who was walking toward the front door of his workplace. "Can I *help* you?" he said pugnaciously.

Junior was certainly vastly better off than he had been living on the street, but his continued employment within the drug rehabilitation industry begged the question of whether he had fully left the street behind or merely migrated to a different role within the same social world. His discourse had not changed so much either. Despite his talk of disease, he still cleaved close to the moralistic binaries of "street" and "straight," even though now he had left the "wolves" for the ranks of the saved.

JJ

JJ, an African American shift manager at a transitional shelter, explained his own take on the clash between sin-talk and sick-talk in the culture of one of the major transitional shelters. "It's true that we often have problems coming up between the case managers and the other staff. It's not *all* the case managers, but . . . well, they tend to be a certain kind of a person, very softhearted—naive, you might say. And I respect them, you know. They are doing their best. But if you really know these people (the clients), like if you have spent a lot of time around them, you know that they don't need someone else giving them another chance—they don't need to be given too much space to let loose with a load of bullshit. What they need is a firm hand—kind, yes, but firm. I think half of them, three-quarters of them, didn't get the discipline that they needed when they were kids, and they are still needing it. It's like they say, tough love—tough love is going to be more effective in this kind of situation. . . . If they misbehave, they are out. That's the way it has to be. You can't have your case manager fresh out of college saying, 'You know, so-and-so just needs special considerations—he can't help it because he's disturbed,' all that. They are *all* disturbed. They are *all* messed up. That's what happens when you make bad choices and when you are *allowed* to make bad choices. Our job is to teach them to follow some simple rules. Other people have to follow rules, and that's what they'll have to do if they are gonna get off the street."

If we take a look at JJ in action, we can see how his take on how to treat the homeless was not unkind, but emphasized straightforward authoritarian behavioral modification over individualized diagnosis and treatment.

It was 8:45 p.m., and JJ stood surveying the large dormitory that housed the clients most recently recruited from the street. His eyes scanned the room, looking to see who was missing. The men sat or lay on the low beds, talking softly to each other.

"If you don't turn that radio off *now* you won't see it again," he growled to a couple in the corner. As they lay down on the low beds, most of the men kept their clothes on to sleep. He walked over to one of the empty beds. "Gone?"

"Uh-huh," said the man in the next bed.

JJ looked over to another empty space. "Jed, where's Charles?"

"Had to make a call," said Charles's neighbor Jed, a scrawny speed freak.

"That's the third time. If he don't get his sorry ass up here in five minutes, he's out. I don't care *what* he says." Jed left the room quickly.

Noticing another man inspecting holes in his socks, JJ called over, "We should be able to help you out with some new socks. Go see Linda in the morning."

Jed and Charles returned. "Sorry, man . . ." began Charles.

"I *don't* wanna hear it. I'm sick of your bullshit," said JJ, loud and severe. Charles grinned.

"Lights out in three minutes!" JJ shouted to the rest of the room.

The benign sin-talk embodied by JJ made him relatively well liked by the clients. He was quick to flash with anger, but also quick to laugh. Many of the homeless men, especially the numerous ex-cons, were long habituated to being treated as naughty children and seemed to be more at ease with his bluff, take-no-bullshit attitude than with the intrusive sick-talk of the more middle-class case managers.

A good example was the offending Charles, an African American heroin addict from the Fillmore.

When I asked Charles what it was like staying in the shelter, he shrugged. "I dunno. It beats the street. I like to keep myself clean, you know."

"But what about the program? Do you think you will stick it out?"

"Hard to say. I don't really..." Charles broke off. "Wouldn't say there's much they can teach me about my problem with dope. I got Steve (as case manager). He ain't got a clue, if you don't mind me saying. You couldn't believe the bullshit," he snorted. "Wanted to talk about my mom, that I ain't seen in a million years, like she has anything to do with my stupid shit. Talks like I could get hired as sales assistant. What planet is he from? You know, it makes me tired, dealing with someone like him.... JJ, now, I'd rather deal with him. He knows the score. You know where you are coming from."

Again we can see how sin-talk's simple binary of street versus straight could function as a surprisingly successful form of social control. The street identity of the hustler was dependent on its "straight" counterpart to make sense of the world, and the moment when an authority figure like JJ refused to "take their bullshit" was experienced almost joyfully, as a moment of recognition, of relief at being known. In a fundamental way, both judge and sinner spoke the same language.

When I returned to my earlier notes after years in the field, I found irritatingly naïve my criticisms of JJ's infantilization of grown men. On reflection, I could see how his tactics were not so different from the persona I myself took on to bond with street hustlers. After various instances of being rejected or taken for a fool, I had learned to adopt a similar reliance on a knowing "Yeah, right!" The easiest way that I could get the more hardened hustlers to feel comfortable in my presence was to behave as if I were quite indifferent to their problems and to act as if I took nothing that they said seriously. For sure, these rituals of "trickster" versus "skeptic" were usually softened by humor, but they were no less significant for all that.

To some extent, then, it seems fair to see the sin-talking shelter workers as not just imposing moral judgment, but actually adapting to the culture brought in by their toughest, most resistant clients: the ex-con hustlers. As caseworker Evan implied above, there would need to be a far more extensive training process, and much higher staffing levels, to institute the kind of cultural change he thought desirable.

"Let Me Tell You What Your Problem Is"

Despite the persistence of sin-talk within San Francisco's transitional shelters, it was clear that many homeless men were initially attracted by the better conditions. It was a great relief to have a secure place to stay, your own bed, a locker, and warm food guaranteed for the next few days. Yet these relative luxuries came with a price ticket in terms of loss of autonomy.

This study is hardly qualified to make any quantitative claims about the success rate of the transitional shelter programs. But the experience of my research companions does not instill strong optimism about these institutions' capacity to move people out of homelessness permanently. Although most of the thirty-eight had entered the transitional shelters at one time or other, Junior was the only able-bodied man who moved permanently out of homelessness by working his way through a sequence of programs in transitional shelters and drug rehabilitation facilities. Several more worked transitional programs for a while and did demonstrate some willingness to reframe their life stories in terms of problems of addiction, depression, or bipolar disorder. But short of entering long-term drug rehabilitation, there were sharp limits to the amount of concrete help available to support long-term change.

I listened to unending complaints about the homeless archipelago's emphasis on individual reformation over more practical help.

"You can't even go in those places without getting the three degrees," Julius told me. "All you want to do is lie down, get some peace, but no, they get you doing that intake procedure. Straight off they looking at you like, 'OK, what's the problem with this poor mofo, this loser?' I hate that shit. You have to sit down, think of something like, 'Yes, ma'am, I am ready to make changes.' I've *been* ready. Why is it all about *me,* what I'm doing wrong? I need a break, that's what I need. I can't stand those places. If I have to go to a shelter, like, if it is really cold and somebody took my bedroll, I be better off on the floor, sitting in a chair, whatever. Just don't ask me your stupid questions."

Julius here echoed the comments of Linc in chapter 4, fiercely resenting the idea that helping strategies should be focused on his own dysfunctions. Like Linc, Julius had a strongly systemic analysis that placed homelessness as first and foremost a product of racism in education, the criminal justice system, and the labor market. Julius is not just complaining about medicalization, but also about control. Like other observers of the shelter system, he is arguing that it tended to undermine its own ostensible aims of fostering self-sufficiency with the kinds of intrusive and comprehensive control characteristic of the "total institutions" described by Erving Goffman in *Asylums*.[13]

"Like I Need More Drugs in My Life" showed how Carlos was terminated from a transitional shelter program for getting a painting job. The case manager who forbade Carlos to work was relatively respectful and tolerant of difference compared with parallel institutions in less liberal parts of the country, yet his position was ultimately the same as that of far more morally judgmental drug counselors with whom I later worked in St. Louis. Drugs were the issue, work was not. Carlos's own belief in the crucial role of a break, a job with which he could start to reestablish himself, was taken for fantasy, a delusion that he was what Goffman would call a "normal" rather than a deeply flawed street addict.[14]

"They Want Us All Shelterized, You Know"

The emphasis on pop medicalization, as some of the earlier material implies, not only frustrated men desperate to work, but also reduced the legitimacy of the shelter system. In particular the insistent erasure of systemic critique from shelter discourse infuriated clients already alienated by homeless clearances.

While the social work professionals within the transitional shelters did their best to promote therapeutic self-examination, it may be a mistake to see the new shelters simply as strongholds of sick-talk. Earlier on in the book, we saw Manny arguing that the homeless archipelago was intimately connected with more clearly authoritarian policies of police clearances and imprisonment. "Those shelters will break you down," he said. "They want us all shelterized, you know. . . . They don't want another tent city on Civic Center, for sure, and they reckon these new-style shelters, that's the best way to do it. Then they don't even need the cops."

Manny and his fellow thinkers saw the functions of homeless clearance and shelter warehousing as intimately connected and mutually dependent. They were certainly right that the existence of shelter beds and other rehabilitative programs were used over and over again to justify police clearances. (Hence, for example, years of public argument between the mayor's office and the Coalition on Homelessness over the extent of the shortage of beds.)

My street companions distrusted the capacity of shelters to provide any long-term solutions and experienced the lengthy intake procedures and myriad other forms of questioning as intrusive and insulting. In the conversation below, you can see how doubts about the helpfulness of the self-reformation aspects of the transitional programs led men to meditate on possible structural connections between shelter system and the police clearances.

After some wrangling at the front desk I got permission to go in and visit with recycler Willie, who had become homeless after a fire claimed his apartment. Willie, who was generally not particularly interested in systemic approaches to homelessness, had decided to try a three-month program after a spell of pneumonia. We sat on his dormitory bed, looking at the paperwork he had been given. Willie looked both strikingly clean and rather faded.

"So?"

"S'alright." He smiled and looked me in the eyes. "I'm not crazy about living in here, as you know. It's like the army, but most people are the opposite of in shape."

"And mostly fighting each other?"

"Sure. Each other and the monitors. But not everybody's fighting. There's plenty of people just keeping to themselves, like me, I guess. Have to say, I thought it would be worse. It's definitely a better scene than Hospitality House in the old days."

"Yeah, well, that was more like a basic shelter, right? What about all the programs, your caseworker? How is all that working for you?

Willie paused. "Look, there's some decent folks in here. My case manager is OK, but this action plan . . . I guess it makes sense to some people, but personally speaking, it's kinda dumb—like I don't know how to get clothes and an ID? Give me a break."

"What about the substance abuse meetings?"

Willie grimaced. "Some of what they say makes sense, but you know it's just that 'talk the talk' BS in the end. That's what makes you sick about it. The guys that go all gung ho on recovery in the meetings, they are the same guys trying to sell you crack in the bathroom, the same guys joking around about how they gonna get some SSI scam going. I can't take it seriously."

"So for you, personally, the program doesn't seem to be offering you that much?"

Willie shook his head. "Nah. It's all right not being outside for a spell, but if I'm really honest with myself, I don't see this changing much in my life. You will see me out there again soon enough."

"What could they do to help you more?"

"I don't want to sound paranoid, but it seems like the main reason they made these places more of a daytime thing as well is to get us out of sight. I mean, when they all talk about the homelessness problem in the paper, it's really the mess, right? It's the people asking for money, nutters, the winos, the far-out crackheads, right? Someone like me who keeps a low profile, doesn't rip people off—it's not really about me. . . . I guess I'm rambling."

"No, I think I see where you're going."

"OK, it's like, make a bunch of programs to keep us out of sight, but in the end it's kinda half-assed. Maybe I'm wrong, but that's how it looks from where I'm standing."

As we saw earlier, in *Nobody Loves a Loser,* Willie did ultimately get off the street, but through his own friendship networks rather than by progressing through the homeless archipelago.

"You Need a Safe Place"

Interestingly, many of my research companions' criticisms were reiterated by caseworkers themselves.

Particularly concerned was Timothy, a deeply empathetic African American case manager who himself had survived years of addiction and homelessness. Timothy worried that his clients did not have a stable enough environment in which to take advantage of his counseling skills. In his mind, there was a dangerous disconnect between the vulnerability and self-searching required by the therapeutic model and the survival mode imposed by the state of homelessness. "I'm not sure I feel completely comfortable persuading someone to really get into their issues, you know, if they are just gonna be going out again on the street. That's not what you need out there. It's not gonna help you survive. Out there you need to be strong—fight or flight, you know. . . . You need a safe place if you are going to really get in there, look at yourself. So as a case manager, I want to know that there is something in place for that person, that if they are going to turn their life around, something is gonna be there for them. With some of these guys, a lot of these guys, I can't see it happening. We can get people into rehab if they are patient, if they are willing, but it takes time, and I think you have to face the fact that rehab is not going to work for everybody out there. I wish we had a bigger range of options to offer them, I really do. I worry about it." Timothy's comments (which resonate deeply with Walter's reflections in chapter 4) suggest that the absence of the third phase of the continuum of care could undermine not only the clients' but the caseworkers' ability to pursue the second, rehabilitative phase in good faith.

The San Francisco caseworkers were quite divided about the extent to which their services should be constructed within a therapeutic framework. In particular they expressed quite divergent opinions about the increasingly strong (often compulsory) emphasis on substance abuse within the shelters. Funding priorities had made substance abuse the fastest-growing specialty in the shelters. As Lyon-Callo's Massachusetts study demonstrates in rich detail, this shifting balance between different kinds of professionals could have deep effects on overall institutional cultures. In San Francisco, many of these specialty positions were filled by members of AA and NA—former addicts like Timothy—who had a strong belief that homelessness was primarily a product of addiction.

Some of the other caseworkers, though, were less happy about the priority given to addiction issues. Ricardo, who had been a caseworker for five years, argued that the shelter management seemed more interested in monitoring clients' attendance at substance abuse groups than in listening to his own account of how his clients were doing. He described a case where a client that he considered to be "doing very well" was expelled from the shelter for not attending Alcoholics Anonymous meetings.

"These action plans (the contracts that the clients have to agree to in order to stay in the shelter), they are still way too rigid. I said to Dolores (one of the shelter managers) that John was doing very well, he was taking classes here, even went over to City College to research some other classes, which impressed me a lot. But she said they had to eighty-six (expel) him because he was uncooperative and wouldn't comply with his action plan, basically wouldn't go to his meetings. And it's the managers that decide in the end. We get to have our opinions, but..." Ricardo broke off, then shrugged. "Like I have said, there's always this big tension between the caseworkers and the managers. It doesn't go away, and the reason is that, when it comes down to it, they have different goals from the caseworkers. They want to run a tight ship, have strict control of the clients—that's their number one priority. The managers are not much different from the monitors in that respect. They always assume that if the client doesn't want to do what they are told, it's because they are fucking up. Well, sometimes they are and sometimes they're not. And they don't change their basic attitude about the clients. It doesn't matter how long they have been here, what phase they are in, you still get this assumption of guilt, and it's a pain in the ass for the caseworkers.... Here we are, trying to persuade the clients that the program is working in their best interests, but you have other people in the shelter treating them like children, or worse."

Ricardo, like several of the other San Francisco caseworkers I interviewed, seemed to be generally frustrated and discontent with his work. There was a shortage of qualified recruits for these jobs and the turnover was high. At one large shelter all but two of a team of eight caseworkers left the organization within a three-month period, complaining of the impossibility of doing a "good job" under present conditions. Part of their frustration came from bad relations with the management team of the shelter, but the social workers also shared a more fundamental critique of the way that the idea of "transitional" housing was being conceived and implemented. Like Kim Hopper and others studying the continuities between the shelter system and other institutions, these caseworkers could see that transition was generally functioning in a more circular than linear fashion, and that many of the clients caught up in the circuit between shelters, hospitals, jails, and rehab were getting no closer to moving off the street.[15] Once the caseworkers confronted the precarious level of support for the healthier graduates of their program, they started to reevaluate the process of breaking down clients, of encouraging them to drop their combative ways for introspection. They came to doubt their capacity to liberate through therapeutic truth and to worry that their practices were ineffective or even abusive.

"The Big Ticket"

The key role of disability payments in getting men off the street was confirmed when my companions were severely injured or otherwise incapacitated. In one case, champion recycler Sam was run over by a car on the way to the recycling plant, an accident that badly broke both his legs and left him permanently disabled. I was very surprised by the response of his recycling colleagues, several of whom expressed envy of Sam for "lucking out" and "catching the big ticket," SSI (Supplemental Security Income). The fact that he could no longer walk three steps without pain seemed minor in comparison.

Sam's friends' commentary on his injuries reminded me of a conversation with another recycler, Victor, early on in my fieldwork. I had been nagging Vic that he should not take a particular busy slip road toward the recycling plant. It had no sidewalk, and I thought he could easily get run over. "The cars come so fast. Don't you think it's dangerous?" I asked. Victor shrugged and gave me one of his serious, muted looks, as if there was something he wasn't saying but maybe wished he could. (He had looked at me the same way in the old see-no-evil days before we had started talking about his heroin habit.) At the time I took Victor's response as an expression of despair, an unspoken hint that he was indifferent to physical danger because he really didn't care if he lived or died. He would not have been unique with such an attitude. Twice I had to argue with homeless men not to court death by deliberately lying down in the middle of busy intersections. After the general reaction to Sam's injuries, though, I remembered this incident, wondering if Victor had been hinting that a serious injury might help him escape the street.

Interestingly, Sam moved much closer to a disease discourse on homelessness after his SSI enabled him to leave the street milieu. He got himself clean of heroin and became an enthusiastic member of

Alcoholics Anonymous, and was now scathing about his once honorable career as a street recycler. "Recycling—it was keeping me out there, enabling my heroin habit," he now believed.[16]

Another person whose life was transformed by SSI was James Moss. Formerly a crack dealer in the Tenderloin, James suffered two strokes that left him lame, without the use of his right arm, and with serious difficulties in verbal communication. Unlike Sam, James showed no interest in a twelve-step reconstruction of his life history, yet he did happily adopt a sick role as an important part of his new, non-Tenderloin identity. He joined various groups organized around disease and disability: an antismoking support group and an activity program for people with strokes and other brain injuries. Eventually I managed to get him Section 8 housing in a quiet complex high in the hills near Twin Peaks. In this new setting he was able to leave behind his "TL" style and redevelop a softer interactional style and new interests, such as photography. His full-length leather coat was put away for occasional use; he was now more likely to wear a woolen sweater.

James's new life brought him in turn a new set of friends, including a girlfriend, a brilliant playwright older than himself who was recovering from her own nightmare of depression and attempted suicide. Overjoyed with his good fortune, James expressed very little nostalgia for his days of running the street. "Thank God," he would say any time the Tenderloin came up in conversation, meaning, "Thank God I got out."

Despite James's and Sam's horrible injuries, I did come to understand how the men might see them as an elite: the ones that got away. Certainly none of those who had expressed their jealousy arrived at the same kind of stable income and accommodation over the next couple of years. Short of the "big ticket," the so-called "transition" touted by the shelter programs opened onto a void, and most men tumbled back out to the street. In fact, various important resources became steadily less available to the nondisabled during the late 1990s and early 2000s. It was no longer possible to get SSI for addiction-related problems. SF General's methadone clinic now gave free methadone treatment only to clients who were both HIV-positive *and* addicted to heroin, and the hospital's six-day hotel vouchers for discharged patients were restricted to those with mental illness.

James, during our Greyhound expedition to look for his relatives in Atlanta and Cincinnati.

A consensus had built over the last decade that the transitional shelter system was failing to move many of its clients through to permanent housing. In 2004, in line with new thinking at the federal level, the city took a radical new step. Using the savings from an 85 percent cut to General Assistance entitlements (the controversial Care Not Cash initiative), they opened several hundred hotel rooms for able-bodied homeless people. My own street research did not extend into the Care Not Cash era; by this time, I had finished my fieldwork. I am sure that receiving this basic, few-strings-attached housing was an immense relief to those who were lucky enough to get it. This kind of "housing first" project, though, is expensive and by definition aimed at the homeless people who cause the most disturbance and cost the most in terms of policing, emergency services, and health care.[17] The pilot "housing first" programs have primarily targeted the delusional mentally ill and chronic alcoholics, and this principle is most unlikely to be adopted for the 80 percent of homeless people who do not fall under the chronic homelessness definition.[18] The transitional shelter remains the cornerstone of the archipelago.

"They Say You Got to Go All the Way Down"

Chronic homelessness initiatives would be unlikely to target many of my own street companions. Only a handful, the panhandlers Freddie and EJ, for example, were constantly in battles with the police. Neither were they delusionally mentally ill, except for poor Clarence, who gradually lost his bearings after several years on the street. Those who got into housing were either helped by friends or family, like Willie, Rich, and eventually Morris, or through becoming severely physically disabled, like Sam or James.

The other route into housing was through rehab, which could be accessed either independently or through the transitional shelters' substance abuse programs. (The waiting list rarely dropped below 1,000, generally translating into two weeks to a month.) San Francisco's facilities were definitely above par, offering indigent clients far longer time in rehab, serious job training, better-kept buildings, and much more substantial employment support and placement than the average American down-at-heel rehab center for the uninsured.[19] In return, institutions demanded prolonged subordination to a mass of institutional rules and a continuous demonstration of humility and discipleship. Clients had to not only stay clean, but also forsake completely their old ways, to turn their backs on most of their relationships and revolutionize their previous understandings of their lives.

Drug addiction treatment in the United States was originally developed to help middle-class people with drug and alcohol problems to recover their lives. As Weinberg describes in *Others Inside,* rehab institutions split into a two-tier system, with private care for more redeemable middle-class addicts separated from the public custodial facilities for "irreconcilably other" lower class addicts.[20] Since the 1970s, the National Institute on Alcoholic Abuse and Alcoholism promoted a more uniform approach, heavily influenced by Alcoholics Anonymous. The tendency toward stricter treatment for poor addicts has continued, with most inner-city rehabs pursuing an authoritarian "therapeutic community" model that sees its clients as fundamentally immature and wrongheaded.

One great achievement of the therapeutic community movement was the incorporation of large numbers of recovered addicts as the core of the counseling staff within state-funded rehab facilities, prisons, and shelters, providing one of the few viable career paths for working-class street addicts who have turned themselves around.[21] The disease model of homelessness disseminated by substance abuse counselors from this kind of therapeutic community background tended to be substantially different from that of social workers, far closer to Christianity, and with a much greater emphasis on personal responsibility. (As in the case of JJ, public castigation by drug counselors seemed to resonate well with the sin-talking masculinity of some of the men on the street, although it infuriated many others.)

For the minority who moved through rehab successfully, the therapeutic community model could work well, not only by helping them clean up and stay safe in the short term, but by inserting them into a "recovery" community that would continue to support them in the following years. As caseworker Timothy told me, "Rehab gave me my life back, gave me my friends. And in the end, the learning I did in there gave me the chance to give back. Nothing else is gonna give these guys all that." As he acknowledged earlier, though, for most people, most of the time, rehab did not work out: "You have to be ready. You have to let go your pride, let go all your *stuff,* all that protective BS you been building up. It's *hard.*"

Luther, an African American recycler who had been a heroin addict for many years, recounted just how hard it could be. He decided to try rehab for the third time in the late 1990s. "I was in there eleven weeks, you know, meetings all the time, all sorts of bullshit. It's not easy being locked up with a bunch of addicts, but I tried to work the program. But the way they break you down, treat everyone like he's a liar and a damn fool—all day there's something, some group, somebody getting in your face. I couldn't take it any more. I was starting to go crazy shut up in there.... The building was too hot, you couldn't breathe, and everywhere noise. When you've been used to camping out, not having to deal with people too much, it's not realistic. I could tell there wasn't a snowball's chance in hell I was gonna make it through to when they would give me my own space."

Eventually Luther decided to leave. "I started to feel like I was gonna turn nasty and pop somebody. I was hiding out in the john all the time. It was *not* gonna work out."

When he said he was going to walk, three staff members harangued Luther. "I just got all this shit like, 'Your problem is you're arrogant, you think you're better than the others,' and 'Maybe you haven't gone all the way down.' They say you got to go all the way down before you turn around, before the program will truly work for you. That made me so mad. They refused to see where I was coming from. What the hell do they know? How much further down can you get? I've *got* nothing. Half the time I feel like I *am* nothing. No one's gonna cry for *me* when I am gone."

Luther blinked away angry tears. "If I'm not suffering enough, if I'm not 'tired' enough, then I don't know who the hell is."

Straddlers

The emphasis of the transitional shelters on substance abuse and general personal reformation could be particularly dissonant for the temporarily or episodically homeless, a group that make up the largest number of those experiencing homelessness in any given year, often "passing" among the general population. Such a character was laconic David, a white man who often worked temp jobs as a security guard, as well as collecting two or three large loads of recycling every week. The work was very hard for David, who had some kind of serious disc problem in his lower back. He walked with a bent-kneed, forward lean, in constant pain.

David and I were taking a break after selling a bunch of cans at the Safeway on Market Street. We had worked together several times at this point, and David had used my bathroom for a shower the week before. In general I didn't try to tease out my companions' "stories of the fall" straightaway, preferring to build a more companionable rapport over work. But I felt we were ready, and while David was smoking I asked him how he had become homeless.

"Back in '92, '93, was the last time I had a place, but my landlord didn't pay the rent."

"You mean you were subletting?"

"Yeah. It's been hard for me to find anything decent work-wise for a long time. I don't have the right skills for what they are looking for right now. And there's not so much I can do, with my back. I figure if you don't have something decent going by the time you're my age, you had better forget it. For*get* it. So, yeah, a couple years back I was crashing with this guy, Rick. Bad jobs, bad pay. Nothing permanent, but getting by, you know. My back was killing me, so I couldn't do so many days in a row. But then Rick . . . he had problems with his children, with child support. He couldn't pay the rent and so we were out of that place. I stayed in the shelter a couple of weeks. Then it looked like it was gonna work out. My brother was doing OK, his wife needed a babysitter and everything. . . . I went out of town to go stay with them, but then . . . they caught a lie on the job on him. Well, in fact, it's not like he was lying at work; it was more that he didn't disclose some problems he had had before when he applied. He lost his job, had to move, and they put—OK, they didn't *put* me in the street, but they couldn't take me with them . . . so that put me in homelessness."

"So you came back to San Francisco?"

"Sure. I know people here. It's my home, if I've got one. I figured I could work something out. But it's got so, so fucking expensive. It just blows my mind to think about what we used to pay in the Mission a few years ago. It's literally ten times as much now, I reckon. And there's barely any places going. Crazy.

"So I've been shuffling around for maybe two years now. Pillar to post, Hospitality House, MSC, stayin' outside, staying with this or that buddy, camping in the Presidio, sharing hotel rooms, camping by 280. Had a decent tent for a while that this church gave me, but then the city workers went and slashed it to hell. What a fucking runaround. . . . And the GA—any possible reason they can give to cut you off, they'll try it. And do it too. It's a damn-near full-time job keeping your check, and I could never seem to get MediCal so I could get help with my back problem. Some people told me I should be eligible, but I couldn't figure it out and couldn't get anyone to help me. I'm not so good with forms."

"So I figured, OK, they want me to do one of these programs. Maybe that way I can get some help getting myself together. I need help, that's for sure. So I checked myself in. Put up with a whole load of crap. Teach you how to manage your money when you ain't got a penny. Act like a good citizen. Talk about how I am going to cut down on my drinking. Jesus. Did this Northern California Service League thing. OK, but the most basic kind of shit. I don't need any more worthless certificates. . . . Oh yeah, and anger management! Teach you how to manage your anger so you won't pop the next man in line. I'm not beating down on those people, but you know it's just not useful. They've got a guy in front of them who is saying over and over, 'I've got a real problem with my back and I need to do something about it,' and instead they give me all this rah-rah, turn-your-head-around psychological stuff.

"OK, so I do get some help sorting out my resume, finding places I can apply. Nada. OK, I got some more temp work, but I was already doing that. Pinkertons, Labor Ready, sure ain't any news to me. But something better? *No, señor.* I go the whole fucking nine yards and what did I get out of it? Zilch. Then the woman at the shelter got me this voucher that is supposed to be good for three months' rent. Well, not totally free rent, but something you could pay outta GA. But guess what? You go look at the list, and OK, there's nothing on the list. Not unless you are disabled, you got kids, you got AIDS. . . . I finally got a fix on this place in Oakland. Real rough neighborhood. Spent two weeks there, but . . . some animal in a ski mask busts down my door and beats the shit out of me as I don't have no money for him. I try to get back my voucher, but no dice. Landlord says I'm still living there far as he is concerned."

"I go crash with this girl I used to see for a couple weeks. But her landlord won't have it. Then I come back over here, thinking like the woman at the shelter can help me sort out the voucher situation. And what? She has quit and no one else gives a flying fuck. . . . And, oh yeah, some other guy tells me I got an attitude problem. Can you fucking believe it? Like how old do they think I am? I just walked out. I'm sorry, but I'm not buying it."

"That's when you started recycling?"

"That's right. And that's been better for me, in some ways. I mean, it's hard on you, it's hard on my back. Hella dirty. But I like to work. I'm just sick to death of people saying they wanna help me, and I just gotta do this and that, and fill in this form, and be nice, talk the talk, talk about my problems, and it's all gonna work out. It's not true. Sometimes you think they are just on a power trip, you know?"

David's narrative highlights the day-to-day priority given to the reformation and reeducation of the individual within spaces of the poverty agencies rather than practical help in navigating the real institutions from which he or she is excluded. PRWORA (Personal Responsibility and Work Opportunity Act) and other programs have placed workfare and job searches at the center of their eligibility structure, welfare officers and nonprofit social workers have been forced to become employment counselors, all too often without any real training or expertise.[22] What David really needed was back surgery, according to the doctor he saw through SF General's excellent primary care track, but his injury was apparently not serious enough to qualify him for Medicaid.

With a long work history and no incapacitating problem with drug or alcohol use, David seemed crudely shoehorned into the pop medicalization of the transitional programs. His poverty and illness turned into the label of "homelessness," a narrow and artificial reification superimposed upon the diversity of lived experience. In the process, his own goals of surgery, a job, and an apartment were constantly diverted into anger management, budgeting, and other forms of training light on education and heavy on moral and behavioral reorientation. After two years on and off the street he had filled in hundreds of forms, and attended scores of classes and therapeutic group meetings, but still not succeeded in accessing any form of independent housing beyond the two weeks he spent in Oakland.

From "Deficit" to "Empowerment"?

As you may have noticed, the programs pursued by David often employed the language of education, rather than the comprehensive medicalization described in the work of Vincent Lyon-Callo and Darin Weinberg. In progressive San Francisco, the character of the disease model in the shelters and rehab facilities has been shaped by the unusual strength of system-talk in public discourse. Both individually and collectively, a large faction of the shelter case managers struggled to shift local poverty agencies out of what they worried was a "deficit" model into a more respectful emphasis on "empowerment."

As Jason, an enthusiastic caseworker at one of the multiservice shelters put it, "We try to see people's problems in terms of skills, like what skills do they need if they are going to operate in the mainstream. We find it is less negative that way, so we are not always saying you have this problem and that problem. Instead we say, 'OK, you have certain skills already.' We look at what those are, and then we might say, 'But you need to work on your personal presentation, you need to work on anger management, organizing your time. You need to learn budgeting,' that kind of thing." Jason shrugged. "Of course, there's a lot of people where the most important thing is going to be recognizing and dealing with substance abuse issues. But we always try to make it about the practical issues, the skills you need to get by in a competitive society."

To the extent that the problem of homelessness was still understood as a product of individual shortcomings, the logic of "educational" or "people-centered" models was not necessarily that different from the more common deficit model, yet this kind of language did mitigate the more extreme pathologization of the homeless individual. Instead of emphasizing major dysfunctions, clients were encouraged to see themselves as potential workers who needed only to raise their skill level to integrate into mainstream society. This less invasive lexicon was clearly appreciated by some of my companions, who, as we have seen, often resented the language of "issues" and "problems."

Yet within a field where strong agency was so closely tied into the stigma of sin and "bad choices," the emphasis on "skills" was easily colonized by morally judgmental notions of "personal responsibility." For example, as one of the San Francisco multiservice centers shifted its program toward an intensive six-month transitional scheme during the late 1990s, it reprinted the individual "action plan," changing the term "client" to the term "program participant." The well-worn social worker title of "case manager" was changed to "service plan coordinator," and the planned "improvements" for the client were written up in a "self-directed goal plan," which every resident had to sign. The combination of this new terminology with forceful sanctions for those who did not "self-direct" themselves appropriately ultimately represented a shift toward harsher judgments of client behavior, leading some of those who had pushed for these changes to regret them. Sandrine, an experienced social worker, was one of those who expressed misgivings about the unintended consequences of another institution's 2001 shift toward an educational model.

"It's just amazing to me how hard it is to change ideas about society's losers. You know, you only have to look at the history of those we are now calling 'developmentally disabled.' We've gone through literally dozens of terms trying to destigmatize *that* group, and each term quickly becomes a way to disparage them. It's the same with the homeless. And in a way, I think we haven't been so smart about the incorporation of 'skills' language in our materials. Advocates were coming up with these critiques that we were going overboard applying psychological and medical labels to our clients. And I think they were right, I really do. And I was one of those who was very ready to hear those critiques. I have always been uneasy with the way that we have tended to treat everybody who comes in our doors as if they are so much more dysfunctional than the general population, and it isn't always true.

"So I was one of those who listened to those critiques and pushed for changing our language to some extent. We were trying to make the process more dignifying, to treat people more like adults in charge of their lives. But then you have a lot of people working in homeless services who were very happy to take advantage of that, you know. And in some ways I feel that we have moved toward a less helpful, less sympathetic message that we are giving our clients. So now what we are saying is you are in charge, get yourself together. Of course we are still struggling on, doing our best to get people the right services—it's not as if *that* has changed. But I see some of the staff, even caseworkers, using this new language *against* the clients, which is really the opposite from how we intended it. I am hearing a lot of talk where there is not much sympathy, not much of a spirit of helpfulness, I would say. And on the other hand there is all this 'Hey, it's all up to you—pull yourself together' kind of talk. And in so many cases, there is a long history of trauma, of abuse, of neglect, and I feel that we need to keep the door open, to make it clear that we understand that most of these people have been through worlds of pain, you know."

Sandrine's account shows how trying to shift institutional discourses is an unpredictable and risky business. By moving away from strongly medicalized language toward what they hoped were more neutral narratives about "skills," social workers like her had no intention whatsoever of creating yet more ammunition for moral judgment. Nevertheless, their strategy seems to have played into the hands of those among the staff who felt that homelessness was first and foremost a problem of moral weakness and bad behavior. But the problem was not only their colleagues' assumptions, but the superficial effects or the new terminology on business as usual in the shelter. The definition of skills brought together a strange grab bag, with more neutral tools such as resume writing rubbing up against motivational classes directed toward the reorientation of "attitude," "anger," and other faulty aspects of the homeless personality—what David called "this rah-rah, turn-your-head-around psychological stuff." The "clients" might now be "participants," but a personality makeover was still at the core of the package. Second, the language of skill acquisition was still understood within an overwhelmingly individualistic framework, with the men's own analysis of their skill gap usually contested as unproductive self-pity or just ignored, as we saw with Carlos and David. Third, the staff was not able to ground the new approach within the kind of systemic analysis (still less social justice practice) that might have shifted some of the burden of responsibility for change onto a changing economic or political system rather than the homeless individuals themselves. The "competitive society" remained a given. It was the homeless who had to change, one by one.

If, as Lyon-Callo and some of the San Francisco social workers argued, the more strictly medicalized focus on "diseases of the will," such as depression and addiction, were disempowering (and leading to overuse of medication), the increasing emphasis on classes or groups aimed at anger management and housing readiness had a more complex, double-edged effect. On the one hand these activities amplified the scope of medicalization. Moving beyond the usual view that the shelter population suffered disproportionately from problems of mental illness and substance abuse, the broad pop-medicalization rolled out with the "life skills" approach sent the message that the shelter clientele as a whole was composed of weak and faulty individuals in need of guidance.

Yet this was a diluted, hybrid form of sick-talk: the discourse on homelessness sweeping the shelters at the turn of the twenty-first century had a very different character from the careful, expert diagnostic work recommended by Baum and Burnes. Individuals working on budgeting or anger management, for example, experienced little reprieve from moral judgment. By telling the clients "You are in charge," as Sandrine suggests, the shelter lifted the reprieve offered by narrower, more expert-led forms of medicalization, and handed back responsibility to its clients, telling them that all that stood in their way was lack of willpower and control.

On every level of government, the 1990s saw the moral and disease discourses on poverty triumph over the systemic interpretations of the early 1980s. By supporting the evisceration of welfare entitlements in 1996, the "caring" liberal Democrats joined free-market Republicans in naturalizing the specific social and economic structure of the United States in the 1990s. Jobs and housing became a given, part of a a nonnegotiable "competitive society" to which poor people must adapt. They were not the government's responsibility.

Given these prevailing winds, the failure of the third phase of the 1994 Continuum of Care was doomed before it was printed. While focusing on the homeless as a separate and more needy category than other poor Americans, the administration was turning its back on broader antipoverty and housing programs that would alleviate most street homelessness, restricting money and attention to what was only a small and disproportionately multiproblem subgroup of the poor. Indeed, the Clinton administration that produced HUD's master plan to combat homelessness was at the same time dismantling the most important antipoverty program of the twentieth century, Aid to Families with Dependent Children, and doing almost nothing to reduce the rising tide of incarceration. Expenditures on tax relief for homeowners—in 1978 less than half the amount spent on HUD—now outstripped HUD's budget more than five times over.[23]

This combination of entitlement rollback for the many and authoritarian pop-medicalization for the few represented a major triumph of the disease discourse on poverty over systemic interpretations. As chapter 7 shows, the simultaneous narrowing and pathologizing of poverty rose to a new level in the 2000s, as homeless funding became more tightly funneled toward the clients most immediately problematic for city leaders—those classified as the chronic homeless.

But what were the effects on the ground? First and foremost, the San Francisco shelters did not succeed in creating a strong, consistent therapeutic culture. Even if "clients" were predisposed toward reconstructing their worldview in the direction of sick-talk, the case managers, mental health workers, drug counselors, and other social workers could not provide an environment that would support such a shift. The difficult practice of renewal through self-analysis and personal reformation was constantly threatened by the strong peer culture of distrust and judgment brought in from the street and the criminal justice system only reinforced the hostile behavior of many of the shelter staff.

Second, caseworkers ultimately did not have much to offer for those without serious health problems and were therefore unable to create a strong reward structure for the uptake of therapeutic identities. Even the social workers' attempts to mitigate the stigma of pop medicalization with a more agentic, "dignifying" lexicon only seemed to give more room for the institutional discourse to be recolonized by a powerful mixture of old-fashioned sin-talk and the neoliberal notions of self-management now sweeping American poverty management.

If you accept my contention that the primary discourses on homelessness set up profoundly different notions of human nature and agency, it seems logical that the shelters' uneasy combination of sick-talk and sin-talk produces highly contradictory messages about the potential role of homeless people themselves. Carlos argued this very point as he thought back over his failed "action plan." "They say you gotta be more responsible, more taking charge of your life, all that." Carlos raised his eyebrows. "OK, then why are they making you feel even more *out* of control, like you need help on this and that, like you are not capable of working. Then they get mad at you when you try to make it on your own." This astute commentary on the contradictions between pop-medicalization and personal responsibility suggests that the clumsy confusion of sick-talk and sin-talk in the sheltering industry may have the consequence of making neither particularly persuasive.

A Little Room for Myself

I GOT TO KNOW DECLAN early in my recycling career. I was sitting in a Chinatown alleyway with a meager load of bottles and cans, writing in my notebook, when Declan pushed his cart into the same alleyway. I saw a slight, balding man with a forward lean.

"Just coming through. I'll leave you the findings," he muttered to me, pushing on fast.

"That's OK, take what you can. I'm taking a break."

Declan nodded. "That's right. You can't be getting frantic about this job."

"Do you want to join me? I have a couple of cans of soda."

"Soda! That's a new one. All right, then," he said hesitantly, sitting down nearby.

After a couple of minutes he asked me what I was writing. "I'm doing a study of recycling," I answered.

"So you are doing this for fun?" he said in a neutral tone.

I remarked on his Irish accent and told him that for a while I had made a living playing Irish music in pubs and factory clubs. Declan seemed pleased by the connection and agreed that we should go recycling together on Friday morning, a couple of days later.

These kinds of rendezvous were often unsuccessful, so I was pleased when Declan showed up outside Vesuvio's Friday morning. We worked well together. He was not really nimble enough to vault over into the big dumpsters, so I clambered in and threw bottles and cans out to him. After gathering a substantial load over a three-hour period, we pushed it across the South of Market neighborhood to the recycling company on Rhode Island. Though the cart was piled high and wide, we were able to move fast. Declan pulled strenuously from the front with a "rope" made from two pairs of jeans and I did my best to stabilize the cart from the back.

After the last breathless push up the slope between the freeway and Rhode Island we swung into the great dim expanse of the plant's weighing area. It reeked with stale beer, and more distant clanks and engine sounds from inside the processing zone mixed with the sharper crash of bottles thrown into sorting bins by several other homeless recyclers, already in the process of separating and weighing their loads. Declan seemed wary of contact, keeping his eyes down. I wasn't sure if this was just shyness or fear, but I acquiesced, and we started our sorting in silence and a few yards away from the others.

As we were collecting our sixteen dollars, Desmond and Bill swung their carts into the plant. Bill was a generous middle-aged white man who had befriended me during my first days of fieldwork, teaching me the basic tricks of the trade. African American Desmond, a former musician, was another man I trusted deeply. My feeling was that Declan was isolated and that it would be good for him to get to know these two. Declan stiffened but seemed to be reassured when Bill and I hugged each other vigorously. Though Declan's tentative, polite manner was unusual on the street, Desmond treated him kindly, explaining the intricacies of the rates for different kinds of plastic. "OK, yes, that's good to know," Declan muttered, looking rather dazed.

After getting our money we waited around for Bill and Desmond and shared a couple of cigarettes outside the plant. Bill continued Declan's recycling education, telling him his own tips for how to collect and sell wine bottles without raising the wrath of the weighers. (At that time wine bottles were not covered by the California Bottle Bill's redemption scheme.) Declan paid careful attention, but his look of underlying bewilderment persisted. He seemed to be still in the "shock stage," as some in the recycling scene called it, not quite able to understand or accept that he was really homeless.

Sitting in Washington Park after some more hours of work, Declan and I watched a couple of older Chinese ladies doing their evening tai chi exercises. I didn't want to push him yet on how he had become homeless, so I turned the conversation toward our migrations to America.

"So why did you come?" I asked him.

"It's hard to say now. I can't really remember what I was thinking. . . . I do remember buying the ticket because I was so pleased with myself that I saved the money, because it was expensive. . . . I think really it was less about coming to America and more about leaving Ireland. America was just . . . this place where everyone was supposed to do so well. But I wasn't so sure that I would do well. I never seemed to be cut out for success, but you can't help hoping."

Declan smiled ruefully, avoiding eye contact.

"Why did you want to leave Ireland?"

"That was clear enough. Ireland is awful strong on the family, you know. The family and the religion. And I, well, I had no luck with the first and no taste for the second. Bunch of hypocrites, if you ask me."

Later I found out that Declan was the illegitimate child of an absent and unmentioned mother. As a baby he had been reluctantly taken in by an aunt and uncle in a provincial town. Uncle James and Aunt Kathleen were "lace-curtain Irish," respectable, inhibited folks who never acknowledged Declan as their nephew in front of strangers. If necessary they would tell some vague story about how he was an orphan from Aunt Kathleen's village on the coast. In the evening, Kathleen would serve him food after the other children, and when I got to know him, he was still bitter about the rarity of meat on his plate as a child.

Like many others circulating in and out of homelessness, Declan had grown from unwanted child to isolated adult. At sixteen he found work washing dishes in a hotel: "I was doing all right with my work; that wasn't so much the problem. But, of course, I wasn't making enough for to rent my own place yet. I was lodging with another family for a few shillings a week, but they were a damn miserable lot. The place was so damp; my bed was always soaking.

"So I went to my other uncle, my Uncle Patrick, in the hopes that maybe I could stay with them for while. I was willing to pay my way, of course. He took me down to the pub and was quite friendly, but he said his wife wouldn't want it. They were always ashamed of my existence, all of them. I was a stain on the family."

"Were you the only one?"

"I don't know. They would never speak of my mother, so I don't know what happened to her, but fasure it was no good."

Thirty-five years after immigrating to America, Declan still led a solitary, unloved existence. Although he could talk up a storm when the mood took him, most of the time he seemed deeply depressed, his shoulders bowed and his forehead permanently drawn into a large, central crease.[1]

My impressions turned out to be accurate: Declan had been homeless for only a few weeks. For the previous eleven years, he had been living in a Chinatown SRO hotel, cleaning the hallways and bathrooms in exchange for rent. It was a tiny nest, but he had made it quite cozy, even growing flowers and tomatoes on the roof. In 1994 the hotel manager had decided that Declan needed to come up with some money to supplement his work-for-rent trade.

"I mean, it was outrageous. This fella was already working me thirty hours a week for rent alone, so I was having to work another janitor position for my other living expenses. . . . They put the rent up to $500 a month, and they were getting people in who had that kind of money."

"How much were you making?"

"Ooh, I was making $8.25 an hour at my outside job, but the hours were not regular enough for me. I couldn't get my rent in on time, and they threatened me with eviction . . . like I walked in off the street last week. I didn't want to stay anymore. After that, I was too angry. I could not look the fella in the eye anymore. I wanted to punch him."

"Did you?"

"No. I'm not a violent man."

Far from it. Declan said that he had not had a fight since he was a teenager, and it was easy to believe. If anything, he had not enough fight in him, but seemed browbeaten into passivity by his harsh childhood and a life of lonely, menial labor.

He had accepted the prospect of temporary homelessness, moving some of his possessions into a storage locker and buying a twenty-year-old Corolla for somewhere to sleep. Another man living in a van suggested to him that he start recycling, as the chaos of car living was making it hard for him to keep regular hours with the day labor agencies.

As long as he had his car, where he could sleep or relax with the racing news, Declan was willing to push around a shopping cart without the shame that plagued most of the homeless men. "See," he told me, "you can tell that I'm not really homeless like some of these fellas, because I just have the bottles and cans in my shopping cart. There's no clothes in there. I'm not carrying broken-down pieces of junk. And I keep myself clean. Altogether there's not much reason for anyone to think I was sleeping out on the street."

During this period, Declan was parking overnight in an old industrial section of eastern So-Ma, now pocked with the upscale condominiums classified misleadingly as live-work "lofts." He chose this neighborhood because at that time many of the buildings were still warehouses and there was little competition for parking spaces. He would eat his breakfast on a picnic table in the small park and brush his teeth at the drinking fountain. But even though parking places were still plentiful, new parking restrictions had followed on the heels of the upscale urban pioneers. Frequently posted signs now announced, "NO VEHICLE LIVING 10 PM–6 AM."

"I want to stay in the neighborhood because there's plenty of parking and it feels safe-like. You've got good streetlights, not too many bad characters around. But this law, it's a right pain in the ass. You have to somehow make it look like you're not in the car. Like it's not hard enough fitting your whole life into a little car, you have to even hide the evidence inside the damn car. It's easier if you have a van; you can cover up the windows. But with a car, you look suspicious if you do that. Tinted windows, that's what you need. But you don't see your Civics and Corollas with tinted windows."

Declan decided to get rid of his much-loved plants, which had been stashed along the rear window shelf. He also sold his collections of Father Brown detective novels and Dick Francis thrillers, making more room for basic necessities in the trunk. None of these concessions worked. After police officers woke him three nights in a row, demanding he move on, Declan moved south into Dogpatch, one of the last remaining corners moderately safe from either robbers or nighttime rousting by the police.

The neighborhood's odd mixture of families and loners, wage workers, recyclers, sidewalk peddlers, and thieves provided solitary Declan with a more lively social circle than he had known for years. His prejudice against other homeless people disappeared, and he started talking about some as "neighbors." He befriended one person in particular: a big, shy redhead called Mitch with a lumberjack look to him.

A couple of months later, the Corolla's clutch finally gave out completely, and he had to push it from one side of the road to the other to avoid parking tickets. Mitch came to the rescue, helping Declan acquire and install a replacement clutch, and in return Declan let him use the car to visit his terminally ill father in Antelope Valley. Declan went along, as he had nowhere else to stay.

I did not see Declan for some weeks after this trip. But one morning about eleven o'clock he called me in a state of panic.

"Look, I'm sorry, but I need your help. I'm having a terrible time with my car."

"What's the matter?"

"The bastards towed it this morning. I didn't know what time it was because my watch was stopped."

Declan asked me if I could come down and help him deal with the towing company. I could not afford the $130 he needed to get the car out of the pound, but he thought it would help if I came down. "Dressed nicely like?" he hinted. He was desperate to get his things out of the car. "I can't see why they would mind, you know. They will still have the car and all." Declan's shallow breathing and sweaty fidgeting gave the lie to his optimistic words.

When we got to the towing company, Declan told them respectfully that he did not have enough money for the fine right now, but could he please get his things out of the car.

At first the person at the desk was merely officious in his refusals. I had been trying to reach someone at the Coalition on Homelessness to find out what rights Declan had in this situation. Unfortunately, there was no one around at that moment that knew. There wasn't much that we could do. I tried to appeal to the desk clerk's sympathy.

"It's like being evicted from your house and not being able to get any of your things out," I pleaded.

"That's not our problem," he snapped, hardened no doubt by years of dealing with enraged car owners. "I can't make exceptions to the rule."

Declan asked to speak to a manager, and the clerk pointedly ignored him.

"If you can't handle the responsibility of a car, you shouldn't have one," he told us.

This poverty-as-irresponsibility stab worked wonders. Declan stormed out, his fists clenched. Outside on the street the cars roared by, forcing us to shout.

I could tell Declan had given up on me.

"It's all right, it's all right," he kept repeating. "I'll figure something out. You haven't the time for all this."

I was embarrassing to be so useless, but I had no more authority than Declan did. He wouldn't speak his fear, so I could not easily console him. I offered him a couch for the night. He looked doubtful, but said he would call later, and we parted quickly.

I was not surprised that Declan did not call me that night, but when I had not heard from him in a week I started to worry. I went over to Dogpatch and managed to find Mitch. He also had no information and was equally concerned. I went home and reluctantly picked up the phone to call the usual trinity: the jail, the hospital, and the morgue. Suicide was my biggest worry, but pushing morbid thoughts aside, I called the jail first. To my surprise I was told that he was indeed there. I could not find out the charge, but assumed it was minor, for Declan had never been in trouble with the law.

When I went down to see him, his face looked gray and creased under the fluorescent lights of the jail.

"What did you do, Declan?"

"I don't know what I was thinking. I was wandering round the place for a few hours and, you know, I could see my car. I didn't know what to do. So when it got to about three in the morning I tried to jump the fence and get my papers out of the car. I couldn't see anyone around."

"But you got caught?"

"Mmmm." Declan looked at the table. We sat in silence.

"Are you OK?"

"You can't relax. There's all this fighting and bully-boy tactics like."

I gave Declan some money for cigarettes and phone calls. I was going away for a few weeks, and I was sure that within a week or two he would be out. I could not imagine that a first offender would be given any serious jail time for trying to get his car back. Many of the recyclers cycled regularly in and out of jail for minor offenses, rarely staying more than a few weeks.

What Declan had not told me was that he had got into a scuffle with the security guard who had caught him. He was charged and convicted of both attempted burglary and assault.

I was out of town when his case came up, but I gleaned that Declan's clean record may have stood for something, but his lack of employment and legitimate housing had sent another, more important message. The judge seemed convinced by the security guard's tale of being attacked by a fearsome, demented intruder, though Declan assured me that this was "damn lies." ("Crikey. You never heard such a tall story. And him a big strapping lad, twice my size.")

Declan's courtroom manner would not have helped. When dealing with authority he vacillated between self-deprecation and resentment. Like so many of the always poor, he could not display the righteous indignation of a man who believes he deserves better.

Declan did nine months in the county jail, coming out noticeably grayer and even more stooped, his manner more meek and distracted than ever. He stumbled hopelessly into the shelter system with nothing beyond the clothes on his back.

Mr. Haven,[2] his case manager at MSC South, helped him get some clothes, but although Declan picked up occasional days of work at a day labor agency, it seemed impossible that he would ever get together enough money to move back inside. It was now impossible to find even the meanest studio for less than $800 a month and inconceivable that he could pay such sums without a regular job.

As a client with neither a fiery attitude nor a serious substance abuse problem, Declan had won the sympathy of Mr. Haven, who eventually helped him to find a semipermanent bed in a Marin County shelter in exchange for kitchen work. This was a passable compromise for a while, but the last time I spoke to him, Declan was chafing over the lack of privacy.

"I'm asking myself, is it possible I'll ever have my own room again?" he told me as we sat alone in the shelter's grim cafeteria. "I'm dreaming about it constantly like. That's all I want, just a little room for myself, away from people coughing, people snoring, people fighting. I've never been much of a sociable fella, you know, and I find the noise, the chatter, the quarrelling, and complaining makes me want to shout out BE BLOODY QUIET! ... I'm not sure how long I can do this job without going loony."

"What do you think you will do?" I asked.

"What can you do? Mr. Haven says if I was American he could maybe get me some help to go home. But even if they could send me to Ireland, I don't know where I would go."

Declan looked up at me, shaking his head, then turned away as tears came into his eyes. "I'm finished, if you ask me. I'm finished."

> Home is the place where, when you have to go there,
> They have to take you in.

Thus ruminates the sympathetic farmer's wife in Frost's poignant poem about the death of the old tramp Silas. There was no such place for Declan. He would have to make do with today's poorhouse.[3]

SEVEN

The Old Runaround: Class Cleansing in San Francisco

In many ways, the migratory worker is a man without a country.
By the very nature of his occupation he is deprived of the ballot,
and liable when not at work to arrest for vagrancy and trespassing.
—NELS ANDERSON, *The Hobo*

Sometimes, you wonder if we're really Americans....Whether
we're a citizen or not.... It defines homelessness in the dictionary—
they define it as without a country. You know, you go in the bar, in
the coffee shop, they don't want your money. You go in the park,
they move you on. You try to sit down on the stoop, somebody
calls the cops. It doesn't stop.
—GEORGE, homeless in San Francisco, 1998

THE PURITANS CONCEIVED OF AMERICA AS A PLACE WHERE
they could build a pure community, a "city on a hill" that
would serve as a beacon, beckoning the righteous and leaving
behind the worldliness, miseries, and corruption of old Europe.[1] As
real American cities grew larger, though, they took on a much more
ambivalent role in the national imaginary. Great powerhouses of production and consumption, the nineteenth-century cities drew vast
and diverse armies of workers from across the world as well as the
rural hinterland. City streets became increasingly dense and heterogeneous, places where Jew and Gentile, seamstress and millionaire
shared the same public spaces.

On the one hand, educated Americans were proud of the architectural majesty and productive power of their great metropoli. At the same time they distanced themselves from urban culture, counterposing a nostalgic image of the small town "Main Street" to a wicked city characterized by runaway greed, polarities of wealth, glamour and vice, and the unhygienic mixing of peoples and races.[2] Jefferson's agrarian romanticism found its complement in the literary antiurbanism of Emerson and Thoreau and later in the influential work of sociologist Louis Wirth, who feared that the density and heterogeneity of large cities eroded community, kinship, and any shared moral compass.

Many city dwellers themselves, however, had higher hopes for urban life. As the immoderate exploitation of the Gilded Age fed desires for both reform and revolution, increasingly assertive working classes and their allies started to pressure the city fathers to counteract the human costs of intensive exploitation. Powered by the wealth and technology of the industrial revolution, cities became producers of public goods on a grand scale—with public transportation, libraries, subsidized housing, welfare services, and eventually affordable institutions of higher education. As Neil Smith puts it, the Keynesian city of the 1930s and 1940s was a "combined hiring hall and welfare hall," doubly a magnet for Americans down on their luck.[3]

With the suburbanization of the postwar years, the American downtown started to lose its position as the hub of leisure and consumption. The fetishized instruments of domestic utopia—the car, the TV, and the mechanized kitchen—reoriented leisure and consumption around private, low-density dwelling.[4] Older city neighborhoods lost much of their earlier population and eventually most of their businesses. Among those left behind were many African Americans, blocked from leaving the cities by both poverty and racist housing covenants. Instead, their numbers grew rapidly as southerners continued to migrate into the northern and western cities. City leaders supported their white constituents' efforts to avoid integration, trying to contain their overcrowded ghettos by building concentrations of public housing that all too quickly became vertical slums.

The most significant postwar attempt to mitigate the increasing poverty of the central cities arrived as the mass civil disobedience of the civil rights movement spurred on the Equal Opportunity Act of

1964.[5] But the War on Poverty provided too little too late. It was too late to re-create the New Deal, let alone the Eisenhower boom years, for African Americans — and the piecemeal programs initiated by the poverty warriors of the 1960s collapsed into the fiscal and political crisis generated by the Vietnam War.[6] By the time of the great manufacturing decline of the 1970s, the stage was set for urban crisis. Most of the prosperous members of the white middle and working classes, and many of their former workplaces, had already left the American central cities, the vital mosaic of class, race, and ethnicity of the early twentieth century replaced by a largely depressed terrain sharply segregated between aging white ethnics, growing immigrant enclaves, and African American ghetto tracts now experiencing their own middle-class exodus to the suburbs.

At this point, the strong binaries of American sin-talk became again starkly spatialized within the urban form. Where the European medieval town and the early New England theocracies had used the city wall to exclude the undeserving poor, the American urban crisis of the 1970s segregated the poor in an inside-out or doughnut fashion, corralling them *inside* the limits of the old city. Always under suspicion for their concentrations of racial minorities and fresh immigrants, central cities now became more than ever the primary marker for the social problems of the nation.[7]

As the primary engines of the nation's economy, American cities during the New Deal era had been subsidized at the federal level in a multiplicity of ways. But the de-industrialized cities of the 1970s and 1980s no longer represented the nation's economic engines, and the leaner, meaner federal government of the post-Keynesian era followed Gerald Ford's lead, dismantling the mechanisms of national redistribution, progressively shedding commitments to public housing, preventative health, and the myriad services previously subsidized through block grants.[8]

Urban politicians have been left with fewer and fewer funds with which to maintain their increasingly impoverished residents. Still overwhelmingly Democratic in their affiliation, they have been forced to recognize that they no longer have the power to implement the broad tax-and-spend policies used to mitigate social suffering and disorder in previous decades. Slowly but surely the leaders of former Keynesian strongholds have turned, whether reluctantly or eagerly, to forms of business-led regeneration that entail no significant commitment to social reproduction. The great masses of manual workers that propelled industrial capitalism are largely irrelevant to the real estate developers, financiers, and retailers that are the primary business constituency for the post-Keynesian city. Instead, local politicians have been faced with the paradoxical demand that they deliver a safe and aesthetically appealing environment for shoppers and white-collar workers, despite the disintegration of former institutions of class compromise.

The cornerstone of post-Keynesian urban policy has been gentrification, the remaking of urban space to pull affluent suburbanites back into the city, both as residents and as visitors. Neil Smith's invaluable work on the subject shows the commonalities between older forms of bottom-up gentrification and the more interventionist top-down redevelopment that has proliferated since the 1990s.[9] Whereas bottom-up gentrification encourages middle-class incomers to turn around dilapidated housing stock, top-down gentrifying developments use public/private partnerships to remake urban spaces on a large scale. At the heart of both strategies is the project to produce a physical environment that attracts and calms people uncomfortable with gritty city life. To achieve this, city governments have developed or revived an arsenal of techniques to preserve the value of redeveloped and gentrified spaces by excluding the disorderly poor.

Nowhere is the importance of gentrification more evident than in the radical changes in the practice and philosophy of urban policing over the last two decades. In chapter 2 we saw how police departments and local officials eagerly took up the "broken windows" discourse of Wilson and Kelling across the United States during the late 1980s and 1990s. In thousands of municipal discussions on the problem of homelessness, "broken windows" became the beachhead for the return of a firmly moral discourse on poverty, a narrative with which local politicians and officials could shift the terms of social policy away from the language of rights and equal opportunity bequeathed by the Great Society. The problem of homelessness became the problems created by the homeless, and in particular, the threat to safe and clean urban spaces.

At the core of Wilson and Kelling's argument was the claim that overly permissive environments are more important in creating disorder and crime than "inexorable social forces," as they put it: Vandalism, panhandling, graffiti writing, and "loitering" create an opening for more serious crime.[10] The postwar focus on car-based policing and more serious crimes, said Wilson and Kelling, had left neighborhoods without protection from low-level disorderly conduct that propelled them into criminality and chaos. This retreat from the attempt to create public order had been caused in part, they said, by the activities of the ACLU and other legal defense organizations, whose focus on individual rights blocked the kind of day-to-day policing most effective against nuisance offenses. Instead of dashing around in cars solving high-profile crimes, police officers needed to return to small-scale patrolling, backed by "the legal tools to remove undesirable persons from a neighborhood when informal efforts to preserve order in the streets have failed."[11]

The first cities to mobilize large-scale campaigns against panhandling and sleeping in public space were places where economic inequality is strongly marked by racial difference. The leaders of Atlanta and Orlando, most notably, moved swiftly and firmly against their majority-black homeless populations.[12] But many others swiftly followed them. Small towns that had always been hostile to the vagrant poor revived municipal articles forbidding loitering or sitting on the sidewalk that had not been used since the Great Depression, as well as more contemporary innovations such as banning shopping carts outside of supermarket property and employing undercover cops to catch people panhandling.[13]

Most of the new and revived "quality of life" laws focused on out-of-place home practices,[14] expressing on the principle that public space should be a complement to private space, not a substitute for it. Commercial streets should be used for shopping, not conversations, sleeping, or sitting; public transportation for traveling, not for basic shelter; and parks for playing sports and walking, not sleeping or drinking.[15] The wide mobilization of these codes played an important role in bringing the politics of urban space in line with what Peck and Tickell have called "rollback neoliberalism"—a comprehensive project to destroy and de-legitimize forms of social welfare and political mobilization developed during the Keynesian era.[16] For example, in many cities, the "broken windows" approach drew strong support from new community groups that focused almost entirely on crime. These organizations abandoned the cross-class conceptions of neighborhood articulated by many neighborhood movements of the 1960s and 1970s, redefining community as a collection of stakeholders — merchants and property owners. The city was to be made safe for gentrification.

There were clear continuities between the kinds of "community" sought by the new community organizations of the 1980s and 1990s and the suburban impulse of the postwar period, when vast numbers of whites had left the old heterogeneous, unpredictable city neighborhoods for the glories of clean lawns and the PTA. But now the suburban values of the gentrifiers were being applied back to the wicked city they had fled. While many of the gentrifiers found the city more exciting than the suburbs, they could not help bringing deeply held assumptions about the desirability of clean, class-homogenous neighborhoods. Furthermore, their ability to negotiate a modus vivendi with unruly neighbors was probably hampered by the limited interactional style that Baumgartner characterizes as suburban "moral minimalism."[17]

Under pressure from frustrated merchants and residents disturbed by vagrants sleeping on their doorsteps, city halls across the country revisited the fortress tactics previously only employed by the very rich: architecture to repel invaders, surveillance cameras to watch them, subsidiary police to roust and remove them, sprinklers to drench them, and stadium lighting to prevent them from sleep.

The legislation directed at controlling the movement and behavior of homeless people was supported by many more subtle mechanisms of homeless control. One strategy used in many cities was the leasing of the sidewalks of commercial strips to merchants so that trespassing laws could be enforced. Common also were the destruction of encampments and the confiscation of property, the locking of public bathrooms, and the replacement of bus-stop benches with narrow "flip" or barrel-topped seats on which people could not slump, let alone sleep. Both public institutions and businesses started to use more aggressive lighting, surveillance cameras, spikes on windowsills, and locks on dumpsters to prevent scavenging. In the zones of the most intense battles over public space, anti-homeless tactics moved beyond the piecemeal, becoming a major design parameter for new buildings. Under these principles of "anti-homeless architecture," architects avoided creating discreet nooks and crannies outside of major sightlines and cut out the kinds of window ledges or boundary walls where homeless people might sit or sleep.[18]

The imperative to physically corral the disorderly homeless became another reason for political leaders to expand top-down gentrification: public-private partnerships with real estate developers to create new forms of pseudo-public or "urbanoid" space that would attract shoppers and tourists while keeping out the desperate and unwashed.[19] The first areas sacrificed to such projects were inevitably down-at-heel liminal zones that harbored remaining cheap hotels, further reducing the stock of affordable housing for the single poor.

Cracking Down in San Francisco

As resurrected sin-talk swept the country, it was not only taken up by historically conservative small towns and suburbs, but it also gained considerable strength within the citadels of North American urban liberalism: Manhattan and San Francisco, Seattle and Chicago. Precisely *because* residents of these cities had fought hard to maintain functional, high-density urbanism, they now have vital public spaces vulnerable to devaluation by the presence of homeless people.

San Francisco, a historical stronghold of the labor movement, civil rights activism, and other social movement activity, embodies this tension between valuable public space and progressive politics to a high degree, an important reason for the political centrality of its "homelessness problem" over the last twenty-five years. The city's wealth of Victorian housing stock, expanded by the enforcement of strict building codes after the 1906 earthquake, presents an extraordinarily beautiful built environment, further complementing its magnificent natural setting as a highland promontory colored by rapid sweeps of sun and fog. High residential density and limited off-street parking encourages mass pedestrianism, keeping the sidewalks lively and meaningful, a central sphere of daily life for most of its residents. Fed by a comprehensive and well-used public transportation system, downtown teems with office workers, tourists, and shoppers during the day, and the neighborhood commercial strips beckon with restaurants, all kinds of shops, and sidewalk cafes.

The city's cosmopolitan cachet has attracted cultural industries, financial services, and corporate headquarters, keeping the economy buoyant through the recessions of the last thirty years. Politicians, local businesses, residents, tourists, and hoteliers all recognize that the streets of the city themselves are a priceless commodity, one whose value must be maintained.

Yet the same streets that attract visitors from the world over are also wandered by thousands of homeless paupers. As the 1990s saw the city's rental market become one of the most expensive in the world, the *threshold* of homelessness dropped lower and lower. Top-down gentrification and the destruction of low-income housing progressed steadily over the last twenty years, wiping from the landscape scores of vital single-room-occupancy (SRO) hotels and cheap apartment buildings across the South of Market and North East Mission neighborhoods in favor of large-scale development projects: the Yerba Buena Center, the new SF Museum of Modern Art, the Sony Metreon Mall, and block after block of new "live-work" lofts.[20] For many poor San Franciscans, the extraordinary strain of trying to maintain housing was compounded by an absence of strong social ties. As a great destination of migrants, cultural, economic, and political, more than half of the city's population were born elsewhere and had no local family members to help them in times of trouble.[21] Every year thousands lost tenure in cheap apartments or hotels. Many left, but others resorted to living in cars and vans, homeless shelters, and encampments under freeway bridges.[22]

San Francisco represents a particularly important case of the criminalization of homelessness. In this progressive stronghold, sin-talk of the "broken windows" proponents had to compete with strong opposing systemic and therapeutic arguments articulated by formidable voices among both service providers and activists. Yet even in liberal San Francisco, the construction of homelessness as bad behavior became powerful enough to propel large-scale police campaigns against nuisance offenses, repeated attempts to abolish General Assistance, and numerous other strategies aimed at pushing the "visible poor" back into zones of invisibility.

The following story of how San Francisco came to normalize clearance, incorporating it into a coherent discourse of authoritarian medicalization, speaks strongly to the contemporary politics of homelessness across the United States as a whole. If it could happen there, it could happen anywhere.

In San Francisco, like most major American cities, street homelessness returned to a significant level in the early 1980s, coinciding with rising rents and widespread gentrification. First a handful, then hundreds of ragged, desperate people appeared in the downtown area, panhandling for change or just sitting on steps and benches for hours at a time, backpacks and bedrolls around them. At night those walking the downtown sidewalks became used to the sight of homeless people stretched out on sidewalks or huddled in doorways and stairwells. As numbers steadily increased through the middle-1980s, discomfort rose. Merchants started to grumble and sympathetic citizens started to organize informal soup kitchens and temporary shelters, many of them in the halls of churches and synagogues.

The consensus at the time was that this was only a temporary problem created by the economic slump of the early 1980s. The mayor, Dianne Feinstein, responded by subsidizing rooms in single-room-occupancy hotels run by slum landlords, a precedent that would be repeated by subsequent administrations. The "hotel voucher" strategy helped some off the street, but the problem continued to grow rapidly in scale. The city was already getting itself a name for having one of the worst homelessness problems in the nation. Hundreds of encampments proliferated along prominent arteries—Market Street, Van Ness, and Folsom—and concentrated under freeway bridges and outside construction sites, while panhandlers and street entertainers worked every block in the most heavily frequented tourist areas. The hotelier and merchant associations were alarmed and the city's population as a whole disquieted by these developments.

Feinstein's successor, Art Agnos (1988–1991), took the problem much more seriously, throwing himself into drafting a more comprehensive policy. A former social worker, Agnos attributed the increasing rate of homelessness to shrinking affordable housing, together with insufficient funding for mental health and substance abuse services.

As an old-school Keynesian liberal, Agnos struggled to maintain credibility within a city infected by the new neoliberal zeitgeist. From the beginning his administration was dogged by pressure from residents and merchants in the Haight-Ashbury district, a neighborhood in the process of gentrification that was heavily affected by the return of large-scale homelessness in the city. Agnos's political opponents

Sleeping under cover on Market Street.

demanded immediate solutions to street homelessness, arguing that it was useless to talk about the macrosocial conditions that had led to the problem. "Everyone wants to talk about ancient history, federal history, Republicans . . . and nobody wants to talk about people fifteen feet away. I don't want to hear about what happened a decade ago. I want to know what you're going to do tomorrow," charged Supervisor Richard Hongisto.[23]

Agnos's election roughly coincided with the formation of the San Francisco Coalition on Homelessness, an activist organization led by homeless and formerly homeless people that rapidly rose to prominence within the radical flank of the national advocacy movement. The Coalition was quick to support a group of homeless people evicted from their camp in the Civic Center Plaza outside City Hall in 1989 and organized a "Camp Agnos" vigil there for several months, to much public attention and outrage. When the protests of downtown merchants and hoteliers became too intense, Agnos would order a sweep, but the encampment protest continued throughout his administration, at times mobilizing several hundred homeless people.

Agnos responded to the heat from both homeless activists and business people with "Beyond Shelter," a report that proposed the construction of two multiservice centers. Prefiguring the federal Continuum of Care model, these institutions would centralize homeless management, combining shelter with counseling for substance abuse and mental health problems, and ultimately serving as a conduit into affordable housing and employment training. The multiservice centers were indeed created, and Agnos's vision was given national recognition. He did not, however, keep his leadership long enough to supervise the new system. Camp Agnos had infuriated more conservative constituents, who started to mobilize toward a radical change in policy.

The Battle for Downtown

In the heated mayoral election of 1991, the politics of homelessness took center stage. Agnos was challenged by his former police chief, Frank Jordan. Jordan promised to crack down on the homeless population, rejecting Agnos's combination of structured *system-talk* and therapeutic *sick-talk* in favor of a clearance strategy more in line with the contemporary "broken windows" philosophy and punitive sin-talk. Jordan proposed new restrictions on panhandling and the creation of mandatory mental health and detoxification services. More controversially, he raised the possibility of a "work farm" at the San Bruno jail, to which noncompliant homeless people could be sent.[24] Jordan's anti-homeless platform probably won him the mayoralty; several opinion polls named homelessness as the most important issue of the election.

Jordan's administration, with its aggressive, full-frontal attack on social-democratic notions of citizenship and entitlement, and its determination to wrestle back public space from the poor, epitomized the "revanchist city" delineated by Neil Smith.[25] The mayor's office ordered the police department to adopt the zero-tolerance clearance strategies pioneered in Giuliani's New York, a policy turn explicitly framed within the broader imperative to promote both bottom-up gentrification of the neighborhoods and economic growth through top-down redevelopment.[26]

Jordan immediately moved to introduce "broken windows" policing, reviving various archaic nuisance laws and sponsoring new legislation. With financial support from downtown business interests, he introduced a new ballot initiative against "aggressive panhandling," which passed with a 55 percent majority. The following year the new policies were consolidated into a Quality of Life Enforcement Program, better known as the Matrix Program. Matrix instituted a number of violations subject to citation or arrest, all of them aimed at curbing the behavior and presence of homeless people downtown. The primary offenses cited were trespassing, setting up lodgings, blocking the sidewalk, drinking from open containers, aggressive panhandling, and urinating outdoors. Sleeping in doorways now warranted a ticket for trespassing, while the "setting up lodgings" prohibition kept people from making shanties with shopping carts and tarpaulins or blankets. The average ticket was $76, increasing to more than $180 for offenses deemed more serious. Most homeless people were unable to pay the fines, and many who had not previously been in trouble with the law came to have outstanding warrants.

Homeless advocates met the persistent stream of quality-of-life propositions with fierce countercampaigns. The Coalition's efforts were critical to the narrow defeat of a 1994 proposition that would have made it illegal to sit on downtown sidewalks. Its Civil Rights Working Group challenged many of the practices of Matrix in the courts, from the confiscation of shopping carts with personal possessions to the prohibition against bringing bedding into the parks. During this time advocates also won several less well-reported victories, substantially improving conditions for the homeless population: the right to earn small sums to supplement low-level welfare benefits, an advocacy system for the shelters, and improved rights for workfare workers.

Spearheading San Francisco's exceptionally strong lobby of system-talkers were the Coalition on Homelessness; Religious Witness with Homeless People, led by the indefatigable Sister Bernie Galvin; and the Tenderloin Housing Clinic. Without the unusual political makeup of the city, this small group would have had scant success, but their efforts pulled in a broad network of liberal and radical sympathizers inside and outside city government, people schooled in ways of seeing developed within the hobo tradition, the labor movement, the Beats, the civil rights movement, gay rights, and the many other social and cultural movements that have pulsed through the city over the years. The cause won even more legitimacy through the participation of several competent, even brilliant individuals from the city's homeless and formerly homeless population.

One of the Coalition's most important victories was maintaining the city's continued provision of General Assistance payments. This took on a dual significance, as both crucial assistance to homeless people and symbolic centerpiece of a rights-based approach to homelessness. While other cities across the country were abolishing or vastly reducing cash transfers to single adults, the Coalition and its allies foiled a multitude of similar attempts, either defeating them or fighting tenacious rearguard actions in the courts that prevented their implementation. In 1993, they successfully fought the revival of Mayor Feinstein's Hotline Program, which would have limited homeless GA recipients to hotel vouchers instead of cash. Next, they managed to block the implementation of 1994's Proposition N, which mandated deducting $280 for rent out of the GA recipients' monthly check of $345, as well as the mayor's office's 1996 attempt to circumvent the proposition process with a Mandatory Direct Rent Payment Program.

Under constant fire for its aggressive clearance policies, the Jordan administration retreated from the unashamed sin-talk of the election campaign, now claiming that Matrix represented not clearance alone but a combination of policing and social work, punishment and treatment. They hired seven extra outreach workers, and the police officers assigned to warn or ticket homeless quality-of-life offenders were also authorized to give out vouchers for shelter beds. Advocates complained that this represented little more than musical chairs, as those with Matrix vouchers then took precedence over others standing in line. The Coalition, together with other activists and advocates, succeeded in 1994 in persuading the city's board of supervisors to pass a resolution demanding an end to the program.[27] Mayor Jordan refused to close down the program, instead extending it from downtown to Golden Gate Park,[28] but his opponents had succeeded in discrediting Matrix in the eyes of many city residents, and Jordan's image was now tainted with inhumanity.

Anger and despair on Illinois Street mural, Dogpatch.

The much-ridiculed social welfare element of Matrix was the first attempt to bring together strategies of clearance and treatment vis-à-vis the homeless population, an approach that would be progressively refined over the next ten years. Even this first form represented an important step toward authoritarian medicalization, making the police the arbiters of the fine line between sickness and criminality. For example, when officers in the special Matrix vans came across a homeless person behaving aggressively or strangely, they were authorized to do spot psychological assessments and to forcibly bring people judged to be mentally ill to the hospital.

In practice, the clearance strategy had far more effect on homeless people's lives than the social welfare elements. In the first two years of the program, police gave out 22,000 citations to the thousands of homeless people frequenting the downtown area. Most of the tickets remained unpaid, eventually turning into bench warrants. During this same period, the outreach workers recorded 9,000 encounters with homeless people, but had little power to provide more than a conduit to the limited set of services already available. Generally they simply gave out information about available mental health and substance abuse programs. The most practical service they performed was doling out the aforementioned vouchers and, sometimes for the lucky few, arranging one week's stay at one of the city's dilapidated single-room-occupancy hotels.[29]

Willie Brown and the Institutionalization of Homeless Clearances

The modification of Jordan's policy and rhetoric with the outreach elements of Matrix did not save him from a fatal backlash from the substantial sector of the electorate that was still broadly sympathetic to the homeless. Homeless policy was again a key issue in the 1995 election, with more than 30 percent of those polled by the *San Francisco Chronicle* ranking homelessness as the most pressing problem in the city. Jordan defended what he called his "compassionate but realistic" policies, while his challengers attacked Matrix's focus on quality-of-life crimes. Willie Brown, the wily former state speaker who was to win the election, took advantage of the unpopularity of Matrix, promising that "in my administration, the police will spend their time going after crack dealers, thugs, aggressive panhandlers and other predators, rather than rounding up people whose only crime is being poor."[30]

Brown's new administration immediately announced the end of Matrix and started to work toward a homeless summit that would bring together service providers, academics, advocates, community groups, and merchant associations to create a comprehensive plan. Significantly, this summit never materialized. It became clear that there was not going to be sufficient common ground for any kind of consensus, and that the mayor's office would not countenance the large-scale affordable housing initiative demanded by the advocates. (The Coalition on Homelessness, calling for a "People's Budget Initiative," did push the board of supervisors into funding various more permanent solutions to homelessness in the late 1990s, but affordable housing programs could not keep up with the steady loss of SRO units and other cheap housing to gentrification projects.)

The cost of housing in San Francisco continued to soar through the late 1990s, as the San Francisco Bay Area became the least affordable metropolitan area in the United States. Faced with the difficulty of delivering on promises of affordable housing, the Brown administration maintained the nuisance policing emphasis of Matrix, minus the high-profile rhetoric. Tickets for quality-of-life violations — trespassing, camping, carrying open alcohol containers, and violating park curfews—continued to increase, averaging more than 20,000 a year in 1999 and 2000, and the city attorney set up a special unit charged with prosecuting these offenses.

"There is no room anywhere," complained Randy Shaw of the Tenderloin Housing Clinic, the organization that managed the hotel voucher program. "We used to find rooms for about 150 people a month, and now it's more like 35 or 40. There are no vacancies."[31]

At the time, San Francisco had about 1,400 shelter beds and between 5,000 to 8,000 homeless people. An informal *Chronicle* survey of shelters found an average of 250 people turned away from shelters each night because of lack of space, with the largest shelter reporting about 1,200 turn-aways each month.

The heated struggles over multiple homelessness-related ballot propositions in the 1990s had made it clear enough that the San Francisco population was polarized over the issue of homelessness. Jordan's defeat had showed the danger of taking an overly antagonistic position against the homeless population, yet merchants, hoteliers, and residents associations continued to vociferously demand the class cleansing of the city. While Willie Brown did not offer any radical departure from Matrix, he and other members of the centrist Democratic establishment had clearly realized that a "broken windows" policy toward the homeless should not be overemphasized in public.

As the rollback neoliberalism of the 1980s and early 1990s developed into a more mature "roll-out" phase, politicians at the national and state level moved on to an active program of building new structures of governance that forced local municipalities and public sector institutions at every level to permanently compete for capital investment. Put in the position of "responsibility without power," as Peck and Tickell put it,[32] mayors like Willie Brown and his successor, Gavin Newsom, bowed to the new model of entrepreneurial city management. In the absence of other forms of wealth creation, it became more important than ever to keep the city attractive for tourism, middle-class taxpayers, and corporate investment.

Half of the city's housing projects crumbled to the wrecker's ball of Clinton's Hope VI program, removing all obstacles to gentrification in the Mission, Fisherman's Wharf, and the Lower Haight and further depleting the city's African American population.[33] The supply of

Boom and bust.

affordable housing lurched to a new low. Advocates managed to anchor a handful of hotels by leasing them or converting them into nonprofits, but other independent hotels continued to disappear, redeveloped for tourism and condos or burned in suspicious circumstances.[34]

Fighting for Hearts and Minds in the Haight

Like urbanites in other cities, San Franciscans were divided over the new clearance policies. In the neighborhoods with the largest numbers of visibly homeless these divisions swelled into a bitter conflict during the 1990s. Competing groups of residents mobilized rival community organizations with profoundly divergent ideas about how to define and manage the problem. An old guard remained true to the more broadly defined "community" of urban liberalism, but the new

"stakeholder" organizations had far more resources at their disposal. A particularly prominent battle for the heart of a neighborhood occurred in Haight-Ashbury, where arguments about how to police the popular commercial strip of Haight Street gave concrete and immediate form to the furious debate over the definition of both community and homelessness.

"The Haight" had been home to large numbers of homeless people since the mid-1980s. Some of them were 1960s and 1970s dropouts and acid casualties who had lived entire adult lives in the neighborhood, gradually losing access to housing as rents rose. The others were young runaways drawn by its colorful history and reputation as the epicenter of the West Coast drug culture. Yet more were simply drawn by the neighborhood's excellent service agencies and the critical mass of other homeless people who provided some protection from police attention. Many of these people lived in the neighboring Golden Gate Park, the "gutterpunk" crowd openly claiming the part nearest to Haight Street and many more hiding out in more wooded patches where they could camp in relative privacy.

The long-standing Haight-Ashbury Neighborhood Council (HANC) consistently campaigned for more and better social services for homeless residents and supported the rights of homeless or street people to live in the area and sit or panhandle along the main thoroughfare. In opposition, several organizations emerged in the late 1980s and early 1990s: the Cole Valley Improvement Association, the Haight-Ashbury Improvement Association, and, most explicitly, Residents against Druggies. All these groups were strong supporters of Frank Jordan's Matrix Program and pressured the police to clear the street.

In opposition to HANC's calls for more services for the homeless, their opponents complained that services drew undesirables to the area and that willfully homeless "druggies" were destroying the community. The new groups made an invaluable connection with Ken Garcia, columnist for the *San Francisco Chronicle,* who took a leading role in giving voice to their complaints. The significant clout of this alliance became apparent in the fall of 1997, when Garcia wrote an impassioned article claiming that the homeless people living in the park included a number of dangerous parolees who represented a significant danger to the welfare of neighborhood residents.

Mayor Willie Brown held a news conference a few days later, where he and the director of the parks department charged the media with exaggeration and distortion. But Garcia and other reporters pushed back aggressively, claiming its homeless residents were destroying the park. A local TV station joined the investigation, showing lurid pictures of people using drugs in the park. At this point, Mayor Brown recognized his danger and made a lightning about-turn. He apologized to the media, the director of parks resigned, and he gave the police instructions to start a series of nightly sweeps into the farthest reaches of the park, handing out citations, confiscating property, and sending most of it to the city dump.

In retrospect, this incident marked a clear turning point for the politics of homelessness in San Francisco. The following year saw the narrow victory of Proposition I, which subjected the approval of new facilities dealing with the homeless to further community oversight, suggesting that the politics of NIMBY (not in my back yard) had finally won a crucial political edge.

The Coalition and its allies were far from defeated, but it now seemed Brown's de facto continuation of Matrix was perhaps less a political liability than he thought; maybe he had more to lose than win by appearing "soft on the homeless." (Here it may be worth noting that Willie Brown, previously Democratic speaker of the California Legislature, had a long record as a progressive, even radical politician. That he was now administering homeless clearances and other characteristically "neoliberal" policies is perhaps less evidence of his personal outlook than of the impossibility of returning to Keynesian city management.)

San Francisco's system-talk, and its political radicalism in general, was far from dead, as shown by the astoundingly successful write-in mayoral campaign of Tom Ammiano in 1999. But Ammiano's proposals to tax corporations to pay for broad-based services and affordable housing could not survive a gloves-off second-round election against the far richer and more institutionally powerful Brown. The balance of power had turned, and the class cleansing of San Francisco would continue.

The clearance of United Nations Plaza, one of the only open spaces in the downtown area, continued day and night. After several years of endlessly rousting homeless people from the twenty-four benches, city workers sawed the benches off at their bases in 2001. By then it was illegal to sit anywhere in the area. Signs indicated that the lawn was closed for maintenance and that it was prohibited to sit on the low wall around the grass or on the fountain blocks. (Non-homeless people sitting on the wall or fountain were rarely disturbed. I myself spent countless hours in the late 1990s sitting on the wall, writing field notes without so much as a questioning look from a police officer.)

Around the same time that the benches were removed, city officials debated a plan to remove the central fountain itself, at a cost of $1 million. The justification for this proposal was that the fountain, an ungainly composition of concrete slabs set at different angles, was being used by homeless people as both bath and latrine. The mayor himself suggested lighting the plaza so brightly that it would be impossible to sleep there.

Another innovation in 2001 was the so-called HOMETEAM unit (Helping Officers Maintain the Environment through Enforcement, Accountability, and Management). The intention was to direct more resources to "quality-of-life code violators," the common police euphemism for the street homeless. From the beginning, the unit focused on destroying "encampments" (anything from one person sleeping under a freeway bridge to fifteen people sleeping under tarpaulins in an alley), clearing 300 in their first two weeks.

Nowhere to Go

Away from the channels of elite discourse and policy, what were the effects of the homeless clearances on those at the bottom of the class ladder? Most deeply affected were those sleeping outside and the people who made their cash panhandling. The endless moving on, the tickets for encampment, the slashing of tents, and destruction of possessions all combined to further disturb and disorganize already difficult lives, provoking anger, despair, and bitter alienation.

During the most intensive sweeps it became a battle even to sit downtown, let alone lie down. Between 1995 and 1998, the ten of my street companions who spent most time downtown were collectively given more than eighty tickets. One of the perpetrators was Julius, the middle-aged African American who spent much of his time collecting bottles from garbage cans in the Theatre District on the edge of downtown. Julius was given seven tickets for lodging, camping in public, and trespassing. In the case of two of the camping tickets, he was sleeping in the doorways of shops or office buildings after hours, a violation of Police Code 25. (The police had successfully criminalized taking this kind of rudimentary shelter by encouraging business owners to post signs indicating that they did not permit after-hours trespassing.)

To avoid citations for creating a "structure," Julius usually slept with most of his things in the cart beside him, using only his sleeping bag and an old sweater for a pillow. He kept his ID and any cash in an inside pocket. The downside of his strategy was that the cart made it easy for police officers to confiscate his possessions, which had happened on several occasions.

A few days after one of these episodes, I met up with him in the Central Library, where he had gone to read the newspaper.

"I didn't get any sleep last Wednesday night, it was so damn cold," he said quietly, keeping an eye on the security guard. "I have to keep moving when it's like that, go out, do some extra recycling. So I sell my bottles Thursday morning, the sun comes up, cash in my pocket, feeling OK, but I'm tired. I know I can take the bus over Bayshore[35] and get me some shut-eye, but I'm waiting for an appointment with this social worker at 10:45 a.m. Of course, there is nowhere to go. I'm not going to go get picked on by some dope fiend in the Tenderloin, so I sit down on one of the benches in the Civic Center.

"Next thing I know, this cop is banging on my arm with his baton. His buddy has already taken my cart and everything in it. I'm all sleepy, you know, like, 'Hey, what the hell's going on?' I want to run after the other cop to see if I can get some of my things, but my guy won't let me. He's shouting, 'Just try it. I'll take you down, you better believe it.' Like I'm what, a bank robber? He's writing out a ticket and I say, 'What's the charge, Officer?' He says, 'Encampment.' Like I set up camp. I just fell asleep for a few minutes. They don't want you there even a few minutes. I guess it's too close to City Hall. The mayor doesn't want to be reminded about all the people they are leaving out in the cold."

Julius's experience with Matrix and later waves of ticketing heightened his sense of exclusion. It seemed evident to him that this direct crackdown was only one element in a much broader range of strategies. As he said, there was "nowhere to go."

"Have you noticed there's barely any benches anymore?" he asked me. "No bathrooms, no benches, and the one place they got benches you ain't allowed to sit down. Nowhere to lie on the grass, not if you're homeless. Like the Yerba Buena Center. Very pretty, but you know that the second you sit your butt down in *there* you in big trouble. They don't want any more Union Squares. Then you got some people go to the Golden Gate Park, and what do they get? More of the same. It's *cold*, you know."

As downtown public spaces were steadily replaced by large-scale "urbanoid" public-private developments[36] places to sit became sparse indeed.

The clearances during Brown's terms in office were particularly hard on those living in vans and cars. People living in vehicles get relatively little attention in the literature on homelessness, but they make up a significant proportion of the American population outside conventional housing. One national survey has suggested that this less visible fraction could even constitute the majority of the literally homeless.[37] Certainly in the San Francisco Bay area, car and van living, temporarily or semipermanently, was a common strategy for economic survival. As the police intensified efforts to clear, first, residential neighborhoods and, then, edge areas with little other demand for the space, people living in vans and cars found themselves ticketed, towed, and roused in the night. The vignette following this chapter shows how crackdowns on vehicular living steadily eroded the marginal but initially sustainable existence of Emory, a middle-aged Chinese American and San Francisco native — one of countless vehicular dwellers to

Walking all day, nowhere to go, nowhere to rest. Finally nodding off against some scaffolding on Twenty-fourth Street.

be displaced during the 1990s. Bit by bit, the old communities were pushed out of the Panhandle, the roads bordering Golden Gate Park, China Basin, Mission Rock, Illinois Street, even the dubious refuges of Alemany Boulevard and Sunnydale.

Contributing to this crackdown was a development juggernaut that, as it advanced around the northeast corner of the city, threw up whole neighborhoods of new townhouses and lofts, the seemingly obligatory new skybox stadium, and a new University of California biotech center. Thanks to the new light-rail line, Dogpatch, now touted in *Men's Journal* as one of the coolest "nabes" on the West Coast, became a fifteen-minute commute to the financial district. The swelling population of loft dwellers soon increased pressure for clearances that wiped the van communities of misfits, artists, stoners, and mad visionaries off the map so thoroughly they seemed like a dream that disappears as soon as you try to think of it.

By making it hard to panhandle, scavenge for food, sit, sleep, or go to the bathroom, Matrix was supposed to reduce the attractions of downtown areas for homeless people. But it would take an extended war of maneuver to wear down the sense of entitlement to downtown public space shared by many of the poorest residents of the city. After all, young and old, patrician and immigrant, black and white, tourist and old-timer have long mingled in San Francisco's downtown without giving each other a second look.

Downtown was certainly the place where panhandlers, sidewalk vendors, and street entertainers could make the most money, but the region's homeless and indigent did not congregate there simply to make money. Like the book vendors in Mitchell Duneier's *Sidewalk*, they also went there because they felt that city streets were for everybody. Neighborhoods might be claimed by residents, but downtown and the main arteries of the city were by their nature open, diverse spaces where anyone had the right to be.[38]

Freddie, as a longtime panhandler, was one of the most vociferous in this respect. "This is downtown! Anyone has the right to be downtown. Whatcha think this is, Palo Alto?" he snarled at a police officer that was telling him to leave Market Street or get ticketed.

In contrasting lively, heterogeneous San Francisco with sleepy, upscale Palo Alto, Freddie took for common sense the distinction between the sidewalk democracy of a large, vital city and the enforced homogeneity of an exclusive suburb. Similarly, when recycler Desmond was first told not to sit on the sidewalk on Fourth Street, he couldn't believe it. "It is downtown, for God's sake! If you can't go downtown, where the hell *can* you go?"

The resistance of many San Franciscans to open victimization of the homeless meant that San Francisco's quality-of-life legislation and policing, both downtown and in the neighborhoods, was less comprehensive than what went on in many other American cities and towns. Yet in some ways this relative restraint only encouraged the city to develop less publicly transparent anti-homeless practices. Where the Las Vegas homeless were legally prohibited from showering, shaving, or other forms of cleaning up in public bathrooms, San Francisco merely got rid of most of its bathrooms. Where the Orlando homeless were cordoned off into confined areas by the police or forced to apply for licenses for panhandling, San Franciscans sleeping outside were jolted awake by freezing water sprayed by Department of Public Works trucks or returned to their encampments to find their tents irreparably slashed or their shanties flattened.[39]

Radicalization

The excesses of Matrix created a permanent buzz of resentment on the street. Several of my street companions felt that harassment by GA, the hotels, and most of all by Matrix had risen to a point where they had lost any sense of citizenship. "That bastard Jordan" and the "fucking cops" came up in conversation all the time. Clearance, needless to say, felt like persecution, plain and simple, not the "compassionate realism" claimed by Jordan.

As we saw earlier, the recyclers had constructed a street subculture in explicit opposition to the backbiting character of much street life. In doing so, they developed a collective version of system-talk that was far more consistent and embodied than the sporadic furies of Tenderloin hustlers like Del and Sammy (see Part II). It was not unexpected, then, that recyclers became some of the most prominent activists against "broken windows" policing in the neighborhoods.

In their public persona as recycler or canner they felt more able to assert their rights to freedom from official harassment than if they had been panhandling or lying on the sidewalk. Panhandlers Jim, Freddie, and Sass, for example, would respond to police officers with resentful grumbles and curses, but inevitably did what was asked. In contrast, the more radical recyclers could sometimes fight back, leaving behind the repertoire of the disgruntled lumpen proletariat for the indignation of the mistreated citizen.

George, a Greek American ex-con who worked as a delivery driver before serving a long stretch in prison, would regularly intervene with police officers on the behalf of his colleagues. One time I was with him when an officer overturned the cart of an older recycler. George sped toward the scene like a superhero. "You call this keeping the peace?" he angrily repeated until the other officer righted the cart. George's outrage at the humiliation of homeless people by the police and criminal justice system had a slightly different character than the resentment expressed by those African Americans—most of them—who had always been poor. Legal harassment was not new to them. A more common response to ticketing or cart confiscation was less shocked than world weary—"Just the cops getting their kicks" said Dobie sullenly. George, however, had experienced another reality and tenaciously held onto his pre-prison understanding of the respect due to a (white male) American citizen.

In the following conversation, Ray—last seen with the Dogpatch dumpster divers in *Moorings*—and George compared Matrix policing with "real" crime-fighting. (George found Ray a willing interlocutor, but while they were talking Ray maintained a state of physical relaxation and a philosophical smile that strongly contrasted with George's tight voice and clenched fists.)

"You know, I get quite a bit of harassment," said George. "I've got a few tickets for disturbing the peace [by rattling bottles], for having an unauthorized, stolen, shopping cart. . . . Then certain things, like a couple of times they kicked over my shopping cart. I had to bite my tongue because I wanted to kill them. I'm real serious. When I got arrested that one time I told them, 'If you want me out of this dumpster, you're just gonna have to come in and get me out of this dumpster.' . . . I added a few other things, like, 'What would your mother think, you doing this kind of work, instead of a real policeman's work?' I told them back in the seventies a lady would be able to go up the Tenderloin in a wheelchair. Now, even *without* a wheelchair they can't do it here, and the macho policemen are harassing *me*. I told them they made me sick to my stomach."

"Uh-huh, real sick," nodded Ray accommodatingly. "You're right on, man, they should be going after the big dealers, the violent criminals. But we are easier to pick on, 'cause we've got nowhere to hide our asses. Like that fat-ass white officer, that Dickinson[40]—he couldn't run after a real bad mofo to save his life. But he is all over us. He took DT's sleeping bag yesterday, and that was the second time."

George's eyes flashed. "I could *kill* that fucking asshole. One of the kids was making a phone call down by the market and Dickinson gives him a ticket for blocking the phone booth. What the fuck does *that* mean? Like we can't use the fucking phone?"

"And his buddy, Ramirez, his shit about loitering." Ray shook his head. "He searches me like *I'm* gonna be carrying a gun. And there's a couple of herone (heroin) dealers on the other side of the street and he don't even look at *them*."

"He'd be scared," said George scornfully. Ray laughed.

Of the recyclers, George was the most organized opponent to Matrix, becoming something of a community leader. Unlike many of the recyclers, George was willing to see common cause with the younger gutterpunk crowd; he was not interested in drawing normative divisions among the homeless. He socialized with both middle-aged street denizens and young runaways, taking on the role of roving legal adviser. Most notably, he distributed legal rights leaflets produced by the Coalition on Homelessness. With the title "When you're homeless, knowing the law sometimes keeps the law from stepping on you," these handouts gave the exact wording and established usage of the various police codes used on the Matrix tickets. To those too blurred with drink or blunted by inertia to read, George would declaim key paragraphs of the text aloud.

If some of the African Americans were less surprised by how they were treated, they still fought back. Morris, as I described in Part II, was the indigenous intellectual of the Dogpatch community—helping his handful of friends and companions to understand their experience within the tread of Californian history. Luther and Dobie, both veterans of Camp Agnos, also proved themselves capable leaders of collective action on occasion. Dobie had a magnificent presence. Negotiating a delay of execution on a clearance, he would stay quiet, looming down on the officers from his rangy six-foot-three, never letting his anger reach more than a subterranean flicker. As the sweeps of Golden Gate Park gathered in frequency, Dobie's camp was surrounded by a cluster of others, more than a dozen people hoping he would help to shield them from disruption and further dispossession.

Luther was furious when he was sent to work off his General Assistance by clearing the encampments of other homeless people in the park. After a couple of hours he walked off the job, taking the two other workers with him. "I may be a poor man, but I've got my limits," he told the supervisor. "It's evil, setting us on each other," he told me later. "It's like slavery, when they took the biggest guys and got them to beat up on the rest. We supposed to throw out other folks' shit, they

Workfare detail outside the Hilton, Geary Street.

blankets, they clothes, so they come back and it all gone. Can you imagine what that's like? It's the worst. Like you starting all over again." Luther was nearly thrown off GA for this protest but managed to persuade them to change his detail. Others were not so lucky. Word on the street, maybe apocryphal, had it that some GA recipients were forced under pain of arrest to clear their own possessions into a dump truck.

The men's sense of grievance and injustice tended to taint even those elements of the local homelessness industry that were genuinely aimed at providing help. This feeling of alienation was well articulated by George.

"You're not an American, you have *no country!*" he stormed at me one day in a cafe. "How could you not—how could you not feel like that when you're, when supposedly someone's trying to help you get off the merry-go-round and actually what they're doing is pushing you onto a worse one."

George was highly suspicious of the pairing of police officers and outreach workers in the Matrix teams. "Like, with the Matrix, they say they want to help, but it's, like, go to the shelter or get beat up or sent to jail. . . . It's all the same bullshit, when you come down to it. They want to get you out of sight, then get in your business, quiz the hell out of you, and tell you it's all your own goddamn fault. That's why I don't bother with welfare, and I'm not asking anybody for nothin'. Period. That way I don't owe them an explanation for anything, because . . . even if I did give them the right explanation, their questioning would be a crock of shit anyway." George swore under his breath. "I have my problems, but who says *they* got the right to judge *me*?"

While George was ready to admit to "problems," his experiences on the street made him so angry with the city that he was alienated from homelessness services altogether. There was no way, he said, that he was going to relinquish his right to privacy and his sense of self-determination to try the new transitional programs opening up during that time.

As we have seen in previous chapters, many others shared George's feelings. In particular, many felt that the shelters relied on police action to bring them clients and therefore funding.

"They say they want to help," said Carlos, who at that time was staying frequently at MSC South, "but you get the feeling it's all about numbers. You know, the more of us in there, the more money they get. You know, a lot of guys would only stay in there in the worst weather. . . . I mean, yeah, it's dangerous outside, for real, but if you put the effort into finding a decent place to sleep, I'd say it's safer than MSC. It's more healthy, that's for certain. Place is crawling with bugs. I'm looking for a new place to stay right now, but whoa—with this Matrix crap I dunno. You gotta be real creative. What I'm saying is, like, if the cops didn't make it so damn difficult to sleep out, maybe the shelters wouldn't get paid. See what I mean?"

The men's critique of the links between quality-of-life policing and the shelter system served as a counterdiscourse to both the criminalization of street homelessness and the sick-talk promoted within the transitional shelters. David (last seen frustrated with one of the transitional programs in *The Homeless Archipelago*) took Carlos's system-talk one step further, seeing a clear connection between the "problems" he was labeled with in the shelter and the city's clearance policies.

"OK, so generally in the daytime I keep busy recycling. I am done with the programs, that's for sure. No GA, no so-called life skills. I'm not going through that again. I won't say it isn't a hard life. I could deal, only they won't leave me alone. I guess I'm getting to be one of the scum the mayor keeps talking about. How we are 'littering' the city? How we are all useless druggies, scum, criminals. The cops just don't fucking stop. Ever. You have a nice comfortable camp spot where you can go out, recycle, leave your stuff unattended without being able to get ripped off and what do you have? . . . 'You are messing up the area—you have to pack it up and move.'

"Fuck it, not everyone's on drugs and alcohol; they *keep* sayin' that. Not everybody is. There's plenty people wanna eat, sleep, just get by, and they can't pay that high rent by themselves. It's too hard."

Another of the recycling pros, Anthony, had come up while we were talking. Picking up on David's last comment, Anthony, who was a hard drinker, butted in. "Well, you know drinking just relaxes things. Because people that live on the street—man! It gets them depressed. So they go up to Tenth and have a beer and relax. If they were home they might not even be drinking. They got something to do, you know. They have a TV. They can clean their bathroom, their kitchen. They got somethin' to do."

"Uh-huh, right," said David, who was himself not immune from sporadic but fearsome binges on "MD" (Mad Dog malt liquor). "I'm not disrespecting anybody. It's just, like, they *use* it, you know? If they see you drinking, then, hey, they can say, just wino scum, drek. *You* are the problem, you know. . . . Who's looking at what *they're* drinking?"

The Convergence of "Sin" and "Sickness"

In San Francisco, as in other large American cities, the systemic narratives about homelessness (system-talk) developed by activists and advocates in the 1980s gradually lost ground over the next fifteen years. The early emphasis on unemployment and poor wages was drowned out by the kind of aggressive sin-talk exemplified by San Francisco's Frank Jordan, painting men and women living outside as dirty, dangerous blights on the social landscape. Equally important, though, was the rise of sick-talk—the construction of homelessness as a symptom of individual pathologies, especially substance abuse and mental illness. Nurtured within the professionalizing agencies and shelters, medicalized discourses on homelessness were developing a formidable institutional base, unlike the systemic critique of the cash-strapped activists. As sick-talk permeated the public sphere, filtered by the changing voice of the *San Francisco Chronicle,* it was taken up by many residents frustrated with the intractability of the problem.[41]

Willie Brown's administration may have energetically pursued clearance, but the mayor still seemed conflicted about his position on the city's persistent homeless problem. The old California speaker seemed to be caught between system and sin, between his old discursive comfort zone of civil rights talk and the pro-development realpolitik of his later years. Even though he proved willing to expand treatment and services, he did not apply the twelve-step lexicon of denial and tough love to the homeless—perhaps out of principle or perhaps because he failed to recognize the potential of transforming the tension between sin-talk and system-talk into a productive hybrid. In any case, Brown's public statements on homelessness remained split between primarily aesthetic justifications of the police sweeps and his continued project to present himself as the defender of the poor. In a typically oblique move, he eagerly promoted a complete rebuilding of Union Square, the heart of the war of maneuver between the homeless and the merchant associations. Construction kept the square closed for two years, to reopen in 2002 as a public-private plaza anchored by businesses with patio seating.

At this point, many other Democratic public officials had already abandoned system-talk about poverty and homelessness. Bill Clinton was skillfully navigating the shoals of welfare reform at a national level, and Democratic politicians all over the country were developing parallel strategies for withdrawing citizenship rights and existing social entitlements in the name of tough love. It was only a matter of time before San Francisco's leaders created their own Clintonesque mixture of therapeutic and punitive discourses on homelessness.

San Francisco would get there in the end, but at the moment what was more noticeable was that such medicalized narratives were becoming standard operating procedure in Bay Area municipalities less encumbered by San Francisco's weighty social movement legacy. From the early 1990s onward, officials in smaller towns and suburbs all over California had started to present acts of punishment and exclusion within a therapeutic register. Police clearances became a kind of tough love, a necessary push to help people change their unhealthy lifestyle.

For example, during 1997 the city of Menlo Park, a suburb south of the city, decided to clear the small homeless shantytown under the San Francisquito Creek Bridge. The police chief and the director of the local multiservice agency unanimously framed the clearance as aid to those evicted. "This isn't a place to live," said Bruce Cumming, the Menlo Park police chief. "We're actually doing these folks a favor. They need to make changes in their lives."

The homeless men experienced the eviction as an act of exclusion, complaining that they had been hunted down even in a place where they were "out of the way,"[42] but Daryl Ogden, executive director of the local multiservice center, agreed with the police chief.

"It's a reality check for the homeless," he told reporters. "For too long, we've been enabling them, not helping them climb up the ladder to attain the lifestyle they need to be normal. This isn't normal."[43]

This example illustrates not only the discursive convergence of sin-talk and sick-talk, but a developing interdependence between the key practices of homeless management that follow from these two discourses. As quality-of-life policing and transitional shelter programs developed, they grew in mutual dependence. The existence of the services, as David and Carlos argued, provided local politicians with vital legitimacy for their clearance policies: conversely, without these clearance campaigns, it was far from clear that transitional shelters would attract enough of the client base to justify their existence. Street life had to be made as difficult as possible so that clients would choose to come inside and submit themselves to rehabilitation.

Underpinning this extraordinary marriage of sin-talk and sick-talk was the professional lexicon of the rehab industry, with its constant depiction of "out there"—the street—as the ground zero of drug damage. Within this broad pop-medicalization homeless people *as a category* could be constructed as fundamentally out of touch with their own interests, needing to be physically coerced out of "denial" into "treatment."

Back in San Francisco, the power of sick-talk made it harder and harder for the coalition to rally public support against clearance policies. As discussions of substance abuse and mental health moved to the fore within the media, the radicals of the Coalition on Homelessness found themselves fighting on two fronts, forced to acknowledge that many homeless people had serious problems with addiction and mental illness, yet insisting that they still deserved the human rights accorded to other citizens. The Coalition staff demonstrated their usual resilience, producing their own surveys and harnessing evidence about the medical needs of many homeless people into rights talk by instituting their own Substance Abuse and Mental Health Work Group to campaign for more and better treatment slots. In 1998 they pushed through a Single Standard of Care, guaranteeing the uninsured the same mental health treatment as the insured, a crucial gain for the homeless mentally ill. Yet within the discourse wars, the emphasis on access to mental health and substance abuse treatment was not a straightforward issue to play. It took a lot of effort to combat the common assumption that the homelessness of addicts and the mentally ill was purely a product of their individual problems, and politicians were becoming ever more sophisticated at harnessing sick-talk in the service of clearance.

Spearheading the breakthrough of authoritarian medicalization in the early 2000s was the ambitious young city supervisor Gavin Newsom. Visible homelessness was still creating consternation among both business interests and the electorate, and there was more talk of emulating Rudy Giuliani's famous cleanup of Manhattan. "If New York can do it, why can't San Francisco?" fulminated Bob Begley of the San Francisco Hotel Council. Newsom decided to prepare his bid for the mayoral race of 2003 with a breakthough campaign to reform homelessness policy.[44]

Newsom was no Frank Jordan. From the beginning he was extraordinarily careful to couch his positions in terms of authoritarian sick-talk rather than punitive sick-talk. For example, when discussing the $200 million a year spent on dealing with homelessness in San Francisco in 2001, he adopted technocratic yet caring language. "It's inexcusable that we have performed so badly. People are suffering because of our inability," he said.

Newsom argued that the homeless population needed more oversight and tighter control, proposing a central shelter intake procedure, with fingerprinting, and the adoption of work requirements for transitional shelter programs. But the centerpiece of his mayoral strategy was the 2002 campaign to finally abolish the General Assistance entitlement, "Care Not Cash." San Francisco was one of the last large cities in the nation (and one of only two counties in California) to still provide more than minimal pocket money to indigent single adults, and several similar attempts to slash it had been blocked by the all-out efforts of system-talking advocates. At the time of Newsom's proposal (Proposition N), the San Francisco homeless on GA were still drawing between $320 and $395 a month, while their equivalents across the Bay in Oakland were receiving a maximum of $24 a month. Newsom proposed that payment be cut by 85 percent to $57 per month, and that the money saved by the cuts would go into a fund to support permanent supportive housing for recipients.

The Care Not Cash campaign was heavily advertised, with a major grassroots effort from not only Frank Jordan's constituency but also the incomers who had so profoundly altered the city's demographic and political makeup over the previous decade, many of whom volunteered for the campaign. In November 2002 it passed with 60 percent of the vote. Voters were impressed, and Newsom was elected the following year. After a long legal battle, the proposition was fully implemented in May 2004. (The homelessness rate in the impoverished city of Richmond, across the bay, veered sharply upward.)[45]

The mayor's office continued to mobilize volunteers for monthly Homeless Connect events, creating compelling moments of collective effervescence around an anti-political narrative of disability and compassion. The San Francisco Chronicle, which had continued to give some space to systemic perspectives on homelessness through the 1990s, at this point placed its weight squarely behind the mayor, staff writer Kevin Fagan producing a steady string of puff pieces about the city's new homelessness initiatives.[46]

Where Brown's homelessness policy had been fragmented and prone to U-turns, Newsom layered a skillfully coherent discourse over a set of policies that were, if anything, even more equivocal. For example,

Billboard promotion for Care Not Cash.

as a supervisor Newman had stood up for treatment on demand and other supportive services. Once in power, he continued to frame his discourse around care, but in reality was unwilling to dedicate the resources. He tried to reduce treatment funding, which had doubled under Brown, and reduced psychiatric beds and made large cuts to mental health services.

In the meantime, he vigorously pursued his quality-of-life agenda, instituting centralized shelter intake and fingerprinting and pushing through a new proposition (M) tightening up legislation against "aggressive" panhandling and panhandling near ATMs.[47] Now "spare-changing" was forbidden in parking lots, on median strips, outside check-cashing businesses, and on buses. Again, punitive sanctions were couched in terms of care. Offenders were to be fined or, if appropriate, diverted to substance abuse or mental health programs, where they would be given precedence over others on the waiting list.

"The idea is not to just throw the homeless into cells, but to help them," said Newsom. "The main thing is we don't want them suffering on the streets, and if they're not suffering it's better for everyone, including them."[48]

Both Care Not Cash and Proposition M shifted city resources toward pulling the most visible and rowdy off the street, especially those in the downtown and tourist areas. For justification, the administration placed increasing emphasis on the need to serve the "chronic homeless"—a new category traveling the policy circuit. From the outset, this group was defined in the characteristically neoliberal terms of cost-benefit analysis; these were the single, long-term homeless individuals with "disabling conditions" who accounted for a strongly disproportionate outlay of homeless assistance dollars.[49]

Here again San Francisco was at the forefront of national homelessness policy initiatives. During the 2002 mayoral race the *San Francisco Chronicle* received an open letter from President Bush's so-called "homelessness czar," Phil Magnano. The administration was prepared to spend $200 million next year on a range of new homelessness initiatives "targeted to supportive housing, services, and employment for those on the streets and in shelters," and Magnano encouraged San Francisco, perhaps the most prominent example of the "national disgrace," to compete aggressively for the funding. "We stand ready to deepen our partnership with San Francisco," Mangano wrote. "San Francisco is positioned to demonstrate that if there's a will, there's a way to end this national disgrace."

The principal target of this money, to be released to municipalities through the "10-Year Plan to End Chronic Homelessness" model, were the chronic homeless, a group often treated as synonymous with those who "spent most of their time outside."[50] (I hope readers of this book will understand by now the problematic character of this assumption. True, my own study of recycling had drawn me to some of the healthier people living outside, but these men were far from unusual. Perhaps the rough sleepers were disproportionately mentally ill and severely addicted, but they also included many who were healthier than more regular shelter-users and certainly used less resources.

Magnano, former manager of the pseudo-folk-revival group Peter, Paul, and Mary, sent out an inspirational PowerPoint document encouraging local ten-year plans that were to be "driven, shaped, and implemented by a business mindset" and oriented to strict benchmarks of "visible, measurable, quantifiable change on the streets, in neighborhoods, and most important in the lives of homeless people." Magnano's emphasis on quantifiable reductions in visible street disorder well matched Newsom's own urgent desire to finally clean up the visible homeless, and he enthusiastically attended the announcement of San Francisco's 10-Year Plan in 2004. The plan followed the standard cost-benefit construction, aiming its money at 3,000 individuals, roughly 20 percent of the current homeless population, who they estimated to cost the city 63 percent of its annual homeless budget.

The therapeutic rationale behind the chronic homelessness push was "Housing First," an approach pioneered by New York's Pathways to Housing program in the 1990s for people with mental illness.[51] Housing First reversed the "Treatment First" model of the Continuum of Care (the former federal orthodoxy), instead moving clients directly into independent housing supported by on-site services. Evaluation studies so far have generally been very favorable, yet as Drs. Kertesz and Weiner have shown, the cost-benefit incentive for cities to promote this approach quickly decreases when Housing First is offered to less severely debilitated individuals.[52]

The national turn to Housing First is replete with ironies, contradictions, and possibilities. This is not the place for a detailed investigation of how or why this explicitly anti-moralistic harm-reduction strategy—hitherto most strongly represented in the United States by underfunded and marginalized needle exchanges—came to be taken up by the Bush administration. Key for the politics of homelessness, though, is the way that Housing First has come to dovetail with the class cleansing of the central city.

The principle behind Newsom's Care Not Cash was to offer SRO hotel rooms to all the homeless General Assistance recipients whose benefit was cut—more than 1,200 people.[53] A lucky 15 percent of the single homeless population had gained basic housing, but the conditions were now even harder for the rest. With the designated Care Not Cash rooms filled, new homeless GA claimants were left forfeiting most of their check just to stay in the city shelters.[54] The General Assistance rolls predictably fell sharply following the cuts, yet the annual homelessness count showed little change.[55]

Newsom astutely incorporated elements of system-talk—talking about "putting people directly in housing" and even arguing that "there is no such thing as housing resistant"—ideas long used by the Coalition in its criticisms of the authoritarian medicalization of the transitional shelters. Just as his support for gay marriage had won the hearts of liberal San Franciscans, his promotion of the progressive Housing First principle seemed to inoculate him from stronger criticisms of his homelessness policy.

The "broken windows" agenda within the Housing First initiative became more apparent as officials started grumbling about Care Not Cash recipients still spending time hanging out on the street. They quickly started a Homeward Bound bus-ticket program that gave out thousands of free bus tickets away from the city. Most seriously, though, the 1,441 citations for sleeping outdoors in the first year of the Newsom administration tripled the count of the previous year. City hall geared up for the next initiatives: a return to Matrix-style combinations of policing and "outreach," a downtown Community Justice Court aimed at pushing quality-of-life violators into services, and a radical reduction of the emergency shelter beds, drop-in centers, and soup kitchens available to those outside the transitional shelter programs.

As Trent Rhorer, director of the city's Human Services Agency put it in 2007, "The idea of expecting something for nothing is not a direction the Mayor wants to go any more. It's a two-way street, and you have to meet us halfway. The idea would be that if you're in a shelter, you're in a care-management plan."[56]

San Francisco was no longer the famous radical outlier within the field of the American politics of homelessness. With Care Not Cash, the name of which so neatly symbolizes the inexorable shift of American poverty management from cash transfers to authoritarian medicalization, Newsom had pulled the city closer into line with the national zeitgeist.

Cognitive Mapping

The earlier conversation between David and Anthony gives a sense of the way that those living on the street tried to grapple with the confusing combination of "cold" punishment—the tickets, the destruction of their camps, the early morning soaking from the DPT trucks—with the caring discourse of the social workers and other professionals.

One evening Pipe, ex-con and thief, held forth on the subject to a group of his friends while sitting on the broken pier at Mission Rock, just north of their camp in Dogpatch. "If those politicians in city hall want to really help us, why don't they just give us housing, or at least let folks camp in peace without being kicked around by idiot cops? I'll tell you why. Because all their friends running the shelters and all these other programs would lose their jobs."

"Right!" "Ain't *that* the truth!" chorused companions Manny and Tom.

Manny took the line of thought further, setting up the disease model itself as a form of social control designed to prevent collective action. "It's not just about the money, you know. Those shelters will break you down. They want us all shelterized, you know, like depressed and sniffling around, snitching on each other, that's the idea. They don't want another tent city on Civic Center for sure, and they reckon these new-style shelters, that's the best way to do it. Then they don't even need the cops."

Derick in South of Market, Morris, Spike, and Valentino in Dogpatch, Anthony in the Mission, George in the Haight, Dobie on the west side of the city—all seem to have a similar project. They were building a cognitive map of the homelessness industry, which linked it to their critiques of policing and the criminal justice system. There must be a connection, they felt, between punitive and supposedly therapeutic aspects of homelessness management, between the ticketing and tent-slashing *clearance* from the streets and *corral* in the shelter. Manny's way of seeing it persuaded some of his friends in Dogpatch. First the police kept them "off their feet" and pushed them toward the shelters, they argued, then the same shelters further broke down their independence. For the icing on the cake, the politicians used the shelters to justify their clearance policies.

Unlike those who raised more than half a million dollars to promote the 2003 anti-panhandling legislation, these men had few resources to get their discourse out.[57] As the city continued to gentrify rapidly, and as the patches of liminal turf grew smaller, some of the homeless activists with more wherewithal—the van livers of HANC and Food Not Bombs, the political squatters of Homes Not Jails, and the organic intellectuals of the street homeless scene—finally gave up and left town. University-educated dumpster diver Quentin, for example, went to live in the garage of a friend in a small town north of the city. A period of exhaustion hit the indefatigable few running the Coalition on Homelessness. The media presence of system-talk was quieter than before, and its constituency among the housed was shrinking, many of the more progressive residents embroiled in their own struggles to hold onto affordable housing.

This chapter has followed the journey of Wilson and Kelling's discourse of "broken windows" from the national politics of urbanism to its specificities in San Francisco, and then from Frank Jordan's deliberately confrontational Matrix Program to the increasing normalization of clearance under Brown and Newsom. In an endless war of maneuver, the police and other public agencies moved in on the fragile urban spaces made by the placeless, denying their right to share the city's busy pedestrian nodes and destroying their makeshift shelters in obscure corners. As they walked this path, politicians and officials learned to temper the exclusionary language of sin-talk—which remained unacceptable to the general population—first, with the shift toward the aesthetic, and second, with an authoritarian medicalization that focused on chronically homeless lost souls in need of a firm hand.

I argued in *The Homeless Archipelago* that the medicalization of the transitional shelters seemed particularly dissonant when applied to the more "high-functioning" among the homeless—the straddlers moving in and out of homelessness as their fortunes rose and fell, the temp workers, the pro recyclers. But once we see these policies in the context of the class cleansing of San Francisco, they take on a different aspect. The relentless drive to cleanse the city of even the most out-of-the-way and self-sustaining of its homeless tells a different story, a more straightforward one. It was not only the most scabrous and disreputable, the Freddies and the Dels, who threatened the ritzy urbanoid imaginary of the new San Francisco, but any and all of the shabby dreamers and aging drag queens, humble isolates, and grumpy blue collar relics lacking the wherewithal to roll with the tide of change. The clearances might be driving many further down into the most desperate layers of the lumpen proletariat, but as long as these people continued their downward trajectory in a lateral direction—in Oakland, Richmond, or farther off—then the policy could indeed be deemed successful. In the broader policy context, the decision by Newsom, and indeed of Magnano and Bush's HUD, to make a high-profile push toward getting the "chronic homeless" Housing First makes more sense.

Through gentrification and redevelopment, the reduction of public housing, and quality-of-life policing, neoconservative politicians have reversed the three-decade abandonment of the central cities to "tax-and-spend" Democrats, forging a new pro-urban conservatism that reappreciates the city and claims it back from the deviant and unruly.[58] Within this context, the push toward authoritarian medicalization of the homeless serves a dual strategy. First, the focus on overcoming the self-destructive delusions and denial of the sick justifies the steady progress of quality-of-life policing and vehicle confiscation against all those living outside, whether flamboyant or discreet, cleansing valuable urban space for more profitable uses. Second, by throwing a media floodlight onto the most visible, desperate, and degraded tip of the homeless iceberg, it creates a chasm between homelessness and mundane poverty. High-profile initiatives like Housing First and Homeless Connect demonstrate compassionate action in aid of the most needy without disrupting continued divestments in more broad-based programs and public goods.

"The law, in its majestic equality, forbids the rich as well as the poor to sleep under bridges, to beg in the streets, and to steal bread," runs Anatole France's aphorism, suggesting the inherent violence of a civil moral order imposed on a vastly unequal population. We have now learned to make these rulings in a different register, adding to the majestic impartiality of class rule a bombastic, intrusive compassion. We spray our fellow men and women with freezing water, slash their tents, destroy their shanties, and tow their cars, all in the name of a compassionate crusade to save them from their inner demons.

The Road to Nowheresville

EMORY, AN AGING CHINESE AMERICAN HIPPIE with a flamboyant mustache and a long ponytail, had lived in the Haight since he was in his early thirties. He didn't make much at his job in a rehearsal studio where he set up fuzzy sound systems for would-be rockers in bandannas and leather trousers, keeping the ledger and sorting the cash. In the early 1990s, he was sharing an apartment with four younger speed freaks, the only living situation he could afford in the ever more expensive housing market.

Exhausted from the bassy cacophony at work, Emory craved quiet, but living with his hyped-up roommates got more and more crazy. In 1994 he decided to save for a van instead. The legacy of the "summer of love" still lingered in his neighborhood, Haight-Ashbury, and at that time, there were still other stalwarts of the San Francisco counterculture living in ramshackle vans around Panhandle Park. By joining them, Emory could continue living near his old apartment.

All in all, Emory didn't regret the decision to leave the crazy apartment. He really liked living on his own, a luxury that few can afford in San Francisco. Being naturally tidy, he was able to manage his possessions within a very limited space without getting claustrophobic. He still knew lots of people in the neighborhood, and friends would come by to chat when they saw his distinctive green van. One friend, Hector, gave him a spare key so he could use the bathroom whenever he needed.

But parking the van in the Haight became harder and harder. First of all, as the neighborhood continued to gentrify, parking spaces became increasingly scarce. Emory's old Ford needed a big space, and some nights he found himself driving around for hours after work. But still he persisted. Without the proximity of his friends, especially Hector, he knew that van living would be a lot less attractive.

About a year after Emory quit his apartment, the police returned to their episodic targeting of those sleeping in cars and vans. They would wake people at night and ask them to move on, and sometimes give them a ticket for living in a vehicle, an offense under San Francisco Police Code 97. This time the mayor's office had declared all-out war on would-be urban campers. All over the city, in the areas most popular with van and car dwellers, the Department of Parking and Transportation changed parking regulations. Even out in the relative desolation by Mission Rock, where there was never any competition for parking, the DPT put up signs prohibiting parking between 2:00 a.m. and 6:00 a.m.

Emory held out in the Haight for another couple of years, parking along the edge of Golden Gate Park, where his van was rocked by heavy traffic. But here too the cops eventually showed up. Mayor Brown's fall 1997 campaign to clear the park of homeless people included the van dwellers on its edge, and Emory and his neighbors found themselves hounded for petty violations like urinating in bushes or sleeping in the park during the afternoon. (The police were told to treat sleeping with a sleeping bag or other possessions as "encampment," which was a violation of San Francisco's Park Code 3.12.)

After a few weeks, Emory was exhausted. Wandering the Haight in search of my street companions, I found him lying on the grass near his van, dark rings under his eyes. "I'm beat, man. I'm too old for this bullshit. I get back from work one-thirty, two in the morning, grab maybe four hours of sleep, and the old runaround starts again. The rush hour traffic is crazy. There's no way I can sleep, not even with plugs, ya know? Then having to move the van all day—it's so fucking stressful. If I try to catch a bit more shut-eye here away from the road, I might be getting myself into more shit. Some of the cops are out ticketing folks in the park for camping. Camping! With just a blanket! Something's gotta give, somehow."

Some police officers seem to relish being given a mandate to clear the area of "lowlife scum," as I heard one of them call the recycler George. But others were themselves frustrated with the clearance campaign in the Haight. Not only was the rousting of the homeless a low-status task in police life, it was widely recognized to be a futile one. Emory introduced me to one Officer Vasquez, who told me that he personally didn't see the point in bothering people living in vans.

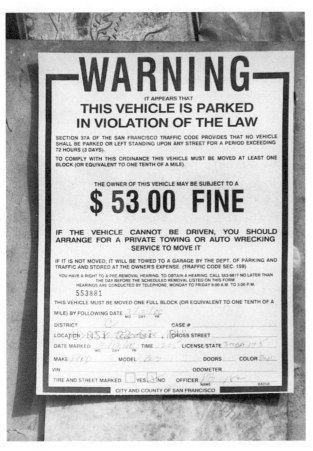

"Your starter motor's gone and you're supposed to lose your friggin' home?"

"Some of these [homeless] people are real troublemakers, you know, but most of the ones living in the vans are OK. They don't make much mess. This town is very expensive right now. It's no wonder some guys are living out of vans. It's the same with some of the other homeless. Some of them really make an effort to keep out of the way. There is a couple I know who are really harmless, you know. You don't see them out drinking and cursing and spoiling the park for the public. But we have to treat everybody alike. I don't really see it as a policing issue myself if somebody is keeping to himself and not making any trouble, but this is what they want us to do."

"Why do you think city hall is cracking down on the homeless?" I asked.

"It's a difficult question. Partly the residents don't like it; they don't like having people sleeping on the doorsteps or making it so they can't take their kids to the park. And they are right. The neighborhood is for everyone, and you can't let a few druggies take over. So in general it's good that they are putting pressure on open beverages (public drinking), aggressive panhandling, those kinds of things. What I don't get is why we have to go after those ones who aren't in anyone's way. I'm not comfortable with it, personally."

Vasquez told Emory to "just chill for a few weeks, go visit family or something. City hall will get tired of all this soon enough." Another officer suggested a place he might park unmolested on the edge of a local army base.

The ambivalence of Vasquez and the other relatively sympathetic police officers Emory encountered made a welcome contrast to the insolence of many of their colleagues. All the same, even Vasquez did not reject the basic tenet of quality-of-life policing, the idea that homeless people had a duty to "keep out of the way," invisible to the eyes of more prosperous people. Van dwellers like Emory, so long as they kept their doors closed most of the time, were doing the right thing by keeping themselves incognito.

Emory, still unwilling to leave the Haight, his neighborhood for fourteen years, decided to try to move back inside. He reckoned he could afford $300 a month for a room if he took on some more hours of work and started working early shifts at a local coffee shop two or three times a week. Getting his own place was out of the question, he knew, but maybe he could find something in a shared apartment again. Selling the van could raise enough money for "first, last, and deposit," he hoped. This plan, however, proved impossible. There were very few rooms available at that price, and in every case the mostly young and white occupants did not choose him.

"With the first couple of places, I made the mistake of saying I was living in my van," Emory explained. "You know, you can forget that for some people—that means there's something wrong with you. They can seem to be kind of knowledgeable about the system, like maybe they bitch about the government, the economy, but it doesn't mean they really get it. They still see a guy like me, not much money, living in his van, and they think I've got to be crazy or antisocial or something. They don't think maybe this is a guy who really tries to stay out of the same system they are sitting there complaining about. . . . It wasn't much better when I said I was living in Hector's place. Like with the apartment on Masonic, they seemed like cool kids, but they were in their early twenties, I should think. A couple of them were students at State. They were friendly, we hung out for about an hour, but I knew they would never choose me. They want people their own age, into the same music, all that. I didn't look right to them."

Meanwhile, the police offensive against van dwellers was intensifying, and Emory found it more and more difficult to stay out of trouble. One officer threatened (illegally) that he would have Emory's van towed if he ever saw it around the Panhandle again. As Emory became increasingly anxious about losing his van, the studio folded, unable to renew their lease, and he lost his primary source of income. He still had his coffee shop hours, but his income was now barely enough pay for gas and repairs. Emory started eating at soup kitchens.

At first he was bewildered to find himself treated as another street person. "I never really thought of myself as, you know, on the street, when I first moved into the van," he said. "I felt sorry for some of those guys out there, but I didn't have much to do with them." But as months became years and the initial feasibility of van living turned into a stressful runaround, Emory started to see himself as a victim of harassment and discrimination.

While Emory was working in the coffee shop, his loyal friends Hector and Nina lost their apartment through another of the "move-in" evictions plaguing the city's renters. They reluctantly left the city to move in with Nina's mother in the flatlands of East Oakland. Emory now had no bathroom access beyond the toilet at work, and keeping clean and well kempt became more of a struggle.

Eventually his boss, Hamid, told him he could not continue to employ him unless he found an apartment. "I feel humiliated, you know," Emory said later. "I shouldn't have told him I was living in the van, but he was asking me why I couldn't get a phone. But I had my pager, so it wasn't really a problem for him.

"I guess I feel discriminated against. And he made a fuss about me coming to work early to clean myself up. 'I don't want you looking after your personal hygiene here,' he said. Why should he care? I'm clean, I know how to clean up. He told me the place looked better than ever. I dunno. It's like it's a crime to not have money these days. Everybody makes you feel like shit, disrespects you, like you should just piss off to Nowheresville. It's worse than growing up Chinese on Divisadero, I tell ya. Honestly. It is starting to get to me, big time."

While Emory was becoming progressively alienated from housed society, he was also getting closer to some of the other van dwellers of the Haight. As they shared grievances and strategies for avoiding the police, this group developed a discourse around homelessness and gentrification that galvanized the usually laid-back Emory into earnest indignation.

"Can you believe this bullshit?" he told Foxy, one of his new comrades in misfortune. "I've lived my whole life in San Francisco. Why should I be pushed out because a bunch of dot-commers want to come to the city?"

"Uh-huh," nodded Foxy, a heavy white woman in her late thirties with striking green and black tattoos. "We gotta stand up for ourselves. We gotta fight back."

But then the conversation trailed off. Emory and Foxy seemed unclear about what kind of fighting back could work at this point.

Foxy's much older boyfriend, Smiler, was a canny Vietnam vet who had been involved on and off with the radical Haight-Ashbury Neighborhood Council (HANC) for many years. He had been evicted two years ago from his apartment of twelve years when his building was sold to a "dot-commer." Ever since he had been looking for another place he could afford on his irregular income as a cash-in-hand house painter. By this point Smiler seemed exhausted and had little faith left that collective action could improve their situation. HANC had lost much of its political clout to the new, more conservative neighborhood groups, and Smiler had returned from the latest meeting with nothing but rumors of more local crackdowns to come.

Two weeks later, Emory, Smiler, Foxy, and several others decided to give up the struggle. Together they left the neighborhood and crossed the city to postindustrial China Basin. The mood was somber. "Twenty-six years and it comes to this," muttered Smiler. "Never thought I would leave this neighborhood." He stared across the park, then up at the cloudless spring sky. Both Emory and Smiler seemed dazed with the

"No one lives out here except us. So that one-hour parking, it's hard not to take it personally."

pain of leaving, barely able to tell their decades-old network of neighborhood acquaintances what was happening.

For the next few months, the three of them settled down on Illinois Street in Dogpatch. Then the city instituted another large-scale clearance over there and I lost track of them. I had one garbled phone message from Emory, but his pager was no longer working.

It was not until a year and a half later that I ran into him at the Berkeley BART station. We went to catch up over coffee. We had both had a difficult time since we last saw each other, and we traded news for over two hours. Emory was still living in his van.

"It's been hard," he said. "I've tried to get a few gigs here and there, but it's hard without a phone, without a street address. I don't even know if I woulda gotten anything even if I had that, though. I have filled in a lot of forms. At this point I'd take anything, really. I've tried Comp-USA, Guitar Center, Circuit City. The only place I got an interview was

Pay Less, and the supervisor didn't seem to like the look of me. It's been really hard to keep the van."

"What are you living on?"

"Right now, I'm back on GA, in the city. Doing workfare bullshit with all the crackheads. But they keep making reasons to cut me off. I got, I dunno, four months of GA all of last year. The only reason I'm still on the road is I've got some help from my uncle."

"Couldn't he help you get together a first and last?"

Emory looked dubious.

"It's possible. I don't like to ask him. But until I've got work there's no point, I could never pay the rent."

"So all you are getting is GA?"

"I'm dealing a bit of weed. But it's risky, very risky. And expensive. I wouldn't do it if I wasn't so hard up. I'm running scared, to be honest. Smiler got picked up, you know?"

"For dealing weed?"

"Yeah. They got him driving down from Humboldt. He's in the joint at San Luis Obispo and Foxy's really messed up. She got beat up and raped by some son of a bitch when we were staying on Illinois, you know? He followed her off the bus. Since then she's been going way downhill. She lost the van." Emory raised his eyebrows eloquently. For people in his situation, it was common sense that "losing the van" signaled utter disaster, the end of any hope of safety, personal space, or autonomy. "Last time I saw her she was sitting out on Haight Street, hanging with a bunch of hardcore winos."

We talked for a while about Smiler and Foxy. While Foxy had gone "way downhill," Emory seemed to be well aware that he himself was hanging on only by the skin of his teeth. With the other Bay Area cities passing their own anti-camping laws, it was hard to imagine that he could hold out much longer. I wondered if he was suffering his difficulties alone.

"Have you teamed up with anyone lately?"

"Not really. It's hard to trust people these days." Emory sighed. "There were some cool folks in Dogpatch, but we all got cleared out of there and kinda split up. I got majorly ripped off by a black dude when I was staying down on Alemany Boulevard. I've been keeping to myself, I guess. When I've got stuff to sell, I go up to the Haight. There's still a bunch of people I know up there, mostly musicians. Still see Hector and Nina from time to time, but honestly, I wouldn't say I was close with anyone."

"Sounds lonely."

"Sure it is." Emory locked his fingers together and stretched them backwards. "Sometimes I think I'm getting weird. I'm getting kinda freaky—unsociable, you know? I don't even want to see people anymore. I feel like my life is on hold until I get back in somehow, but nothing seems to give. I had to sell my guitars. And I can't find a decent place to park."

"Where do you go?"

"Most nights I stay down on the frontage road. Generally they let you stay there, but it's hella noisy and it stinks. I have to keep my windows closed and then it stinks inside too."

"It makes you feel nauseated?"

"Yup." He shrugged. "But it's better than the shelter. I can't find anywhere better. Not here, not in the city, for sure. The cops are getting hard-line around China Basin now. First there was the stadium, now they're building that genetics center thing. There isn't anywhere safe in the city you can park anymore. Ya know, sometimes I don't even care. It's not San Francisco anymore. It's still beautiful, but it's not the city I grew up in. There's no soul anymore."

Conclusion

"THE HOMELESSNESS IN THE GREAT DEPRESSION—THAT was a whole different thing, you know," opines shelter worker Jim. "The thing that really gets to me about the Coalition on Homelessness and those types is how they make out that the homeless now are like the people who were homeless in the depression. You know, 'they are just very poor, they are out of work.' But these are not just regular people out of work. These people have got *big problems.* We're not talking about *The Grapes of Wrath* here. No one who worked here for a *week* would believe that," he says, laughing and tipping his head toward the next room and the sound of a rapid-fire cursing match.

Though populist representations of homelessness in the Great Depression have had a lasting legacy, providing resonant touchstones for systemic ideas about poverty, the shadow of the *Grapes of Wrath* can work in the other direction, as shown by Jim's commentary. For him it was common sense that the indigent behaved far better in the 1930s than they do now. *That* was about poverty; *this* is about pathology. Yet Jim's reference to the self-evidently "economic" nature of homelessness in the Great Depression is unwarranted. The 1930s, in fact, saw extensive efforts to study homeless men using the categories of psychopathology. Sociologists, psychologists, ministers, and politicians discussed over the best way to deal with this unruly population.[1] For the influential psychopathologists of the day, the major causes of homelessness were alcoholism, mental instability, wanderlust, and physical and mental disability.[2]

What we also do not remember is that the homeless crisis of the 1930s provoked widespread fear and violent repression. Gangs of thugs met migrant workers at the California state line, and transients all over America found themselves warned out of towns with signs of "NO WORK, NO RELIEF, KEEP MOVING," backed up by police sweeps. In the long term, Steinbeck, Dorothea Lange, and other progressive artists and activists succeeded in shaping the dominant retrospective trope on the homeless or transient of the Great Depression. System-talk had proved more powerful, for a time. But apparently it is easier to accept systemic arguments about poverty when separated by time or space. In-your-face degradation and desperation is another thing entirely.

In 1923 Nels Anderson had proposed a systemic solution to the hobo problem. Anderson argued for a "decasualization of labor," to be achieved by instituting a well-funded national employment system with the task of regulating employment agencies and providing public works for periods of business depression.[3] And indeed, this is what came to be with the advent of the New Deal. The mass layoffs following the Wall Street crash pushed huge numbers of the population into homelessness or desperate migration. Widespread unemployment spurred unprecedented sympathy for the "forgotten man," eventually producing federal transient camps: the Works Progress Administration and the Civilian Conservation Corps. These antipoverty measures were ultimately consolidated by the wartime mobilization and the economic boom of the postwar years; the new Social Security entitlements rescued the elderly from penury. The skid rows of America shrank to a fraction of their old glory, the radical tramps of the IWW died out, and the majority of the white working class found the means for marriage and stability in the new tax-and-spend commonwealth.

But times changed again. Over the last thirty years, American government, corporations, and transnational governmental organizations have restored class power to business elites worldwide. The "forgotten man" evoked by this project was no longer the unemployed worker, but the overtaxed entrepreneur. David Harvey succinctly summarizes this neoliberal turn as "the maximization of entrepreneurial freedoms within an institutional framework characterized by private property rights, individual liberty, unencumbered markets, and free trade."[4]

Inequality is bound to be inversely correlated with legal and social protection for wage earners: economic regulation and labor rights reduce inequality, while deregulation and labor repression increase it. It was inevitable that the neoliberal turn would produce striking polarization. The United States is still be the richest country in the world, but inequalities of wealth and income have exploded, propelled by unrestrained profits and salaries at one end, and at the other, a transition from heavy industry to low-paid and rarely unionized service work.[5]

Countries have adopted different strategies in response to global neoliberalism. Several European states, for example, have tried to mitigate inequality and social suffering within the free market model by investing heavily in a "social economy."[6] The U.S. business class, as prime instigator and enforcer of the neoliberal world order, has instead resurrected the social Darwinist belief in the market as the judge of moral worth, forswearing subsidies to those who fail.[7] The bottom-line response to the poverty and despair of those abandoned by footloose capital has been to reconceive this now massive surplus population as criminals and incompetents.

The violence, both symbolic and all too concrete, of the incarceration strategy was highly visible in homeless San Francisco. Imprisonment and homelessness had become a mutually reinforcing nexus, one through which thousands moved both backward and forward with little respite.[8] Every day men were released from the system with little money, damaged social ties, and minimal job prospects, and many fell fast, even instantly, to the street. In turn, living on the street was very likely to send them back inside, sanctioned for quality-of-life offenses and parole violations.

On the symbolic level, the revolving door between imprisonment and homelessness supercharged the moral discourse on poverty, spurring a defiant celebration of deviance and marginality. As Sammy, Lee, and Del had moved between juvenile hall, the street corner, and bout after bout of incarceration, their embattled worldview had solidified into a more and more inflexible, incurably marginal notion of man versus system, us versus them, have-nots versus haves. In their intimate dance with the police and other forces of coercion, they moved within a powerful consistent totality. The streets were theirs, they claimed, insisting that they were still "takers," rather than losers or

Smoke break.

passive recipients. They scornfully rejected the therapeutic approach of the homelessness archipelago, slyly ridiculing attempts to liberate them of the burden of sin.

The defiance of the homeless hustlers demonstrates how the United States' emphasis on incarceration over integration, on punishment over rehabilitation, works a double function. Its brutally material lockdown physically controls its targets, but it also simultaneously reaffirms their outlaw subjectivity; in turn, ensuring the reproduction of the "bad behavior" that legitimizes the continued reliance on lockdown.

Incarceration may be the cornerstone of contemporary American social policy, but highly dramatized force makes for a volatile form of social control. Our demonic representations and authoritarian handling of poor men and women, especially African Americans, leaves risky "free spaces" that can in turn fuel a passionate resistance. By rendering large segments of the population metaphorically outside the walls, the overt violence and coercion of the prison system breeds hostility and cultural separation, a flipping of the binaries into a powerful outlaw code that attracts the disaffected of all stripes and creates the danger of widespread alienation or even rebellion—a storming of the scaffold. Our unprecedented reliance on incarceration could not stand without the support of softer, more therapeutic forms of state intervention that offer the marginal some kind of pathway back into normality and citizenship. For the poorest Americans, the way back in has become the homelessness industry.

The shelter archipelago is fundamentally different from publicly subsidized housing, in principle and in practice. In a determined withdrawal from the cash transfers and means-tested housing subsidies of the Great Society era, the billions spent on homelessness-related programs over the last fifteen years have remained in the hands of institutions providing heavily surveilled sheltering, drug rehabilitation, and other forms of group reeducation, as well as long-term warehousing for the irretrievably disabled. Funding for rehousing the homeless remained segregated under "homeless assistance," firmly differentiated from the shrinking HUD commitment to public housing and subsidization.[9]

With the collapse of rent control and disappearance of public or government-subsidized housing, moving into a shelter has become the single strongest way for the poor to demonstrate serious need, one of the most immediate and significant ways to qualify for basic resources from the shrunken state. Once in the shelter, though, the task of reintegration is primarily defined as a project of spiritual conversion.[10] For those without serious physical and medical problems, the goal is to wrestle their lives back onto a sustainable track through reformation of the will. System-talk is discouraged. It is not racism, the housing market, the job market, or any other force keeping them in poverty, they are taught. Within this compelling hybrid of sin-talk and sick-talk—moralism and pop-medicalization—those shelter residents willing or able to "work" a program are exhorted to take responsibility, deal with their issues, and remake themselves to fit the rigors of the economy."

The American homelessness industry prevents the development here in the United States of the shantytowns endemic to many parts of the global south. It provides a major loophole within the austerity imposed by welfare reform, a crucial last-ditch resource for poor Americans in crisis, perhaps especially for women with children. Yet if the creation of the homeless archipelago has served as a crucial mechanism for the state to mop up some of the problems created by the destruction of welfare reform and other forms of social protection, the representation of its clients as incompetent, deeply flawed individuals has simultaneously accelerated the transition away from the New Deal era's emphasis on rights and entitlements. The recent push toward Housing First, while more inclusive in principle, in practice is targeting only the most disturbing or recalcitrant of our public indigents, leaving even fewer resources for rehousing the far larger numbers lost in the shelter system.

In places where public space is the most valuable commodity, the contemporary corral of the shelters has worked hand-in-hand with a rebirth of old-fashioned vagrancy control. While these institutions have become centers of crucial services, especially to the sick and disabled, they have simultaneously legitimized the class cleansing of public space (rural as well as urban) by proving that people without housing have "somewhere to go." Government thus refuses commitment to regulating or providing affordable housing, and simultaneously demands that those unable to stay inside do not pursue their own makeshift spaces of affordability. If people cannot somehow squeeze back inside, there is little space left between the "three hots and a cot" of jail and the stigmatized neediness and imperfection of the shelterized role.

Many of the men profiled in this book pushed back against these limited possibilities, avoiding both the shelters and the jails. "Jail is not an option," said angry young Derick, for example, but he also did his best to avoid "bowing down to the poverty pimps." Together with the other pro recyclers, he struggled to maintain independence from institutional control, exploiting the economic niche of bottle and can sales. They produced not only cash but a self-conscious statement against both criminalization and medicalization, their material practice grounding

Canner under the 280 Freeway.

their discursive claims. Yet many, though, sank more into panhandling and petty crime. Once engaged in these activities it was far easier to drift in the great current of sin-talk than to maintain, let alone develop, alternative ways of thinking. Since 2008, a renewed assault on recycling "theft" has thrown even this slender niche into crisis.[11]

Like its more aggressive twin, hyper-incarceration, authoritarian medicalization relies on the symbolic separation of the poor from the rest of the population. But such divides are always unstable and tend to break down in times of economic instability. Since the 2008 collapse of the international property bubble propelled the global economy into the deepest economic crisis of the last fifty years, there have been signs of an opening in American homeless policy. Once again, the broadening of homelessness may have created the space for a revitalization of system-talk. A 2009 tent city in Sacramento drew hundreds of journalists eager to find a symbol of the hardships of the financial crisis. With more lasting significance, President Obama's American Recovery and Reinvestment Act of 2009 designated $1.5 billion for "homelessness prevention and rapid re-housing activities," in a form diverging significantly from the federal funding priorities set over the last fifteen years. At the top of the list stood "short-term or medium-term rental assistance" and "housing relocation," with no explicit targeting to specific populations beyond "persons who have become homeless" or are in danger of becoming so. Funds could also be used for credit repair, utility payments, final rent payments, moving costs, or security payments and deposits. Back in San Francisco, Mayor Newsom seemed to have lost interest in pursuing his latest crackdown on street homelessness.

It remains to be seen, though, whether system-talk is really back again and whether the ARRA funding or other recession measures will create any lasting changes within American social policy. Over the last thirty years, homelessness has taken on a crucial role, becoming both the *product of* and simultaneously *justification for* a great shedding of collective responsibility for inequality and social suffering. We will not change our ideas about homelessness and the poor without fundamental shifts in how we conceive the relationship between politics, economics, and "the social."

Yet history does not stand still. Radical changes in our ways of life and patterns of consumption are inevitable over the next generation, whether imposed by human action or by our damaged environment. Can we turn to a more democratic, cross-class model of community, one that recognizes our essential interdependence and values the skills of those who can live on little? Or will we only intensify the model we have been developing for the last thirty years, a "gated" construct of citizenship that stigmatizes, punishes, and excludes those who fail to prosper?

Notes

Introduction

1. A similar breakdown was suggested in an article about homeless advocacy by Rob Rosenthal. He suggests labels or images applied to homeless people: "lackers," "slackers," and "unwilling victims" (Rosenthal, "Imaging Homelessness and Homeless People").

2. Irwin, *The Jail*.

1. Urban Ethnography beyond the Culture Wars

1. Cresswell, *The Tramp in America*; DePastino, *Citizen Hobo*; M. Katz, *In the Shadow of the Poorhouse*; Monkkonen, *Walking to Work*.

2. Blau, *The Visible Poor*; Burt, *Over the Edge*; Rossi, *Down and Out in America*.

3. Rossi, *Down and Out in America*, 22. O'Flaherty's more recent study concurred that inequality of incomes is ultimately the most compelling cause of contemporary homelessness (O'Flaherty, *Making Room*).

4. The combination of real estate speculation and mortgage debt have consistently driven up housing costs, as well as occasionally throwing the entire economy into crisis. (Both were major factors in the Wall Street crash and 1970s stagflation, as well as the savings and loan crisis of the 1980s.) Even the FHA, VA, and HUD loans given by the government, according to Michael Stone, pushed up rents and housing costs in general, even while they helped millions of working class and lower middle class Americans move into home ownership (Stone, *Shelter Poverty*).

5. Blau's calculation used what is now the standard definition of affordable housing: a rent of (or mortgage) of 30 percent or less of the income of a family at the federal poverty line (Blau, *The Visible Poor*, 74). The federal poverty line itself has been questioned for several decades, based as it is on unrealistic and

dated notions of the relationship between food costs and income (M. Katz, *The Undeserving Poor*, 115–18).

6. For a thorough quantitative study of the relationship of homelessness to the contemporary shortage of affordable housing, see Ringheim, *At Risk of Homelessness*. Rather than making up the shortfall of affordable housing, the federal government has steadily decreased its role in housing provision, consistent with the broad reduction of federal aid to the cities since 1980 (M. Katz, *The Undeserving Poor*, 189–90).

7. Blasi's survey of studies of homelessness across discipline areas found two-thirds of the articles emanating from psychiatry, psychology, or medicine (Blasi, "And We Are Not Seen," 580). See also Snow, Anderson, and Koegel, "Distorting Tendencies in Research on the Homeless."

8. Buckley and Bigelow, "The Multi-Service Network."

9. Baum and Burnes, *A Nation in Denial*, 4–5.

10. Snow and Anderson, *Down on Their Luck*, 73–87.

11. Golden, *The Women Outside;* Liebow, *Tell Them Who I Am;* Passaro, *The Unequal Homeless.*

12. Bourgois, Lettiere, and Quesada, "Social Misery and the Sanctions of Substance Abuse"; Desjarlais, *Shelter Blues;* Dordick, *Something Left to Lose;* Liebow, *Tell Them Who I Am;* Lyon-Callo, "Medicalizing Homelessness"; Passaro, *The Unequal Homeless;* Weinberg, *Of Others Inside.* See also Marvasti, "Being Homeless"; Stark, "The Shelter as 'Total Institution' "; J. Williams, "Domestic Violence and Poverty."

13. Hopper, *Reckoning with Homelessness,* chapter 6; Hopper et al., "Homelessness, Severe Mental Illness, and the Institutional Circuit."

14. O'Flaherty, *Making Room;* Susser, "Creating Family Forms."

15. Susser, "Creating Family Forms."

16. Duneier, *Sidewalk;* Gowan, "Excavating 'Globalization' from Street Level"; Snow and Anderson, *Down on Their Luck;* Snow et al., "Material Survival Strategies on the Street"; Waterston, *Street Addicts in the Political Economy.*

17. Borchard, *The Word on the Street;* Gagnier, "Homelessness as 'an Aesthetic Issue'"; Mitchell, "Annihilation of Space by Law"; Snow and Mulcahy, "Space, Politics, and the Survival Strategies of the Homeless"; Vitale, *City of Disorder;* Wolch and Philo, "From Distributions of Deviance to Definitions of Difference"; Wright, *Out of Place.*

18. Gowan, "The Nexus"; Metraux and Culhane, "Homeless Shelter Use and Reincarceration Following Prison Release."

19. O'Flaherty, *Making Room;* Susser, "Creating Family Forms."

20. R. Wright, "Out of Sight, Out of Mind." See also Blasi, "And We Are Not Seen"; Bogard, *Seasons Such as These;* Snow and Cress, "Mobilization at the Margins"; Takahashi, "Out of Place."

21. For a developed account of Sam and his workaholic routine, see Gowan, "Excavating 'Globalization' from Street Level."

22. See commentary by Blasi, "And We Are Not Seen," 581; Hoch, "Sheltering the Homeless in the United States."

23. The number of African Americans in San Francisco decreased by another 23 percent, from 79,039 in 1990 to 60,515 in 2000, driven out by a combination of high housing costs, almost zero availability of Section 8 housing in the 1990s, and the destruction of several large housing projects through the federal HOPE VI program (U.S. Census Bureau, 2000). See also Belluck, "End of a Ghetto"; Nieves, "Blacks Hit by Housing Costs Leave San Francisco Behind"; Weston, "San Francisco Bayview."

24. Sassen, *The Global City.*

25. Solnit and Schwarzenberg, *Hollow City.*

26. The proportion of renters stood at 84 percent in 2009. The proportion of renters is always higher than the proportion of rental units (65 percent), as owners tend to have much smaller households.

27. Jeff, a gay man suddenly evicted from his already illegal unit in a South of Market warehouse, moved his twenty years' worth of possessions into a U-Haul van, even though he had nowhere to go. "I'm a homelessexual," he cracked, embarrassed. He circled the neighborhood for weeks, desperately trying to come up with a plan and using up all his money.

28. For example, Los Angeles's skid row is notorious on the West Coast for its homicides and beatings.

29. The recyclers were deliberately unthreatening and many became trusted companions. Two of the San Francisco thieves, Manny and Pipe, were the best friends I ever made on the street, and I had no fear of spending the night in their encampment. With the other thieves and the drug dealers I was more cautious. However, they spent most of their time in the Tenderloin, a very dense skid row neighborhood where the sheer volume of people on the street in the daytime created a sense of relative safety.

30. Golden, *The Women Outside;* Passaro, *The Unequal Homeless.* Historically, poor women have been differently positioned vis-à-vis the law, benefit entitlements, and the state. At the cost of close monitoring by social services, they have been given limited financial support and shelter on the basis of their status as mothers and/or victims of domestic violence (Abramovitz, *Regulating the Lives of Women;* Piven and Cloward, *Regulating the Poor*).

31. Calsyn and Morse, "Homeless Men and Women," 602; Kisor and Kendal-Wilson, "Older Homeless Women." For a qualitative account with a rich exploration of the particular forms of mental distress for homeless women, see Golden, *The Women Outside.*

32. Many of the men took it for granted that women down on their luck would work as prostitutes if they needed money. They were often wrong, but it was certainly true that the economic potential of prostitution far outstripped other forms of hustling and that women and teenage boys trading flesh were generally able to find themselves a place to sleep.

33. The men had very few heterosexual relationships, or even encounters, and most seemed to take it for granted that things would stay that way while they were homeless.

34. Dennis was making a valiant attempt to stabilize his heroin habit, forcing himself to take only twenty dollars a day for copping off. I was helping him out

with cigarettes, one of the more dubious ways that I produced immediate reciprocity in the field.

35. My hunch is that my decision to steer away from the more spectacular deviance of the densest encampments was, in fact, roughly consonant with the range of street life in San Francisco. Many of the city's homeless men did not regularly participate in the city's larger shooting encampments or "bottle gangs."

36. Passaro, *The Unequal Homeless;* Snow and Anderson, *Down on Their Luck;* Susser, "Creating Family Forms"; Wilson, *Declining Significance of Race;* Wilson, *The Truly Disadvantaged.*

37. Burawoy, "Extended Case Method"; Clifford and Marcus, eds., *Writing Culture;* Stacey, "Can There Be a Feminist Ethnography?"

38. O'Connor, *Poverty Knowledge.*

39. Banfield, *Moral Basis of a Backward Society;* Lewis, *The Children of Sanchez;* Moynihan, *The Negro Family,* 47; Rainwater, *Behind Ghetto Walls.* On the surface of it, Moynihan's report smacks more of sickness than sin, in that Moynihan and his colleagues saw "faulty" culture as a matter for careful expert analysis and intervention more than for castigation and punishment. In the late 1960s, the moralistic "bad choices" explanation of poverty was at a low point, and the report's elaboration of "Negro" pathology was articulated in a technocratic voice, with a less judgmental timber than such arguments have taken in more recent years.

40. Lewis, "The Culture of Poverty," 188.

41. Ryan, *Blaming the Victim,* 82.

42. Bourgois, *In Search of Respect,* 17.

43. Ethnographers themselves have endlessly disputed the question of their true mission—whether ethnographers should content themselves with detailed analysis of the microsetting or whether they should mobilize their fieldwork as a window on the intimate workings of the wider society (Burawoy et al., *Global Ethnography;* Denzin, *Interpretive Ethnography;* Fine, "Towards a Peopled Ethnography"; J. Katz, "From How to Why" (parts 1 and 2).

44. A typical example was the *New York Times* review of Bourgois's *In Search of Respect.* The book, said Richard Bernstein, was "irritatingly didactic, especially in those numerous instances when Mr. Bourgois, rather than cope with the shocking nature of his material, simply veers off into an abstract, politically correct jargon identifying 'class exploitation, racial discrimination and, of course, sexist oppression' as the underlying causes of everything." While he praised Bourgois's "remarkable" description, he felt free to dismiss the anthropologist's own analysis (Bernstein, "Entering the Minds of a City's Young Drug Dealers").

45. Sullivan, "Absent Fathers in the Inner City."

46. From 1965 to 1980 government demand for research on poverty rose fast, driven by every increase in the costs of its social programs. (Annual federal spending on poverty research increased from $2.5 million to $160 million, more than 30 percent of all federal research expenditures.) The bulk of the new funding went to economists, anointed and blessed by the principles of hard science, which were becoming increasingly essential within policy circles. The intimate

complexities of qualitative research were clipped by large data sets, predictive models, and program evaluation according to easily quantified measures. Under these conditions, even "hard" sociology lost much of its former influence on social policy (M. Katz, *The Undeserving Poor*, 118–19).

47. Liebow, *Tally's Corner;* Rodman, "The Lower-Class Value Stretch"; Stack, *All Our Kin.*

48. W. Wilson, *Declining Significance of Race;* W. Wilson, *The Truly Disadvantaged.*

49. Gans, "Deconstructing the Underclass"; Hochschild, "Politics of the Estranged Poor"; Niemonen, *Race, Class, and the State in Contemporary Sociology;* Small and Newman, "Urban Poverty after *The Truly Disadvantaged*"; Young, "Social Isolation and Concentration Effects." Wilson responded that his tightly theorized notion of the underclass was precisely what was needed to counter the overly racialized and culture-heavy use of the term in the mass media (W. Wilson, "The Truly Disadvantaged Revisited").

50. Wacquant, "Scrutinizing the Street," 1469. I address this argument and other elements of Wacquant's analysis in more detail in Gowan, "New Hobos or Neoromantic Fantasy?"

51. Kim Hopper has complained that too many ethnographers of homelessness have prided themselves on *Braving the Street,* as Glasser and Bridgman put it, producing no more than field guides to sequestered, exotic subcultures with all the "convenient foreignness" of a third world within. Although his criticisms have a very different flavor, Hopper shares Wacquant's worries that ethnography is not doing enough to elaborate the connections between pernicious social policy and social suffering. While Hopper's criticisms may be well deserved in some cases, it seems to me that many researchers working in the field have taken considerable pains to make strong connections beyond the petty degradations of homeless life (Hopper, *Reckoning with Homelessness,* 204).

52. More recent examples might include the work of Venkatesh (*American Project*) or Edin and Lein (*Making Ends Meet*). The study of poverty in the less industrialized countries went through a similar process. Social scientists wary of the political pitfalls of culture-of-poverty arguments rejected the cultural interpretations of economic and technological backwardness that had been developed in the 1950s and 1960s by Lewis, Banfield, Samuel Huntington, and others. Qualitative research on poverty declined, and, outside anthropology, "culture" became a dirty word. Many turned instead to political economy, most notably dependency theory, which unpacked the external, structural causes of third world poverty (Cardoso and Faletto, *Dependency and Development in Latin America*). Anthropology, however, was quicker than sociology to return to the investigation of cultural structures. While some anthropologists of poverty followed Clifford in turning away from fieldwork altogether, others returned to getting their hands dirty, exemplified by Nancy Scheper-Hughes's magisterial study of rural poverty in Brazil (Clifford, *The Predicament of Culture;* Scheper-Hughes, *Death without Weeping*).

53. An earlier example is Jay MacLeod's widely read ethnography *Ain't No Makin' It*, which compares a relatively respectable group of African American and black immigrant youth with a more delinquent set of young whites.

54. Berrick, *Faces of Poverty;* Duneier, *Slim's Table;* Duneier, *Sidewalk;* Kaplan, *Not Our Kind of Girl;* Newman, *No Shame in My Game;* Stoller, "Spaces, Places, and Fields."

55. This problem is particularly notable in some journalistic accounts. See, for example, Sheehan, *Life for Me Ain't Been No Crystal Stair.*

56. Ong, *Spirits of Resistance and Capitalist Discipline;* Scott, *Weapons of the Week.*

57. Fiske, "For Cultural Interpretation"; Kelley, *Yo' Mama's Disfunktional.*

58. Abu-Lughod, "The Romance of Resistance"; Gilroy, *Against Race.*

59. Willis, *Learning to Labor.*

60. Bourgois, *In Search of Respect,* Introduction; Salzinger, *Genders in Production.*

61. Even if riven with conflict or difficulty in reality, the concept of home symbolizes rest, safety, and familiarity, a state of being as much as a physical place. (For an interesting exploration of how marginally housed women themselves think about home, see Wardhaugh, "The Unaccommodated Woman.") The precarious sleeping arrangements of homeless people place them inescapably in a zone of risk, strangeness, and chaos, whether in unpleasant shelter dormitories, under bushes, on the bare ground, or in often-destroyed encampments. Just as important, their consciousness of the label "homeless" forces them to ruminate on the issue.

2. Managing Homelessness in the United States

1. The "constructions of poverty" could equally well be called discourses, in the sense that I use the word, but I have decided to keep the terms distinct in the interest of easy comprehension.

2. Davis, *Prisoners of the American Dream;* Roediger, *The Wages of Whiteness;* Takaki, "The Tempest in the Wilderness."

3. J. Miller, *Search and Destroy;* Tonry, *Malign Neglect;* Wacquant, "'Suitable Enemies'"; Wideman, "Doing Time, Marking Race."

4. Quadagno, *The Color of Welfare.*

5. T. Miller, "The Knights of St. John and the Hospitals of the Latin West," 712.

6. Ibid., 713. The story of Dives and Lazarus (Luke 16:19–31) was an immensely popular trope for class relations in medieval Britain, and it has endured in the form of various folk songs, the most well known set to the melody used for "The Star of the County Down."

7. The lack of distinction between sickness and poverty was a product of the undeveloped level of medical knowledge. European care of the sick was extremely rudimentary until the end of the twelfth century, when the Knights of St. John brought in the more scientific methods used in the great hospitals

of the Islamic world (ibid., 719–26). Cities such as Constantinople, Damascus, Baghdad, and Cairo all were bigger than any of the European cities during the early Middle Ages and were therefore forced to deal with the problem of disease in a systematic way much earlier.

8. Luther, Preface to *Liber Vagatorum*, 19, 21, 29. Although Luther's primary intention was to discredit begging by associating it with fraudulent priests, he also tried to employ anti-Semitism, arguing that "Beggars' Cant has come from the Jews, for many Hebrew words occur in the vocabulary" (ibid., 3).

9. Ibid. The pamphlet is believed to derive from the great trials at Basel in 1475, when hundreds of blind beggars, strolling musicians, and other vagabonds were arrested, cross-examined, and classified.

10. The Poor Law of 1601 mobilized central authority to generate local solutions to extreme poverty by requiring parishes to tax parishioners to provide a safety net for local inhabitants fallen into poverty (Cowherd, *Political Economists and the English Poor Laws;* Lees, *The Solidarities of Strangers*).

11. In her history of transients in New York State, Joan Crouse describes how colonial legislation required that new arrivals had to post a "security" (a substantial fee) one week after arrival. The authorities would keep this money for two years, against the risk that the transients would become burdens to the county (*The Homeless Transient in the Great Depression,* 16).

12. M. Katz, *In the Shadow of the Poorhouse,* 21; Wyllie, "The Search for an American Law of Charity, 1776–1844," 207.

13. Cowherd, *Political Economists and the English Poor Laws.*

14. Garland, *Punishment and Modern Society: A Study in Social Theory.*

15. A common task for women and children was picking oakum (M. Katz, *In the Shadow of the Poorhouse,* 23–24).

16. Ibid., 93.

17. Monkkonen, *Walking to Work: Tramps in America, 1790–1935,* 8.

18. During the late eighteenth and early nineteenth centuries, many observers noted the irrationality of using laws originally designed to prevent the mobility of feudal serfs to a modern capitalist society. Rather than staying put, industrial workers in the United States were increasingly not only permitted, but also expected, to move to find work. In fact, the father of capitalist social theory, Adam Smith himself, had complained back in 1776 that the British Poor Laws inhibited economic development by holding back the emergence of a free labor market: "Whatever obstructs the free circulation of labor from unemployment to another obstructs that of stock likewise: the quantity of stock which can be employed in any branch of business depending very much on that of the labor which can be employed in it. . . . It is everywhere much easier for a wealthy merchant to obtain the privilege of trading in a town corporate, than for a poor artificer to obtain that of working in it" (*The Wealth of Nations,* 122). Mid-nineteenth-century American manufacturers reliant on seasonal labor agreed, arguing that their workers were unfairly penalized by settlement laws and that municipalities should give the unemployed some aid out of season rather than treat them as criminals. Calling for a new, up-to-date, moral differentiation between deserving

and undeserving poor, they claimed that the passive, long-term poor were the truly undeserving, whereas the seasonal poor were merely victims of economics. Mobility was a positive sign of initiative and should not be discouraged (Crouse, *The Homeless Transient in the Great Depression*, 18).

19. Ibid., 19.

20. Settlement laws were not outlawed until 1969, and my research companions have told me that the practice of warning off was alive and well in the smaller towns of Missouri and California.

21. M. Katz, *In the Shadow of the Poorhouse*, 5.

22. Ibid., 6.

23. Montgomery, *The Fall of the House of Labor*, 132.

24. M. Katz, *In the Shadow of the Poorhouse*, 15–17.

25. Samuel Bishop, reviewing the great achievements of the first thirty years of the charity organization movement for the *American Journal of Sociology* in 1901, felt that the most important insight of its founders was that "the development of intense life in localities, and of personal and vital relationships between men and women of varying gifts and acquisitions, by which good men and gracious women can inspire goodness and graciousness in other men and women, is the highest form of charity" ("The New Movement in Charity," 596).

26. M. Katz, *In the Shadow of the Poorhouse*, 68–71.

27. Ibid., 71.

28. Quoted in Stanley, "Beggars Can't Be Choosers," 1270.

29. M. Katz, *In the Shadow of the Poorhouse*, 84.

30. Many of the children in the orphanages of the Gilded Age were placed there by their parents. For example, during the depression of the late 1870s, the majority of children entering New York orphanages had two parents living. Often not only men, but women would split up from their children, hoping to retrieve them when their fortunes improved. While men would go on the road, women would often take on residential domestic service work.

31. Stanley, "Beggars Can't Be Choosers," 1267.

32. A few judges around the country resisted enforcing the vagrancy codes to the satisfaction of the police, arguing that the laws were unconstitutional, but in general the judicial system went along with the crackdown on poor men (ibid., 1278).

33. Ibid., 1279.

34. M. Katz, *In the Shadow of the Poorhouse*, 94–95.

35. See Daniel, "The Metamorphosis of Slavery, 1865–1900," 90–95.

36. Ibid., 90.

37. Anxious to prevent dependency and idleness, the federally instituted Freedmen's Bureau did little to prevent the development of debt peonage, insisting that the former slaves moved quickly into wage labor. Although it contested some of those statutes and laws that explicitly disadvantaged African Americans on the basis of race, the bureau collaborated with the planter class in forcing African American workers back into disadvantageous contracts. Amy Dru Stanley

quotes a Mississippi bureau agent's instructions to freedmen: "I cannot ask the civil officers to leave you idle, to beg or steal. If they find any of you without . . . means of living, they will do right if they treat you as bad persons and take away your misused liberty" ("Beggars Can't Be Choosers," 1286–87).

38. Davenport, *The Feebly Inhibited*.

39. Ira Steward, labor reformer, quoted in Stanley, "Beggars Can't Be Choosers," 1272.

40. Ibid., 1281.

41. Ringenback, *Tramps and Reformers 1873–1916*.

42. N. Anderson, *The Hobo*, 10, 15.

43. Starr, *Endangered Dreams*, 226.

44. Ibid., 227–28.

45. Ibid., 236.

46. Cresswell, *The Tramp in America*, 198.

47. Hofstadter, *The Paranoid Style in American Politics;* Perlstein, *Nixonland*.

48. MacLeod, "Street People."

49. For an account of the most prominent early activism around homelessness, that of Mitch Snyder and the Community for Creative Non-Violence in Washington, D.C., see Rader, *Signal through the Flames*.

50. Bogard, "Claimsmakers and Contexts in Early Constructions of Homelessness"; Bogard, *Seasons Such as These*.

51. Community for Creative Non-violence.

52. Bogard, *Seasons Such as These*, 125–26.

53. From the beginning, the homelessness advocacy movement was primarily focused on using the mass media more than on building a movement of homeless people. As such, it was vulnerable to the notoriously fickle attention span of news editors and television producers, who mostly turned away from positive images of the homeless by the late 1980s.

54. Gary Blasi has argued that the national advocacy groups' earnest attempts to create an image of the "deserving" (and therefore by implication "white") homeless backfired, as it implicitly accepted the principle that the homeless should be morally evaluated. Instead, he says, activists should have merely shown that homeless people represented a slice of the very poor, somewhat diverse, but far more likely to be African American, addicted, or mentally ill than the average individual ("And We Are Not Seen").

55. Two-parent families do not figure highly in statistics of the homeless. Apart from the huge stresses that poverty and insecurity put on relationships, institutions such as AFDC, safe houses, and family shelters have encouraged poor women to leave their partners.

56. *Suspect*, 1987, dir. Peter Yates; and *Hard Target*, 1993, dir. John Woo.

57. Bogard, *Seasons Such as These*.

58. Allahyari, "The Micro-Politics of Worthy Homelessness."

59. M. Katz, *The Undeserving Poor*, chapter 5.

60. Snow and Anderson, *Down on Their Luck*, chapter 3.

61. Gary Blasi goes further, speculating that homelessness advocacy may have even exacerbated the problem of homelessness: "The final record may suggest that advocacy aimed at ending homelessness actually prolonged it by diverting attention and resources from the wider issues of poverty and inequality" ("And We Are Not Seen," 569).

62. Atkinson, "Domestication by *Cappuccino* or a Revenge on Urban Space?"; Buckley and Bigelow, "The Multi-Service Network."

63. Baum and Burnes, *A Nation in Denial.*

64. Bunis, Yancik, and Snow, "The Cultural Patterning of Sympathy toward the Homeless," 393.

65. Michael Katz, writing in the late 1980s, compared the "deserving" homeless with the "undeserving" underclass. Given the subsequent rise of homeless clearances and the racialization of street people, I doubt that he would have seen the same distinction fifteen years later (*The Undeserving Poor,* chapter 5).

66. Leo, "Distorting the Homeless Debate"; Raspberry, "Telling the Truth about Homelessness"; Thomas, "The Rise and Fall of the Homeless."

67. Gagnier, "Homelessness as 'an Aesthetic Issue'"; Mitchell, "Annihilation of Space by Law"; Snow and Mulcahy, "Space, Politics, and the Survival Strategies of the Homeless."

68. Blasi, "And We Are Not Seen."

69. Brosch, "No Place Like Home."

70. Pear, "Clinton Cites Welfare Gains and Defends Overhaul Plan."

71. Koegel, "Economic Resources of the Homeless"; Snow et al., "Material Survival Strategies on the Street"; Zlotnick and Robertson, "Sources of Income among Homeless Adults."

72. States with the one-month limit: Kentucky, Idaho. Counties with the same limit: Harris County, Texas. Miami allowed applicants benefits for ninety days once every three years. New York specified a twenty-four-month lifetime limit for cash assistance with certain exceptions. All state and county programs also periodically review each case or require that recipients reapply every one, three, or six months, regardless of whether they have time limits. If receiving food stamps, recipients also had to work for their food stamps, and the two processes were not coordinated in most cases.

73. DeVerteuil, Lee, and Wolch, "New Spaces for the Local Welfare State?"

74. See, in particular, a fascinating interview in Giamo and Grunberg, *Beyond Homelessness.*

75. Danziger and Kossoudji, *When Welfare Ends;* DeVerteuil, Lee, and Wolch, "New Spaces for the Local Welfare State?"; Halter, "Homeless in Philadelphia."

76. An enthusiastic elaboration of the "broken windows" perspective (Siegel, *The Future Once Happened Here*). A more social scientific exploration can be found in Skogan, *Disorder and Decline.* There exist numerous excellent critiques, including the following: Duneier, *Sidewalk;* Harcourt, *Illusion of Order;* Hopkins and Nackerud, "An Analysis of Atlanta's Ordinance Prohibiting Urban Camping"; Mitchell, "Annihilation of Space by Law"; Rutheiser, "Making Place in the Nonplace Urban Realm"; Siegel, *The Future Once Happened Here.*

77. A revaluation of homeless advocacy from two leading academic activists can be found in Hopper and Baumohl, "Held in Abeyance — Rethinking Homelessness and Advocacy."

3. Moorings

1. Carlsson, "The Progress Club"; Groth, *Living Downtown;* Issel and Cherny, *San Francisco, 1865–1932;* Walker, "California Rages against the Dying of the Light."

2. Issel and Cherny, *San Francisco, 1865–1932,* lv.

3. Groth, *Living Downtown,* 1.

4. Figures from the Tenderloin Housing Clinic.

5. The city also maintains a close financial relationship with various hotels still in private hands through the Master Lease program, recently expanded by the "Care Not Cash" hotels (see chapter 7).

6. Since the early 1990s, the most basic welfare entitlement, General Assistance, has not come close to covering the rent for one room, even if residents eat in the soup kitchens only. As a consequence there were always comings and goings, a quick turnover of those able to pay for only one week before their check ran out and they hit the shelter again, others with short stays paid for by temporary housing vouchers.

7. Irwin, *The Jail.*

8. See Pippert, *Road Dogs and Loners.*

9. Bourdieu, *The Logic of Practice.*

10. Drake and Cayton, *Black Metropolis;* Dubois, *The Philadelphia Negro;* Liebow, *Tally's Corner.*

11. Light, "The Ethnic Vice Industry, 1880–1944."

12. W. Wilson, *The Declining Significance of Race.*

13. Mauer and King, *A Twenty-Five-Year Quagmire.*

14. Wacquant, "The New 'Peculiar Institution.'"

15. Wacquant, *Punishing the Poor;* Wideman, "Doing Time, Marking Race."

16. Even with juveniles, psychological criteria make barely any impact within the overwhelmingly moral discursive framework of the contemporary American criminal justice system. Repentance and respect for authority remain the only yardstick of rehabilitation. For example, the great majority of reports written up by probation officers about juvenile offenders are squarely situated within a moral discourse on crime. Psychological interpretations are rare, with the most important criteria remaining the degree to which the young person has either expressed or failed to express either remorse or respect for authority. Bridges and Steen, "Racial Disparities in Official Assessments of Juvenile Offenders."

17. R. Anderson, "Homeless Violence and the Informal Rules of Street Life."

18. "James Moss" is not a pseudonym. James was always extremely opposed to the idea of pseudonyms, and when he was dying from emphysema he extorted a promise that I use his true name in this book.

19. In the case of the heroin users, many chose to steady their habits by teaming up with shooting or "running" partners. This way they could share smaller

proportions of one bag rather than roll in a dangerous cycle from shooting large quantities to heavy nodding to monster cravings. (Reciprocity among San Francisco street heroin addicts is discussed in detail in Bourgois, Lettiere, and Quesada, "Social Misery and the Sanctions of Substance Abuse.") The practicalities of heroin use therefore pushed addicts new to the street in the direction of their fellows. They might move to one of the encampments on the western edge of the Tenderloin or beyond to the streets around Van Ness Avenue, to the Haight's Buena Vista Park, or the Mission's Thirteenth Street, or San Jose and Arlington, or down by the Cesar Chavez/101 underpass, each of which had a somewhat different character.

20. Some of those living in Golden Gate Park and the Presidio woods tried to grow marijuana.

21. Lefebvre, *The Production of Space*, 288.

22. Eighner, *Travels with Lizbeth*.

23. Weinberg, "'Out There.'"

24. In fact, Del's opinion that the recyclers were showing obstinate self-delusion in their refusal to acknowledge the extent of their marginality has been echoed by several academics after reading my articles on the subject.

25. Dordick, *Something Left to Lose*.

4. Word on the Street

1. Snow and Anderson, *Down on Their Luck*, chapter 3.

2. N. Smith, *New Urban Frontier*.

3. Vitale, "Enforcing Civility."

4. See, for what is now a classic discussion of this point, Sayer, *Method in Social Science*.

5. In some parts of the English-speaking world, "gang-banging" has come to mean gang rape, but the aging hustlers of the Tenderloin did not use the term in this sense. To them, "gang-banging" was a generic term for drinking, drugging, "wilding," fighting, and generally raising hell with other boys.

6. "Bad news," "bad scene," and "bad eye" are negative, for example, but "bad-ass nigger," "bad boy," and plain "baad" tend to be highly positive. The Black Power years in particular produced a whole host of terms incorporating "bad" with a positive spin—"bad-mouth," "bad rags," and "bad-doing," for example. Some scholars trace this characteristic of African American speech back to Africa, pointing to similar reversals in the languages of the Sierra Leone area (Major, *Juba to Jive*, 15).

7. The connection of blackness with nighttime among San Franciscan street addicts has also been noted in Bourgois, Lettiere, and Quesada, "Social Misery and the Sanctions of Substance Abuse," 164.

8. Hopper, *Reckoning with Homelessness*. In the early twentieth century, African Americans were, if anything, underrepresented among the homeless. Now they are significantly overrepresented, making up from 40 to 50 percent of single homeless people.

9. Ibid.

10. While the Vietnam connection was strained, it was no stretch to believe that these men's participation in the military was connected to their homelessness. Most of the homeless men who had been in the military for a long time had lost contact with their families beyond the rare letter or phone call at Christmas. When they later became homeless, there was not much likelihood that they would be able to draw on those back home for support.

11. Margolis, "Samurai beneath Blue Tarps."

12. San Francisco Department of Public Works.

13. Weinberg, *Of Others Inside.*

14. The Coalition on Homelessness tried to bring system-talk into the shelters with an outreach program designed to listen to people's problems with the shelters, as well as providing information about legal rights and various training or employment possibilities. In general, though, system-talk was weak within the shelters, as others have noted. See, most notably, Lyon-Callo, *Inequality, Poverty, and Neoliberal Governance.* To the extent that these institutions were successful in shifting the grip of sin-talk, it was in the direction of sick-talk.

15. Tiny, *Criminal of Poverty.*

16. It will come as no surprise that in my own eyes I was far more a captive of system-talk.

17. Bakhtin, *The Dialogic Imagination;* Kristeva, *The Kristeva Reader;* Volosinov, *Marxism and the Philosophy of Language.*

18. Rice and Waugh, *Modern Literary Theory,* 199.

No One Loves a Loser

1. Identity disguised.

2. The San Francisco Fire Department released a report on the notorious Delta Hotel fire of August 11, 1997, in which one resident died and several were injured. The report stated that the upper floors of the building were destroyed due to the nonfunctioning of both of the most important fire protection mechanisms in the building, that is, the sprinkler system and the standpipe from which the firefighters should have been able to douse the flames. Wallace, "Sprinklers Blamed in Fatal Fire: S.F. Hotel Standpipe Didn't Deliver Water Either, Probe Finds." Willie and his ex-neighbors were convinced that the owner had deliberately disabled the sprinkler system in hopes of a large insurance payout.

5. The New Hobos

1. My fieldwork supported the estimates of the Coalition on Homelessness, namely that no more than 20 percent of the street homeless were likely to be receiving General Assistance at any given time.

2. Hartwell, "Not All Work Is Created Equal"; Rossi, "Minorities and Homelessness"; Snow et al., "Material Survival Strategies on the Street."

3. U.S. Conference of Mayors 2005. If there has indeed been a decrease, this may be connected to the fast-growing proportion of women and children among those counted as homeless.

4. Esbenshade, "The 'Crisis' over Day Labor"; Hartwell, "Not All Work Is Created Equal"; Parker, *Flesh Peddlers and Warm Bodies;* Rossi, "Minorities and Homelessness." Theodore has estimated that at least 50 percent of the day laborers in Chicago are homeless, which supports Cook's impressions of the workforce of Labor Ready in San Francisco. Cook, "Street Corner, Incorporated." Theodore, "Political Economies of Day Labor."

5. Snow et al., "Material Survival Strategies on the Street." In another article, Snow and Anderson do note a small minority of dumpster divers who "pridefully identified themselves in terms of this activity." Snow and Anderson, "Identity Work among the Homeless."

6. Snow and Anderson, *Down on Their Luck.*

7. I have already made this case in the context of somewhat different arguments: Gowan, "American Untouchables"; Gowan, "Excavating 'Globalization' from Street Level."

8. My 1994–1995 research with San Franciscans using vans and pickup trucks to recycle suggested that the work was particularly attractive to immigrants with poor language skills or lack of legal residency, and in some cases to refugees (mostly Laotians and Cambodians) who could not take official work without losing their refugee status. Most of the van recyclers cited in the city's 1995 crackdown were undocumented immigrants.

9. Statistics based on research by *San Francisco Chronicle* journalist Kevin Fagan and my own interviews with city recycling officials and local recycling companies in 1994–1995. See Fagan, "Heavy Load"; Gowan, "American Untouchables."

10. Latinos and Asian Americans, many of them first-generation and undocumented immigrants, use pickups and small trucks to collect large quantities of cardboard and bottles.

11. This is an extremely conservative estimate, based on several spot surveys of those entering the city's major recycling plants from 1995 to 2001. The number of recyclers clearly increased during these years, and my most thorough survey, taken in 1998, suggested there were at least 850 homeless people making their primary income from recycling at that time. As my qualitative fieldwork indicated that those bringing in large loads were usually full-time recyclers, I used the size of the load to distinguish between the serious or pro and casual recyclers.

12. While shelters now cater to large numbers of women and children, street homelessness remains mostly the province of men. This divide between "men on the streets" and "women in their place" is well described by Joanne Passaro (Passaro, *The Unequal Homeless*).

13. Translated from Spanish.

14. Derick was referring to the reflective jackets worn by GA recipients when cleaning the streets for their compulsory "workfare" detail.

15. Snow and Anderson, "Identity Work among the Homeless."

16. As many of those studying labor have pointed out, the accuracy of this perception is highly debatable. Exploitation can be all the more successful for being hidden.

17. Aluminum remains the most popular recyclable, the only material to reach a recycling rate of more than 50 percent in the United States. According to the Institute of Scrap Recycling Industries, 55.6 billion aluminum cans were recycled in 2001 for a payout of $850 million.

18. On January 1, 2000, the law changed to include containers for water and other noncarbonated drinks such as wine, reinforcing the bottle as the preeminent target for the homeless recyclers. But the small number of recyclers who lived in vans and cars and used their vehicles for transportation were less dependent on bottles. For example, those with pickup trucks were able to use their large amount of space to successfully specialize in cardboard or large pieces of scrap metal.

19. "Copping" is the standard street term for buying drugs.

20. Where did this knowledge of hobo lore come from? Most authors writing on the subject considered that the hobos of the West Coast had more or less died out in the postwar period, with the exception of a few apple tramps who worked the fruit harvests in the northwest, described by Douglas Harper in Harper, *Good Company*. I pursued the ghostly line of hobos leading to Morris like a detective on a case, determined to uncover a living local hobo tradition, talking with him repeatedly and grilling other men living near the train lines. Morris had indeed gleaned some fascinating details from a few encounters with older tramps, but he had learned more of his information about hobos from the same sources as I had. For example, he too had read Dean Stiff's *The Milk and Honey Route: A Handbook for Hobos,* as well as the more sociological *The Hobo* by Nels Anderson (N. Anderson, *The Hobo*); Stiff, *The Milk and Honey Route*.

21. Wine bottles didn't bring in a redemption fee so were not officially accepted at the recycling plants. However, those bringing in big loads could successfully mix in some wine bottles or pieces of glass from broken lamps or dishes.

22. For the classic account of "emotion work," see Hochschild, *The Managed Heart*.

23. See Gowan, "Excavating 'Globalization' from Street Level" for a fuller account of Clarence's movement from informalizing the military to formalizing the informal recycling economy.

24. *La migra* is the colloquial name for the U.S. Immigration and Naturalization Service (INS).

25. The situation was rather different for recyclers with vans or trucks. While most Anglo-run businesses seemed indifferent to the question of who was going to gain money from their recycling, immigrant-run businesses showed substantial evidence of ethnic enclaves. Many Latino-run bars and restaurants would have exclusive relationships with particular Latino van recyclers, and Chinese-run establishments tended to save their recycling for their own relatives or friends.

26. Working-class families, on the contrary, tended to make their own trips to the small recycling operations on supermarket lots, pushing wire laundry

carts stacked high with tightly packed bottles and cans. Many Latino and Asian American people said that they regularly collected the recycling for their whole building, and that they would request their neighbors and relatives not to put out valuable bottles and cans. On the other hand, Latino businesses were much more likely to give recycling to Latino recyclers.

27. Lankenau's study of Washington, D.C., panhandlers concludes similarly that contact with regular donors is vital for the resistance of stigma and non-personhood (Lankenau, "Stronger Than Dirt: Public Humiliation and Status Enhancement among Panhandlers").

28. Other suppliers did not share these values, but were immigrants from poor countries where scavenging and extreme poverty were more ordinary and less pathologized. While panhandlers bemused them, they saw nothing in need of explanation in the actions of the homeless recyclers.

29. Wacquant, "Scrutinizing the Street."

30. Ibid., 1481.

31. Snow and Anderson, "Identity Work among the Homeless: The Verbal Construction and Avowal of Personal Identities."

32. DePastino, *Citizen Hobo: How a Century of Homelessness Shaped America*; Foner, *History of the Labor Movement in the United States, vol. 4*.

6. The Homeless Archipelago

1. Baum and Burnes, *A Nation in Denial*, 3.

2. Ibid., 110–53.

3. Hoch, "Sheltering the Homeless in the United States"; Snow et al., "Material Survival Strategies on the Street."

4. Interagency Council on the Homeless, Department of Housing and Urban Development, *Priority Home!*

5. One of the earliest academic critiques of the overreliance on emergency shelter in the 1980s was the work of David Snow and Leon Anderson. Snow and Anderson, *Down on Their Luck*, 77–87.

6. Barrow and Zimmer, *Transitional Housing and Services: A Synthesis*, 26.

7. See chapter 2.

8. Baum and Burnes, *A Nation in Denial*, 149.

9. Hospitality House switched its large men's shelter into a case-management model in the mid-1990s. Then, in 2001, the Multi-Service Center North, another of the large male shelters, was transformed into a transitional housing program called the Next Door, which offered more personal space for each resident and a broad range of services in the same building.

10. My interviews with caseworkers, unfortunately, do not constitute any kind of representative sample. Despite valiant attempts by some individuals to help me gain access, I found it extremely hard to get permission for any systematic research within the transitional shelters. Almost all these interviews with caseworkers were held outside of the shelters.

11. Conrad, "Medicalization and Social Control"; Mathieu, "The Medicalization of Homelessness and the Theater of Repression"; Schram, "In the Clinic."

12. In some cases, shelter managers who shared their primarily moral perspective on homelessness often supported the sin-talk of the frontline staff. In *The Homeless Archipelago,* Ricardo, a case manager at a transitional shelter, described an institutional fault line between the sick-talk of the case managers and the sin-talk of the other shelter staff. His characterization of this division supported my own observations and was echoed by several workers at three different shelters. Ultimately, this frequent mutual incomprehension between the social workers and the other senior staff was overdetermined by the weighty combination of differences of race, class, and culture. Many of the caseworkers and senior social workers were white college graduates whose manner contrasted sharply with the more overtly disciplinarian style of their colleagues, often African Americans, who had risen from working-class backgrounds through the ranks of the city bureaucracy or other areas of public administration. In this kind of situation, the therapeutic orientation of the social workers was heavily outnumbered, with even the most sympathetic of their colleagues more likely to understand homelessness in moral terms.

13. Goffman, *Stigma.*

14. See also Stark, "The Shelter as 'Total Institution,'" 553.

15. Hopper et al., "Homelessness, Severe Mental Illness, and the Institutional Circuit"; Wolch and Philo, "From Distributions of Deviance to Definitions of Difference."

16. I heard this comment secondhand from a mutual friend who bumped into the now reformed Sam. Sam was not eager to renew contact with me, it seemed, presumably because I was too strongly connected with his life "out there." Maybe he thought that I had enabled his addiction by not pushing him to place it at center stage.

17. Culhane, Metraux, and Hadley, "Public Service Reductions Associated with Placement of Homeless Persons."

18. Kertesz and Weiner, "Housing the Chronically Homeless."

19. Their peers in many other cities could get only thirty days at a time, barely enough time to register what it felt like to be "clean" before they had to scramble for alternative arrangements.

20. Weinberg, *Of Others Inside,* 70.

21. Ibid. Daytop Lodge in New York City, founded 1963, was the first such state-funded therapeutic community.

22. Hays, *Flat Broke with Children.*

23. Western Regional Advocacy Project, *Without Housing,* chart 7.

A Little Room for Myself

1. As several others have argued, depression in someone who is homeless should not necessarily be taken as a contributing factor to becoming homeless.

It is generally hard to tell what someone who has been homeless for a while was like before he or she hit the streets. As George said in his forceful fashion, "Of course I am fucking depressed. What the hell do you expect?" Once someone is both homeless and depressed, though, depression is likely to make it even harder to get off the street. For a very useful discussion of the uncritical use of psychiatric inventories, see Snow, Anderson, and Koegel, "Distorting Tendencies in Research on the Homeless," 461–75.

2. Name changed.

3. Robert Frost, *Poems by Robert Frost: A Boy's Will and North of Boston*, 73.

7. The Old Runaround

1. This metaphor was at the center of Puritan leader John Winthrop's famous sermon "A Model of Christian Charity," given in 1630. "For we must consider that we shall be as a city upon a hill," said Winthrop. "The eyes of all people are upon us. So that if we shall deal falsely with our God in this work we have undertaken . . . we shall be made a story and a by-word throughout the world." Winthrop, Dunn, and Yeandle, *The Journal of John Winthrop, 1630–1649*, 10.

2. P. Smith, *As a City upon a Hill*.

3. N. Smith, "New Globalism, New Urbanism."

4. Goldberger, "The Rise of the Private City"; Groth, *Living Downtown*; Sibley, *Geographies of Exclusion*.

5. The War on Poverty's expansion of federal transfers to the inner-city poor was influenced by a constellation of diverse conditions. Piven and Cloward emphasize the dramatic civil rights context—the Birmingham civil rights campaign and the 1963 March on Washington—arguing that Democratic leaders were forced to act to maintain social stability and the African American vote. Others have insisted that the Kennedy Democrats were equally informed by the Progressive tradition and the contemporary works of Harrington and Galbraith. Those who have studied closely the institutional picture have pointed to how federal spending was driven upward by agency jockeying between the Council of Economic Advisers, the Labor Department, the Social Security Administration, and the President's Commission on Juvenile Delinquency. See accounts by M. Katz, *The Undeserving Poor*; O'Connor, *Poverty Knowledge*; Piven and Cloward, *Regulating the Poor*.

6. Fraser and Gerstle, *The Rise and Fall of the New Deal Order, 1930–1980*.

7. Beauregard, *Voices of Decline*.

8. Castells, *The Informational City*; Davis, *City of Quartz*; Jacobs, *The Death and Life of Great American Cities*; Kain, "Housing Segregation, Negro Unemployment, and Metropolitan Decentralization"; Marcuse, "The Ghetto of Exclusion and the Fortified Enclave"; Siegel, *The Future Once Happened Here*.

9. N. Smith, "New Globalism, New Urbanism."

10. "[A] lot of serious crime is adventitious, not the result of inexorable social forces or personal failings. A rash of burglaries may occur because drug users have found a back alley or an abandoned building in which to hang out. In their

spare time, and in order to get money to buy drugs, they steal from their neighbors. If the back alleys are cleaned up and the abandoned buildings torn down, the drug users will go away." Wilson, "Making Neighborhoods Safe."

11. Ibid., 47.

12. Hopkins and Nackerud, "An Analysis of Atlanta's Ordinance Prohibiting Urban Camping"; Rutheiser, "Making Place in the Nonplace Urban Realm"; Williams, "The Public I/Eye."

13. Nieves, "Prosperity's Losers."

14. B. Wright, *Out of Place,* 40.

15. Snow and Mulcahy describe street homelessness as "a rupture of the spatial bedrock and the associated cultural imagery on which the urban order rests." By panhandling, scavenging, and holding sidewalk sales, street people break powerful social norms. This is even more the case when they show signs of mental illness or extreme dirtiness. Yet, as Talmadge Wright and others have argued, many of the behaviors of homeless people in public spaces are the kinds of "home practices" that are not universally deviant but merely "out of place." Sleeping, sitting, teeth cleaning, drinking, urinating, eating, and the kinds of activities defined as "loitering" are all acceptable within private space (and licensed campgrounds), but become suspect in public. Mitchell, "The Annihilation of Space by Law," 310–12; Snow and Mulcahy, "Space, Politics, and the Survival Strategies of the Homeless," 154; Waldron, "Homelessness and the Issue of Freedom," 301–2.

16. Peck and Tickell, "Neoliberalizing Space."

17. Baumgartner, *The Moral Order of a Suburb.*

18. Amster, *Lost in Space;* Atkinson, "Domestication by *Cappuccino* or a Revenge on Urban Space?"; Brosch, "No Place Like Home"; Davis, *City of Quartz;* Gagnier, "Homelessness as 'an Aesthetic Issue,'" 168; Hopkins and Nackerud, "An Analysis of Atlanta's Ordinance Prohibiting Urban Camping"; Marcuse, "The Ghetto of Exclusion and the Fortified Enclave"; Mitchell, "The Annihilation of Space by Law"; Rutheiser, "Making Place in the Nonplace Urban Realm."

19. Goldberger, "The Rise of the Private City."

20. By exploiting a loop in the housing code designed to help struggling artists to stay in the city, Joe O'Donoghue and the Residential Builders Association threw up luxury "live-work spaces" over large sections of eastern San Francisco without the usual requirements to either pay taxes toward public schools or to include a certain number of affordable units.

21. National Low Income Housing Coalition, "Out of Reach 2001: America's Growing Wage-Rent Disparity."

22. San Francisco merchants and community associations hostile to the homeless have frequently claimed that homeless people come from all over the country to take advantage of the city's superior service provision. No large-scale study has properly examined the origins of the homeless population, but several advocates and service providers I interviewed agreed that the majority of San Francisco's homeless, like most residents of the city, appeared to have moved there as adults, in many cases from nearby cities in northern California.

23. Cited by Vitale, "Enforcing Civility," dissertation, City University of New York, 2001.

24. Paddock, "S.F. Sense of Pride an Issue."

25. N. Smith, "New Globalism, New Urbanism."

26. Godfrey, "Urban Development and Redevelopment in San Francisco."

27. The board of supervisors is San Francisco's selected legislative branch, designed to balance the power of the mayor, but in many areas the mayor's office holds far more power.

28. For another account of the San Francisco clearances, see Parenti, *Lockdown America*.

29. During this period, the Salvation Army shelter reserved forty beds for Matrix referrals and the other large shelters also gave preferential treatment to those referred through Matrix. 1993–1995 statistics from Cothran, "Matrix's Happy Face."

30. Epstein, "Homelessness No. 1 Problem, S.F. Voters Say: They Want Issue Given Mayor's Highest Priority."

31. Nieves, "Prosperity's Losers." It is possible that a small proportion of these tickets were not given to homeless people, but other "quality-of-life code violators."

32. Peck and Tickell, "Neoliberalizing Space," 384.

33. National Housing Law Project, *False Hope.*

34. This strategy proved a lifesaver for many poor people on disability or social security, but left no place for the able-bodied poor.

35. Bayshore is a low-income, largely African American neighborhood outside the purview of the Matrix Program.

36. Goldberger, "The Rise of the Private City."

37. Link et al., "Lifetime and Five-Year Prevalence of Homelessness in the United States."

38. Duneier, *Sidewalk.*

39. Borchard, "Fear of and Sympathy toward Homeless Men in Las Vegas." Brosch, "No Place Like Home."

40. Name changed.

41. One place where this discursive take-up was evident was in the online forums run by the *San Francisco Chronicle,* where readers earnestly debated how to differentiate the sick from the criminal homeless.

42. "Push has definitely come to shove," one man said. "There's nowhere to go. You can't walk around upstairs—on top of the creek—with bags and a shopping cart." Zinko, "Homeless Haven Cleared Out."

43. Ibid.

44. Vitale, "Enforcing Civility."

45. Fagan, "Fewer Homeless People on Streets of San Francisco."

46. Fagan, "Newsom Details Plan for Homeless"; Fagan, "Attacking Hard-Core Homelessness"; Fagan, " 'Supportive' Housing Seen as Good Start."

47. Aggressive panhandling was defined in the following terms: causing fear in a person being solicited or using violent or threatening gestures; persisting

once a person has refused, or following a person while panhandling; purposely blocking a vehicle or person.

48. Fagan, "New Panhandling Law—S.F. to Take It Easy."

49. The full definition given by Culhane and Kuhn takes any chronically homeless person to be an "unaccompanied individual with a disabling condition who has either been continuously homeless for a year or more, or has had at least four episodes of homelessness in the past three years." Culhane and Kuhn, "Patterns and Determinants of Public Shelter Utilization among Homeless Adults in New York and Philadelphia"; Culhane, Metraux, and Hadley, "Public Service Reductions Associated with Placement of Homeless Persons with Severe Mental Illness in Supportive Housing." See also "The 10-Year Plan to End Chronic Homelessness in San Francisco," at http://www.sf-planning.org.

50. See, for example, Fagan, "Feds Say S.F. Just Needs to Decide."

51. Tsemberis, Gulcur, and Nakae, "Housing First, Consumer Choice, and Harm Reduction for Homeless Individuals with a Dual Diagnosis."

52. Kertesz and Weiner, "Housing the Chronically Homeless."

53. The city set aside 793 hotel rooms at the outset of the program, adding another 484 over the next two years. Once the General Assistance payments to each client were reduced, the bulk of the money saved was put into a central fund to pay for hotel rooms. After three checks, an individual's checks could fund a hotel room in one of the welfare hotels designated for the program.

54. The program had a problematic effect on the shelters themselves, exacerbating the long-standing problem of turn-aways from shelters that were not in reality filled to capacity. A third of the beds (or mats) were now held until late at night for Care Not Cash recipients, regardless whether they were using them or not. Homeless General Assistance recipients were already paid through the County Adult Assistance Program (CAAP), and it was CAAP recipients that received the large cuts in entitlement. As of June 2009, 1,321 hotel rooms were provided through Care Not Cash.

55. Knight, "Homelessness?"

56. Nevius, "Newsom's Hints at New Plans for Homeless."

57. The opponents of the proposition, led by the Coalition on Homelessness, raised $8,000.

58. Beauregard, "The Politics of Urbanism."

Conclusion

1. One notable large-scale study was Sutherland and Locke, *Twenty Thousand Homeless Men.*

2. Cresswell, *The Tramp in America;* DePastino, *Citizen Hobo.*

3. N. Anderson, *The Hobo,* 72.

4. Harvey, "Neoliberalism as Creative Destruction."

5. Fantasia and Voss, *Hard Work: Remaking the American Labor Movement;* Loba and Hooks, "Public Employment, Welfare Transfers, and Economic Well-Being across Local Populations."

6. Jessop, "Liberalism, Neoliberalism, and Urban Governance."

7. The notable exception here is the agricultural sector.

8. Gowan, "The Nexus: Homeless and Incarceration in Two Cities."

9. Western Regional Advocacy Project, *Without Housing.*

10. Weinberg, *Of Others Inside;* Dordick, "Recovering from Homelessness"; Skoll, *Walk the Walk, Talk the Talk.*

11. California State Assembly AB 1778, introduced by San Francisco Assemblywoman Fiona Ma.

Bibliography

Abramovitz, Mimi. *Regulating the Lives of Women: Social Welfare Policy from Colonial Times to the Present.* Boston, Mass.: South End Press, 1988.

Abu-Lughod, Lila. "The Romance of Resistance: Tracing Transformations of Power through Bedouin Women." *American Ethnologist* (1990): 41–55.

Allahyari, Rebecca Anne. "The Micro-Politics of Worthy Homelessness: Interactive Moments in Congressional Hearings." *Sociological Inquiry* 67, no. 1 (1997): 27–47.

Amster, Randall. *Lost in Space: The Criminalization, Globalization, and Urban Ecology of Homelessness.* New York: LSB Scholarly Publishing, 2008.

Anderson, Nels. *The Hobo: The Sociology of the Homeless Man.* Chicago: University of Chicago Press, 1961 (1923).

Anderson, Ralph. "Homeless Violence and the Informal Rules of Street Life." *Journal of the Social Distress and the Homeless* 5, no. 4 (1996): 369–80.

Atkinson, Rowland. "Domestication by *Cappuccino* or a Revenge on Urban Space? Control and Empowerment in the Management of Public Spaces." *Urban Studies* 40, no. 9 (2003): 1829–43.

Bakhtin, Mikhail M. *The Dialogic Imagination: Four Essays.* Translated by Holquist, Michael M., and Caryl Emerson. Austin: University of Texas Press, 1981.

Banfield, Edward. *The Moral Basis of a Backward Society.* New York: Free Press, 1958.

Barrow, Susan, and Rita Zimmer. *Transitional Housing and Services: A Synthesis.* Washington, D.C.: U.S. Department of Housing and Urban Development, 1999.

Baum, Alice S., and Donald W. Burnes. *A Nation in Denial: The Truth about Homelessness.* Boulder, Colo.: Westview Press, 1993.

Baumgartner, M. P. *The Moral Order of a Suburb.* New York: Oxford University Press, 1988.

Beauregard, Robert. "The Politics of Urbanism: Mike Davies and the Neo-Conservatives." *Capitalism, Nature, Socialism* 10, no. 3 (1999): 40–45.

——. *Voices of Decline: The Post-War Fate of U.S. Cities.* Oxford: Oxford University Press, 1993. Belluck, Pam. "End of a Ghetto: Razing the Slums to Rescue the Residents." *New York Times,* September 6, 1998, sec. 1, p. 1, col. 4.

Bernstein, Richard. "Entering the Minds of a City's Young Drug Dealers." *New York Times,* 1997, C7.

Berrick, Jill Duerr. *Faces of Poverty: Portraits of Women and Children on Welfare.* New York: Oxford University Press, 1995.

Bishop, Samuel H. "The New Movement in Charity." *American Journal of Sociology* 7, no. 5 (1902): 595–610.

Blasi, Gary. "And We Are Not Seen: Ideological and Political Barriers to Understanding Homelessness." *American Behavioral Scientist* 37, no. 4 (1994): 563–86.

Blau, Joel. *The Visible Poor: Homelessness in the United States.* New York: Oxford University Press, 1992.

Bogard, Cynthia J. "Claimsmakers and Contexts in Early Constructions of Homelessness: A Comparison of New York City and Washington, D.C." *Symbolic Interaction* 24, no. 4 (2001): 425–54.

——. *Seasons Such as These: How Homelessness Took Shape in America.* New York: Walter de Gruyter, 2003.

Borchard, Kurt. "Fear of and Sympathy toward Homeless Men in Las Vegas." *Humanity and Society* 24, no. 1 (2000): 3–18.

——. *The Word on the Street.* Las Vegas: University of Nevada Press, 2005.

Bourdieu, Pierre. *The Logic of Practice.* Translated by Richard Nice. Part 1, ed. Stanford, Calif.: Stanford University Press, 1990.

Bourgois, Philippe. *In Search of Respect: Selling Crack in El Barrio.* New York: Cambridge University Press, 1995.

Bourgois, Philippe, Mark Lettiere, and James Quesada. "Social Misery and the Sanctions of Substance Abuse: Confronting HIV Risk among Homeless Heroin Addicts in San Francisco." *Social Problems* 44, no. 2 (1997): 155–73.

Bridges, George S., and Sara Steen. "Racial Disparities in Official Assessments of Juvenile Offenders: Attributional Stereotypes as Mediating Mechanisms." *American Sociological Review* 63, no. 4 (1998): 554–70.

Brosch, Eric. "No Place Like Home." *Harper's,* April 1998, 58–59.

Buckley, Ralph, and Douglas A. Bigelow. "The Multi-Service Network: Reaching the Unserved Multi-Problem Individual." *Community Mental Health Journal* 28, no. 1 (1992): 43–50.

Bunis, William K., Angela Yancik, and David A. Snow. "The Cultural Patterning of Sympathy toward the Homeless and Other Victims of Misfortune." *Social Problems* 43, no. 4 (1996): 387–402.

Burawoy, Michael. "The Extended Case Method." *Sociological Theory* 16, no. 1 (1998): 4–33.

Burawoy, Michael, Joe Blum, Sheba George, Zsuzsa Gille, Teresa Gowan, Lynne Haney, Maren Klawiter, Steve Lopez, Seán Ó Riain, and Millie Thayer. *Global Ethnography: Forces, Connections, and Imaginations in a Postmodern World.* Berkeley: University of California Press, 2000.

Burt, Martha R. *Over the Edge: The Growth of Homelessness in the 1980s.* New York: Russell Sage Foundation, 1992.

Calsyn, Robert J., and Gary Morse. "Homeless Men and Women: Commonalities and the Service Gender Gap." *American Journal of Community Psychology* 18, no. 4 (1990): 597–608.

Cardoso, Fernando Henrique, and Enzo Faletto. *Dependency and Development in Latin America.* Berkeley: University of California Press, 1979 (1971).

Carlsson, Chris. "The Progress Club: 1934 and Class Memory." In *Reclaiming San Francisco: History, Politics, Culture.* Edited by James Brook, Chris Carlsson, and Nancy J. Peters, 67–88. San Francisco: City Lights Books, 1998.

Castells, Manuel. *The Informational City: Information Technology, Economic Restructuring, and the Urban-Regional Process.* Oxford: Blackwell, 1989.

Clifford, James. *The Predicament of Culture.* Cambridge, Mass.: Harvard University Press, 1988.

Clifford, James, and George Marcus, eds. *Writing Culture: Poetics and Politics of Ethnography.* Berkeley: University of California Press, 1986.

Conrad, Peter. "Medicalization and Social Control." *Annual Review of Sociology* 18 (1992): 209–32.

Cook, Christopher D. "Street Corner, Incorporated." *Mother Jones* (March/April 2002): 65–69.

Cothran, George. "Matrix's Happy Face: Few Statistics Contradict Jordan's Spin on Homeless Crackdown." *San Francisco Weekly,* March 22–28, 1995, 4.

Cowherd, Raymond G. *Political Economists and the English Poor Laws: A Historical Study of the Influence of Classical Economics on the Formation of Social Welfare Policy.* Athens: Ohio University Press, 1977.

Cresswell, Tim. *The Tramp in America.* London: Reaktion Books, 2001.

Crouse, Joan M. *The Homeless Transient in the Great Depression: New York State, 1929–1941.* Albany: State University of New York Press, 1986.

Culhane, Dennis P., Stephen Metraux, and Trevor Hadley. "Public Service Reductions Associated with Placement of Homeless Persons with Severe Mental Illness in Supportive Housing." *Housing Policy Debate* 13, no. 1 (2002): 107–64.

Culhane, Dennis P., and Randall Kuhn. "Patterns and Determinants of Public Shelter Utilization among Homeless Adults in New York and Philadelphia." *Journal of Policy Analysis and Management* 17, no. 1 (1998): 23–44.

Daniel, Pete. "The Metamorphosis of Slavery, 1865–1900." *Journal of American History* 66, no. 1 (1979): 88–99.

Danziger, S., and S. Kossoudji. *When Welfare Ends: Final Report of the General Assistance Project.* Ann Arbor: University of Michigan, School of Social Work, 1995.

Davenport, Charles B. *The Feebly Inhibited: Nomadism, or the Wandering Impulse, with Special Reference to Heredity.* Washington, D.C.: Carnegie Institute of Washington, 1915.

Davis, Mike. *City of Quartz: Excavating the Future in Los Angeles.* London: Vintage, 1990.

———. *Prisoners of the American Dream.* New York: Verso, 1986.

Denzin, Norman K. *Interpretive Ethnography: Ethnographic Practices for the Twenty-first Century*. Thousand Oaks, Calif.: Sage Publications, 1997.

DePastino, Todd. *Citizen Hobo: How a Century of Homelessness Shaped America*. Chicago: University of Chicago Press, 2002.

Desjarlais, Robert. *Shelter Blues: Sanity and Selfhood among the Homeless*. Philadelphia: University of Pennsylvania Press, 1997.

DeVerteuil, Geoffrey, Woobae Lee, and Jennifer Wolch. "New Spaces for the Local Welfare State? The Case of General Relief in Los Angeles County." *Social and Cultural Geography* 3, no. 3 (2002): 229–45.

Dordick, Gwendolyn A. *Something Left to Lose: Personal Relations and Survival among New York's Homeless*. Philadelphia, Pa.: Temple University Press, 1997.

Drake, St. Clair, and Horace Cayton. *Black Metropolis: A Study of Negro Life in a Northern City*. Chicago: University of Chicago Press, 1993.

Du Bois, W. E. B. *The Philadelphia Negro*. Philadelphia: University of Pennsylvania Press, 1899.

Duneier, Mitchell. *Sidewalk*. New York: Farrar, Straus, and Giroux, 1999.

———. *Slim's Table: Race, Respectability, and Masculinity*. Chicago: University of Chicago Press, 1992.

Edin, Kathryn, and Laura Lein. *Making Ends Meet: How Single Mothers Survive Welfare and Low-Wage Work*. New York: Russell Sage Foundation, 1997.

Eighner, Lars. *Travels with Lizbeth*. New York: St. Martin's Press, 1993.

Epstein, Edward. "Homelessness No. 1 Problem, S.F. Voters Say: They Want Issue Given Mayor's Highest Priority." *San Francisco Chronicle*, 1995, A1, A6.

Esbenshade, Jill. "The 'Crisis' over Day Labor: The Politics of Visibility and Public Space." *Working USA* 3 (2000): 27–71.

Fagan, Kevin. "Attacking Hard-Core Homelessness; Plan Envisions 3,000 Housing Units within Next Six Years." *San Francisco Chronicle*, July 1, 2005a, B4.

———. "Feds Say S.F. Just Needs to Decide: Homelessness Funding Awaits 10-Year City Plan." *San Francisco Chronicle*, December 17, 2003a, A1.

———. "Fewer Homeless People on Streets of San Francisco." *San Francisco Chronicle*, February 15, 2005b, A1.

———. "Heavy Load: Cart-Pushers Recycle Tons of Bottles and Cans." *San Francisco Chronicle*, November 27, 1999, A19.

———. "New Panhandling Law—S.F. to Take It Easy." *San Francisco Chronicle*, May 25, 2004, A1.

———. "Newsom Details Plan for Homeless." *San Francisco Chronicle*, December 14, 2003b, A1.

———. "'Supportive' Housing Seen as Good Start." *San Francisco Chronicle*, May 14, 2006, A3.

Fantasia, Rick, and Kim Voss. *Hardwork: Remaking the American Labor Movement*. Berkeley: University of California Press, 2004.

Fine, Gary Alan. "Toward a Peopled Ethnography: Developing Theory from Group Life." *Ethnography* 4, no. 1 (2003): 41–60.

Fiske, John. "For Cultural Interpretation: A Study of the Culture of Homelessness." *Critical Studies in Mass Communication* 8, no. 4 (1991): 455–74.

Foner, Philip S. *History of the Labor Movement in the United States.* Vol. 4. New York: International Publishers, 1965.

Fraser, Steve, and Gary Gristle. *The Rise and Fall of the New Deal Order, 1930–1980.* Cambridge, Mass.: Harvard University Press, 1990.

Frost, Robert. *Poems by Robert Frost: A Boy's Will and North of Boston.* New York: Signet Classics, 2001.

Gagnier, Regina. "Homelessness as 'an Aesthetic Issue': Past and Present." In *Homes and Homelessness in the Victorian Imagination.* Edited by Murray Baumgarten and H. M. Daleski, 167–86. New York: AMS Press, 1998.

Gans, Herbert J. "Deconstructing the Underclass: The Term's Danger as a Planning Concept." *Journal of the American Planning Association* 56 (1990): 271–349.

Garland, David. *Punishment and Modern Society: A Study in Social Theory.* Chicago: University of Chicago Press, 1990.

Giamo, Benedict, and Jeffrey Grunberg. *Beyond Homelessness: Frames of Reference.* Iowa City: University of Iowa Press, 1992.

Gilroy, Paul. *Against Race: Imagining Political Culture beyond the Color Line.* Cambridge, Mass.: Harvard University Press, 2000.

Godfrey, Brian J. "Urban Development and Redevelopment in San Francisco." *Geographical Review* 87, no. 3 (1997): 309–33.

Goffman, Erving. *Asylums: Essays on the Social Situation of Mental Patients and Other Inmates.* New York: Anchor, 1961.

———. *Stigma: Notes on the Management of Spoiled Identity.* New York: Simon and Schuster, 1963.

Goldberger, Paul. "The Rise of the Private City." In *Breaking Away: The Future of Cities.* Edited by Julia Vitullo-Martin, 135–47. New York: Twentieth-Century Fund, 1996.

Golden, Stephanie. *The Women Outside: Meanings and Myths of Homelessness.* Berkeley: University of California Press, 1992.

Gowan, Teresa. "Excavating 'Globalization' from Street Level: Homeless Men Recycle Their Pasts." In *Global Ethnography: Forces, Connections, and Imagination in a Postmodern World.* Edited by Michael Burawoy, Joseph A. Blum, Sheba George, Zsuzsa Gille, Teresa Gowan, Lynne Haney, Maren Klawiter, Steven H. Lopez, Seán Ó Riain, and Millie Thayer, 74–105. Berkeley: University of California Press, 2000.

———. "New Hobos or Neoromantic Fantasy? Urban Ethnography beyond the Neoliberal Disconnect." *Qualitative Sociology* 32, no. 3 (2009): 231–57.

———. "The Nexus: Homelessness and Incarceration in Two American Cities." *Ethnography* 3, no. 4 (2002): 500–535.

Groth, Paul. *Living Downtown: The History of Residential Hotels in the United States.* Berkeley: University of California Press, 1994.

Halter, A. "Homeless in Philadelphia: A Qualitative Study of the Impact of State Welfare Reform on Individuals." *Journal of Sociology and Social Welfare* 19 (1992): 17–19.

Harcourt, Bernard. *Illusion of Order: The False Promise of Broken Windows Policing.* Cambridge, Mass.: Harvard University Press, 2001.

Harper, Douglas. *Good Company*. Chicago: University of Chicago Press, 1982.

Hartwell, S. W. "Not All Work Is Created Equal: Homeless Substance Abusers and Marginal Employment." *Research in the Sociology of Work* 9 (2000): 115–25.

Hays, Sharon. *Flat Broke with Children: Women in the Age of Welfare Reform*. New York: Oxford University Press, 2003.

Hoch, Charles. "Sheltering the Homeless in the U.S.: Social Improvement and the Continuum of Care." *Housing Studies* 15, no. 6 (2000): 865–76.

Hochschild, Arlie. *The Managed Heart: The Commercialization of Human Feeling*. Berkeley: University of California Press, 1983.

Hochschild, Jennifer. "The Politics of the Estranged Poor." *Ethics* 101, no. 3 (1991): 560–78.

Hofstadter, Richard. *The Paranoid Style in American Politics*. New York: Vintage, 2008 (reprint edition).

Hopkins, Ellie, and Larry Nackerud. "An Analysis of Atlanta's Ordinance Prohibiting Urban Camping: Passage and Early Implementation." *Journal of Social Distress and the Homeless* 8, no. 4 (1999): 269–89.

Hopper, Kim. *Reckoning with Homelessness*. Ithaca, N.Y.: Cornell University Press, 2003.

Hopper, Kim, and Jim Baumohl. "Held in Abeyance: Rethinking Homelessness and Advocacy." *American Behavioral Scientist* 37, no. 4 (1994): 522–52.

Hopper, Kim, John Jost, Terri Hay, Susan Welber, and Gary Haugland. "Homelessness, Severe Mental Illness, and the Institutional Circuit." *Psychiatric Services* 48, no. 5 (1997): 659–65.

Interagency Council on the Homeless, U.S. Department of Housing and Urban Development. *Priority: Home! The Federal Plan to Break the Cycle of Homelessness*. Washington, D.C., 1994.

Interagency Council on the Homeless, White House Domestic Policy Council. *Homelessness: Programs and the People They Serve. Findings of the National Survey of Homeless Assistance Providers and Clients*. 1997.

Irwin, John. *The Jail: Managing the Underclass in American Society*. Berkeley: University of California Press, 1986.

Issel, William, and Robert W. Cherny. *San Francisco, 1865–1932: Politics, Power, and Urban Development*. Berkeley: University of California Press, 1986.

Jacobs, Jane. *The Death and Life of Great American Cities*. New York: Vintage Books, 1992 (1961).

Kain, John F. "Housing Segregation, Negro Unemployment, and Metropolitan Decentralization." *Quarterly Journal of Economics* 82 (1968): 175–97.

Kaplan, Elaine Bell. *Not Our Kind of Girl: Unraveling the Myths of Black Teenage Motherhood*. Berkeley: University of California Press, 1997.

Katz, Jack. "From How to Why: On Luminous Description and Causal Influence in Ethnography (Part 1)." *Ethnography* 2, no. 4 (2001): 443–73.

———. "From How to Why: On Luminous Description and Causal Influence in Ethnography (Part 2)." *Ethnography* 3, no. 1 (2002): 63–90.

Katz, Michael B. *In the Shadow of the Poorhouse: A Social History of Welfare in America*. New York: Basic Books, 1986.

——. *The Undeserving Poor: From the War on Poverty to the War on Welfare.* New York: Pantheon Books, 1989.

Kelley, Robin. *Yo' Mama's Disfunktional: Fighting the Culture Wars in Urban America.* Boston, Mass.: Beacon, 1997.

Kertesz, Stefan G., and Saul J. Weiner. "Housing the Chronically Homeless: High Hopes, Complex Realities." *JAMA* 301, no. 17 (2009): 1822.

Kisor, Ann J., and Lynne Kendal-Wilson. "Older Homeless Women: Reframing the Stereotype of the Bag Lady." *Affilia Journal of Women and Social Work* 17, no. 3 (2002): 354–71.

Knight, Heather. "Homelessness: What Happened?" *San Francisco Chronicle,* October 21, 2007, A9.

Koegel, Paul. "Economic Resources of the Homeless: Evidence from Los Angeles." *Contemporary Economic Policy* 16, no. 3 (1998): 295–309.

Kristeva, Julia. *The Kristeva Reader.* New York: Columbia University Press, 1986.

Lankenau, S. E. "Stronger Than Dirt: Public Humiliation and Status Enhancement among Panhandlers." *Journal of Contemporary Ethnography* 28, no. 3 (1999): 288–318.

Lees, Lynn Hollen. *The Solidarities of Strangers: The English Poor Laws and the People, 1700–1948.* Cambridge: Cambridge University Press, 1998.

Lefebvre, Henri. *The Production of Space.* Oxford: Blackwell, 1991 (1974).

Leo, John. "Distorting the Homeless Debate." *US News and World Report,* November 8, 1993, 27.

Lewis, Oscar. *The Children of Sanchez.* New York: Random House, 1961.

——. "The Culture of Poverty." In *On Understanding Poverty: Perspectives from the Social Sciences.* Edited by Daniel P. Moynihan, 187–200. New York: Basic Books, 1968.

Liebow, Elliot. *Tally's Corner.* Boston, Mass.: Little, Brown, and Co., 1967.

——. *Tell Them Who I Am: The Lives of Homeless Women.* New York: The Free Press, 1993.

Light, Ivan. "The Ethnic Vice Industry, 1880–1944." *American Sociological Review* 42, no. 3 (1977): 464–79.

Link, B., J. Phelan, M. Bresnahan, A. Stueve, R. Moore, and E. Susser. "Lifetime and Five-Year Prevalence of Homelessness in the United States: New Evidence on an Old Debate." *American Journal of Orthopsychiatry* 65, no. 3 (1995): 347–54.

Lobao, Linda, and Gregory Hooks. "Public Employment, Welfare Transfers, and Economic Well-being Across Local Populations: Does a Lean and Mean Government Benefit the Masses?" *Social Forces* 82, no. 2 (2003): 519–56.

Luther, Martin. Preface to *Liber Vagatorum: The Book of Vagabonds and Beggars, with a Vocabulary of Their Language.* Translated by John Camden Hotten. London: John Camden Hotten, 1860.

Lyon-Callo, Vincent. *Inequality, Poverty, and Neoliberal Governance: Activist Ethnography in the Homeless Sheltering Industry.* Broadview Ethnographies and Case Studies. Peterborough, Ontario: Broadview Press, 2004.

———. "Medicalizing Homelessness: The Production of Self-Blame and Self-Governing within Homeless Shelters." *Medical Anthropology Quarterly* 14, no. 3 (2000): 328–45.

MacLeod, Celeste. "Street People: The New Migrants." *The Nation*, October 22, 1973, 395–97.

MacLeod, Jay. *Ain't No Makin' It*. Boulder, Colo.: Westview Press, 1995.

Major, Clarence. *Juba to Jive: A Dictionary of African-American Slang*. New York: Penguin, 1994.

Marcuse, Peter. "The Ghetto of Exclusion and the Fortified Enclave: New Patterns in the United States." *American Behavioral Scientist* 41, no. 3 (1997): 311–27.

Margolis, Abby Rachael. "Samurai beneath Blue Tarps: Doing Homelessness, Rejecting Marginality, and Preserving Nation in Ueno Park." Ph.D. dissertation, Cultural Anthropology, University of Pittsburgh, 2002.

Marvasti, Amir B. "Being *Homeless:* Textual and Narrative Constructions." Gainesville: University of Florida, 2000.

Mathieu, Arline. "The Medicalization of Homelessness and the Theater of Repression." *Medical Anthropology Quarterly* 7, no. 2 (1993): 170–84.

Mauer, Marc, and Ryan S. King. *A 25-Year Quagmire: The War on Drugs and Its Impact on American Society*. Washington, D.C.: Sentencing Project, 2007.

Metraux, Stephen, and Dennis Culhane. "Homeless Shelter Use and Reincarceration Following Prison Release." *Criminology and Public Policy* 3, no. 2 (2004): 139–60.

Miller, Jerome G. *Search and Destroy: African-American Males in the Criminal Justice System*. New York: Cambridge University Press, 1996.

Miller, Timothy S. "The Knights of St. John and the Hospitals of the Latin West." *Speculum* 53, no. 4 (1978): 709–33.

Mitchell, Don. "The Annihilation of Space by Law: The Roots and Implications of Anti-Homeless Laws in the United States." *Antipode* 29, no. 3 (1997): 303–35.

Monkkonen, Eric C. *Walking to Work: Tramps in America, 1790–1935*. Lincoln: University of Nebraska Press, 1984.

Montgomery, David. *The Fall of the House of Labor: The Workplace, the State, and American Labor Activism, 1865–1925*. Cambridge: Cambridge University Press, 1987.

Moynihan, Daniel P. *The Negro Family: The Case for National Action*. Washington, D.C.: U.S. Department of Labor, 1965.

National Housing Law Project. *False Hope, or A Critical Assessment of the Hope Vi Public Housing Redevelopment Program*. Oakland, Calif.: 2002.

National Low Income Housing Coalition. *Out of Reach 2001: America's Growing Wage-Rent Disparity*, 2001. http://www.nlihc.org/oor/oor2001/.

Nevius, C. W. "Newsom's Hints at New Plans for Homeless." *San Francisco Chronicle*, December 6, 2007, B1.

Newman, Katherine S. *No Shame in My Game: The Working Poor in the Inner City*. New York: Alfred A. Knopf and the Russell Sage Foundation, 2000.

Niemonen, Jack. *Race, Class, and the State in Contemporary Sociology: The William Julius Wilson Debates*. Boulder, Colo.: Lynne Reinner Publishers, 2002.

Nieves, Evelyn. "Blacks Hit by Housing Costs Leave San Francisco Behind." *San Francisco Chronicle,* August 2, 2001, see A; p. 12; col. 1.

————. "Prosperity's Losers: A Special Report; Homeless Defy Cities' Drives to Move Them." *New York Times,* December 7, 1999, A1.

O'Connor, Alice. *Poverty Knowledge: Social Science, Social Policy, and the Poor in Twentieth-Century U.S. History.* Princeton N.J.: Princeton University Press, 2001.

O'Flaherty, Brendan. *Making Room: The Economics of Homelessness.* Cambridge, Mass.: Harvard University Press, 1996.

Ong, Aihwa. *Spirits of Resistance and Capitalist Discipline: Factory Women in Malaysia.* Albany: State University of New York Press, 1987.

Paddock, Richard C. "S.F. Sense of Pride an Issue." *Los Angeles Times,* October 5, 1991, A1.

Parenti, Christian. *Lockdown America: Police and Prisons in the Age of Crisis.* London and New York: Verso, 1999.

Parker, R. E. *Flesh Peddlers and Warm Bodies: The Temporary Help Industry and Its Workers.* New Brunswick, N.J.: Rutgers University Press, 1994.

Passaro, Joanne. *The Unequal Homeless: Men on the Streets, Women in Their Place.* New York: Routledge, 1996.

Pear, Robert. "Clinton Cites Welfare Gains and Defends Overhaul Plan." *New York Times,* December 8, 1996, sec. 1, p. 35, col. 1.

Peck, Jamie, and Adam Tickell. "Neoliberalizing Space." *Antipode* 34, no. 3 (2002): 380–404.

Perlstein, Rick. *Nixonland: The Rise of a President and the Fracturing of America.* New York: Scribner, 2008.

Pippert, Timothy D. *Road Dogs and Loners: Family Relationships among Homeless Men.* Lanham, Md.: Lexington Books, 2007.

Piven, Frances Fox, and Richard A. Cloward. *Regulating the Poor: The Functions of Public Welfare.* New York: Vintage Books, 1993.

Quadagno, Jill S. *The Color of Welfare: How Racism Undermined the War on Poverty.* Oxford: Oxford University Press, 1994.

Rader, Victoria. *Signal through the Flames: Mitch Snyder and America's Homeless.* Kansas City, Mo.: Sheed and Ward, 1986.

Rainwater, Lee. *Behind Ghetto Walls: Black Families in a Federal Slum.* Chicago: Aldine Publishing Company, 1970.

Raspberry, William. "Telling the Truth about Homelessness." *Washington Post,* December 29, 1992, A21.

Rice, Philip, and Patricia Waugh. *Modern Literary Theory: A Reader.* London: Hodder Arnold, 2001.

Ringenback, Paul. *Tramps and Reformers 1873–1916: The Discovery of Unemployment in New York.* Westport, Conn.: Greenwood Press, 1973.

Ringheim, Karin. *At Risk of Homelessness: The Roles of Income and Rent.* New York: Praeger, 1990.

Rodman, Hyman. "The Lower-Class Value Stretch." *Social Forces* 42 (1963): 205–15.

Roediger, David R. *The Wages of Whiteness: Race and the Making of the American Working Class.* London: Verso, 1991.

Rosenthal, Rob. "Imaging Homelessness and Homeless People: Visions and Strategies within the Movement(s)." *Journal of Social Distress and the Homeless* 9, no. 2 (2000): 111–26.

Rossi, Peter H. *Down and Out in America.* Chicago: University of Chicago Press, 1989.

———. "Minorities and Homelessness." In *Divided Opportunities: Minorities, Poverty, and Social Policy.* Edited by G. D. Sandefur and Marta Tienda, 87–115. New York: Plenum Press, 1988.

Rutheiser, Charles. "Making Place in the Nonplace Urban Realm: Notes on the Revitalization of Downtown Atlanta." In *Theorizing the City: The New Urban Anthropology Reader.* Edited by Setha M. Low, 317–41. New Brunswick, N.J.: Rutgers University Press, 1999.

Ryan, William. *Blaming the Victim.* New York: Vintage, 1976 (1971).

Salzinger, Leslie. *Genders in Production: Making Workers in Mexico's Global Factories.* Berkeley: University of California Press, 2003.

Sassen, Saskia. *The Global City: New York, London, Tokyo.* Princeton, N.J.: Princeton University Press, 1991.

Sayer, Andrew. *Method in Social Science: A Realist Approach.* 2nd ed. London: Routledge, 1992 (1984).

Scheper-Hughes, Nancy. *Death without Weeping: The Violence of Everyday Life in Brazil.* Berkeley: University of California Press, 1992.

Schram, Sanford F. "In the Clinic: The Medicalization of Welfare." *Social Text* 18, no. 1 (2000): 81–108.

Scott, James C. *Weapons of the Week: Everyday Forms of Peasant Resistance.* New Haven, Conn.: Yale University Press, 1985.

Sheehan, Susan. *Life for Me Ain't Been No Crystal Stair: One Family's Passage through the Child Welfare System.* New York: Vintage, 1994.

Sibley, D. *Geographies of Exclusion.* London: Routledge, 1995.

Siegel, Fred. *The Future Once Happened Here: New York, D.C., L.A., and the Fate of America's Big Cities.* New York: The Free Press, 1997.

Skogan, Wesley. *Disorder and Decline: Crime and the Spiral of Decay in American Neighborhoods.* New York: The Free Press, 1990.

Small, Mario Luis, and Katherine Newman. "Urban Poverty after *The Truly Disadvantaged:* The Rediscovery of the Family, the Neighborhood, and Culture." *Annual Review of Sociology* 27 (2001): 23–45.

Smith, Adam. *The Wealth of Nations.* London: Dent, 1910 (1776).

Smith, Neil. "New Globalism, New Urbanism: Gentrification as Global Urban Strategy." *Antipode* 34, no. 3 (2002): 427–50.

———. *New Urban Frontier: Gentrification and the Revanchist City.* London: Routledge, 1996.

Smith, Page. *As a City upon a Hill.* New York: Knopf, 1966.

Snow, David A., and Daniel M. Cress. "Mobilization at the Margins: Resources,

Benefactors, and the Viability of Homeless Social Movement Organizations." *American Sociological Review* 61, no. 6 (1996): 1089–1109.

Snow, David A., and Leon Anderson. *Down on Their Luck: A Study of Homeless Street People.* Berkeley: University of California Press, 1993.

———. "Identity Work among the Homeless: The Verbal Construction and Avowal of Personal Identities." *American Journal of Sociology* 92, no. 6 (1987): 1336–71.

Snow, David A., Leon Anderson, and Paul Koegel. "Distorting Tendencies in Research on the Homeless." *American Behavioral Scientist* 37, no. 4 (1994): 461–75.

Snow, David A., Leon Anderson, Theron Quist, and Daniel Cress. "Material Survival Strategies on the Street: Homeless People as *Bricoleurs.*" In *Homelessness in America.* Edited by Jim Baumohl, 86–96. Phoenix, Ariz.: Oryx, 1996.

Snow, David A., and Michael Mulcahy. "Space, Politics, and the Survival Strategies of the Homeless." *American Behavioral Scientist* 45, no. 1 (2001): 149–69.

Solnit, Rebecca, and Susan Schwarzenberg. *Hollow City: Gentrification and the Eviction of Urban Culture.* London: Verso, 2001.

Stacey, Judith. "Can There Be a Feminist Ethnography?" *Women's Studies International Forum* 11, no. 1 (1988): 21–27.

Stack, Carol B. *All Our Kin: Strategies for Survival in a Black Community.* New York: Harper and Row, 1974.

Stanley, Amy Dru. "Beggars Can't Be Choosers: Compulsion and Contract in Postbellum America." *Journal of American History* 78, no. 4 (1992): 1265–93.

Stark, Louisa R. "The Shelter as 'Total Institution': An Organizational Barrier to Remedying Homelessness." *American Behavioral Scientist* 37, no. 4 (1994): 553–62.

Starr, Kevin. *Endangered Dreams: The Great Depression in California.* Oxford: Oxford University Press, 1996.

Stiff, Dean. *The Milk and Honey Route: A Handbook for Hobos.* New York: Vanguard Press, 1930.

Stoller, Paul. "Spaces, Places, and Fields: The Politics of West African Trading in New York City's Informal Economy." *American Anthropologist* 98, no. 4 (1996): 776–88.

Stone, Michael. *Shelter Poverty: New Ideas on Housing Affordability.* Philadelphia, Pa.: Temple University Press, 1993.

Sullivan, Mercer. "Absent Fathers in the Inner City." *Annals of the American Academy of Political and Social Science* 501 (1989): 48–58.

Susser, Ida. "Creating Family Forms: The Exclusion of Men and Teenage Boys from Families in the New York City Shelter System 1987–1991." In *Theorizing the City: The New Urban Anthropology Reader.* Edited by Setha M. Low, 67–82. New Brunswick, N.J.: Rutgers University Press, 1999.

Takahashi, Lois M. "Out of Place: Homeless Mobilizations, Subcities, and Contested Landscapes." *Journal of the American Planning Association* 64, no. 2 (1998): 239–40.

Takaki, Ronald. "The Tempest in the Wilderness: The Racialization of Savagery." *Journal of American History* 79, no. 3 (1992): 892–912.

Theodore, Nik. "Political Economies of Day Labor: Regulation and Restructuring of Chicago's Contingent Labor Markets." *Urban Studies* 40, no. 9 (2003): 1811–28.

Thomas, Andrew Peyton. "The Rise and Fall of the Homeless." *The Weekly Standard,* April 8, 1996, 27.

Tiny, aka Lisa Gray-Garcia. *Criminal of Poverty: Growing up Homeless in America.* San Francisco, Calif.: City Lights, 2006.

Tonry, Michael. *Malign Neglect: Race, Crime, and Punishment in America.* Oxford: Oxford University Press, 1995.

Tsemberis, Sam, Leyla Gulcur, and Maria Nakae. "Housing First, Consumer Choice, and Harm Reduction for Homeless Individuals with a Dual Diagnosis." In *American Journal of Public Health* 94 (2004): 651–56.

U.S. Conference of Mayors. *A Status Report on Hunger and Homelessness in American Cities.* Washington, D.C.: 2004.

Venkatesh, Sudhir. *American Project: The Rise and Fall of an American Ghetto.* Cambridge, Mass.: Harvard University Press, 2002.

Vitale, Alex. "Enforcing Civility: Homelessness, Quality of Life, and the Crisis of Urban Liberalism." Dissertation, Graduate Center, City University of New York, 2001.

———. *City of Disorder: How the Quality of Life Campaign Transformed New York Politics.* New York: New York University Press, 2008.

Volosinov, Valentin N. *Marxism and the Philosophy of Language.* Cambridge, Mass.: Harvard University Press, 1986.

Wacquant, Loïc. "The New 'Peculiar Institution': On the Prison as Surrogate Ghetto." *Theoretical Criminology* 4, no. 3 (2000): 377–89.

———. *Punishing the Poor: The New Government of Social Insecurity.* Durham, N.C.: Duke University Press, 2008.

———. "Scrutinizing the Street: Poverty, Morality, and the Pitfalls of Urban Ethnography." *American Journal of Sociology* 107, no. 6 (2002): 1468–1532.

———. "'Suitable Enemies': Foreigners and Immigrants in the Prisons of Europe." *Punishment and Society* 1, no. 2 (1999): 215–22.

Waldron, Jeremy. "Homelessness and the Issue of Freedom." *UCLA Law Review* 39, no. 2 (1991): 295–324.

Walker, Dick. "California Rages against the Dying of the Light." *New Left Review* 209 (1995): 42–74.

Wallace, Bill. "Sprinklers Blamed in Fatal Fire: S.F. Hotel Standpipe Didn't Deliver Water Either, Probe Finds." *San Francisco Chronicle,* September 5, 1997, A18.

Wardhaugh, Julia. "The Unaccommodated Woman: Home, Homelessness, and Identity." *Sociological Review* 47, no. 1 (1999): 91.

Waterston, Alisse. *Street Addicts in the Political Economy.* Philadelphia, Pa.: Temple University Press, 1993.

Weinberg, Darin. *Of Others Inside: Insanity, Addiction, and Belonging in America.* Philadelphia, Pa.: Temple University Press, 2005.

——. "'Out There': The Ecology of Addiction in Drug Abuse Treatment Discourse." *Social Problems* 47, no. 4 (2000): 606–21.

Western Regional Advocacy Project. *Without Housing: Decades of Federal Housing Cutbacks, Massive Homelessness, and Policy Failures.* San Francisco, Calif.: 2008.

Weston, Kevin. "San Francisco Bayview: Residents Blast Housing Proposal." *San Francisco Chronicle,* July 15, 2001, A21.

Wideman, John Edgar. "Doing Time, Marking Race." *The Nation* (July 28/August 4 1995): 503–5.

Williams, Brackette F. "The Public I/Eye: Conducting Fieldwork to Do Homework on Homelessness in Two U.S. Cities." *Current Anthropology* 36, no. 1 (1995): 25–39.

Williams, Jean Calterone. "Domestic Violence and Poverty: The Narratives of Homeless Women." *Frontiers* 19, no. 2 (1997): 143–59.

Willis, Paul. *Learning to Labor: How Working Class Kids Get Working Class Jobs.* New York: Columbia University Press, 1977.

Wilson, James Q. "Making Neighborhoods Safe: Sometimes 'Fixing Broken Windows' Does More to Reduce Crime Than Conventional 'Incident-Oriented' Policing." *Atlantic Monthly* (February 1989): 46–52.

Wilson, James Q., and George L. Kelling. "Broken Windows: The Police and Neighborhood Safety [online]," *Atlantic Monthly,* March 1982. http://www .theatlantic.com/magazine/archive/1982/03/broken-windows/4465/.

Wilson, William Julius. *The Declining Significance of Race: Blacks and Changing American Institutions.* Chicago: University of Chicago Press, 1978.

——. *The Truly Disadvantaged: The Inner City, the Underclass, and Public Policy.* Chicago: University of Chicago Press, 1987.

——. "The Truly Disadvantaged Revisited: A Response to Hochschild and Boxill." *Ethics* 101, no. 3 (1991): 593–609.

Winthrop, John, Richard S. Dunn, and Laeticia Yeandle. *The Journal of John Winthrop, 1630–1649.* Cambridge, Mass.: Harvard University Press, 1996.

Wolch, Jennifer, and Chris Philo. "From Distributions of Deviance to Definitions of Difference: Past and Future Mental Health Geographies." *Health and Place* 6 (2000): 137–57.

Wright, R. "Out of Sight, Out of Mind: Homeless Children and Families in Small-Town America." *Annals of the American Academy of Political and Social Science* 559 (1998): 202.

Wright, Talmadge. *Out of Place: Homeless Mobilizations, Subcities, and Contested Landscapes.* Albany: State University of New York Press, 1997.

Wyllie, Irvin G. "The Search for an American Law of Charity, 1776–1844." *The Mississippi Valley Historical Review* 46, no. 2 (1959): 203–21.

Young, Alford A. Jr. "Social Isolation, and Concentration Effects: William Julius Wilson Revisited and Re-Applied." *Ethnic and Racial Studies* 26, no. 6 (2003): 1073–87.

Zinko, Carolyn. "Homeless Haven Cleared Out: 15 Rousted from Mid-Peninsula Creek-Bed Camp." *San Francisco Chronicle,* October 8, 1997, A13, A17.

Zlotnick, Cheryl, and Marjorie J. Robertson. "Sources of Income among Homeless Adults with Major Mental Disorders or Substance Use Disorders." *Psychiatric Services* 47, no. 2 (1996): 147–51.

Index

TERESA GOWAN is assistant professor of sociology at the University of Minnesota.